Enigma Books

Also published by Enigma Books

Hitler's Table Talk: 1941–1944
In Stalin's Secret Service
Hitler and Mussolini: The Secret Meetings
The Jews in Fascist Italy: A History
The Man Behind the Rosenbergs
Roosevelt and Hopkins: An Intimate History
Diary 1937–1943 (Galeazzo Ciano
Secret Affairs: FDR, Cordell Hull, and Sumner Welles
Hitler and His Generals: Military Conferences 1942–1945
Stalin and the Jews: The Red Book
The Secret Front: Nazi Political Espionage
Fighting the Nazis: French Intelligence and Counterintelligence
A Death in Washington: Walter G. Krivitsky and the Stalin Terror
The Battle of the Casbah: Terrorism and Counterterrorism in Algeria 1955–1957
Hitler's Second Book: The Unpublished Sequel to *Mein Kampf*
At Napoleon's Side in Russia: The Classic Eyewitness Account
The Atlantic Wall: Hitler's Defenses for D-Day
Double Lives: Stalin, Willi Münzenberg and the Seduction of the Intellectuals
France and the Nazi Threat: The Collapse of French Diplomacy 1932–1939
Mussolini: The Secrets of His Death
Mortal Crimes: Soviet Penetration of the Manhattan Project
Top Nazi: Karl Wolff—The Man Between Hitler and Himmler
Empire on the Adriatic: Mussolini's Conquest of Yugoslavia
The Origins of the War of 1914 (3-volume set)
Hitler's Foreign Policy: 1933–1939—The Road to World War II
The Origins of Fascist Ideology 1918–1925
Max Corvo: OSS Italy 1942–1945
Hitler's Contract: The Secret History of the Italian Edition of *Mein Kampf*
Secret Intelligence and the Holocaust
Israel at High Noon
Balkan Inferno: Betrayal, War, and Intervention, 1990–2005
Calculated Risk: World War II Memoirs of General Mark Clark
The Murder of Maxim Gorky
The Kravchenko Case: One Man's War On Stalin
Operation Neptune
Paris Weekend
Shattered Sky
Hitler's Gift to France
The Mafia and the Allies
The Nazi Party, 1919-1945: A Complete History
Encyclopedia of Cold War Espionage, Spies, and Secret Operations
The Cicero Spy Affair

A Crate of Vodka
NOC
The First Iraq War: Britain's Mesopotamian Campaign, 1914-1918
Becoming Winston Churchill
Hitler's Intelligence Chief: Walter Schellenberg
Salazar: A Political Biography
The Italian Brothers
Nazi Palestine
Code Name: Kalistrat
Pax Romana
The De Valera Deception
Lenin and His Comrades
Working with Napoleon
The Decision to Drop the Atomic Bomb
Target Hitler
Truman, MacArthur and the Korean War
Working with Napoleon
The Parsifal Pursuit
The Eichmann Trial Diary
Stalin's Man in Canada
Cold Angel

H. James Burgwyn

Mussolini Warlord

Failed Dreams of Empire

1940–1943

Enigma Books

Enigma Books
New York, NY
www.enigmabooks.com

First Edition

Copyright © 2012 by H. James Burgwyn

ISBN 978-1-936274-29-1
e-ISBN 978-1-936274-30-7

Printed in the United States of America

Publisher's Cataloging-In-Publication Data

Burgwyn, H. James, 1936-
    Mussolini warlord : failed dreams of empire, 1940-1943 / H. James Burgwyn. --
1st ed.

    p. : ill., maps ; cm.

    Issued also as an ebook.
    Includes bibliographical references and index.
    ISBN: 978-1-936274-29-1

    1. Mussolini, Benito, 1883-1945--Political activity. 2. Dictators--Italy--20th
century--Biography. 3. Italy--History, Military--1914-1945.   4. Warlordism--Italy--
History--20th century. 5. World War, 1939-1945--Diplomatic history. I. Title.

DG575.M8 B87 2012
945/.091/092

To Enrico Ferranti

Contents

Acknowledgments

It is my pleasure to acknowledge the help I have received from many sources.

Several respected colleagues generously agreed to read portions of the book that pertained to their areas of expertise, despite the demands of their own professional commitments and scholarly projects.

Thomas Schlemmer graciously shared with me the gold-mine of information he has gathered on the Italian campaign in the Soviet Union. He offered cogent insights on military events, war crimes, and Fascist troops enamored of the Fascist creed. No better place to do this than in a Munich Bierstube during Oktoberfest!

Pier Paolo Battistelli accorded me the full benefit of his unsurpassed mastery and understanding of the Italian military during World War II, putting to rights many factual errors. With unfailing patience, he responded to every request or question I had.

The gifted young Italian scholar Amedeo Osti Guerrazzi, in addition to providing me with important information on Italian occupation policies in Yugoslavia, shared his insights into Mussolini and Fascism, as well as his passion for scholarly studies. I remember with pleasure the many lunches we shared after navigating the narrow, snaking roads outside the German Historical Institute in Rome.

Filippo Focardi, who, along with the distinguished German historian Lutz Klinkhammer, pioneered studies on the general cover-up of Italian war crimes, offered me sage advice on how to strengthen my discussion of Italian counterinsurgency.

Elisabeth Giansiracusa provided valuable research assistance in Rome. She skillfully mastered the labyrinthine archives in the Italian Foreign Ministry, ferreting out important information from the recently opened—but still disorganized—Albanian papers. Likewise the Greek files in the military archives.

Writing mostly in isolation on this side of the Atlantic, I am all the more grateful for the advice, help, and friendship I received in Italy from the aforementioned individuals. They greatly advanced whatever merit this study possesses. Any sins of omission, commission, errors in fact, or misjudgments that remain in this book are mine alone.

I owe a particular debt of gratitude to my editor at Enigma Books, Robert L. Miller. This charming and gifted editor—scholar, translator, and novelist—has been a pleasure to work with. His critique of my manuscript was astute and sound, as was his advice on how to reorganize the book so that it would have a more coherent narrative.

My wife, Diana, freshened my enterprise by bringing to it crucial qualities of mind and spirit. In overcoming a deadly hematoma, she gave me inspiration by her courage and indomitable will to recover. During her convalescence she summoned the strength to give the manuscript a careful reading, correcting my sometimes infelicitous and awkward prose. I have benefited greatly from Diana's love and plucky spirit.

My longtime friend Enrico Ferranti has provided me over the years with a wonderful sanctuary in his Rome and Tolfa residences. His inexhaustible hospitality—as well as that of his wife, Giovanna—has given every trip to Italy a special meaning. A true Renaissance man, Enrico has engaged me in many a penetrating discussion on Italian history and politics. It is to him, my charismatic Italian "brother," that I dedicate this book.

Abbreviations

ACS	Archivio centrale dello stato
ADAP	Akten zur deutschen auswärtigen Politik 1919-1945
AP	Affari politici
ARMIR	Armata italiana in Russia
ARS	Archives of the Slovene Republic, Ljubljana
ASMAE	Archivio storico del ministero degli affari esteri
AUSSME	Archivio ufficio storico dello stato maggiore dell'esercito
AVII	Institute of Military History, Belgrade, Serbia
CC.NN	Camicie nere
CC.RR	Carabinieri reali
CIAF	Commissione italiana di armistizio con la Francia
CSIR	Corpo di spedizione italiano in Russia
DDI	*Documenti diplomatici italiani*
DGFP	Documents on German Foreign Policy
DS	Diario storico
GABAP	Gabinetto armistizio-pace, ministero degli esteri
MAE	Ministero degli affari esteri
MI	Ministero dell'interno
MVAC	Anti-Communist voluntary militia
NAW	National Archives Washington (cited as microcopy, followed by reel number, and frame(s) only, sender and receiver, and date.
NDH	Nezavisne Države Hrvatske
OKW	Oberkommando der Wehrmacht
OO	Benito Mussolini, *Opera Omnia*
PC	Presidenza del consiglio, cited by year and file number
PCM	Presidenza del consiglio dei ministri
PP	Pietromarchi papers
CS	Comando supremo
SIM	Servizio informazioni militare
SMG	Stato maggiore generale
SME	Stato maggiore dell'esercito
SMRE	Stato maggiore regio esercito
USSME	Ufficio storico dello stato maggiore dell'esercito
Zbornik	*Zbornik dokumenata I podataka o Narodnooslobodilačkom ratu naroda Jugo-slavije* (Belgrade: Vojnoistorijski Institut, 1949-86)

Mussolini Warlord

Chapter I

The Hour Marked By Destiny

Imperialist Muse

At 6 p.m. on Monday, 10 June 1940, the balcony doors of the Palazzo Vene-zia swung open for the first time in nine months, and Benito Mussolini, the Duce of Italian Fascism, appeared to address the assembled crowd. Standing behind the balcony's stone railing with hands placed firmly on hips, Mussolini spoke in a staccato voice, his lower lip quivering. "Fighters on the ground, the sea and in the air! Black Shirts of the revolution and the legions! Men and women of Italy, of the Empire and the kingdom of Albania! Listen! The hour marked by destiny is about to strike in the sky above our homeland. The hour of irreversible decisions. The declaration of war has already been handed to the am-bassadors of Great Britain and France. We enter the fray against the reactionary and plutocratic western democracies that have always hindered the advance and often threatened the very existence of the Italian people... Having solved the problem of our borders on the continent, we shoulder our weapons to deal with the issue of our maritime frontiers; we want to break the chains of a territorial and military nature that are strangling us inside our sea because a people of 45 million souls cannot be truly free if it doesn't have access to the Ocean..."

The war, said Mussolini, was the war of "the poor and numerous peoples" against those who "hang on to their monopoly of all the wealth and gold on earth, of the young and prolific nations against the sterile and declining ones, of two centuries and two ideas." Exhorted the Duce, his jaw set and chest swelling: "Rush to arms and show your tenacity, your courage, and your valor!" Fascist Italy, the first ally of Nazi Germany, had entered the Second World War.

Had Mussolini fumbled his cards or had he played them cleverly? The country was ill prepared to fight a modern war. The soldiers, many of whom were semi-literate and half-trained, bore equipment that was old and inefficient. But the Duce's timing seemed right. Who could question his calculation that England, after the debacle of Dunkirk, would not be able to stand alone against Hitler's wrath? Indeed, Germany, having overrun Norway, the Low Countries, and France, appeared to have already won the war. Italy, in Mussolini's calculations, would join Hitler in a tough but brief battle and, "after a few thousand dead," would share in the final victory. Then he would co-author a rearrangement of power in the Mediterranean. The idea that America and the Soviet Union would eventually join in a crusade against the dictators was at that point unimaginable. It is worth noting that Mussolini consulted neither his cabinet nor the Fascist Grand Council on these matters.

It is not unusual in Italian history for decisions on war and peace to be made secretly. The two schemers, Prime Minister Antonio Salandra and Foreign Minister Sidney Sonnino, did the same thing back in 1915 when they hatched a plan to move the nation from neutrality to war against the former Triple Alliance partners, Germany and Austria-Hungary. In signing the Pact of London with the Allies, Sonnino aimed to gain territory from the sprawling Habsburg Empire. Little could he have guessed that at the end of the war the Empire would break up.

Mussolini was not the only one in Europe who thought that Britain and France were finished. The noted historian Richard Bosworth writes: "It is at least arguable that, whatever his rhetoric, Mussolini waited longer and displayed more scruples in 1940 than did Salandra and Sonnino in 1915. It is equally arguable that no imaginable Italian leader around which Italian society had been organized since the Risorgimento, would not have entered a Great War at a time when it seemed plain that one side had won a total victory. Because of the myths of the Risorgimento any Italian leader would have declared war on Germany's side in June 1940 because it was by then the only step that could possibly lead to the survival of Italy's pretensions to be a Great Power."[1] There is wisdom in this passage. Still, one wonders. Would a traditional monarchist, in the style of Sidney Sonnino, who wore his cuffs and stiff collar proudly and felt a deep nostalgia for the defunct Habsburg Empire, have ever gone to war on the side of plebeian Nazis? Was there not a real clash of standards and habit between the Old World and the Axis New Order?

If Mussolini was audacious in entering the war on the side of Nazi Germany, he showed timidity by not demanding sacrifices from his countrymen in fighting it. No general mobilization was declared or emergency proclaimed, and the regime did not dare to increase taxes (many citizens were not in the habit of paying them anyway). Food rationing was not introduced until spring 1941. Nor did Mussolini wisely supervise the selection of arms for his military, whose planners slavishly deferred to the large industrial combines that produced the least effective and most expensive armaments of any major combatant in the Second World War. After enormous military outlays to defray the expenses of wars against Ethiopia and the Spanish Republic, Italy's treasury in 1940 was nearly empty. But the minister of exchange and currency, Raffaello Riccardi, who, on financial grounds advised staying out of the war, was finally stampeded into acquiescence.

Having only recently been unified, Italy seemed barely to hold together. Many regions were locked in poverty. A semi-industrialized north coexisted uneasily with an impoverished south. Handfuls of little "italies" perpetuated parochial loyalties and disrespect for central authority, and northerners referred to Sicilians as an African species that should be confined to their island ghetto. Furthermore, a dearth of raw materials hindered industrial expansion, while agriculture remained mired in feudal practices. It seemed that Italy was doomed to be "the least of the Great Powers," playing way over its head in the European power game. Yet many nationalists were convinced that the Fascist leader would overcome such chronic weaknesses by welding the nation together under the banner of *italianitá*, with the aim of enhancing its role as a strong competitor in imperialist expansion.

Despite his war talk bravado, Mussolini was aware of Italy's industrial weakness and lack of unity and feared that the nation would rise up against him if required to make large sacrifices in a major war. The discomfiting reality was that military exhaustion wrought by wars against Ethiopia and in Spain had left the country in no shape for battle, but Mussolini, counting on a quick German victory, chose to ignore that. If instead the war were strung out, Germany, he

---

1. R. J. B. Bosworth and G. Rizzo, *Altro Polo, Intellectuals and Their Ideas in Contemporary Italy* (Sydney: F. May Foundation, 1983), p. 78.

was certain, would still eventually prevail. Behind all the Duce's calculations was a determination to prove that Italy had backbone; the shedding of blood in that endeavor did not concern him. If blunted on the French frontier or in Libya, Mussolini would hurl his forces on the more weakly defended Djibouti and Kenya. Naval and air offensives in the Mediterranean would convince Hitler that Italy was battle-hardy and worthy of Nazi respect. The time had finally arrived to settle accounts with the country's former allies of World War I.

Italy's burning national grievance against the Allies originated at the Paris Peace Conference of 1919. Instead of receiving imperial prizes from alliance partners for a gallant contribution to the victory at a tremendous cost in lives and resources, it was treated as a grasping and belligerent Balkan state that had fought "Sonnino's war" in a fit of selfish *sacro egoismo*. Worse still, while Britain and France held Italy to account for not acting according to Wilsonian principles, the Western Allies similarly ignored those principles by allocating choice African and Middle Eastern real estate to themselves, leaving Italy largely out in the cold. Anger and humiliation roiled the "Italian street." If the poet laureate Gabriele D'Annunzio was the first to capture the public mood with the slogan "the mutilated victory," no one knew better than Mussolini how to work this legend into national fury. Italy would avenge itself against its erstwhile allies by taking up the "revisionist" cause hand-in-hand with the treaty-breaker par excellence, Germany.

To transform Italy into a feared and dominant power in Europe, Mussolini from the beginning of his reign pondered Italian spheres of influence in the Balkans and along the Danube. No less enticing was an expanded empire in Africa assured by naval supremacy in the Mediterranean. These imperialist aims were not irritable mental gestures but were powered by real ideological imperatives, many of which had been appropriated from the nationalists' creed or borrowed from European disseminators of the "culture of despair." Living in a lawless world, Italy must be among the fittest to survive and compete for power. "Expand or die" in Fascist Italy translated into a radicalized struggle between incompatible political regimes. The "Decline of the West" was seen as the decline of France and England, whose desire for peace and penchant for diplomatic solutions and appeasement, according to the Fascists, had led only to corruption and degeneration. Overcoming these democratic countries, infested with feckless politicians of a bygone liberal era, would be a cakewalk for the resurgent modern-day Sparta.

According to a popular determinist notion, Mussolini set a trap for himself by engaging in an endless cycle of propaganda aimed at building up high expectations that war would bring large returns from imperial expansion. If the Duce failed to walk the talk, he would lose face and Fascism would die out.

Thus, according to this theory, he had cornered himself into the ineluctable necessity to wage war.[2] Yet it must be remembered that Mussolini did closely follow events on the battlefield. He would watch and wait before making any irreversible move. But in declaring non-belligerency, the Duce implied future intervention on the side of Germany. In the run-up to war, never did he honestly consider reconciliation with the Western Powers.

The French military collapse in May 1940 ended Mussolini's internal debate. He would not let Hitler be the sole arbiter of Europe. It looked like a safe bet that Italy would stand to profit from the astonishing victories of the Wehrmacht in Western Europe. If there had been stalemate on the Western Front, there is no telling what Mussolini might have done. Perhaps he would have squirmed impotently on the sidelines. On the other hand, if the two sides appeared to have reached mutual exhaustion, he might have convened an Italian "Munich" from a position of relative strength, handed victory to Hitler, and picked up spoils from the losers as the "mediator" of a "lenient" peace. But there was one thing of which he was sure: defeat for Germany would mean the end of Italy's dream of becoming master of the Mediterranean.

There was no question that most Italians felt trapped in the Pact of Steel, for they feared and distrusted Hitler. But once Italy, by entering the war, had sealed its partnership with the Teutonic behemoth—whose ultimate victory only a few in the Italian leadership doubted—the so-called "moderate" anti-German Fascists fell into line. No one within the propaganda apparatus, military circles, or diplomats of the regime undertook any serious step to challenge the path to war. A few discordant voices questioned the timing and method, but not the substance of Mussolini's imperialist objectives. Caution was overwhelmed by the certainty that the moment was unique and possibly finite for Italy to acquire a Mediterranean empire and glory for the nation at small cost. Not one of the Fascist leaders, except for the discredited Dino Grandi, ventured beyond mildly expressed watchfulness. The view that Mussolini's son-in-law, Foreign Minister Galeazzo Ciano, pursued a line of policy contrary to Mussolini's is purely the invention of conservative apologists. Ciano's off-the-cuff asides and occasional outbursts for restraint against Mussolini's rashness carried little weight, and he made no effort to assemble a following. In truth, Ciano was more anti-German than anti-war, for he did not back away from battle against the "decadent democracies," even though he himself was a "decadent" Fascist.

Like Ciano, the Fascist intellectual Giuseppe Bottai, an old comrade of the Duce, shrank from subordination to the German Moloch. But when push came

---

2. For an interesting discussion on this point, see Gerhard Schreiber's Part I in *Germany and the Second World War* (Oxford: Clarendon Press, 1995), vol. III: 99–126.

to shove, he, too, was swept away by Fascism's irresistible appeal as a revolutionary, anti-plutocratic, and anti-Bolshevik movement, which stilled his doubts over Nazi Germany. War, he felt, would revitalize Fascism and consolidate a consensus behind the Duce.

Pugnacious talk, Mussolini knew, invariably perked up nationalist enthusiasm. On 2 April, in a Council of Ministers meeting, he promised that his countrymen would never act "like whores with the democracies." Neutrality "was for the castrated," and "would diminish the stature of Italy as a great power for a century and as a Fascist regime for eternity."[3]

To justify Italy's entry into the war, Mussolini employed deceit as well as forthrightness. At the end of April he decided to tell the Italian people that the English blockade on coal deliveries denied the country freedom and suffocated industrial development. To strengthen this point, he planned a detailed report to be delivered before the Parliament that would spell out the abuses inflicted on Italy by the Western Powers for adhering to non-belligerency—a clear sign of favoritism towards Germany. Luca Pietromarchi, head of the office of economic warfare, fills in the background details: "I was given the task to prepare material for his [Host Venturi's] speech. The head of the cabinet, Ambassador Filippo Anfuso, gave me this information by handing me the Duce's written orders on a piece of paper on which he, in longhand, wrote out the following: 'Compile a list on the maritime war.' What does he mean by this? I asked. Anfuso replied by giving me a packet of onionskins listing the telephone interceptions of the complaints from persons charged with reporting the damages resulting from [Britain's] control measures. The Duce sent the material to me for safekeeping. I rejected the pile of onionskins. This stuff, I said, I already know; it serves no purpose because it is not reliable. I would prefer documented and detailed *note verbali* that I would send directly to the English and French ambassadors. Bah! 'Do the best you can,' concluded Filippo in his usual cordial, ironic way. Would some notes suffice? I asked. No: you must make up a document that is detailed."[4]

As opposed to dyed-in-the-wool Fascists bent on war, the Italian military dragged their feet. To shake up his hidebound generals, Mussolini delivered an oration liberally seasoned with trumped-up statistics about the monies allocated to put the country on a war footing. On 9 April 1940 the military chiefs met to thrash out the question of Italian intervention in the war and Mussolini's strategic directives. The head of the Joint General Staff (Stato Maggiore

---

3. Count Galeazzo Ciano, *The Ciano Diaries* (Garden City, NY: Doubleday, 1946), 2 April 1940.
4. Cited in *I diari e le agende di Luca Pietromarchi (1938–1940): Politica estera del fascismo e vita quotidiana di un diplomatico romano del '900*, ed. by Ruth Nattermann (Rome: Viella, 2009), p. 426, n. 48.

Generale-SMG), Pietro Badoglio, who recently had told intimates that he pre-ferred fighting Germans to fighting with them, listed the military's deficiencies in tanks, guns, and equipment.[5] He had told Pietromarchi the day before: "We can't even engage in a second war like Spain. We have only fifteen days of ammuni-tion and coal reserves for only a month."[6] Badoglio's advice was clear: stand on the defensive and dodge the Germans. "If we were to receive German help, we would not only lose our dignity, but we would expose ourselves to having to pay our debt very dearly indeed." Navy Chief of Staff Domenico Cavagnari had his doubts too: "One [enemy] fleet will place itself at Gibraltar and the other at Suez, and we shall choke in between."[7] To mitigate Mussolini's enthusiasm for war "all along the line," Cavagnari imparted the uninspiring advice that the fleet should remain anchored in port rather than risk ships against the Royal Navy in the open sea. Air Force Chief-of-Staff Francesco Pricolo questioned whether people were not nourishing "too many illusions about aero-naval offensives, the possibilities of which are few."[8]

As long as he was sure of an imminent Franco-British collapse, the Duce was not loath to bear full responsibility in making decisions. He was already on record in declaring the urgency of "barring the doors of the house." While the military were all for hermetically sealing the Mediterranean, they were not yet prepared to do so by war. The senior military authorities, if given their head, would have preferred to spin out non-belligerency, but not one was prepared to step in against the Duce's express train headed for intervention, which picked up speed after the battle of France began on 10 May. Badoglio in his self-serving memoirs claimed to have been dumbfounded by Mussolini's decision to enter the war, but at an important meeting on 29 May, at which Mussolini declared his intention of marching on 5 June, he uttered no protest. Badoglio had clearly been both critic and supporter of what Mussolini chose to do.

On 5 June Mussolini directed Badoglio to order a defensive strategy on all fronts so that the army and navy would be saved "for future events." The navy was not to bombard the French coast or lay mines. Two days later, he ordered the navy to attack if it encountered mixed British and French forces but not to be the first to fire. Yet he encouraged Italian submarines to torpedo French

5. John Gooch, *Mussolini and His Generals: The Armed Forces and Fascist Foreign Policy, 1922–1940* (Cambridge: Cambridge University Press, 2007), pp. 495–99.
6. *I diari e le agende di Luca Pietromarchi*, 8 April 1940.
7. Citations in Knox, *Mussolini Unleashed 1939–1941, Politics and Strategy in Fascist Italy's Last War* (Cambridge: Cambridge University Press, 1982), p. 90
8. Antonello Biagini and Fernando Frattolillo, eds. Ufficio Storico dello Stato Maggiore (hereafter cited as USSME), Diario Storico (hereafter cited as DS), vol. I, tomo II (Rome: USSME DS 1986), Seduta del 9 aprile 1940: Verbali delle riunioni tenute dal Capo di SMG, pp. 182–89.

warships, "if they can get off a good anonymous shot"[9]—a bizarre way to start a war.

On 10 June the military chieftains, filled with qualms, prepared to march into the maelstrom. Badoglio hesitated until the last. It well might be that in the days shortly before Italy's intervention he believed that France still had a lot of fight left, which would afford Italy more time to see how the wind was blowing before acting. Underestimating the decisiveness of the German Blitzkrieg, Badoglio still hoped that the scope of the German victory would be limited. This was a view shared by Mussolini. Ciano records Badoglio as saying on 8 June: "The Duce is following with anxiety the battle in progress, and is happy over the resistance of the French because 'the Germans are finally being weakened and will not reach the end of the war too fresh and too strong.'"[10] But at the moment of truth, all doubters had no choice but to share the facile view of Graziani at the penultimate chiefs-of-staff meeting before the war began: "When the guns start to go off, everything will automatically fall into place."[11]

King Victor Emmanuel, when assured of a quick victory, swallowed his doubts and consented to the declaration of war. The Catholic Church refrained from challenging the stability of the regime by questioning Mussolini's resolve to define the nation's finest hour.

The industrial leaders, on the whole Fascist fellow-travelers, were hardly likely to oppose Mussolini's descent into the war, although many a top manager with international ties worried that profits would drop should business with the West dry up. Business circles fell in with Fascism's imperialist claims, which coincided with the peripheral aim of Balkan expansion to assure control of the area's raw materials against Germany's ambitions. Not even the doubtful major economic players ever openly challenged the regime.

Aroused by the "community of the trenches" experience of the Great War, many restless Italians longed to relive the memories of bonding with comrades from all regions of the country in a common cause. The word "front," evoking privation, battle, and heroism, inspired nationalist hearts to render justice to the abused motherland through patriotic sacrifices. No longer would the Italian people have to "sit by the window." Stress and strain gave way to certainty. A retired liberal and nationalist diplomat wrote: "Strange to say, the general feeling is one of relief. The trying period of waiting is over. The die is cast for better or for worse."[12] The Duce had finally made a decision that seemed preordained after

---

9. Cited in Gooch, *Mussolini and His Generals*, p. 517.
10. *The Ciano Diaries*, 8 June 1940.
11. Gooch, *Mussolini and His Generals*, p. 518; USSME, *Verbali delle riunioni tenute dal capo di S.M. Generale*, vol. I, Seduta del 5 giugno 1940, p. 58.
12. Cited in R. J. B. Bosworth, *Mussolini* (London: Arnold, 2002), p. 369.

the Dunkirk disaster. That France was on the brink of collapse seemed, for many Italians, to prove his wisdom. A police report summarized the state of mind: "Through all these terrible times, only God alone knows what can happen. Here in Italy we have faith in the genius of Mussolini and this gives us a certain calm."[13]

The workers and peasants, on the other hand, drained by the rigors of daily survival, were not moved by Mussolini's truculent call to the colors. The workers, who continued to be unflinchingly loyal to Socialist ideals, resisted the Fascist unions and their sell-out to the capitalist bosses, while the long-suffering and impoverished peasants held on to their belief that war represented a disaster plotted by an alien central government whose sole aim was to tax and exploit them. Workers and peasants both were haunted by the vague feeling that imperialism did not pay; every territorial conquest and every victory would be followed by a worsening standard of living and by economic stagnation.

The majority of the Italian people, made up of the poor and fatalistic untouched by the futuristic winds blowing through the Italian academies, had no love of combat and wished to stay home. They were joined by many from the middle classes who were appalled at the decision for war and uttered many jokes about Mussolini the peasant killing a man already dead, i.e., France. But numbed by years of conformity, they allowed themselves to be dragged into the war without resistance. If unconditional faith in the Duce had not become an article of faith for many Italians, and if there was no stampede to enlist in the armed forces, they would nevertheless serve their mountebank leader by doing their duty.

Now that the hour had struck for revenge against Britain and France, the old generation, haunted by terrible memories of the slaughters of 1914–18, was understandably dismissive of Fascist talk of war as a regenerative experience. The true Italian patriot, as a child of the Risorgimento, esteemed liberal values and rejected Fascism. Nonetheless, he would not flinch from standing behind the nation in its hour of peril. In abandoning old allies, the cautious braced for a leap into the unknown, grasping the hand of the feared German Colossus in the hope that Italy would be able to hold its own. Unforgettable cinematic scenes of the Wehrmacht's Blitzkrieg victories in Northern France, which foretold a short and easy Axis victory, served to dispel residual prudence. Who now would not place his bets on Hitler? Landing on the winning side without any major sacrifice in a war sure to be over by Christmas sufficed to overcome their dislike of Nazi Germany. Natural skepticism had yielded to dangerous opportunism.

---

13. Pietro Cavallo, *Italiani in guerra: Sentimenti e immagini dal 1940-al 1943* (Milan: Il Mulino, 1997), p. 41.

Michele Lanza, second secretary of the Berlin embassy, summarizes: "Now we are at war and must radically modify our way of thinking. Our soldiers are in the front lines. They cannot ask, or rather they cannot discuss, whether this is a just or unjust war. They do not obey a fiction, a party, but only something far grander: Italy."[14]

For Lanza and his friends, Italy was now involved in a fight to the finish. Domination of the Mediterranean and the founding of a great empire would reward victory, but defeat would allow the Western Powers to take great pleasure in reducing the country to a tourist destination.

If the war was a war of the regime, the *classe dirigente* was an accomplice by doing nothing to remove the muzzle imposed by the dictator on internal debate. It shed the obligation to improve institutional efficiency, define areas of competence, and introduce more modern production techniques. Stagnation prevailed. *Affarismo* lived on as the way of life, and *omertà* reigned. As for the broader cross-section of the privileged and educated who shared Mussolini's fears and aspirations, it is not far-fetched to say that they worked in concord with him during Italy's odyssey from peace to war.

The country's most ferocious Blackshirts, spawned by the sprawling *piccolo borghese* classes, spearheaded the Duce's rush to war. For restless Fascist-oriented youths, old-fashioned patriotism was sterile and unexciting. In their yearning for war they barely questioned whether a German victory would be more dangerous to Italy than continued non-belligerence.

Clearly, contrary to the "one man alone thesis," Italy was not force-marched into war. Besides hotheaded Fascists, Mussolini received broad support for a conflict against the Western Powers, especially when the timing seemed right. A large number of Italians, mesmerized by fear or silenced by intimidation, still fell behind their Duce in his great gamble because he articulated their long-standing grievances and ambitions and seemed to have played his cards cleverly. The intentionalist school's most recent acolyte, the American historian Reynolds Salerno, might consider revising his categorical conclusion that "Mussolini went to war virtually alone."[15]

Many participants and scholars have advanced a "phony-war" theory. General Quirino Armellini noted in his diary that the Duce evidently proposed "to declare war, in order not to fight it, and then sit at the peace table as a belligerent in order to claim his share of the booty."[16] Similarly, according to the

---

14. Michele Lanza (pseudo. Leonardo Simoni), *Berlino ambasciata d'Italia 1939–1943* (Rome: Migliaresi, 1946), p. 127.
15. Reynolds Salerno, *Vital Crossroads: Mediterranean Origins of the Second World War, 1935–1940* (Ithaca, New York: Cornell University Press, 2002), p. 209
16. Quirino Armellini, *Diario di guerra: nove mesi al Comando Supremo* (Milan: Garzanti, 1946), p. 24.

British historian Denis Mack Smith, Mussolini proposed "to declare war, not to make it."[17] This "phony-war" theory holds that Mussolini intended, as Badoglio hoped, to "leave open a rapprochement with France to check German domination occasioned by the Wehrmacht's crushing victories. As MacGregor Knox convincingly demonstrates, these views leave out of the equation Mussolini's determination to fight a genuine, if short, war.[18] No bluff here. Mussolini's imperial objectives, many times stated, included the following: French territory that comprised Savoy, Nice, Corsica, Tunisia, and Djibuti; expansion in the Balkans; domination of the Mediterranean; and creation of an African empire pivoted on Libya and Ethiopia and strengthened by the acquisition of Egypt, the Suez Canal, and the Sudan. Such a grandiose agenda presupposed a crushing victory over Great Britain.

On 8 June Mussolini had indeed crossed the Rubicon and there was no turning back. He was thoroughly committed to live or die with the Führer. In the pages that follow, we will see what was singularly Fascist in the way Italy fought, which will clarify what Mussolini intended to accomplish in his "New Mediterranean Order" founded on the ruins of defeated enemies and of the French and British empires.

What kind of an ally did Mussolini intend to be? Reminiscent of the old refrain "*l'Italia farà da sè*," Italy would fight a "parallel war" not with Germany, not for Germany, but for Italy on the side of Germany. This formula, first employed during a ministerial council on 23 January 1940 and issued as a directive on 4 April, revealed both a decided fear of Teutonic supremacy and Mussolini's awareness that none of Italy's imperialist ambitions could ever be realized without Hitler's victories against Britain or against his will. Yet such resentments as the Nazi-Soviet Pact, which was carried out behind Italy's back, fueled his determination to act aggressively, choosing his own war theaters and fulfilling imperialist goals before the victorious Axis Powers dictated a reapportionment of imperial territory to the fallen enemy. By keeping his distance from Hitler in an Axis fraught with mutual distrust, Mussolini intended to reshape the European balance of power in two separate regions: the Italian Mediterranean World and Germany's New Order. The Italian economy would stagger along and the bedraggled troops, facing shortages of all kinds, would prevail through sheer Fascist élan. In eschewing strategic collaboration with Berlin, Mussolini would demonstrate to the Italian people, the Germans, and the world at large that the military caliber of Italian Fascism was to be emulated, not deprecated. And had Hitler not repeatedly confided in Mussolini that the "Mediterranean World"

---

17. Denis Mack Smith, *Mussolini's Roman Empire* (London and New York: Longman, 1976), p. 217.
18. Knox, *Mussolini Unleashed*, p. 122

belonged to Italy and that Germany's Lebensraum pointed eastward? But it was already too late in the day. The German annexation of Austria in 1938, which opened the floodgates to economic penetration of Yugoslavia and Greece, made Mussolini's boast to realize hegemony in the Balkans by means of a "parallel war" rhetorical whimsy.

Shocking negligence marked Italy's lead-up to the opening of hostilities. As warlord, Mussolini failed to set priorities in his strategic objectives or impose vital sacrifices on the country to fulfill them.

Off to a Bad Start

Contrary to Hitler, Mussolini had the courtesy to declare war. Ciano summoned the French and British ambassadors in Rome, André François-Poncet and Sir Percy Loraine, to inform them that Italy was at war with their nations. The French ambassador responded: "It is a dagger blow to a man [France] who has already fallen. In your place, I would not be proud."[19] Loraine received the news "without batting an eyelid or changing color."[20] In an address delivered at the University of Virginia, President Franklin D. Roosevelt proclaimed: "On this tenth day of June 1940, the hand that held the dagger has struck it into the back of its neighbor."[21]

Mussolini assured Hitler that he would unleash war with fortitude and aplomb. Victor Emmanuel left Rome for the front hoping to recapture the bracing atmosphere of the Great War. Ciano clambered aboard his plane to search for French targets over the Côte d'Azur. But the Italian army, which had already been ordered by the cautious Marshal Badoglio to stay put in their trenches, shrank from storming the French "Alpine Maginot Line." François-Poncet and General Henri Parisot, France's military attaché in Rome, declared that Paris had decided against a *guerre brusquée* against Italy, thus sparing the army the embarrassment of launching an offensive for which it was unprepared.

The most modernized arm of the Italian military, the navy, stayed safely anchored at port far out of harm's way, a prudence partially justified by the realization that heavy losses in a direct encounter with the British fleet would have been hard to make up for. Admiral Domenico Cavagnari limited his major task to the protection of shipping between Italy and Libya. The air force undertook a few harmless sorties. But when the French navy shelled the Ligurian coast and the British bombed Turin and Milan, Mussolini on 14 June ordered aerial

---

19. André François-Poncet, *Au palais Farnèse: Souvenirs d'une ambassade à Rome, 1938–1940* (Paris: Fayard, 1961), p. 178.
20. *The Ciano Diaries,* 10 June 1940.
21. Cordell Hull, *The Memoirs of Cordell Hull,* 2 vols. (New York: Macmillan, 1948), I: 784.

bombardments on metropolitan France and on air and maritime bases in Corsica and Tunisia. Little damage was inflicted. On that same day, while the Wehrmacht marched triumphantly down the Champs Elysées, Italian troops engaged in skirmishes in the Alps against the defiant French. The Fascist intellectual Giuseppe Bottai noted: "It is not the shortage of a great number of means that is striking, but a negligence that is petty and distressing. From every direction one resorts to daily expediencies, mean tricks, and lies."[22]

Growing restless, Mussolini, in his newly self-appointed position as commander-in-chief of all the Italian armed forces, issued orders on 15 June to the chief of the SMG for an attack in the Alps to start on the 18th.[23] Badoglio resisted this peremptory order by pointing out that changing from a defensive position to an offensive one would take twenty-five days. Upon learning from a wiretap involving General Mario Roatta, who emphatically declared that an attack would land Italy in a disaster,[24] Mussolini conceded Badoglio a postponement. Yet he did not hesitate to add: "the decision to attack France is essentially a political question which I alone must decide and bear the responsibility."[25]

The French premier Paul Reynaud resigned on 17 June. Field Marshal Philippe Pétain became prime minister, with the intention of asking the Germans for an armistice. Before dictating terms to the French, Hitler wanted to confer with Mussolini, who was taken by surprise at the suddenness of the French collapse. Ciano records the Duce's reaction: "I find Mussolini dissatisfied. This sudden peace disquiets him.... He would like to go so far as the total occupation of French territory and demands the surrender of the French fleet."[26]

The Italians were sure that Hitler was preparing to impose a harsh peace on France and this, given the anticipated collapse of Britain, whetted Mussolini's thirst for a reallocation of colonies and the power to oversee a New European Order. For a meeting in Munich with the Germans on 18 June, Ciano drafted his country's demands. Italy would occupy France to the Rhône and take possession of Corsica, Tunisia, and Djibouti. It would also have the right to occupy other French territories—metropolitan, colonial, or mandated—and use the naval bases of Algiers, Oran, and Casablanca. (Surprisingly, there was no mention of the long-standing claim to Savoy, the cradle of the Italian Royal House.) The French would be required to disarm and surrender their fleet and air force to Italy.

---

22. Giuseppe Bottai, *Vent'anni e un giorno (24 luglio 1943)* (Milan: Garzanti, 1977), p. 177.
23. *Le operazioni del giugno 1940 sulle alpi occidentali* (Rome: SME US, 1994), pp. 100–1.
24. *The Ciano Diaries*, 20 June 1940.
25. Pietro Badoglio, *L'Italia nella seconda guerra mondiale* (Milan: Mondadori, 1946), p. 46. Giorgio Bocca, *Storia d'Italia nella guerra fascista 1940–1943* (Milan: Mondadori, 1996), p. 153.
26. *The Ciano Diaries*, 17 June 1940.

But before the Axis Powers had a chance to divvy up their anticipated spoils, disturbing news arrived from London. General Charles de Gaulle, leading a small but defiant cartel, had vowed to fight on. It was clear to the Germans that if the Axis imposed a Carthaginian peace on the country, the French navy and government would either defect to England or take flight to North Africa, where many Frenchmen would follow to join de Gaulle's resistance. In contrast with a brutal occupation in Poland, the Germans would grant the defeated enemy certain sovereign rights. By forswearing military control over the entire nation and allowing a compliant government to function in an unoccupied zone, Germany would be spared an expensive occupation by hundreds of thousands of troops.

The fate of England was no less important in determining Hitler's treatment of France. A brutal occupation would hardly convince London that peace was in its own best interests. He therefore insisted that an armistice should be signed, a puppet regime in Paris set up, and Allied resistance ended in Europe to facilitate a global settlement with Britain that would acknowledge Germany's continental conquests. The Führer was hardly in the mood to antagonize potential British interlocutors and French collaborators by satisfying Mussolini's Mediterranean claims at their expense.

Although in Munich Hitler exercised no direct pressure on Mussolini to reduce his demands, Germans behind the scenes began obliquely to cut and trim. The atmosphere chilled. Among the many exchanges in the corridors was German Foreign Minister Joachim von Ribbentrop's aside to Ciano: "One must be moderate; one ought not to have eyes bigger than the stomach."[27] While Ribbentrop spoke to Ciano of the need for a "humane peace" and attempted to divert Italian eyes from Egypt and the Sudan, Hitler talked of a place for Britain in the new world order and the need to end the conflict as rapidly as possible.

Hitler's incongruous conciliation drove Mussolini, stunned by this "peace" atmosphere in Munich, into a corner. Would he dare attack a prostrate France on his own? If he met resistance, he would bear the onus for placing Hitler's armistice plans at risk and be accused of beating up an already tottering opponent. In retaliation, the Germans might proceed at once to a separate peace with England or with France—or with both together, leaving Italy as a mendicant. Hitler asked for few outright territorial acquisitions: Alsace-Lorraine, the Belgian Congo and at least part of Morocco. Occupation of the greater part of France, including the Channel and Atlantic coasts, would for the moment suffice. As Ciano put it, "Germany is in the state of mind of a poker player who,

---

27. Cited in F. W. Deakin, *The Brutal Friendship: Mussolini, Hitler and the Fall of Italian Fascism* (Garden City, New York: Anchor Books, 1966), p. 11; ACS, Graziani Papers, f. 46/5, Conversation between the Duce and General Roatta, 19 June 1940.

far beyond his hopes, finds himself in front of a pile of chips. Would it not be better to close the game?"[28] As a warning, Hitler politely but firmly informed Mussolini that armistice talks would not be engaged in jointly. Only the Germans would witness the Führer's victory celebration.

The Duce took the hint by trimming his demands. Ciano records: "Mussolini is very much embarrassed. He feels that his role is secondary. He reports on his conference with Hitler, not without a tone of bitterness and irony... In truth, the Duce fears that the hour of peace is growing near and sees fading once again the unattainable dream of his life: glory on the battlefield."[29] After having prophesied great Italian military exploits, Mussolini, in his admission that "our troops have not made a step forward," showed how hesitant he was to press exorbitant claims on an unenthusiastic Hitler.[30] Therefore, the notion that Mussolini surrendered to the dictates of a domineering Hitler to abandon his excessive claims is pure legend invented by certain French historians.[31] Nor can much stock be placed in Mussolini's so-called display of sportsmanship, as described by General Roatta, to explain why he did not claim more than he had expected to conquer.[32] With unwonted realism, Mussolini, knowing that he had no support from Hitler in advancing his territorial "rights" against France, had to practice the art of compromise. He could neither offend the Führer nor challenge a hostile French government in North Africa alone, for this would have brought about certain disaster at sea in the Mediterranean and a two-front war in the desert. Mussolini therefore had no choice but to hope that Britain would soon fall, after which nobody—not even his Axis partner—would be able to stand in the way of his claims to French colonies.

Mussolini's restraint caused much consternation among the Italian military, which bristled over the abandonment of claims to Tunisian ports, bases in North Africa plus Djibuti, as well as Nice, Savoy, and Corsica. The army, so unwilling to risk war, had expected to take full measure of Hitler's triumph by exacting a rich harvest of military and colonial advantages from a powerless France. Badoglio, who shied away from aggression toward France, aimed shamelessly to take full advantage of Hitler's triumph. General Giovanni Messe, the Italian military star of the future, deplored a once-in-a-lifetime opportunity to obtain mastery of the Mediterranean.[33] The king gave vent to his disappointment over

---

28. Cited in Deakin, *The Brutal Friendship*, pp. 11–12.

29. *The Ciano Diaries*, 18 and 19 June 1940.

30. Ibid., 21 June 1940.

31. Romain H. Rainero, "La campagna contro la Francia, l'armistizio e la CIAF, in *l'Italia in guerra il 1ª anno – 1940* (Rome: Commissione italiana di storia militare, 1985), p. 265.

32. Mario Roatta, *Otto milioni di baionette: L'esercito italiano in guerra 1940–1944* (Milan: Mondadori, 1946), pp. 103–4.

33. Mack Smith, *Mussolini's Roman Empire*, p. 222.

not gaining Savoy. The navy had perhaps the most legitimate complaint in deploring the loss of Tunisia, whose ports were sorely needed to supply Italian troops in the Libyan Desert. But the highly placed Italians who reviled Mussolini for pusillanimity had rushed to judgment. Their leader would put off, but not forgo, revenge for the *vittoria mutilata*. In the light of this territorial greed, how could any reasonably objective historian still argue that Mussolini dragged an unwilling country into war?

Hitler was relieved by Mussolini's comedown. For now his diplomatic gamesmanship could proceed unimpeded by large Italian demands on France. If Mussolini felt cheated, so much the worse for him. Despite Hitler's continued assurances to the Duce, he cared not a whit for Italy's imperialist ambitions, or for Italians, other than the Blackshirt units willing to fight to the death. Yet he was determined to keep Mussolini, whom he admired, as an ally.

Soon Mussolini was his belligerent self once again. Italy's imperial claims would not come as baksheesh but earned by spilled blood. On 20 June he ordered an attack for the next day against the supposedly already-defeated French, whose representatives were on the point of departure for negotiations with the Germans. Badoglio was dismayed, as was the chief of the air force, Francesco Pricolo. They preferred helping themselves to French territories from Hitler's platter rather than fighting for them. Ciano told the Duce that it was "inglorious to fall upon a defeated army."[34] Unsure of himself, Mussolini first rescinded the attack and the next instant ordered the Italian armies to advance against well-prepared French positions, but only on the northernmost sector of the front.

Hopes of a speedy victory vanished when the Italian military quickly ran into snags on all fronts. The troops, having a commanding advantage of twenty-two divisions against the French six, surged forward in dreadful weather against an adversary that was dug deeply in the formidable Alpine mountain ranges. Mussolini's crisscrossing commands in the movement of troops, supplies, and artillery, did not help military deployment.[35] Faced by a spirited French resistance, the offensive ground to a quick halt. The armistice saved Mussolini further embarrassment and further needless casualties. While the French suffered 37 dead, 42 wounded, and 150 unaccounted for, the Italian losses were far greater, with 631 dead, 2,631 wounded, and 616 unaccounted for. The Fascist newspaper writer Roberto Farinacci concluded: "Ours is like a Mexican army."[36]

---

34. *The Ciano Diaries*, 20 June 1940.
35. V. Gallinari, *Le operazioni del giugno 1940 sulle Alpi occidentali* (Rome: SME US, 1981), p. 135.
36. Marco Innocenti, *L'Italia del 1940: Come eravamo nel primo anno della guerra di Mussolini* (Milan: Mursia, 1996), p. 53.

Hitler proceeded to Compiègne on 22 June where he demanded that the French hand over to Germany a few vitally important territories: Alsace-Lorraine, the Belgian Congo, and part of Morocco. France would be divided into an occupied zone in the North and an unoccupied zone in the South; the army would be demobilized apart from a force of 100,000 necessary to ensure internal order; the fleet would be disarmed and ships locked in their home ports. The French would bear occupation costs, and their prisoners of war, almost two million of them, would remain in captivity until hostilities were over. For security against the British, Germany would occupy the French Atlantic coast. Now that the fighting had ceased, the Armistice would serve as a preliminary to a final peace settlement. Of compassion there was none—one can only say that the French were treated better than the Poles.

The Italians sat down with the French at Villa Incisa on 23 June to thrash out their armistice terms. Bracing themselves for the worst, the French were ready to walk out of the talks and return to the trenches for a fight to the finish against a boastful but feckless enemy. But the Italian delegation, led by Badoglio, treated French General Charles Huntzinger with the utmost courtesy and presented mild terms. Mussolini, since he was not present, was spared this demonstration of Latin fraternity. Although required to disarm and saddled with an inspection team to enforce the demilitarization of naval bases at Toulon, Bizerte, Ajaccio and Mers el Kébir, the French were greatly relieved to hear that the Italians would foreswear occupation of the left bank of the Rhône and annexation of Corsica, Tunis, and Djibouti, limiting themselves to a narrow slice of territory in the mountains between Menton and Savoy.[37] As the only belligerent toward whom the French officers could legitimately feel superior, the new conservative forces grouped around French head of government Marshal Pétain, who were groomed for collaboration with Germany, were greatly relieved to find Italy treating their prostrate country reasonably well.

The Italians were divided in their feelings toward a foe beaten by the Germans. General Badoglio, who had vivid memories of personal camaraderie during the Great War, showed magnanimity, which was shared by moderate Italians who hoped that the supposedly friendly rapport achieved between the Italian and French generals at Villa Incisa presaged a rapprochement between Rome and Paris against the Teutonic hordes. But they stood no chance against Mussolini and the hardliners, who were bent on taking full measure of their claims against the "Latin Sister."

Argument still rages today over whether Hitler made a mistake in failing to

---

37. Mack Smith, *Mussolini's Roman Empire*, p. 224; Bocca, *Storia d'Italia nella guerra fascista*, pp. 183, 188.

occupy the southern coast of France and French North Africa in June 1940. To deliver a shattering blow to England, would it not have been better if he had placed the whole of France under Nazi rule as a stepping-stone to a Mediterranean campaign that would sweep out the British fleet by the seizure of Malta and the Suez Canal? Two high-ranking Germans, Admiral Erich Raeder and General Heinz Guderian, had in vain asked Hitler to postpone the armistice so they would have time to move on to French North Africa with the assistance of Franco's Spain. But historian Andreas Hillgruber argues that Hitler was right. Although a grand-style Axis war in the Mediterranean would have inflicted great damage on Britain and its imperial position, it would not have impaired the vital nerve: communications with the United States in the Atlantic.

As for Mussolini, in 1944 he singled out Hitler's failure to insist that the Axis occupy the southern coast of France and French North Africa in June 1940 as a fatal error because it left the British daring and resolute in the Mediterranean.[38] But Hitler had his own reasons. Already fixated on his conflict with Bolshevism, and unable to bomb the British into rubble—or to invade the island fortress—he dabbled with different proposals to cut a global deal with Britain, which required an armistice with France, not conquest. His overall objective in 1940 was not so much the destruction of the British Empire but construction of a German continental empire consolidated by a Lebensraum in the East. Since the Mediterranean did not loom large in Hitler's immediate scheme of things, "Perfidious Albion" was left to recover its strength following Dunkirk and prepare for another day. Italy would pay a stiff price for Hitler's treatment of the Mediterranean as a secondary theater.

"Quivering" with warlike spirit against the British, Mussolini implored Badoglio to put "wings to everybody's feet."[39] Sitting like a wounded duck on the Italian "sacred sea" was the British fortress island of Malta, undermanned, underarmed, and vulnerable—Britain's only base in the central Mediterranean. Admiral Cavagnari casually perused skeleton plans for the invasion of Malta, but found a paucity of landing equipment, inadequate air support, and insufficiently trained assault troops, as well as no detailed plan for an amphibious action. Imagining that the island bristled with weapons, he took invasion off the books, a decision that would be revisited in 1942.

In the North African desert, Italo Balbo, the Italian governor of Libya, caught the war fever by toying with an offensive aimed at the Suez Canal against the slender British forces arrayed against him. But Badoglio moved quickly to

---

38. Nicholas Farrell, *Mussolini: A New Life* (London: A Phoenix Paperback, 2004), p. 337.
39. Mario Montanari, *Le Operazioni in Africa Settentrionale* (Rome: SME US, 1990), (hereafter cited as *Operazioni*), Vol I: *Sidi el Barrani (giugno 1940-febbraio)*, p. 72.

put Balbo on a short leash, which was not difficult since he was despairing over the lack of equipment, heavy tanks, and motorized infantry and had not yet blocked out any two-front strategy. But when the French colonies on 28 June declared for Pétain, Mussolini assumed that, having been freed of the French threat, Balbo could, in fourteen days, turn full attention to fighting the British. Few supplies, however, reached him, due in large measure to the loss of one-third of the Italian merchant fleet, which was caught in neutral ports upon Italy's declaration of war. Many orders placed abroad for much-needed equipment and raw materials were instantly aborted.

Hampered by Badoglio's veto on offensive action, Balbo watched helplessly while British short but swift attacks in Libya quickly overran several outposts and resulted in the capture of an Italian general. On 28 June Badoglio ordered him to commence an attack on 15 July. Balbo was not destined to read that order or lead the assault, for on that very day his aircraft, on reconnaissance for British armored cars, was shot down by Italian anti-aircraft batteries while heading for a landing to refuel for continuing the search. Mussolini shed no tears over the removal of an imposing rival, and his death did not delay preparation for the attack on Egypt. Libya seemed to be the obligatory destination of Fascist dauphins in disgrace.

Badoglio's main rival, General Rodolfo Graziani, the army chief-of-staff, was sent to Tripoli to be Balbo's successor. The deputy chief of the army, General Mario Roatta, would take care of business in Rome. Only reluctantly accepting his new appointment, Graziani took a cram course in desert warfare before flying off to Benghazi to take up his command; on arrival he found Badoglio's order to attack on his desk. The pressure for an offensive intensified when Mussolini sent a message to Graziani through Badoglio on 3 July that it was "a vital interest for Italy" that he be ready to launch the offensive by the 15th so as to coincide with a supposed German landing on British shores.[40] Mussolini, however, in a sudden turnaround, informed his commander that the 15 July target date was only "*indicative*," which left him free to initiate an offensive at a time of his own choosing.[41] When he had secured the means, a foray into Sollum would do for the moment.

A little later Mussolini granted Graziani a further reprieve because of the hot weather and because many months were needed to amass equipment and supplies for a far ranging campaign that would carry him beyond Marsa Matruh to Alexandria. This confusion of military orders issued, revised, and cancelled

---

40. *Operazioni*, I: 78.
41. Renzo De Felice, *Mussolini l'alleato 1940–1945*, vol. I: *L'Italia in guerra 1940–1943*, Tomo primo: *Dalla guerra "breve" alla guerra lunga* (Turin: Einaudi, 1990), p. 279.

between Rome and Libya amounted to much talk and no action. But Mussolini was in no hurry for he fully expected a quick German conquest of England that would leave Italy master of the Suez Canal. According to Ciano, the Duce considered the "march on Alexandria as practically completed." Even the cautious Badoglio "considers the undertaking easy and safe."[42] Hinging everything on a yet-to-come German amphibious landing on British shores was a bad way to win a war.

Two years later Göring asked Mussolini in Rome "why at the time of the armistice negotiations with France the occupation of Tunis had not been demanded." The Duce replied that he had been far too modest.[43] In truth, his "modesty" toward the French at Villa Incisa stemmed from the near immobility of his armed forces. Now it would be up to the diplomatic arm to defend Italy's parity in the Axis. For Hitler was on the verge of laying the groundwork for what was to become Mussolini's greatest nightmare—an anti-British continental system to include the collaborationist Vichy and a non-belligerent Spain. If the Führer's gambit worked, Mussolini would be robbed of his privileged standing in Berlin and bereft of imperial gain.

The "Latin Sisters"

Fearful that the Pétain regime would hand over its navy to the Germans, the British Royal Navy on 3 July opened fire on French ships anchored at Mers el Kébir on the Algerian coast, inflicting heavy damage and killing almost 1,300 French sailors. General Charles Noguès commented: "The Boches would not have acted more perfidiously."[44] Admiral François Darlan was so enraged by the damage done to his fleet that he pressed for reprisals and suggested that France and Italy should mount a joint attack against Alexandria.[45] Pétain ordered a study for the basing of Italian aircraft in Algeria to help protect French ships. During the first week of July the Vichy regime proposed that the two navies undertake a joint action against the British fleet deployed off Alexandria and liberate the French forces trapped in the harbor.[46] Was France sufficiently outraged to proceed from armistice to alignment with the Axis as retaliation against Perfidious Albion?

For a brief two weeks the Italian military apparently thought so. The navy

---

42. *The Ciano Diaries*, 2 July 1940.

43. Deakin, *The Brutal Friendship*, p. 65.

44. Cited in Julian Jackson, *France. The Dark Years 1940–1944* (Oxford: Oxford University Press, 2001), p. 129.

45. Philippe Burrin, *Living with Defeat: France Under the German Occupation, 1940–1944* (New York: The New Press, 1997), p. 78.

46. Romain H. Rainero, *Mussolini e Pétain: Storia dei rapporti tra l'Italia e la Francia di Vichy (10 giugno 1940–8 settembre 1943)* (Rome: SME US, 1990), I: 104.

pondered cooperation with the French fleet, while Badoglio broached the idea of an Italian air base in Algeria for joint Italo-French operations against British vessels. But in Rome doubts prevailed over the trustworthiness of the French military commanders in North Africa coupled with suspicions of the Germans for eyeing bases in Algeria and Morocco. To deny the French precedent, Mussolini rejected their offers of air bases for Italian use in Algeria and forbade joint Franco-Italian naval operations of any kind.[47] As for Hitler's ploy of a French "non-belligerence" on the side of the Axis, Mussolini regarded the Armistice a fraud and resumed his country's outright intransigence toward the Vichy regime.[48]

On 7 July, hoping to shred the Armistice, Ciano brazenly pressed Hitler for an immediate peace treaty with France. Shamelessly, he added claims to the already hefty list originally submitted in Munich: Italian domination of the Middle East pivoted on a protectorate over Tunisia and occupation of three French ports in the Red Sea. Hitler parried with the usual arguments: further humiliation imposed on the French would not convince London that peace was in its best interests, and an alienated Vichy regime would lack the motivation to resist a British move in French Equatorial and Northern Africa.[49] Ciano backed off. Hitler's unresponsiveness left Mussolini with the unrelieved fear that Germany would suddenly end the war by a settlement with England. The seductive German promise of a quick and easy peace, he feared, would act as a potent anesthetic to dull the warlike sensibilities of the Italian people.

The split between Mussolini and Hitler over Vichy France and the Armistice had widened following the events of Mers-el-Kébir. Hitler took the Royal Navy's blindside attack as marking the existence of a fearsome alliance between Britain and Gaullists in the French colonies. To neutralize such a threat and short-circuit anything that might threaten the survival of the Vichy regime, he aimed to maintain the status quo of the Armistice. As he was weighing options toward England, the last thing he wanted was a revolt in French Africa or a threat to the Vichy regime that would require an Axis military intervention—hence Hitler's determination to keep Mussolini quiet on the subject of Vichy France.

On 30 July Mussolini triumphantly issued a declaration of victory over 20,000 French inhabitants in the small slice of French territory under Italian occupation. Unbowed, Vichy representatives immediately began to hide military equipment from the Italians in violation of the existing armistice provisions.[50]

---

47. Documents German Foreign Policy (hereafter cited as DGFP), D, X, 151, Weizsäcker memorandum, 11 July 1940.
48. Documenti Diplomatici Italiani (hereafter cited as DDI), 9, V, 215, Anfuso to Alfieri, 10 July 1940.
49. Knox, *Mussolini Unleashed*, p. 143.
50. Romain H. Rainero, *Mussolini e Pétain. Storia dei rapporti tra l'Italia e la Francia di Vichy (10 giungo 1940–8*

Such deception driving him to distraction, the Duce wrote Hitler: "I feel sure that you cannot have failed to note the extraordinary psychological phenomenon, so typical of the indomitable pride of the French, that *France does not consider herself defeated.*"[51]

Vichy representatives, essentially anti-British, were willing to collaborate with Germany if given a broad settlement that would barter armistice constraints for a welcome mat leading into Hitler's New Europe. If granted a limited rearmament, Vichy would be able to beat off British attacks on the empire. For his part, Mussolini begrudged the slightest concession that might mitigate French pain. But lurking in the wings was the specter of a Communist and Gaullist-led revanchist conspiracy supplied with Anglo-American gold. To meet this threat, Mussolini bragged that he had eight Italian divisions at the ready to suppress any uprising.

From Mussolini's historical perspective, Italian claims were just and so was he: "We don't claim amputations from France, only restitutions."[52] These "restitutions" were rather small, he insisted—only about 1,000 kilometers.[53]

In this "clash of civilizations," the Fascists, having emerged victorious over the French, believed that their "virile and young" country had proven its superiority over a foe debilitated by social and political decay. They saw France as suffering a perennial rural crisis of under-population and judged its people as leading a slovenly café life. This they compared with the demographic fecundity and selfless heroism found in the indomitable Italian farmer-warrior. "Only in France has the kitchen assumed national importance and been cultivated as a noble art," Mussolini noted: "In Paris there existed before the war 38,000 trattorias, which is the cause and demonstration of French flabbiness today."[54]

The Italian Armistice Commission (CIAF), set up on 27 June 1940 to execute the armistice conventions concluded between Italy and France, institutionalized this triumphalist tone in Fascist Italy's propaganda. Headquartered in Turin, it was a military structure not subject to the SME but responsible to Mussolini. Thus CIAF would be a direct arm of the Duce in his pursuit of a radical policy of "victory."

General Badoglio needed no persuasion to discard his long-standing francophilia. The French, he told the German military attaché in Rome Enno von Rintelen, in August, should be punished for cheating on the armistice by their

---

settembre 1943, Vol. II: *Documenti* (Rome: SME US, 1992), pp. 91–96.

51. DGFP, D, X, 388, Mussolini to Hitler, 24 August 1940; DDI, 9, V, 484, Mussolini to Hitler, 24 August 1940.

52. Pietromarchi Papers (hereafter cited as PP *Diario*), 15 January 1942.

53. PP, *Diario*, 15 January 1942.

54. Rainero, *Mussolini e Pétain,* II: 311–12.

refusal to demobilize in North Africa. Roatta was more vocal still; it was time to "act with the mentality *of victors.*" Provoked by French "conspicuous arrogance," he yearned to teach them a lesson they would not soon forget.[55]

Outfoxed by Franco

With Italy's conquest of Ethiopia back in May 1936, Mussolini had arrived at a crossroads. Contemporary observers asked: would he undertake a rapprochement with the Western Powers offended by Fascist aggression or gravitate toward an alliance with Hitler? The chance opening of the Spanish Civil War and Mussolini's decision to aid the fellow would-be dictator Francisco Franco propelled Italy into the arms of Nazi Germany. At the outset, however, it was not clear that this would be Italy's destiny. For one thing, Italy's involvement occurred largely by accident and in the belief that a victory over Spain's weak Republican forces would be speedily won. In taking no heed of history's warning that interventions in a civil war usually create more problems than they solve, Mussolini paid a price. The proud Franco was standoffish, and Fascism's fragile prestige suffered a blow when the Garibaldi Brigade of expatriate anti-Fascist Italians contributed to the defeat of the Black Shirt units at Guadalajara in March 1937.

Did Mussolini hope to forge a tie with, and eventually a patronage over, a kindred Spanish authoritarian movement? Initially, he was influenced by strategic considerations. Of highest import was to forestall a Popular Front encirclement of Italy in the Mediterranean; a slightly lesser aim was to acquire the Balearic Islands. As the conflict in Spain dragged on, Realpolitik yielded to ideology, with Mussolini posing as a Fascist crusader against democracy and Bolshevism.

Following the collapse of Republican Spain, Franco threw a goodbye party for the Italians in Madrid on 19 May 1939. In the victory parade, General Gastone Gambara and the Fascist Blackshirts were given the place of honor at the head of more than 100,000 Nationalist troops who marched past Franco's reviewing stand. The two countries anticipated a future division of French North Africa: Morocco to Spain, and Tunisia plus Algeria to Italy.[56] On 27 March 1939 Spain adhered to the anti-Comintern Pact and on 8 May left the League of Nations.

When World War II broke out in September 1939, Franco had been sorely tempted to join the Germans. But lacking a navy, Spain was quite defenseless

---

55. Cited in Massimo Borgogni, *Mussolini e La Francia di Vichy* (Siena: Nuova Immagine Editrice, 1991), p. 131.
56. John F. Coverdale, *Italian Intervention in the Spanish Civil War* (Princeton, NJ: Princeton University Press, 1975), pp. 384–85.

against the British fleet while Spanish Morocco lay wide open to an attack by French colonial troops stationed in Algeria. Impoverished by the long and bloody civil war, Spain was dependent on trade with the Atlantic Powers, which left Franco no choice but to observe grudging neutrality.

In the aftermath of the Spanish Civil War, many Italians wondered whether the effort had been worth the cost. The tangible rewards were paltry, and the Spanish refused to own up to the large debts incurred during the Italian intervention. When Spain declared neutrality at the outbreak of World War II, Mussolini was not unhappy, for if Franco had joined Hitler, he would infringe on *mare nostrum* and lay claims to areas in North Africa tentatively demarcated as Italian. On 10 April 1940, writing Franco that Italy could not allow a war that would "strangle" Germany, Mussolini asked only for Spain's "support."[57] In early June he issued Franco a half-hearted invitation to join in the conflict by promising that Gibraltar would be returned to Spain when adjustments were made in the Mediterranean at the end of hostilities.[58]

On 10 June, the day that Italy entered the war, Franco wrote Mussolini that Spanish destiny was "indissolubly tied to the destiny of Italy," which left the Duce to mull over the contrast between Franco's risk-free words of spiritual affinity and Italy's willingness to sacrifice arms and money for the Nationalist insurgency against the Spanish Republican government in 1936. Franco edged closer to the Axis by passing from neutrality to non-belligerency on 12 June and by seizing the international enclave at Tangiers two days later—the first imperial conquest of the "new" Spain.

When German legions cruised into Paris, Franco prepared to climb aboard the Wehrmacht express. Without any encouragement from either Berlin or Rome, he presented his terms on 19 June. Spain would enter the war if given Gibraltar (which he had long demanded), a united Morocco under Spain's protection, the Oran district of Algeria, an extension of Rio de Oro to the twentieth parallel, and an enlargement of Spanish Guinea. But before Spain could take the field, Germany would have to deliver extensive economic aid and military supplies.[59] At this point Hitler, thinking he had the Western Powers in his grasp, saw no reason to bid for Franco's intervention in the war at such a high price.[60]

Meanwhile, Mussolini, after a period of indecision regarding Spain, pushed ahead by securing the use of Spanish air bases for bombing runs on Gibraltar.[61]

57. Stanley G. Payne, *Franco and Hitler* (New Haven and London: Yale University Press, 2008), p. 61.
58. DDI, 9, IV, 827, Mussolini to Franco, 9 June 1940.
59. Norman J. W. Goda, *Hitler, Northwest Africa, and the Path Toward America* (College Station, TX: Texas A & M University Press, 1998), p. 60.
60. DGFP, D, X, 73. Conversation between Hitler and Alfieri, 1 July 1940.
61. De Felice, *Mussolini l'alleato*, I:179, n. 1.

But Franco, who feared that Germans would join Italians already stationed on Spanish soil, would not let the Duce rush his country into war against Britain until a final settlement had been worked out in Berlin. Hence the Spaniards insisted on 2 July that the small squadron of twenty Italian planes geared up for action be sent home.[62] Confronted by Franco's timidity, Mussolini's ardor in abetting Spain's imperial ambitions cooled noticeably; correspondingly, there was no letup in the Caudillo's suspicions regarding Italian designs on French Morocco and bases in the Balearics.

On 1 October Mussolini advised Ramón Serrano Suñer, the Spanish minister of the interior, that before entering the war Spain would have to upgrade its military, ease food shortages, and intervene at a time convenient for the Axis. "As far as the aid which Italy can give is concerned," the Duce concluded, "it is out of the question—in view of the scanty grain harvest—for us to help to make up the large Spanish deficit."[63]

Three days later Mussolini met with Hitler, who complained that dickering with the Spaniards made him feel "as if he were a little Jew who was haggling about the most sacred possessions of mankind." Given that clear sign of Hitler's disgruntlement, Mussolini, for the first time in his company, openly expressed his reluctance to satisfy Spanish claims on French Morocco. As a jealous guardian of his privileged status in Berlin, the Duce was not unhappy to see Franco sidetracked.[64] But neither did he want Germany to plant a big footprint in French North Africa. Since Hitler agreed with him that the Spaniards were horse-traders who demanded much and offered little, Mussolini suggested that Spanish non-belligerency was better than Spanish intervention in the war. Franco, in turn, feared—not without reason—that if Spain joined the war, Mussolini would claim French Moroccan territory and the Balearic Islands for Italian air and naval bases as payment for Italy's assistance in the war.

Mussolini was just as anxious to head off a suspected German move that would upgrade Vichy to equal standing with Italy in the grand alliance against Britain. While as distrustful of the French as Mussolini, Hitler persisted in pursuing the fiction that the conflicting colonial claims of France, Spain, and Italy could be sorted out to everyone's satisfaction by legerdemain.[65] At the peace table France would be shorn of territory in Africa that would be handed over to Spain but receive compensation from the British Empire. Neither Spain

62. Archivio Centrale dello Stato, (hereafter cited as ACS), Graziani Papers, b. 58, f. 47, sotto f. 9.

63. DDI, 9, V, 660, Conversation between Mussolini and Suñer, 1 October 1940.

64. DGFP, D, XI, 199, Mussolini to Hitler, 19 October 1940; DDI, 9, V, 753, Mussolini to Hitler, 19 October 1940.

65. Franz Halder, *The Halder Diaries, 1939–1942*, 2 vols. (Novato, CA: Presidio Press, 1988), I: 609, 3 October 1940.

nor France would fully learn what they were due until after the war. Hitler's quixotic diplomacy and Mussolini's rampant suspicions did not augur well for the Führer's ability to sell a continental coalition to Franco and Pétain.

On 20 October Hitler set out on his special train *Amerika* to Hendaye, expecting to finagle Spain into an attack on Gibraltar. Franco met him with his usual extravagant demands on French colonies in North Africa, which almost certainly would have precipitated an end to German collaboration with Vichy France. Hence Hitler refused to be pinned down regarding Spanish colonial claims on France. Naturally he carefully avoided sharing with Franco his own designs on African coastal areas from which he intended to launch a showdown with the United States. Unwilling to alienate Vichy France to gain Spanish belligerency, Hitler had little to offer.

And so on to Montoire where Hitler met with Vichyite authorities. Since Dakar had proved to him that Vichy France was willing to take up arms to defend its empire against Gaullists and the English, he persevered with his "new policy" toward Vichy. Nothing much else happened except a stiff exchange of pleasantries. Hendaye and Montoire seemed to have been a waste of time, but Hitler was not too disappointed since simple collaboration with France would continue, allowing Germany to milk the economy at will.

A face-saving and nonbinding tripartite protocol finally emerged on 4 November. Franco would take his country into the war after being provided with the military support necessary for an effective mobilization. Spain would annex Gibraltar and receive areas in French North Africa. The Vichy regime would be compensated with British colonial territories of equal value, but German and Italian claims against France in North Africa would remain unaffected.

Hitler disembarked from his train in Florence on 28 October for a meeting with Mussolini, hopeful of bonding Italy to his continental system. But Mussolini, rather than desiring collaboration with the "duplicitous" French, urged Hitler to drag them to the peace table for full settlement of Italy's claims. Determined to preserve his privileged place, he would persuade Hitler to spurn both Pétain and Franco. The Führer repeated the promise for the nth time that no eventual settlement with the French would leave Italy's demands unfulfilled, but he rejected the idea of a separate peace for the moment since it would kill French incentive to collaborate. Not so surprisingly, Mussolini offered no help in bringing the Spanish to reason on their vast territorial demands, and he showed not the slightest interest in participating in the invasion of Gibraltar. Doubtless, Hitler's "grand deception" to catch Spain and Vichy France in his anti-British net was dead on arrival thanks to the irreconcilable imperialist claims of all concerned. But it was Mussolini, confined to a grandstand view, who sealed the coffin.

The question of Spain abruptly resurfaced in early December 1940 when Hitler came up with "Operation Felix," the invasion of Gibraltar, to be facilitated by Spanish entry into the war. But on 7 December Franco put a damper on German plans to capture the Rock. "Felix" was cancelled three days later. Peeved at the refractory Spanish, Hitler set Mussolini up to bring Spain around. The Duce obliged by wining and dining Franco at Bordighera in February 1941, but he never moved beyond pleasantries since he was convinced more than ever of the untimeliness of a Spanish entry into the war. The Duce told Pietromarchi: "How does one bring into war a nation that has a bread reserve of only a day?" Franco made clear that he would not be talked down to: "Spain cannot tolerate padroni; nor does it intend to pass from an English hegemony to a German." In a "verbose" presentation, "disorganized, lost in petty details and long digressions about military issues," Franco boasted: "Now it is very clear that the Gibraltar enterprise is neither a German nor Italian undertaking, but exclusively a Spanish one that the Spaniards intend to accomplish with their own arms."[66] But since Germany was unwilling to meet his needs, Franco did admit that if Spain entered the war his country would be a liability: "An army that doesn't eat can't fight."[67]

Unlike Mussolini, Franco was lucky to eventually emerge from the war unscathed. In the Great Power sweepstakes, the Duce had entered the conflict at a time when a British defeat seemed imminent, but without any written guarantee on territorial gain with the Third Reich. Franco, too, was ready for a rush to arms in June in spite of the deplorable shape of his country, but first wanted his avaricious demands guaranteed by the Axis in a written document. This document was not forthcoming. That Franco refrained from entering the war was not so much because he was more prescient than the Duce, or that he was playing a shrewd double game with the Allies, or that his price was studiously excessive. Rather it was mainly because the Germans had nettled him by their outlandish demands for economic concessions and military privilege in North Africa. If the notoriously pro-Nazi Serrano Suñer could not bring the stiff-necked Germans around, who could? Hitler only developed a serious interest in Gibraltar in December 1940. By then it was too late, for Franco had learned to navigate diplomatic shoals deftly. In insisting on written guarantees from the Germans, the Caudillo was perhaps fortunate that he never received them.

Mussolini's shortsighted diplomacy was there for all to see. By dragging his feet on a speedy Spanish entry into the war, the Duce forgot that the capture of Gibraltar might have gone a long way in cutting down British raids on Italian

---

66. Quotes above taken from PP, *Diario*, 11 February 1941.
67. Payne, *Franco and Hitler*, p. 112.

shipping in the Mediterranean. Moreover, he made no effort to resolve conflicting Italian and German claims on military bases and mineral concessions in Spain and its overseas colonies. Nor did the Duce venture the advice that neither power should infringe on Spanish claims on French North Africa for fear of offending Franco. Axis rapacity and unwillingness to coordinate diplomacy left Franco an open lifeline to the Allies.

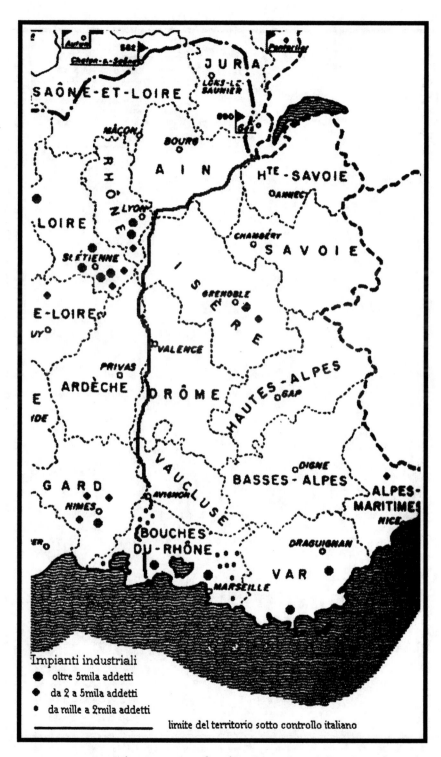

Italian occupation of southern France, June 1940 to September 1943.

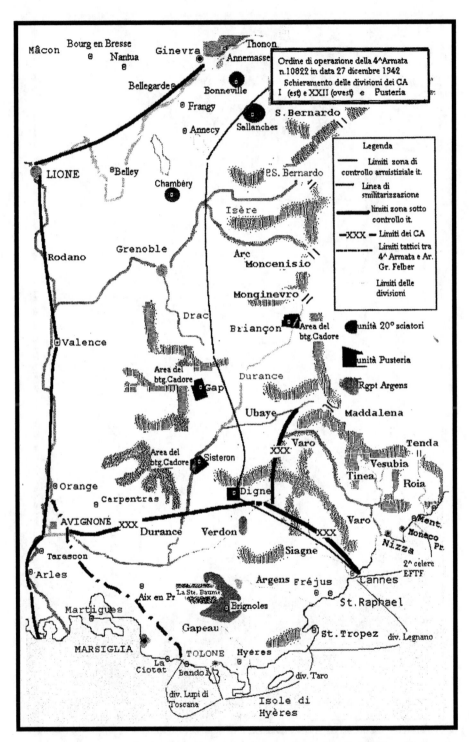

Italian zone of occupation in France: detail by military unit.

Chapter II

The Short War Gets Longer

A Pained Restraint
Stalled in the African Sands
Planning Aggression
A Shambling Military
The Greek Fever

A Pained Restraint

Prior to Italy's intervention in World War II, Mussolini had sought restlessly to advance Italian power and influence in the Balkans by support of kindred insurrectionary movements in a *revisionismo fascista*. With the exception of Albania, however, he had always stopped short of outright military invasion. Once the guns of war sounded, hopes were rekindled in Rome that the time to strike was fast approaching. But the long arm of Germany kept Mussolini under a pained restraint. Having assured the Yugoslavs that they need not fear attack, Berlin was busily negotiating with the Balkan countries for much-needed raw materials at a favorable rate of exchange. He wanted no Italian "parallel war" to upset an undisturbed *Drang nach Südosten*.

Mussolini was not about to leave unchallenged Germany's intrusion into the polyglot kingdom that he considered part of Italy's sphere of influence. It was a question of timing. In early July Hitler inadvertently seemed to give Mussolini an opening by informing Dino Alfieri, the Italian ambassador in Berlin, that the

Wehrmacht had discovered a treasure trove of documents belonging to French and Allied commands that had been abandoned in a railway car at La Charité-sur-Saône. These captured materials contained evidence that the Yugoslav and Greek governments had surreptitiously bid for Allied support in language full of enmity toward the Fascist creed. Delighted to share this damaging revelation with his fellow dictator,[1] Hitler had no idea that his small talk would fuel Mussolini's impetuosity. The Duce could hardly wait to destroy the "artificial contrivance" created by ungrateful former allies at the Paris Peace Conference. Yugoslavia had no place in a Europe remodeled by Fascism. The first steps were taken for an invasion by the movement of men and equipment from the frontier with France to the plains in the Po valley.

Greece vied with Yugoslavia for Mussolini's attention. He was still smarting over the Corfu incident of 1923 that had besmirched Italian pride. In that year an Italian official, who was part of an international surveying team demarcating the border between Greece and Albania, was killed on Greek territory by unidentified brigands. Holding the Athens government responsible, Mussolini retaliated by ordering the bombardment of Corfu followed by a landing of troops. Under British prodding, the League of Nations successfully applied pressure on Mussolini to withdraw his military, but relations between the two countries remained tense. The atmosphere improved somewhat in 1936 when General Ioannis Metaxas seized power and established a dictatorship. Since Mussolini regarded his government as ramshackle and reactionary, he deigned to lecture Metaxas, whom he regarded as a pupil, on the virtues of Fascism. But the Duce's imperial ambitions, suffused by historical resentments and geopolitical imagery, precluded Greek-Italian partnership based on ideological affinity, which cooled relations between Rome and Athens.

In this spirit Ciano in early July 1940 dressed down the Greek minister for permitting the British to use his country as a military base, a charge heatedly denied. Ciano records: "Mussolini is furious. If this music should continue he is decided to take action against Greece. The Greek minister tried weakly to deny it, but he left with his tail between his legs."[2]

It finally struck Hitler how his devilry—sharing news of the captured French documents with the Italians—was actually making Mussolini more eager for war in the Balkans and thus upsetting his diplomacy and military timetables. Still, in spite of gentle warnings to observe abstinence from aggression, Hitler left him a

---

1. Knox, *Mussolini Unleashed*, pp. 140–41; DGFP, D, XI, 73, Conversation between Ribbentrop and Ciano, 20 September 1940.
2. *The Ciano Diaries*, 3 July 1940.

ray of hope. If war broke out "spontaneously" in the Balkans, or after "England had been broken," Italy would be free to undertake military action.[3]

Stalled in the African Sands

War on the high seas started no more auspiciously for Italy than the land offensive against France. In fulfilling a mission that was more or less defined by control of the middle Mediterranean, the navy was hobbled by a lack of aircraft carriers, no fleet air arm, and no radar. On 9 July Italian naval units bound for North Africa and a British convoy headed for Malta ran into each other at Punta Stilo. The results were inconclusive. British Admiral Andrew Cunningham had not succeeded in inflicting serious damage on Italian warships, and the Italians were unable to boast any important hits. The battle showed up defects in the armament of Italy's heavy cruisers, inferiority of its renovated battleships compared to Britain's capital ships, and a manifest lack of cooperation between the Italian navy and air force. While London granted Cunningham freedom to make decisions, the Italian commander, Admiral Inigo Campioni, had to take orders from Cavagnari in Rome before every move, a cumbersome chain-of-command that paralyzed local initiative. Cavagnari's decision to break off the battle showed that he had little taste for head-on collisions with the British navy. The mission of simply protecting supply routes from Italy to North Africa was for the bold navy men a decidedly unheroic assignment. Although the morale of Italy's sailors remained steady following the standoff at Punta Stilo, they must have watched askance as Italian aircraft strafed their own ships.[4]

In the desert Mussolini let matters drift. Instead of fine-tuning an offensive against the British, he chose a waiting game to synchronize an attack with a German landing on British shores. When informed that German invasion plans had been postponed, he would give the unadventurous Graziani the decision to initiate an offensive at a time of his own choosing.[5] But Graziani's army was in no shape to cross 500 kilometers of desert. It consisted of a dozen divisions with 2,506 trucks, 70 badly designed medium tanks, artillery of World War I vintage, and over 300 fighters and bombers whose motors lacked filters and frequently were clogged with sand. Still, Graziani possessed military intelligence indicating that the British forces were composed essentially of only the 7th Armored Division, plus one Indian and one New Zealand division—167,000 Italian soldiers facing 36,000 British troops, with the rest spread out in Egypt guarding against a

---

3. DDI, 9, V, 274. Ciano to Mussolini, 20 July 1940; Martin L. Creveld, *Hitler's Strategy 1940–1941: The Balkan Clue* (Cambridge: Cambridge University Press, 1973), p. 18.
4. *The Ciano Diaries*, 13 July 1940.
5. Ibid., 8 and 19 August 1940.

potential uprising on the part of a hostile native population.[6] Ignoring Graziani's inaction, Mussolini wrote Hitler on 17 July: "The preparation for a large-scale attack on Egypt is now completed. To reach Alexandria it is necessary to traverse 600 kilometers of real desert during a season when the thermometer records 56 degrees [C] in the shade. This fact has weakened the English units, who are unable to cope with such temperatures. I hope I can begin the offensive at the same time as your attack on England."[7]

But Graziani, not predisposed to undertake bold action, was, it must be admitted, burdened by problems not of his own making. Innovative thinking on the part of his military subordinates had been stunted by years of rigid schooling in World War I tactics. They therefore lacked the technical training and imagination for planning or fighting a modern war of movement. Graziani also was faced by a shortage of tanks and their penchant for breaking down. Neither did he have any answer for the lack of trucks and water to supply an excessive number of foot soldiers doggedly plodding across endless stretches of barren desert.

On the other hand Graziani could have called on his own experience for a more aggressive solution to desert warfare. During the latter stages of the reconquest of Tripolitania in 1925, he had assembled a mobile force of trucks driven by indigenous recruits who transported munitions, water, oil, and food supplies. These native drivers could have been used for operations behind British lines to carry out sabotage and reconnaissance. Certainly the British were a far more formidable and modernized enemy than brave but ill-equipped Libyan tribesmen, but such a hit-and-run strategy might have helped to keep the British off-balance.[8] Graziani received no help from Mussolini, who hinged Italy's moves in the Mediterranean and North Africa on an unreliable ally's decision on whether or not to invade England. While the Italians dilly-dallied, the British filled out their skeletal forces in Egypt.

The situation was different in the Ethiopian theater, where Italian armies under the command of the youthful Amedeo II of Savoia-Aosta took bold measures. The Duke of Aosta outlined a gigantic pincers movement designed to crush the small and spread-out British forces by launching a major offensive through the Sudan to Egypt. The purpose was to link up his forces with the Italian army in Libya headed for Suez. Badoglio responded negatively to Amedeo's grandiose scheme, which forced him to settle for the considerably easier task of clearing out the weak British force stationed in Somaliland. Musso-

6. Knox, *Mussolini Unleashed*, p. 155.
7. DDI, 9, V, 264, Mussolini to Hitler, 17 July 1940; DGFP, D, X, 185, Mussolini to Hitler, 17 July 1940.
8. Luigi Goglia, "La guerra in Africa nel 1940," in *L'Italia in guerra: il 1ª anno—1940* (Rome: Commissione italiana di storia militare, 1992), p. 181.

lini gave the plan his blessing, and an Italian army under the command of General Guglielmo Nasi, with a five-to-one advantage in numbers and clear air superiority, wound up the campaign on 19 August. After having stonewalled for so long Amedeo's idea of linking military offensives launched from Libya and Ethiopia, Badoglio belatedly made an effort to coordinate strategy for Italian forces in the Middle East with the goal of conquering Egypt. But it would only be activated if Germany successfully invaded England. By the end of August, Badoglio had lost interest in this combined offensive.

Planning Aggression

Inspired by Ciano, who yearned to enlarge his Albanian satrapy, General Carlo Geloso on 16 July 1940 drew up what was to be called Contingency "G," a limited offensive operation against Greece, whose objective was the occupation of Epirus, of Akarnania as far as Missolonghi, and the Ionian islands.

At the same time Mussolini, in defiance of Hitler's warning to keep the peace across the Adriatic, ordered the military to prepare an offensive against Yugoslavia, which was to be called Contingency "E." Since the logistical problems of attacking Yugoslavia through the Julian Alps were insuperable owing to the rugged terrain, Hitler, it was presumed, would allow Italian military transit through Carinthia and Styria in coordination with a drive across the Adriatic. Italy put in a request for 5,000 German trucks, which provoked German General Franz Halder's dismissive reply: "Italians propose to invade Yugoslavia, and want German help: German transport for the build-up, German supply organization…. What incredible nerve!"[9]

Having received discouraging news from Berlin, Mussolini told Badoglio to "slacken the tempo." Roatta complied by slowing the pace of orders already issued. Relieved, Badoglio put the plan to attack Yugoslavia "in a drawer to be taken out at an opportune moment"—after England had been "liquidated."[10]

There was no letup in deceit between the two Axis partners. The Führer created angst in Rome when, before the Reichstag on 19 July, he appealed to the British for an end to the war. Was Germany about to divide the world with Italy's major imperial enemy? Moreover, Hitler took care to conceal his goal of invading the Soviet Union from Italy. Mussolini, in turn, repeatedly alleviated German fears of an Italian military move in the Balkans that he had no intention of giving up. Nothing would deter him from viewing Greece as fair game since it bordered on the Mediterranean, "Italy's sea."

---

9. *Halder Diaries*, I: 549, 14 August 1940.
10. ACS, Graziani Papers, 18 August 1940.

In this spirit on 12 August Ciano called to Rome the governor of Albania, Count Francesco Jacomoni di San Savino, and General Sebastiano Visconti Prasca for an audience with Mussolini. The chief of the Albanian army corps, Visconti Prasca took pride in his manly physique, though actually, with his monocle and dyed eyebrows, he appeared merely eccentric.[11] The purpose of the meeting was to prepare an action against Corfù and the Greek province of Ciamuria (the northern part of Epirus about up to the Arta River), which Italy's Albanian minions claimed to be rightfully theirs; the action would be launched after Germany's expected invasion of Britain. Jacomoni and Visconti Prasca considered this possible, even easy. Speed was essential to catch the Greeks by surprise. Note that at this stage there was no plan for the conquest of the entire Greek mainland, only satisfaction of Albanian irredentism and a deepened Italian foothold in the lower Balkans.

To prepare the Italian public, the propaganda ministry orchestrated an irredentist campaign in Ciamuria without realizing that intimidation publicly asserted conflicted with the military need for surprise. On 11 August the Italian radio reported that "the Albanian patriot" Daut Hoggia had been savagely murdered by Greek assassins, who cut off his head and paraded it through Athens.[12] This report was misleading and incomplete. Hoggia was a notorious cattle rustler with a prominent police record. The two assassins were Albanians, who had entered Greek territory and had admitted killing Hoggia for reasons entirely unrelated to any political motivation. Heightening the tension between Rome and Athens, an Italian submarine sank an aged Greek cruiser, the *Helle*, in the harbor of Tinos on 15 August, the day of the Greek Feast of the Assumption. The casualties were one dead and twenty-nine wounded. Both place and occasion suggested provocation and sacrilege, which united the country as never before in its modern history.[13] Rome feigned innocence, but the Greeks recovered fragments of the torpedo that proved it was Italian. Emanuele Grazzi, the Italian minister in Athens, who was one of the few forthright members of the Italian diplomatic corps, vigorously denounced the event to his superiors as a piratical action.[14] Embarrassed by the public outcry, Ciano foisted blame for this "intemperance" on the crude and impulsive Fascist Cesare Maria De Vecchi, the

---

11. Mario Cervi, *The Hollow Legions: Mussolini's Blunder in Greece* (New York: Doubleday, 1971), p. 34; Ray Moseley, *Mussolini's Shadow: The Double Life of Count Galeazzo Ciano* (New Haven CN: Yale University Press, 1991), p. 114.

12. W. Vincent Arnold, *The Illusion of Victory. Fascist Propaganda and the Second World War* (New York: Peter Lang, 1998), p. 82.

13. John G. Bitzes, *Greece in World War II to April 1941* (Manhattan, Kansas: Sunflower University Press, 1989), p. 67.

14. Emanuele Grazzi, *Il principio della fine (L'impresa di Grecia)* (Rome: Editrice Faro, 1945), pp. 172–182.

Italian commander in the Dodecanese.[15] Whoever was responsible, a deathblow had been delivered to the already brittle relationship between the Greeks and Italians.

Ribbentrop, aware that Italy was crackling with violence, told his trigger-happy ally on 16 August that an attack on Greece might set the area on fire. Unstated, but fundamental to Germany's plans, was keeping the Balkans quiet so that much-needed raw materials—chrome, manganese, copper, lead, nickel, tin, and aluminum—which were indispensable for the production of arms, would flow into Germany uninterrupted in the build-up for the invasion of the Soviet Union. Ciano agreed to a "complete order to halt all along the line."[16] As for the Greeks, the Germans told them to keep the British at a distance and ignore the Duce's provocations.[17]

In spite of Germany's efforts to defer Italian war plans, Rome continued to pursue them, but unsystematically. At this point Mussolini was unsure over what to do about Greece. Badoglio, who knew that the military was unprepared for a Balkan war, hoped that Ribbentrop and Rintelen would do what he sought to avoid having to do himself: prevail on Mussolini to avoid Balkan complications of any sort.

Mussolini finally yielded to German pressure, which gave Badoglio the opportunity to override Ciano's dangerous coterie. Jacomoni was told to cool his heels and Visconti Prasca warned to be circumspect regarding his contacts with the foreign ministry; he must scrupulously follow the orders of the army general staff.[18] The "Duke of Albania" stepped back from the brink: "Naturally we accept the Berlin point of view. Italy would resolve its dispute with Greece diplomatically and would take no military steps other than reinforcing the Albanian garrison."[19] In a letter filled with ambiguities and hedging, Mussolini reassured Hitler on 24 August that Italy's military measures against Yugoslavia and Greece were simply precautionary. But in reality he was determined to bring the Germans around to an Italian aggression in the Balkans whether by deception or other means.

At various times during August and September Mussolini issued orders to prepare for actions against Greece, Yugoslavia, and France. These simultaneous and frequently changed directives, especially those regarding Greece, caused dis-

15. *The Ciano Diaries*, 15 August 1940.
16. Ibid., 17 August 1940.
17. DGFP, D, X, 334, Weizsäcker memorandum, 13 August 1940; 363, Erbach to Foreign Ministry, 18 August 1940; 372, Erback to Foreign Ministry, 21 August 1940; 377, Woermann to Legation in Greece, 22 August 1940; 386, Woermann to Legation in Greece, 24 August 1940; 387, Woermann memorandum, 24 August 1940; 391, Erback to Foreign Ministry, 25 August 1940; 394, Sonnleithner memorandum, 27 August 1940.
18. De Felice, *Mussolini l'alleato*, I: 197–98.
19. *The Ciano Diaries*, 17 August 1940.

array in military circles. At one point in September, Badoglio declared that plans for Greece were "on the wane" and told Roatta that he was "patiently dismantling" the Greek operation, while Yugoslavia would receive highest priority.[20] But there was a plan on the table that aimed at occupying the Greek province of Ciamuria, for which nine divisions would suffice. Apparently Visconti Prasca and Jacomoni did not believe that troop numbers mattered, for they envisaged "victory" to consist of an Italian military parade into Ciamuria cheered on by friendly disaffected Albanians who comprised the majority of the population. The spiritless Greek army would simply slink away.

Such foolish thinking revealed the inability of the Italian military to develop coherent battle plans. General Quirino Armellini attributes this to an establishment riddled with intrigue, selfishness, overblown egos, and backbiting, which encouraged the top commanders to act out their own fantasies. For Badoglio, everything was manipulation. Unwilling to see Italy involved in Balkan wars, he foisted the task of restraining Mussolini on Germany. For Roatta, everything was bluff. Believing that an attack on Greece was far from inevitable, on 4 September he sent Visconti Prasca Contingency "G," which authorized him to begin a skeleton deployment that would be completed "at the last moment." Then he hedged further by telling Visconti Prasca: "operations are as of now under study and will be implemented following explicit orders from this SME."[21] As for Ciano, there was no manipulation or bluff; he bull-headedly sought war.

In typically listening to his own intuition rather than facts, Mussolini swung from limited objectives to all-out war, failing to take into account the enormously difficult logistical problems of tripling the number of troops and equipment needed for a sustained campaign. The Greeks, for their part, alarmed by the invective directed toward their country by the Italian press, plus Italian troop maneuvers in Albania, calmly began to call up reserves and hasten work on military defenses. By the beginning of September, Contingency "G" had lost the element of surprise.

A Shambling Military

While Balkan tensions simmered, Mussolini in mid-August urged an attack in North Africa. It appeared that Badoglio had won a victory over the various cliques arrayed against him.[22] But Graziani was not ready. Aware of the lack of water, he warned: "we move toward a defeat which, in the desert, must inevitably

---

20. Knox, *Mussolini Unleashed*, pp. 180–81.
21. NARS, T-821, 127, 000342, Roatta to Visconti Prasca, 31 August 1940; 000345; Roatta to Visconti Prasca, 000342–43, 31 August 1940; 000192, Roatta to Visconti Prasca, 26 September 1940.
22. Armellini, *Diario*, p. 64.

develop into a rapid and total disaster."[23] His generals were similarly pessimistic.[24] But the impatient Mussolini, wanting "to move fast in Egypt,"[25] sent out orders on 19 August for Graziani to attack "the day that the first platoon of German soldiers touches English soil."[26] He cited no fixed territorial objectives. "It is not a question of pointing toward Alexandria, and not even Sollum. I ask you only to attack the English forces facing you."[27] Such a step forward would gain the military credibility that Italy had lost in the failed attack against France in 1940. Graziani's task was therefore simplified to testing enemy strength.

When in August Mussolini came to believe that Germany's bombing raids on London were aimed more at softening up the British for a friendly compromise with Berlin rather than bringing them to their knees, he gave way to panic. Poking about the desert would no longer do; only a major offensive launched by 9 September that brought victory was deemed acceptable. Graziani, supported by Badoglio, begged for a month's postponement.[28] Mussolini reacted by telling the Council of Ministers that he would sack Graziani if he continued to shilly-shally.[29]

On 13 September General Graziani finally roused himself to action. In a parade set piece, he advanced across the Egyptian frontier sixty miles to Sidi el Barrani, an objective that served no real strategic purpose. In an orderly manner the British fell back to better defensive positions. (The Egyptians saw this retreat as a sign that the days of their imperialist oppressors were numbered.) Mussolini was "radiant with joy."[30] But nothing could conceal the lumbering and amateurish nature of the Italian advance by seven infantry divisions that lacked a sufficient number of motor vehicles, tanks, and artillery. In the battle, the British lost 50 soldiers, the Italians 120.

Though toasts were exchanged and brandy flowed in this transient moment of glory, Graziani would not budge from his new positions before the necessary equipment arrived and an aqueduct of 150 kilometers was built from Bardia.[31] His demands were legitimate, but his hyperbole ridiculous: "the enemy, after making every resistance imaginable, fighting every inch of the way, has finally been overcome by the maneuver that trapped it…. One can calculate that more

---

23. *The Ciano Diaries*, 8 August 1940.

24. Ibid., 20 August 1940; Bocca, *Storia d'Italia nella guerra fascista*, p. 184.

25. *The Ciano Diaries*, 18 August 1940.

26. DDI, 9, V, 467, Il Capo del Governo, Mussolini, 22 August 1940; *The Ciano Diaries*, 22 August 1940: "Mussolini gives me a copy of certain military directives he has formulated, in which the actions against Yugoslavia and Greece are indefinitely postponed."

27. *Operazioni*, I: 95.

28. *The Ciano Diaries*, 7 September 1940.

29. Knox, *Mussolini Unleashed*, p. 163.

30. *The Ciano Diaries*, 17 September 1940.

31. Knox, *Mussolini Unleashed*, p. 191.

than half of their armor has been lost owing to air strikes and troops lost in the desert following a disorganized retreat.... One wonders when the English will begin to understand that they have just dealt with the best fitted-out colonial army in the world, and when they finally learn to appreciate the valor of the Italian soldier."[32]

At the beginning of September the Germans offered one armored and motorized division to assist Graziani on a drive to reach Alexandria; Hitler made this official during the Brenner meeting with Mussolini in early October. As proud defenders of their "parallel war," the Italians replied by asking for modern weaponry but no soldiers. The Germans, however, refused to countenance military assistance without the Wehrmacht to supervise use of the equipment. The German offer was allowed to lapse. Stukas were tendered as well, but they were turned down too. Roatta noted that the transport of a single German division would require six months due to Libya's already over-strained ports, while Badoglio observed: "We ought to keep in mind that we have plenty of men and that these men are superior to the German soldiers."[33] Had the Italians availed themselves of Hitler's panzers and planes, the combined Axis armies most likely would have easily broken through a paper-thin British force (which had only 85 tanks) and reached the Suez Canal within months if not weeks.[34] Graziani's position was made even worse by decisions taken in Rome. He would not receive the motorized transportation required for a serious offensive.

An advance in the desert by successive stages to Mersa Matruh with the sole objective of reaching a position from which to bomb Alexandria confirmed the Italian strategy of a "small Italian parallel war." General Messe questioned whether Mussolini and Badoglio, seemingly satisfied with the occupation of useless sand dunes, intended to conduct a serious campaign in Egypt. Where was the ultimate aim of capturing the Canal clearly spelled out?[35] But for Mussolini, who expected an imminent British defeat by Germany, wresting a piece of desert would suffice in proving Italian military prowess and parity with Hitler at the "peace table."

The Greek Fever

As the Italian offensive in the desert ground to a halt, Ribbentrop arrived in Rome on 19 September 1940 to see Mussolini. After presenting a windy *tour*

---

32. Cited in *Africa Settentrionale. La preparazione al conflitto-L'avanzata su Sidi el Barrani* (Rome: SME US, 1955), p. 131; Bocca, *Storia d'Italia nella guerra fascista*, pp. 185–86.
33. *Operazioni*, I: Allegato 31, 25 September 1940.
34. *Germany and the Second World War*, III: 273.
35. Giovanni Messe, *La mia armata in Tunisia* (Milan: Mursia, 2004), p. 48.

d'horizon on the Nazi view of the world, he conceded that Yugoslavia and Greece lay in Italy's sphere. But no attack, he added, should be undertaken until England had been beaten. There was no cause for alarm, replied Mussolini, because Italy's military moves were merely precautionary. The two men parted with differing conclusions: the Duce that Ribbentrop had not denied Italy the right to act on its own in Yugoslavia and Greece, Ribbentrop that Mussolini had agreed to concentrate on England.[36]

Having Ribbentrop's premise in mind, Badoglio, thankful that he did not have to worry about Greece, told his military leaders on the 25th to focus on Northern Africa.[37] What would he have thought had he been privy to Ciano's gift for gab? For on the same day Ciano confided to Monsignor Francesco Borgongini Duca, the apostolic nuncio at the Quirinale: "Soon but not immediately," Italy would occupy all of Greece because "they are people whom we can in no way trust, and they are maintaining an absolutely disgusting attitude."[38] Whether the war was short or prolonged seemed to make no difference so long as the Axis won and Italy arrived as a dominant force at the peace table. With that goal, why not open a new war theater in Greece? Badoglio held precisely the opposite view: "the situation would become hopeless if the war were to be protracted."[39]

Acting on the belated discovery that England would survive the German blitz, Mussolini on 29 September pressed Graziani to march on Marsa Matruh no later than mid-October. His inflated expectation was that Italian bombers, escorted by fighters, could reach Alexandria to drive the Royal Navy from Egyptian ports.[40] No one could so rapidly dampen the Duce's enthusiasm as Graziani, who informed his leader that it was impossible to complete logistical preparation by year's end, Mussolini's deadline.[41] The official Italian military historian Mario Montanari finds Graziani's behavior to have been "absolutely incomprehensible."[42]

On 2 October Ciano challenged Graziani: "And if the Duce gives you the order to move?" Should he refuse, Graziani replied dramatically, he would risk violating the military penal code; should he obey, he would risk defeat and be

---

36. DGFP, D, XI, 73, 20 September 1940, Conversation between Ribbentrop and Mussolini, 19 September 1940; DDI, 9, V, 617, Conversation between Mussolini and Ribbentrop, 19 September 1940.

37. *Germany and the World War*, III: 404.

38. *Actes et documents du Saint Siège relatifs à la seconde guerre mondiale*, IV, n. 87, p. 162; *Operazioni*, I: 94.

39. Enno von Rintelen, *Mussolini e l'alleato. Ricordi dell'addetto militare Tedesco a Roma, 1936–1943* (Rome: Corso, 1952), p. 98.

40. *The Ciano Diaries*, 28 September 1940; Knox, *Mussolini Unleashed*, p. 199; Armellini, *Diario*, pp. 98–99.

41. Knox, *Mussolini Unleashed*, p. 199, n. 43; Armellini, *Diario*, pp. 98–99.

42. *Operazioni*, I: 131.

blamed for it.[43] To avoid this predicament, he implied, it behooved Mussolini to provide him the wherewithal to accelerate the tempo of preparations. So long as contingency plans for the invasion of Greece were on the books, however, Graziani would receive no reinforcements. Badoglio was just as appalled as Graziani over Mussolini's hurry-up order, but would not pressure the Duce to reconsider. Thus unchallenged, Mussolini, lusting for "a success of a glorious war that we have searched in vain over the last three centuries," airily dismissed the problems facing Graziani in reaching the Suez Canal.[44]

War preparations were unexpectedly set back on 2 October when General Ubaldo Soddu issued a directive calling for a far-reaching demobilization of Italian troops that would commence on 10 November and be completed by the 15th. There was precedence for this. On 11 July the Italians had placed 100,000 soldiers on leave. (The Wehrmacht had likewise furloughed troops for the fall harvest.[45]) From the economic standpoint the 2 October demobilization order was not entirely illogical. The army was looking for budget relief, and peasant soldiers were needed in the fields harvesting crops to make up for cut-off overseas food imports. Increasing shortages had compelled the government on 1 October to introduce rationing of cooking oil and fats, a move that caused widespread grumbling and unrest. Of the 1,500,000 men under arms in Italy, the army dismissed more than half. (The troops deployed outside the country were untouched by the demobilization order.)[46] Badoglio acquiesced in this measure since it seemed to signal an end to the dangerous talk of war against either Greece or Yugoslavia.[47]

The effect on the army's structure and efficiency was immediate and dramatic. Demobilization by class rather than by unit was disruptive and had far-reaching psychological ramifications. The Italian people, in a war they only dimly understood, were immensely relieved by a measure that seemed to suggest the fighting would soon cease. But they were in for a rude shock when Mussolini expanded the war by flinging his soldiers against Greece on 28 October.

The Italian military reacted to Mussolini's partial demobilization order with the usual differing opinions: dismay, relief, and obstructionism. Horrified, Roatta implored Soddu to suspend leaves in the units destined for Albania in order to flesh out the divisions earmarked for the war against Greece. But since Soddu

43. Ibid.: 131–32; Rodolfo Graziani, *Una Vita per l'Italia: "Ho defeso la patria"* (Milan: Mursia, 1994), pp. 100–1.
44. Ibid.: 130.
45. I want to thank Pier Paolo Battistelli for bringing the earlier German demobilization order to my attention.
46. Pier Paolo Battistelli, "The Road to Defeat: The Reorganization of the Italian Army after the Winter of 1940–1941," unpublished manuscript.
47. MacGregor Knox, *Hitler's Italian Allies: Royal Armed Forces, Fascist Regime, and the War of 1940–1943* (Cambridge: Cambridge University Press, 2000), p. 79.

was Mussolini's obedient tool, he turned a deaf ear.[48] Badoglio had no objection to the demobilization because it seemed to rule out any sudden buccaneering in the Balkans. Finally he reined in Visconti Prasca, who had begun to shift one of his three newly arrived divisions to an advanced position on the Greek border in contravention of Roatta's orders and in flagrant disregard of the verbal directives Badoglio had personally given to him during the latter's visit to Rome.[49] In General Armellini's description of the jostling for influence and power among the generals, he depicts Badoglio as a lone wolf who tried to neutralize the hawks and "work" the Duce toward less menacing policies.[50] Following the issuance of the demobilization order, it did appear that Badoglio would have success in taming Mussolini's swashbuckling proclivities.

At a summit conference at the Brenner on 4 October 1940, Mussolini informed the Führer that he had just given orders for the execution of the second phase of the campaign against Egypt aimed at the conquest of Mersa Matruh. The operation would begin between 10 and 15 October and, he bragged, would be concluded the same month by tough Italians who would flourish in the desert heat as opposed to the cowardly English seeking escape from the merciless sun. Although Italy did not need any assistance in this second phase of the campaign against Egypt, Mussolini averred, he did admit that German trucks, tanks, and dive-bombers might be required for the dash to Alexandria in the third phase. This was the first time Mussolini formally accepted Hitler's offer of troops.[51]

Mussolini and Hitler hardly touched on Balkan affairs if at all. But the Duce, encouraged by renewed German attention to the Mediterranean,[52] took the view that Hitler would grant him more latitude in moving against Greece in the event of any British military moves in the area. The German veto of August and Ribbentrop's cautionary language of 25 September were conveniently forgotten. Ciano records: "Rarely have I seen the Duce in such a good humor and good shape as at the Brenner Pass today."[53]

The next day, 5 October, Mussolini informed Badoglio: "When we get to Mersa Matruh we shall see which of the two pillars of the Mediterranean will be the first to fall: the Egyptian or the Greek."[54] He sent out the order for an attack in the desert between 10 and 15 October because he was convinced that Italy had sufficient and superior forces to the British, taking no notice of a report by

48. Emilio Faldella, *L'Italia nella seconda guerra mondiale, revisione di giudizi* (Bologna: Cappelli, 1967), p. 267.
49. Knox, *Mussolini Unleashed*, p. 195.
50. Armellini, *Diario*, pp. 99–100.
51. DGFP, D, XI, 149, Conversation between Mussolini and Hitler, 4 October 1940
52. Gerhard Schreiber, "The Mediterranean in Hitler's Strategy in 1940: 'Program' and Military Planning," in *The German Military in the Age of Total War*, ed. Wilhelm Deist (Dover, NH: Berg, 1987), pp. 251–58.
53. *The Ciano Diaries*, 4 October 1940.
54. Armellini, *Diario*, pp. 105–6, 5 October 1940.

SIM that they had built up a force of 13-14 divisions in North Africa superior in armor and anti-tank guns to the under-equipped Italian infantry.[55] Since Mussolini would not hear of Graziani's ongoing problems in equipment breakdowns and port congestion, he thought that his irresolute general's misgivings were more of an obstacle to an offensive than British resistance.

On 12 October a news flash from Bucharest stunned Rome. As interpreted by the excitable Italian press, German armed forces were moving into Romania. The facts, however, were less dramatic. Romania had invited a military mission and air units of the Luftwaffe to protect the Ploesti oil wells mainly against Soviet machinations and, not incidentally, against British efforts to bomb them. Stung by Berlin's neglect in forewarning him, Mussolini exploded: "Hitler always faces me with a fait accompli. This time I am going to pay him back in his own coin. He will find out from the papers that I have occupied Greece. In this way the equilibrium will be re-established."[56] The Duce had no reason to be surprised, for he already knew that German advisers were in Bucharest and that German military units had crossed into Romania. Only faintly aware of any German plan to invade the Soviet Union, he was unable to distinguish between Berlin's move to control Romanian oil and its wish to use the country as a military staging area. Would Hitler ever treat him as an equal in the alliance? General Armellini's pithy observation: "Hitler is occupying Romania; Mussolini cannot remain at ease."[57]

The Romanian affair caused Mussolini to ruminate on his various grievances toward Germany. Most upsetting were Hitler's determination to dominate the Yugoslav economy and Nazi machinations with the Croatian Ustaša. Hardly less disconcerting was the Führer's silence over Sea Lion. Had the landing been postponed for reasons of weather or to keep open a compromise peace with London? Then there were Hitler's attempts to persuade Vichy to obtain bases in Morocco and thwart Italy's territorial demands. In Eastern Europe, Berlin called the shots in relations with the Soviet Union and advanced toward supremacy along the Danube. While Germany had devoured much of Europe, Italy, in sad contrast, held only small areas in France and in British Somaliland, and was stuck in the sand dunes surrounding Sidi el Barrani.

Now there was nobody to restrain Ciano. General Paolo Puntoni, the king's aide-de-camp, noted: "Ciano showed an impatience to give a lesson to Greece for its conduct which, he says, is ambiguous."[58] Ciano told Giuseppe Bottai:

---

55. *Operazioni*, I: 132; Mario M. Montanari, "Politica e strategia nella campagna di Grecia," in *L'Italia in Guerra: il 1° Anno—1940*, p. 210.
56. *The Ciano Diaries*, 12 October 1940.
57. Armellini, *Diario*, p. 111.
58. Paolo Puntoni, *Parla Vittorio Emanuele III* (Bologna: Il Mulino, 1993), p. 17.

"The Germans are turning infiltration of Romania into an outright occupation. Did anyone bring this up at the Brenner? No. And now the Germans place us before a fait accompli. Of the pact with Japan, they negotiated unbeknownst to us for a couple of months and summoned us to come and sign. We must counterbalance the Romanian occupation by a blow against Greece. Since August, as you know, I have insisted on this. We could have liquidated Greece in a couple of weeks. Today it will be more difficult, but we can be assured of success. The problem is that Badoglio hesitates, he's thwarting me."[59]

That Ciano was so sure he would get his way on an invasion of Greece was, as his *chef de cabinet* Filippo Anfuso noted, based on his success in lobbying for the occupation of Albania in 1939. Having finally realized that nothing would stop Hitler from waging war with or without Italy, Ciano was determined to block any further German incursion into Italy's Balkan spheres.[60] Less loyal to the Axis than Mussolini, Ciano insisted to Jacomoni that Albania's claims on Greece provided him a "bargaining counter" in a darkening European environment.[61]

If Ciano had begun to learn Hitler's ways, he showed a startling frivolity in assessing the strength of his Greek opponent. "Inside" information informed him that Greek military commanders were corrupt and readily bought; the people were so indifferent to their government of royalist toadies that they would not lift a finger to defend it. "Two hundred airplanes over Athens," Ciano told the Italian diplomat Raffaele Guariglia, "would suffice to make the Greek government capitulate."[62] Only Emanuele Grazzi, the Italian minister in Athens, challenged these glib assumptions. While the Greeks wanted to avoid a conflict with Italy, he was sure that, if invaded, they would rally around their infirm dictator Ioannis Metaxas and put up a strong resistance. The army's morale was high and the population annoyed by Fascist Italy's bullying. But Grazzi's forthrightly written reports received no hearing from his war hawk foreign minister.[63] In Rome, the spirit of *omertà* dictated against any criticism of war against Greece.

Egged on by Ciano's craving for war and Hitler's unwelcome move into Romania, Mussolini on 13 October ordered Badoglio to set in motion Contingency "G," which at this point had the limited aim of seizing Epirus down to the

59. Giuseppe Bottai, *Diario 1935–1944* (Milan: Rizzoli, 1989), p. 227.
60. Anfuso, *Roma, Berlino, Salò* (Milan: Garzanti, 1950), p. 163.
61. Knox *Mussolini Unleashed*, p. 197.
62. Raffaele Guariglia, *Ricordi, 1922–1946* (Naples: Edizione scientifiche italiane, 1950), p. 478.
63. DDI, 9, V, 293, Grazzi to Ciano, 23 July, 634, 23 September, 670, 3 October 1940; Cervi, *Hollow Legions*, pp. 49–50.

Arta River while skirting the rest of Greece.[64] Eight divisions would suffice for hostilities to commence on 26 October. The army chiefs, who had recently informed Visconti Prasca that Plan "G" had been postponed in favor of a desert offensive against the British, were stunned—not for the last time—but Badoglio appears to have lodged no objection.

In a meeting with Badoglio and Roatta at the Palazzo Venezia, it seemed suddenly to occur to Mussolini that an attack limited to Epirus would either trigger a British occupation of Greek ports and airdromes, or cause the Greeks to grant the British permission to utilize the country as a military staging area in the ongoing struggle for mastery over the Eastern Mediterranean. Ergo, instead of a limited action, Mussolini would undertake an all-out invasion, for which twelve divisions would have to be added to the eight already assembled in Albania for a grand total of twenty. He counted on a strong Albanian irredentist movement in Epirus to paralyze the Greek army stationed there and assumed that Bulgarian King Boris would join the Italian attack in order to seize Thrace, a long-standing objective.[65] The astonished generals were required to place a new invasion plan on Mussolini's desk in ten days.

While the army was caught in the middle of demobilization, Mussolini presented his expansive scheme in more detail on the 15th at a conference stacked with fervent supporters of the war: Ciano's two minions, Visconti Prasca and Jacomoni, the foreign minister himself, and Ubaldo Soddu, the undersecretary of war.[66] The two doubters were Badoglio and Roatta, while Cavagnari and Pricolo were conspicuous by their absence, an oddity in that Mussolini was about to present a plan for a sea-borne operation for which command of the air was essential. Also not invited was the head of the SIM, Cesare Amé, who apparently had intelligence on Greek war preparations that differed markedly from Jacomoni's. Obviously those not present might have encouraged Badoglio and Roatta to speak their minds.

Mussolini outlined his objectives: occupation of the whole southern coast of Albania and the Ionian islands of Zante, Cefalonia and Corfu in a first phase, then a knockout blow against the Greeks, and total occupation in two stages to take place no later than 26 October. He showed little concern for the realities of the campaign: it was to take place in difficult mountainous terrain at the opening of the rainy season, the transportation system was practically nonexistent, and port facilities were inadequate to handle a large influx of men and supplies. The

---

64. Knox, *Mussolini Unleashed*, p. 209.
65. Armellini, *Diario*, p. 113.
66. A full report of the 15 October meeting can be found in Carlo Mazzaccara and Antonello Biagini, eds., Verbale della riunione tenuta dal Duce a Palazzo Venezia il 15 October 1940, *Verbali delle riunioni tenute dal capo di SME* (Rome: USSME, 1985), vol. IV: 231–41,

Duce assumed that Italy's 70,000 troops would easily overwhelm an enemy numbering only 30,000—a drop in the bucket to what the Greeks were eventually to mobilize. Bulgaria, which knew nothing of Italy's battle plans, was supposed to attack toward the prized port of Salonica to take pressure off the Italian front.[67]

Ciano declared: "There is a clear distinction between the population and the ruling political, plutocratic class, which animates the spirit of resistance and keeps alive the country's Anglophile spirit. It is a small and very rich class, while the rest of the population is indifferent to everything, including the prospect of our invasion."[68] Similarly confident, Jacomoni guaranteed Mussolini that he had perfectly laid the groundwork for the invasion. The Greek population was "profoundly depressed" and the Albanians were eager for war. But he did point out the cramped landing facilities at the port of Durazzo and the primitive condition of the roads, and he predicted Greek resistance if the Italians did not move quickly.[69]

Mussolini took on full responsibility for the attack and assured his generals that no one need worry about casualties. The problem had been examined from every angle and there was nothing more to be said. An offensive in Epirus, announced the Duce, would be followed by a march on Athens.[70]

Badoglio did not lift a finger to oppose Mussolini at this meeting, and he did nothing to stop the other military commanders from falling in behind him. Nor did he question the spurious premises and faulty logistics of Visconti Prasca's strategy but rather emphasized the importance of seizing Crete and Morea along with occupying the entire country. The British, he thought, would be preoccupied with Egypt and therefore unable to attempt naval landings in Greece. Only the RAF might offer resistance, which could be lessened if Graziani simultaneously advanced on Mersa Matruh in Egypt. The one stand Badoglio took was his insistence on three months for completing the military build-up rather than Mussolini's eleven days.[71]

On 17 October Cavagnari and Pricolo finally were given the opportunity to lay out their objections to the invasion plans. The landing ports were too shallow they claimed, and there was no time to build additional airports in Albania to handle the supply problems. Mussolini's "two-phase" plan was, therefore, quite

67. Mario Montanari, *La Campagna di Grecia* (Rome: SME US, 1980), D. 3; USSME, DS, vol. II, D. 49, Verbale della riunione tenuta nella sala di lavoro del Duce a Palazzo Venezia, 15 October 1940, pp. 823–32.
68. Montanari, *Grecia*, D. 3. Verbale della riunione tenuta nella sala di lavoro del Duce a Palazzo Venezia il 15 Ottobre 1940, pp. 823–27.
69. Ibid.
70. Ibid.
71. Ibid.

unfeasible. Badoglio agreed and promised to thrash the matter out again in an audience with the Duce in the company of the other heads of the General Staff. "All of Badoglio's talk has a pessimistic tinge," Ciano reports. "He foresees the prolongation of the war and with it the exhaustion of our already-meager resources. I listen, and do not argue.... Badoglio must, without any hesitation, repeat to Mussolini what he has told me."[72]

On the 17th Badoglio asserted at a military meeting: "I say to you quite frankly that I am not in a position to explain the political dimension of the operation to you, because such is not part of my responsibilities and I never interfere in the fields of others. The Duce has judged and declared that for him the occupation of Greece is of the highest importance. Therefore there is nothing more to be said."[73] For him the political calculations that the policy-makers handed down to the military must be respected: that there would be insurrection in Ciamuria, the Greek army would not fight, the Greek generals were hopelessly corrupt, Bulgaria would intervene, and the Metaxas government would be overthrown by a pro-Italian cabal lead by the opposition leader Eleutherios Venizelos.[74]

Badoglio had his chance the next day, the 18th, to consult with the Duce directly. Ciano summarized their encounter: "I go early to see the Duce. I find Soddu in the anteroom. He has spoken with Badoglio, who declared that if we move against Greece he will resign. I report to the Duce, who is already in a very bad mood on account of Graziani. He has a violent outburst of rage, and says that he will go personally to Greece 'to witness the incredible shame of Italians who are afraid of Greeks.' He is planning to move at any cost, and if Badoglio presents his resignation it will be accepted immediately. But Badoglio not only does not present it, he doesn't even repeat to Mussolini what he told me yesterday. In fact, the Duce states that Badoglio only brought this up in order to obtain a postponement of a few days, at least two."[75]

At this point Badoglio seemed to be quite aware of the many problems facing his country. In the scalding African sands Italy had mainly foot soldiers, which faced an enemy equipped with superior weapons being reinforced by the day. In Albania Italy lacked adequate port facilities and had to deal with craggy mountain terrain where dirt roads would turn into a muddy quagmire at the first heavy rainfall. But during the last week of October the usually cautious Badoglio was swept away by the idea of a two-pronged attack: invasion of Greece and

---

72. *The Ciano Diaries*, 17 October 1940.
73. Montanari, "Politica e strategia nella campagna di Grecia," p. 199.
74. Ibid., p. 205.
75. *The Ciano Diaries*, 18 October 1940.

Crete coordinated with Graziani's advance on Mersa Matruh. Split between the two fronts, the British would give ground to Graziani's legions.[76] In his excitement, he tossed aside a German proposal to send an armored division to Libya.[77]

In a letter to De Vecchi on 24 October the newly combative Badoglio wrote of a "punitive expedition" against the Greeks, who "will get the treatment they deserve." At the final meeting of the chiefs that same day, he outlined an ambitious plan for launching divisions in the direction of Salonica and expressed the view that there was little likelihood of a Greek counteroffensive since a 5th column had already sapped the will to resist. King Boris' refusal to intervene on the side of Italy, which presumably would allow the Greek generals to take troops from the Bulgarian frontier to face the Italian attack, did not trouble him.[78] No one at the meeting challenged Badoglio or made any realistic and detailed comparison of the relative strength of the opposing forces.[79] On the collision course to disaster, perhaps the generals knew that nothing they said would change Mussolini's mind or bring him down to earth. For example, when told that the air arm had been given orders for a limited action, Mussolini demanded a very "vigorous attack" so that everything would "go to pieces at the first clash."[80] Graziani stepped in to save both Badoglio and Mussolini from such catastrophic measures by refusing to move for at least two months. In frustration Mussolini told Graziani to do as he liked.[81]

Mussolini's "diplomacy" was as frivolous as his military planning. Finally, on 18 October, after his military plans had been set, he offered King Boris a "historic opportunity" to pursue Bulgaria's goal of an outlet on the Aegean by participating in Italy's "settling of accounts with Greece." Boris wrote back that Bulgaria, militarily unprepared and fearful of Soviet and Turkish reaction, was "forced to abstain from any military action."[82] Mussolini was furious: "These gutless royalties will never do anything.... We shall manage without him. Visconti Prasca's march will be so rapid that it will draw the Greek forces from the north to Athens unless they disintegrate and all go home."[83]

Ciano drove forward blindly at breakneck speed: "With General Pricolo I examine the plan of the air attack on Greece. It is good, because it is energetic and bold. By a hard blow at the start, it will be possible to bring about a com-

76. *Germany and the Second World War*, III: 412; ACS, Graziani Papers, 17 October 1940.

77. Battistelli, unpublished manuscript.

78. Montanari, *Grecia*, pp. 117–120.

79. *Germany and the Second World War*, III: 423.

80. *The Ciano Diaries*, 22 October 1940.

81. *Germany and the Second World War*, III: 412

82. DDI, 9, V, 738, Mussolini to Boris III, 16 October 1940; 746, Boris III to Mussolini, 18 October 1940.

83. Badoglio, *L'Italia nella seconda guerra mondiale*, p. 54.

plete collapse within a few hours."[84] He spelled out three hypotheses to Bottai: "either [the Greeks] will not resist, or they will feign an initial resistance, or put up a real resistance of three or four weeks."[85] He told the governor of Dalmatia Giuseppe Bastianini the same day: "It will be a military walkover. Everything is arranged....it will all go very well," paying no heed to Bastianini's retort that the Greeks "will resist like lions."[86] Nothing could stop Ciano now, not even a telegram from Grazzi on the 26th that belied the argument that war against the Metaxas regime was necessary to thwart Greek-British military cooperation against Italy. Greece, Grazzi reported, would not fail to consider joining an anti-British alignment that would include all the Mediterranean powers. Why such overconfidence? Perhaps Ciano had been influenced by a series of recent capitulations by small and threatened nations to demands of powerful neighbors prepared to use overwhelming force. Romania buckled to Stalin's will by giving up Bessarabia and Southern Bukovina to the Soviet Union; Lithuania, Latvia, and Estonia surrendered without firing a shot before advancing Stalinist legions; and Romania, under heavy pressure by the Axis Powers, meekly turned over much of Transylvania to Hungary. Why shouldn't a dinky and backward Balkan nation like Greece similarly cave in to mighty Fascist Italy?

In a letter to Hitler dated 19 October, but sent on the 23rd (Hitler received it on the 25th), Mussolini defiantly challenged salient features of German policy. He rejected admission of France to a continental coalition, refused to countenance German ground units in North Africa, expressed no interest in Spanish entry into the war, and justified his intention to advance on Greece by citing Greco-British collusion: "In short, Greece is to the Mediterranean what Norway was to the North Sea, and must not escape the same fate... In any event, I hope I shall be able to launch operations simultaneously on the Greek and on the Egyptian front."[87] The Duce would conduct a "parallel war" no matter what.

Mussolini once again had tried German patience. The state secretary of the German foreign office, Ernst von Weizsäcker, noted: "Rather than throwing itself on Balkan villages, Italy should be conquering Egypt."[88] He prepared instructions to restrain Germany's Axis partner from bringing new countries into the war without "our advice and consent." Ribbentrop approved this idea, but quieted his subordinates from fear of crossing his ally.[89]

---

84. *The Ciano Diaries*, 24 October 1940.
85. Bottai, *Diario*, p. 228.
86. Giuseppe Bastianini, *Volevo Fermare Mussolini: Memorie di un diplomatico fascista* (Milan: BUR, 2005), p. 287.
87. DGFP, D, XI, 199, Mussolini to Hitler, 19 October 1940.
88. Ernst von Weizsäcker, *Die Weizsäcker-Papiere 1933–1950*, ed. Leonidas E. Hill (Frankfurt a.M., 1974), p. 221.
89. Ibid., p. 244.

Though Mussolini had expressed the concern that "once again an order might come to halt us,"[90] he was determined to confront the Führer with an irrevocable call to arms. He wrote Visconti Prasca: "Dear Visconti, you know, and if you do not I am telling you now that I have opposed all attempts to take your command away from you on the eve of operation. I believe that events and above all your actions will justify me. Attack with the greatest determination and violence. The success of the operation depends above all on its speed."[91]

When Hitler received Mussolini's letter on the 25th, he ordered his train home from Hendaye and Montoire diverted for a stopover in Florence to discover for himself what the Italians were up to. In the wee hours of 28 October as the German train neared Florence, it dawned on Hitler that Italy was actually about to launch a war against Greece. As recorded by the German Army Adjutant Gerhard Engel: "F[ührer] raging when he hears of the Italian attack on Greece. Complains about Gmn. Liaison staff and attachés, who only 'went to lunch-parties' and were not proper spies.... Judges that the Duce is afraid of our economic influence in the Balkans, and doubts whether Italians can defeat Greece as the Greeks are not bad soldiers in themselves. The F. says verbatim: 'This is their revenge for Norway and France.' But he, F., had been forced to act secretly since every second Italian was a traitor or a spy. Angry words about Rintelen, who let himself be conned. Only advantage is that now the British will be forced to stand their ground there too.... Greatly alarmed that Italy's action may involve the entire Balkans and give the British a welcome excuse to set up an air-base there."[92] But Hitler could hardly have claimed that he was innocent of Italy's warlike intentions. In spite of Roatta's and Badoglio's many denials that an attack against Greece was pending, Berlin had obtained abundant information about the imminent Italian aggression from listening posts in Italy, Albania, and Greece.[93]

Beaming, Mussolini greeted his German guest on the station platform in Florence on the 28th, telling him: "Early this morning, in the dawn twilight, victorious Italian troops crossed the Greco-Albanian border." The Duce had indeed paid back the Führer "in his own coin." Hitler nimbly adjusted to Mussolini's pronouncement since it was the timing rather than the aggression itself that upset him. Apart from an offer of parachutists to help in a preventive strike against Crete to keep it out of the hands of the British,[94] which enjoyed no

90. *The Ciano Diaries*, 22 October 1940.
91. Cervi, *The Hollow Legions*, pp. 73–74.
92. Cited in *Germany and the Second World War*, III: 414.
93. Ibid.: 413.
94. DGFP, D, XI, 246, Conversation between Hitler and Mussolini, 28 October 1940; DDI, 9, V, 807, Conversation between Mussolini and Hitler, 28 October 1940.

response from Mussolini, Hitler had little to say on the matter of Greece except an offer of grudging solidarity.[95] Weizsäcker growled: "I have the good conscience of having proposed to bridle Italy before the Greek imbroglio."[96] While Ciano observed that the Florence conference had proven "that German solidarity has not failed us,"[97] he seems to have overlooked the fact that Germany did not break off relations with Athens.

Greece, Mussolini once said, was "skin and bone." It had no noteworthy raw materials or modern resources and was not a food basket. The country was not the plaything of the British enemy, had marginal influence in the Mediterranean, was bereft of allies, and wanted desperately to stay neutral. But Mussolini was determined (as explained to his generals on 15 October) to expand Italy's Balkan empire beyond Albania to include its southern coastline and the Ionian Islands—Zante, Cefalonia, Corfu—and perhaps even Salonica and Athens too, aims that were long-standing. It was only a question of time. Mussolini's fury over the stationing of German troops in Romania, and his fear of a German *Drang nach Südest* were real, and conveniently provided him with a pretext, but this did not provide the underlying reason for the invasion of Greece. Finally the Duce had his chance, by waging aggression, to show that Fascism had transformed Italians into superb warriors and to show the Germans that he, like Hitler, was a military genius.

Ciano wanted to fight so badly that he fooled himself into believing that Albanian "partisans" were straining at the leash to rise against the Greeks in Epirus, and that the Greek army would vanish at the first sight of an Italian Blackshirt. On the threshold of the attack, "he radiantly entered the Colonna house to announce 'his war.'"[98] Ciano did everything imaginable to keep Mussolini on a collision course with Greece by behind-the-scenes maneuvering with two irresponsible co-conspirators, Jacomoni and Visconti Prasca. Their false and tendentious reports that the Greeks would easily give in became the accepted vulgate. This scheming trinity formed the basis of a powerful lobby in Rome hyping the war, which was music to the Duce's ears and unquestionably goaded him on.

Of the three service chiefs, none wanted the war that Mussolini was determined to unleash on 28 October. But not one of them dared say this to him directly. SMG Chief General Badoglio was a man who wanted both to land on the winning side and keep avenues open for a safe retreat. While the question of

95. DGFP, D, XI, 477, Conversation between Hitler and Alfieri, 8 December 1940.
96. Weizsäcker, *Die Weizsäcker-Papiere*, p. 223.
97. *The Ciano Diaries*, 28 October 1940.
98. Bocca, *Storia d'Italia nella guerra fascista*, p. 213.

war still trembled in the balance, he raised doubt but acquiesced, hoping that the mercurial Duce would soon figure out the folly of such a scrambled enterprise or simply lose interest. But once the war had become a certainty, Badoglio came to the belief that things would work out splendidly because the Duce was surely right in thinking that the Greeks lacked the will to fight. As for the Italian brass, whatever doubts they had about the war, they fitfully tagged along. In any event, Mussolini would not be stopped, even when worrisome reports were handed to him and the military by SIM.[99]

In a long report of over two hundred pages entitled *Grecia*, SIM compiled a fairly accurate assessment of the Greek army's capabilities. It was instructed by French officers, did well in training exercises, showed high morale, and would be no pushover. The Italian army had an intelligence source in the person of the military attaché in Athens, Luigi Mondini. Originally Mondini shared the received stereotypical prejudices of Greeks in Rome, but in time came to the view that they would put a competent army in the field and fight bravely. Giuseppe Conti, the current expert on SIM, has not been able to say with certainty that Mussolini ever read the 566 S. *Grecia* report, but it was there for all to consult in the final lead-up to the war.[100] Mussolini was the archetypical example of a hubristic political leader who was inspired almost exclusively by considerations of a political character and had no patience for puzzling through abstruse questions of military strategy and competence. He habitually brushed aside the cautious opinions of generals whom he regarded as stiff-necked, unimaginative, and part of an old-fashioned military establishment.

Armellini had the last word. Noting that while Mussolini was about to throw Italy into a war against Greece, Hitler had had the aplomb to postpone the invasion of Britain. The Germans, he wrote, "have in their blood organization and military awareness whereas we are simpletons who in 1940 wanted to make war according to the doctrines of the *Squadristi*."[101] This, of course, was said before Operation Barbarossa.

---

99. Badoglio later admitted that further objections "would not have served to avert the war Mussolini wanted." Cited in Knox, *Mussolini Unleashed*, p. 213.
100. Giuseppe Conti, *Una guerra segreta: Il Sim nel secondo conflitto mondiale* (Milan: Il Mulino, 2009), pp. 175–87.
101. Armellini, *Diario*, p. 123.

North Africa 1940-1943.

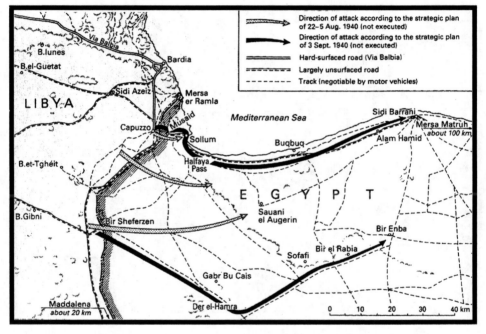

Italian plans for the attack on Egypt, Summer of 1940.

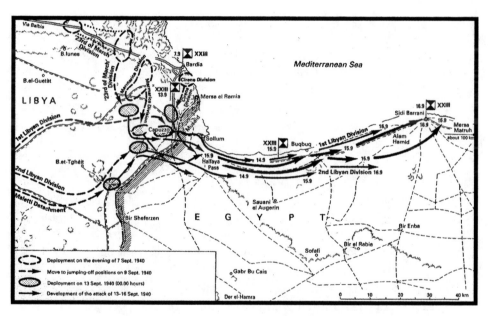

Actual Italian attack on Egypt, September 1940.

Chapter III

Tailspin

Disagreeable Surprises
Setback at Sea and in the Air
Finger-Pointing
Loss of Face in Greece
Agony in the Desert
Greek Quagmire

Disagreeable Surprises

At the outset of hostilities against Greece, an Italian newspaper reported: "The Italian soldiers march raising an illustrious dust. We laugh at Greece as it is and what it was. Olympus had fallen, Hellas has died, and the fiery Achilles has had the funeral he deserved." While the press waxed lyrical, the Italian army of 140,000 trudged grimly across the frontier into Greece on 28 October 1940, the anniversary of Caporetto. "The sky was clear and calm, dotted with the myriads of stars that make the sky of Attica so marvelous, and the temperature was mild," the military attaché in Athens Mondini recorded.[1]

Mussolini rushed to his general headquarters in Puglia to be on hand. Ciano abandoned the foreign ministry to join his air squadron for a bombing run on Salonica. Other ministers hurried over expecting to win war medals. But the excitement was brief, for they landed in the middle of chaos. Thanks to the un-timely demobilization order of 600,000 soldiers in October, the army had to make haste, shipping partially trained men and green recruits to Albania. They

---

1. Cited in Cervi, *The Hollow Legions*, p. 114.

arrived mainly at Durazzo, the only port that could handle large quantities of heavy equipment. But many of the landing ships ran into docked vessels unloading marble for Fascist buildings. Sent to the front immediately, the infantry was bereft of supporting weapons and cut off from supply lines. Instead of the twenty divisions earmarked for the campaign, only roughly half were battle-ready. In pouring rain the sodden dirt roads sagged under the ceaseless traffic of boots, wheels, and hooves. Vehicles floundered in a sea of mud. Troops were dispatched to the wrong places and frequently lacked adequate transport and services. Morale flagged, exacerbated by the social gap between the rank and file and officers. In miserable weather the troops stood in long soup lines for their tasteless rations while their superiors consumed hearty meals in separate mess halls.

Without the advantage of surprise, the invading Italians ran into stiff opposition. Led by the dogged General Alexandros Papagos, the Greek troops advanced relentlessly against the disorganized and bewildered Italians. An aroused population, determined to rid the country of the imperialist invader, gave the army unstinting support. Just as in World War I, when the Italian command heartlessly sent waves of brave soldiers up bullet-sprayed, craggy mountains against fortified Habsburg troops, the officers in Albania hurled their men into battle without concern for casualties. Mussolini's generals were as incompetent as General Cadorna of Caporetto fame.

On 1 November the Greeks tore open a large gap in the thinly defended Italian lines. Quickly they drove to the Albanian frontier. This should not have come as a surprise since the Greeks at the outset enjoyed superiority in numbers, were equipped with weapons not inferior to the Italian, and, as homegrown soldiers, enjoyed a decided advantage in their familiarity with the terrain. The psychological impact of retreat on Italian morale was disastrous.

To take pressure off his hard-pressed troops, Mussolini hoped to outflank the enemy by an amphibious landing at Prevesa, which, as a usable port, would ease the congestion at ports further north. Based on the coastline layout the idea had merit, but was impractical since there were no experienced troops, no infrastructure, and no waters deep enough for large landing craft. Nor would cooperation among the military branches required for such a complex operation suddenly emerge from the relentless internecine squabbling and rivalry.

Although Mussolini and Badoglio had given their new Balkan theater priority over North Africa by diverting to Albania the trucks ticketed for Libya, by early November the haggard divisions faced military catastrophe. Was an Italian Dunkirk in the making? Mussolini forged a new army team to face the crisis. On 9 November Visconti Prasca was let go as commander of the Italian troops in Albania in favor of General Ubaldo Soddu, who was named army group commander while keeping the title of undersecretary of war. General Carlo Geloso received command of the 11th Army.

At a 10 November meeting of his top military brass, which included Badoglio, Cavagnari, Pricolo, and Roatta, Mussolini blamed Visconti Prasca and Jacomoni for the nonexistent Albanian uprising in Ciamuria and the unexpectedly stiff Greek resistance. He vowed to renew the offensive along the coast by 5 December to prevent Great Britain from giving effective support to Greece and "above all for reasons of prestige." His ardor for war undiminished, Mussolini, to spread panic, announced that Greek cities would be carpet-bombed: "All urban centers of over 10,000 population must be destroyed and razed to the ground."[2]

At this meeting Badoglio summoned the courage to point a finger at Mussolini: "You took the decision to attack on 26 October." In the next breath he exonerated himself and Roatta from any misjudgment: "I have made these remarks in order to demonstrate that neither the SMG nor the army staff had anything to do with this affair, which was carried out in a manner that totally contradicts our whole system, which is founded on the principle of first preparing oneself well, and then taking risks."[3]

Addressing a collection of provincial leaders in Rome on 18 November, Mussolini described the current conflict as a latter-day Punic War that would end with "the annihilation of the modern Carthage, England." Italy would break the backs of the Greeks no matter how long it took to overcome the barren mountains and muddy valleys of Epirus. The Greeks, he wound up, "hated Italy like no other people."[4] Words were followed by action: on 22 November Mussolini declared general mobilization.

Setbacks at Sea and in the Air

The debacle in Albania was followed by a disaster at sea on 11 and 12 November. Slow and elderly open-cockpit Swordfish biplanes from the aircraft carrier *Illustrious* swooped down on the Italian fleet anchored at Taranto, sinking a dreadnought and crippling two battleships at the loss of only two aircraft. Defensive measures had been lax: no dispersal of the ships at sea, derisory anti-aircraft defenses, and a lack of adequate torpedo netting guarding the docked ships. Since the British were unable to follow up this audacious strike, the Italians eventually managed to repair the damaged ships and regroup the fleet to

---

2. USSME, Verbali delle riunioni tenute dal capo di SM Generale, IV, Verbale 3, p. 247.
3. Ibid., p. 249.
4. Edoardo and Duilio Susmel, *Opera Omnia di Benito Mussolini* (Florence: La Fenice, 1966), (hereafter cited as *OO*), XXX: 30–38.

contest the enemy another day. At the same time the British bombarded Durazzo and sank an Italian convoy of three ships. Heads rolled. Mussolini replaced the do-nothing Admiral Cavagnari with Admiral Arturo Riccardi, and his equally unimaginative commander of the fleet, Admiral Inigo Campioni, with Admiral Angelo Iachino. This transfer of authority did not presage an overhaul in the top-heavy chain of command.

The trouncing the Italians took at Taranto cast legitimate doubt on their ability to control the central Mediterranean and made infinitely more difficult their mission of cutting off the British sea routes to Greece. No longer having to circumnavigate the Cape of Good Hope to send reinforcements for its troops in North Africa, the British navy could take the "shortcut" directly across the Mediterranean. Henceforward, the Italian fleet, to avoid the risk of defeat, would only reluctantly leave port, which handed the initiative to the British navy. Practically unopposed, the British raided Italy's coasts and disrupted convoy routes from the Peninsula to North Africa. On 9 February 1941 the navy and carrier-based planes wrought destruction on Genoa. Thanks to heavy fog, Italian aerial reconnaissance was not able to locate the British ships heading back to Gibraltar. Admiral Iachino, stationed at La Spezia, had no choice but to weigh anchor. Hoping to intercept the adversary with a large fleet headed by battleships, he followed mistaken orders and faulty intelligence, and ended up wandering about.

The Germans, counting on the Italian fleet to disrupt British convoys ferrying troops and supplies between Greece and Alexandria, urged Iachino to act more vigorously. In spite of a serious fuel shortage the Italian admiral obliged, setting out with the battleship *Vittorio Veneto* surrounded by eight cruisers and seventeen destroyers to raid Allied shipping in the Eastern Mediterranean. Thanks to information provided by Ultra, Admiral Cunningham wheeled around to intercept the unsuspecting Iachino. At Cape Matapan, off the coast of southern Greece, British torpedo bombers, benefiting from ULTRA intercepts, hit the *Vittorio Veneto* on 28 March and sunk three heavy cruisers and two destroyers. The British suffered only little damage. Italian losses in sailors were heavy: 2,303 perished and 1,411 prisoners were taken.[5] Along with an edge in equipment and resources, radar played an important role in the British victory. Unbowed, the Italian navy regrouped and resumed its major task of protecting the convoys bound from Italy to Northern Africa and interdicting British ships sailing to Malta—tasks well acquitted. Between 6 February and 25 May 1941

---

5. Jack Green and Alessandro Massignani, *The Naval War in the Mediterranean 1940–1943* (London: Sarpedon, 1998), p. 159.

fifteen Italian merchantmen transporting troops and equipment to the German and Italian troops in North Africa were lost.[6]

Besides the lack of radar, Matapan exposed further deficiencies in Italian naval procedures. Night operational capability and usable intelligence were mediocre. There was only a dim awareness that the air arm should operate in close tandem with naval gunnery to provide battleships protection. A residue of stubborn pride persisted among the independent-minded naval people who disdained unified doctrinal strategy. In the end it was lack of leadership that caused the Italians to lose the battle of Matapan. Iachino took poorly calculated risks and could not match Cunningham's instincts. Having yielded control of the Eastern Mediterranean to the British navy, the Italian fleet was in no position to challenge the British evacuation from Greece and Crete that would have been turned into a complete debacle had Italian planes and ships been able to join the Luftwaffe. The Germans, who had goaded the Italian admiralty to take on the British navy, were so dismayed by these events that they hardly concealed their wish to take over the Italian fleet.

The Italian air force fared no better. On the same day that the Swordfish struck, 200 obsolete Italian planes flew in a daylight raid on Harwich, England; ten were shot down. Since the Italian aircraft, unsuitable for cold weather, were thought to be more a hindrance than an asset, Hitler asked that they be withdrawn, which wound up Italy's air war over the Channel. Worse still, by early February 1941, the Italian air force in Libya had lost nearly 700 aircraft.

Since its founding in 1923, the Italian air force had been praised as the quintessentially Fascist service. Mussolini banked on air power to overcome Italy's strategic and economic confinement. To enhance the prestige of his regime, he showcased the latest aircraft to advertise his country's technical achievements. During the 1930s Balbo flew beautifully crafted planes around the world that aroused the praise of air enthusiasts everywhere for their aerobatic virtuosity. But planes designed by craftsmen did not progress to efficient mass production inside huge assembly plants, which guaranteed inadequate numbers of aircraft and the failure to produce high-powered engines on a large scale. Since there was a marked lack of machine tools essential for mass production, Italian manufacture was rendered dependent on a small number of highly skilled artisans who dominated the air industry workforce. Owing to the multiplicity of aircraft types, Italian stocking for spare parts turned into a miasma of confusion.[7] A disconnect, therefore, existed between a strategic vision for the Italian air force and

---

6. James J. Sadkovich *The Italian Navy in World War II* (Westport, CN: Greenwood, 1994), p. 137.
7. Brian R. Sullivan, "Downfall of the Regia Aeronautica, 1933–1943," in Robin Higham and Stephen J. Harris, eds., *Why Air Forces Fail* (Kentucky: The University Press of Kentucky, 2006), pp. 135–76.

the technical capabilities of the planes that were purchased. When the war broke out Italian models were wanting in fundamental aerodynamic requirements. High-altitude bombing proved ineffective over Malta and North Africa thanks to rudimentary bombsights and a lack of radio contact between pilot and bombardier. Navigational aids were almost nonexistent. Engine design was faulty, and the quality of fuel fell short of acceptable standards thanks to the shortcomings of the petrochemical industry. The *regia aeronautica* was not prepared to attack moving ships. Although having forged ahead with torpedo bomber designs and models, the Italians had not yet formed a combat unit that contained them. Moreover, they lacked dive-bombers like the German Stuka. These failings stemmed originally from the inability of air force planners to shake free of the guiding philosophy laid out by General Giulio Douhet: the destruction of enemy cities and industrial ports. In addition, given the existing rivalry characterizing inter-service relations, there was no integrated system of air defense radar, fighters, and anti-aircraft artillery. In fact, there was hardly any air defense at all; whatever anti-aircraft artillery existed was manned by Fascist militia using the elderly and those unfit for duty. Only at the last minute did the navy and air force improvise the liaison arrangements for the fleet sortie that led to the Matapan disaster.

Finger-Pointing

Battered by failed war policies, the government was subjected to behind-the-scenes sniping. On 12 November the radical Fascist *Ras* of Cremona, Roberto Farinacci, delivered a letter to Mussolini chastising Badoglio for declaring innocence in a war he claimed had been started irresponsibly by the regime. Farinacci turned to allies like the disgruntled Fascist Emilio De Bono for support. Ciano, wanting to save his own skin, was ready to join this anti-Badoglio cabal, but his country-club snobbery hardly meshed with the boorish Farinacci and his following.

Either because he thought himself untouchable, or because he was unmindful of the political forces gathering against him, Badoglio, in a meeting with OKW Commander Wilhelm Keitel on 14–15 November, heaped blame for the Greek fiasco on the "politicians"; that is, on Mussolini and Ciano. The Bulgarians did not tie up the Greeks in Thrace, he said, and the expected uprising in Epirus that would assure a smooth Italian landing in Albania did not occur. Worse yet, Mussolini had failed to devolve major responsibility onto the military for planning the war. Word of this reached Hans Georg von Mackensen, the

German ambassador in Rome, who summarized Badoglio's assertion of blame-lessness.[8] Ciano records: "The Duce's reaction was like a flash. He called Badoglio names like 'enemy of the regime' and 'traitor,' which are strong epithets for him to use about his own Chief of Staff in wartime."[9]

What had been titillating gossip in the corridors finally came out in the open when on the 23rd Farinacci, in his personal newspaper the *Regime Fascista,* accused the SMG of a "certain lack of foresight and proper timing" in under-taking the Greek operation. Farinacci made public what he had written Mussolini privately: Badoglio must go. Even an old ally like the king turned on him for having failed to comport himself loyally in talks with Keitel.[10] The group around Ciano and Jacomoni joined in by slyly passing on to the "Marchese di Capo-retto" their own errors of judgment. But their malice hardly matched that of the Germans, who hated Badoglio because he was the king's man, a friend of the French, and a faithless ally who had the audacity to remind Keitel of the British lion's ongoing roar.

On 30 November, when Mussolini personally faulted Badoglio for the Greek fiasco during a Council of Ministers meeting, the SMG chief claimed that the Duce's rebuke represented an attack on the integrity of the military. The beleaguered general's allies rushed to his support by pointing out the unfairness in holding the military responsible for the Greek failure. But when the king judged Badoglio "physically a wreck and intellectually stunted,"[11] Mussolini cashiered him on 4 December. Cavagnari was sacked three days later. The governor of the Aegean Sea, Cesare Maria De Vecchi, worried about his future, hurried in for an audience. Mussolini asked: "What do you want"? De Vecchi replied: a high military command. For this audacious request he was dismissed. Humiliated, he withdrew to Turin.[12] Why, the military asked, was Ciano allowed to get off scot-free? Hitler shared the military's aversion to Ciano, but hesitated to ask Mussolini for his removal, fearing that Grandi, a "firm enemy" of Germany, would replace him.[13] In any event, the Duce stood behind his son-in-law.

After a desultory search, Mussolini replaced Badoglio as head of the SMG with the "profiteer general" Ugo Cavallero,[14] who was close to Farinacci and had long served as a senior industrial manager at the Ansaldo corporation. The new

---

8. *The Ciano Papers*, 18 November 1940.
9. *The Ciano Diaries*, 22 November 1940.
10. Puntoni, *Parla Vittorio Emanuele III*, p. 22.
11. Ibid., p. 26.
12. Bocca, *Storia d'Italia nella guerra fascista*, p. 251.
13. Rintelen, *Mussolini e l'Alleato*, p. 115.
14. Cervi, *The Hollow Legions*, p. 72.

appointee moved easily in non-military circles, had the king in his corner, was politically well connected (he was Jacomoni's father-in-law), and exuded optimism regarding Albania.[15] A long-standing enemy of Badoglio, he told the general's son: "We find ourselves again at Caporetto, and as happened then I must repair the errors of Badoglio."[16] However, Cavallero was not without enemies and had few devotees in the military establishment. Ciano distrusted him for being pro-German. No wonder that von Rintelen was more accepting: "Within the limits of the possible, he meets every German desire."[17] As a man conversant with the world of business, Cavallero had acquired knowledge of modern industrial warfare that was lost on his dated military acquaintances.

Many fingers pointed at Ciano as the major culprit for the Greek disaster; his unpopularity in Italy fell to a new low. Believing that their sons had died in a vain war instigated by Ciano to expand his "grand duchy," many Italians called on the Duce to fire him. But such did not happen.

Everything seemed to be going wrong in Italy's war effort: chaos on the Albanian piers, embarrassing defeats on the battlefield, and incompetent military leadership. This outcome was contrary to what Mussolini had thought would be a short war that precluded elaborate military preparations, full mobilization, or civilian sacrifice. Still, the Duce was determined to give the impression that Italy could win handily without disrupting ordinary life. So long as Allied bombing raids remained sporadic, and shortages and rationing did not noticeably lower the quality of life, this was possible. With theaters and movie houses providing escapist entertainment and soccer teams playing in stadiums overflowing with cheering fans, people could live in the illusion that life was normal and the war far off. Fascist propaganda generated confidence that the armies would bring home swift victories against the Greeks, and Mussolini would arrange a home-coming celebration for the conquering heroes.

Escapism became increasingly difficult to maintain as time passed. When caskets bearing the dead from Albania began to pile up on seaport wharves, expectations of a military romp transmogrified into a war without end. Allied bombing raids began to punish Italy's major cities, and shortages occurred that were exacerbated by the Allied blockade. On 1 December the government im-posed rationing of pasta, rice, and flour. Prices rose inexorably and the black market flourished. Mussolini's plan to disconnect the mainstream populace from the war in order to prevent any serious sag in public support of the regime had gone awry. Ciano leaves us with a telling remark: "He [Mussolini] listens to my

---

15. *The Ciano Diaries*, 30 November 1940.
16. Cited in Indro Montanelli and Mario Cervi, *L'Italia della disfatta* (Milan: Rizzoli, 1979), p. 58.
17. Rintelen, *Mussolini e l'Alleato*, p. 176.

suggestion about doing something to raise the morale of the people. We must speak to the hearts of the Italians. We must make them understand that what is at stake in the game is not Fascism—it is our country, our eternal country, the country of all of us, which is above men and times and factions."[18]

Military Breakdown

On 4 December the Greeks broke through the Italian lines and seized the important town of Pogradec. The Italian troops were driven backwards toward ports jammed with equipment and reinforcements. Hitler remarked a day later that Italy's misfortune "has had the healthy effect of once again reducing Italian claims to within the natural limits of Italian capabilities."[19] Ciano claimed that it was still possible to form a bridgehead at Valona. "What counts now is to resist....if we give up it is the end."[20] However, Soddu opined that further military action was "impossible;" to save the day, one would have to find a political solution.[21] Ciano told Alfieri: "This made a great impression on the Duce.... he's very despondent," and quotes Mussolini: "This is grotesque and absurd, but it is a fact. We have to ask for a truce." Ciano replied: "I would rather put a bullet through my head than telephone Ribbentrop."[22] According to Bottai and Alfieri, Ciano took credit for eventually prevailing on Mussolini to persevere rather than beg Hitler to mediate a diplomatic settlement between Italy and Greece.

But there is another side to the story. In the heat of crisis on 4 December, General Alfredo Guzzoni, the SME deputy chief, was among the few who kept his composure. Prepared to ride out the storm, he implored Mussolini to stand firm. According to the official military account, it was Guzzoni's advice that buoyed Mussolini to issue promptly the order that the ground must be held to the last.[23] Both Soddu and Pricolo dismiss as absurd the notion that Mussolini would ever have asked for an armistice.[24] In any case, General Cavallero was sent to the front in Albania to shore up the Italian defenses.

If certain generals like Guzzoni and Cavallero kept steady nerves under fire, the gentlemen at the Palazzo Chigi led by Ciano gave way to panic. In the presence of Mussolini, Ciano asked an ailing Alfieri to take the next train back to

18. *The Ciano Diaries*, 12 December 1940.
19. *The Halder Diaries*, II: 212.
20. *The Ciano Diaries*, 4 December 1940.
21. Montanari, *Grecia*, p. 321.
22. Dino Alfieri, *Dictators Face to Face* (London: Elek, 1954), pp. 81–82; *The Ciano Diaries*, 4 December 1940.
23. Montanari, *Grecia*, pp. 321–27.
24. De Felice, *Mussolini l'alleato*, I: 352–53.

Berlin where he should ask for immediate military assistance. "At these words," Ciano reported, "Mussolini started like a man who has been suddenly roused from sleep. It was as if the thought of the mighty German armies had had a tonic effect on his spirits." What kind of help was he to seek? "Any assistance, so long as it's prompt," Ciano told Alfieri. "There is no need to be specific or to voice any preferences.... The situation is such that the dispatch of a few airplanes, a few guns, a few battalions may make all the difference. It's a question of gaining time—a few days, perhaps even a few hours..."[25] But beyond about fifty transport Junkers to help in the airlift of reinforcements (by mid-December the Germans were shuttling troops and supplies from Foggia in southern Italy to Tirana), Hitler would not go. The Führer was outspoken in advocating punishment for the miscreants in the Italian military: "A man with iron nerves" should resort to "barbarism." Officers who deserted their posts should be shot and the military should not refrain from carrying out selected troop decimation as collective punishment for cowardice.[26] Beyond the reminder that the Italian soldier lacked the unmitigated cruelty of the Nazi warrior, it was clear that Hitler would not provide Mussolini with direct German support for his troops.[27]

Preparing for the invasion of the Soviet Union, Hitler trusted neither the Greeks nor the Italians to keep the lower Balkans secure against a future build-up of British air squadrons on the Greek mainland.[28] Hence on 13 December he activated Operation Marita, a German invasion of the lower Balkans, whose purpose was to deny the Royal Air Force runways for bombing raids on the Ploesti oil fields in Romania. On learning of Operation Marita, which Mussolini took as a Trojan horse for a *Drang nach Südosten*, he discarded any lingering notion of a *guerra di coalizione* under the Italian masterminds in the Balkans in favor of a vigorously pursued military offensive to occupy Italy's *spazio vitale* before the Germans got there.

Agony in the Desert

After having given way to Graziani's stilted march into Sidi el Barrani on 13 September, the British hatched no big surprises in desert warfare, which the Italians took as proof that they did not have the spine to launch offensives. But neither were the Italians inspired to prepare their own attack. It was far simpler to dig in. In a typical deployment suitable for an army of colonial occupation,

25. Alfieri, *Dictators Face to Face*, pp. 84–85.
26. DGFP, D, XI, 477, Conversation between Hitler and Alfieri, 8 December 1940.
27. DDI, 9, VI, 258, Alfieri to Ciano, 8 December 1940.
28. *Germany and the Second World War*, III: 454.

Graziani established a system of elaborate camps around Sidi Barrani. As desert architecture goes these camps were lavish. Scooping holes in the sand and stretching camouflaged canvas across the roofs of the structures created mess halls, hospitals, and sleeping quarters. The camps were surrounded by stonewalls and geometrically spaced lookout posts. Extensive minefields and anti-tank traps were laid in front of the camps, and machine guns and artillery nozzles, peering through niches chiseled out of the stone walls, stood at the ready to cut down any enemy soldiers who got through. Graziani's military artwork seemed to have been taken from a handbook of the Napoleonic era where it became clear that a static army would have no chance against a moving enemy adroit at encircle-ment. Nor did Graziani pay heed to the warnings of SIM, which assessed enemy strength in the theater at thirteen or fourteen divisions and three in the western desert between Marsa Matruh and Alexandria. Since Graziani refused to consider the looming threat of an enemy attack at Marsa Matruh, he undertook few pre-cautions, neglected reconnaissance, and did little in consolidating forces spread out over 150 kilometers.[29]

On 9 December 1940 General Sir Archibald Wavell, the British commander-in-chief in the Middle East, gave General R. N. O'Connor the go-ahead to launch Operation Compass. The stolid Graziani faced a nimble adversary in Wavell, who ably deployed light and fast mobile forces. While Wavell stabbed with many lances from different directions, Graziani stood his ground holding a stationary shield. Faced with a static defense, the British easily infiltrated the Italian lines, circled around, and attacked from the rear. Thickly armored Matilda tanks quickly pierced the lines, and the rout was on. The famed "Desert Rats," who passed through the twisted wreckage of Italian military hardware cheerfully whistling the Australian anthem "Waltzing Matilda," led the conquering soldiers. The Italian "tankettes" might have done well in crowd control or in terrifying Ethiopian horsemen but were no match for the lumbering British giants. Within days the Italian troops straggled out of Egypt utterly demoralized.

To avert a complete military collapse, Mussolini finally swallowed his pride by seeking German assistance on 17–20 December. With the help of his ministers, he drew up a huge list of raw materials that Italy would require through the following year.[30] In addition, to blunt the advancing British in Libya, a German military cohort was needed—one or two armored military divisions, air support, and a vast supply of artillery, anti-tank weapons, trucks, and anti-

---

29. DGFP, D, XI, 597, Rintelen report, 2 January 1941.
30. Cavallero, *Diario*, 19 December 1940; Montanari, *Grecia*, p. 418.

aircraft guns.[31] Under duress on both the Albanian and North African fronts, the Italian command quietly discarded the plan for a "parallel war" in favor of an Axis *guerra comune* against the primary enemy, Great Britain, which hardly concealed the reality that Germany was being asked to intervene in an Italian sphere to save the battered *regio esercito* in North Africa.[32] After some hesitation Hitler agreed to assist his beleaguered comrade, but it would take between ten to twelve weeks to organize and send a relief force to North Africa.

Unwisely, Graziani chose to make a stand at Bardia, whose defense was essential to the salvation of Cirenaica in lieu of a fallback to a better defensive position. Lieutenant-General Annibale Bergonzoli, called "Electric Whiskers" by his troops for his spiky white beard, put up a stiff resistance that momentarily stopped the British offensive. But the under-equipped Italians could hold out only so long. An aggressive British infantry attack on 3 January broke through the Italian lines and captured the town along with 40,000 Italian troops, 120 tanks, 400 artillery pieces and 650 trucks. Graziani wrote despairingly to the Duce on 6 January: "For those inexorable laws that dominate war in the desert, where an initial mayhem is not remediable, defeat will inevitably be total."[33] At the same time British foreign secretary Anthony Eden derisively commented: "Never before has so much been surrendered by so many to so few."[34] Tobruk, one of the best-fortified towns in the colony, fell on 22 January, which gave the Royal Navy a useful port to supply the advancing British troops. In a brilliant encircling movement, O'Connor destroyed the remnants of the Italian 10th Army on 7 February. After making a brief last stand at Beda Fomm, what remained of the Italian army fled from Cyrenaica.

In areas abandoned much looting occurred. Taking advantage of the Italian settlers left defenseless by the retreating Italian army, local Arabs indulged in pillage and arson before the arrival of the Commonwealth forces. The helpless settlers pleaded for protection against the roving bands. But having been dispossessed of their lands or thrown off communal holdings to make way for Italians, the Arabs were, understandably, vengeful.

In ten weeks' campaigning O'Connor's 30,000 men had advanced over 500 miles, destroyed 400 tanks and 845 artillery pieces, routed an army five times their number, and taken 130,000 prisoners at the cost of 476 British dead and 1,225 wounded. The victorious British filed into Tripolitania. At this point they

---

31. DGFP, D, XI, 541, Rintelen and Mackensen to Berlin, 20 December 1940; Jens Petersen, "L'Afrika-Korps," in *L'Italia in Guerra: il 1ᵃ anno–1941* (Rome: Commissione italiana di storia militare, 1992), p. 389.
32. I am indebted to Pier Paolo Battistelli for pointing out this subtle change in thinking at the Italian High Command.
33. *Operazioni*, I, Allegato 57, Graziani to Mussolini, 6 January 1941, pp. 635–36.
34. Winston S. Churchill, *The Grand Alliance* (Boston: Houghton Mifflin, 1950), p. 13.

were compelled to stand down, not because of Italian resistance but because British prime minister Winston Churchill stopped operations in North Africa by transferring troops from the desert to halt Operation Marita bearing down on Greece. This decision gave the Germans an opportunity to reinforce the struggling Italians, which would rob the British of their victories.

Churchill, in an address to the Italian people, noted that the British armies were "tearing the African empire to shreds and tatters.... People of Italy, I want you to know the truth. It is because of one man alone. One man and only one man has launched the Italian people in a deadly struggle with the British Empire and has deprived Italy of the friendship and good will of the United States of America."[35] While it might have been true that Mussolini had "brought the heirs of the glory of the Roman Empire to the side of the bloodthirsty pagan barbarians," and while he might have hoped that his speech would inspire an uprising against the regime, Churchill overlooked the essential patriotism of many Italians who, stolid believers in "my country right or wrong," continued to regard Mussolini as leader of the nation. While fumbling the ball in war, the Duce was thought to be the only one who could salvage Italian honor from the wreckage of military defeat.

This chapter of the North African campaign provided the Italians an education: static defenses could not stand up to piercing frontal attacks by superior British tanks coordinated with flanking movements by speedy, light armored vehicles. Poorly trained and badly deployed infantry invited demoralization and defeat when thrown against a motorized enemy. Graziani might have done better by concentrating his armored units on violent and well-timed counterattacks instead of spreading them out thinly where they could be easily picked off and surrounded.

On 14 December Graziani wrote Mussolini "from man to man" in what promised to be a critique of the Duce's military strategy that had doomed him to a struggle of "a flea against an elephant." Instead, the letter was filled with lame excuses.[36] As the lines crumbled around him in early February, Graziani wrote Mussolini on the 8th: "Duce, recent events have strongly depleted my nerves and energy so much that I no longer can hold the command in the fullness of my faculties. I ask you therefore to be recalled and replaced."[37] The disconsolate general flew back to Italy three days later. How such a mediocre character could arrive at a lofty position of power appears strange until it is remembered that Graziani's ardent Fascism made him a man of the Duce. From this experience

35. Winston S. Churchill, *Their Finest Hour* (Boston: Houghton Mifflin, 1950), pp. 527–28.
36. *OO*, XXX: 41–42.
37. Cited in Bocca, *Storia d'Italia nella guerra fascista*, p. 269.

Mussolini learned nothing, for he would appoint the same disgraced commander to lead his paper army at Salò.

Further disasters struck Mussolini's "pearl of the Fascist regime" in East Africa, an enclave that consisted of Ethiopia, Eritrea, and Italian Somaliland. In command of the Italian forces there, Prince Amedeo of Savoy, the Duke of Aosta, possessed a force of approximately 250,000 troops (seventy percent native), a few hundred aircraft, and about 60 tanks and 100 armored cars against a British army that numbered barely 40,000. In the early spring of 1941, the British attacked and swiftly forced the Italians out of Kenya, the Sudan, and British Somaliland. Ethiopia's turn came next. By April 1941, the badly equipped and led Italian troops in Ethiopia abjectly surrendered to the British whom they vastly outnumbered. His country set free, Haile Selassie triumphantly mounted his throne again on 5 May after five years in exile. Between 20 April and 15 May the duke stubbornly resisted but was finally obliged to surrender on 19 May. Not only were the Italian troops faced by a competent enemy; they were threatened with native uprisings and mutinies on the part of the indigenous soldiers in their ranks. The Italian destroyers and submarines at Massawa did not successfully perform their task of blocking the arrival of British reinforcements by sea.

Greek Quagmire

While the British troops were knifing through the Italian lines in North Africa, the Greeks launched an attack on 14 December that posed a serious threat to Valona. Sensing victory, they paid little heed to the German threat of invasion to bail out the crippled Axis ally.[38] Homer was not the only Greek to be carried away by hubris. When Metaxas died on 29 January, he was replaced as prime minister by Alexandros Koryzis, which did not diminish the Greek will to fight.

Deteriorating conditions on the Albanian battlefield caused recriminations in Rome. For Mussolini, fault rested with the military. "Our forces are not fighting back," he told Ciano, "and their officers are low in morale." Cultivating a good image at the Palazzo Chigi had more value for Mussolini than performance on the battlefield.[39] Now it was Ciano's turn: "Jealousies among generals are worse than among women. One should hear Soddu's telephone calls to General Antonio Sorice. He demolishes all the generals. Geloso has softening of the brain, Perugi is a disaster, Trionfi is bankrupt. Today, for some unknown reason, he speaks well of Vercellino, saying, 'Poor Vercellino! He is such a dear man. He

38. Creveld, *Hitler's Strategy 1940–1944*, p. 90.
39. *The Ciano Diaries*, 20 December 1941.

came to see me and wept.' Also it seems that Soddu spent his free time, even during the most anxious hours in Albania, composing film music."[40] Soddu was recalled to Rome on 29 December and never returned to Albania. He retired in mid-January, ostensibly for reasons of health.

In addition to his regular duties as chief of the SMG, Cavallero on 30 December assumed command of the troops in Albania. His first task was to overcome the chaos at the ports. The next step would be the establishment of a more orderly supply system to smooth the way for the movement of new divisions into Albania. While visualizing future offensives, he set about the more prosaic chore of preparing for the worst by construction of a defensive "wall" in front of the ports of Valona and Tirana. Cavallero needed a last-gasp defense in case a future Greek offensive should shatter the Italian lines. Arctic conditions and rugged terrain came to his rescue by stalling such an offensive. Troops on both sides settled into a grinding war of attrition. Given this reprieve, the Italians no longer worried about a further immediate Greek drive to the Adriatic, which gave Mussolini heart that the Italian troops would be able to pass through this critical phase without German reinforcements. In the comfort of his office in the Palazzo Venezia, Mussolini showed no concern for the hardships his troops faced: "This snow and cold are very good because as a result the pipsqueaks will die and this mediocre Italian race will be improved."[41]

The sacrifices that were required for fighting a parallel war, that is, a war free of German interference, constituted a higher priority in Mussolini's mind than a battle plan that avoided needless sacrifice of Italian troops. The dreaded Operation Marita loomed, which he wanted to head off by a brilliantly successful offensive in Albania, whatever the cost and despite a lack of preparation. To prevent the Germans from robbing Italy of its rightful Balkan sphere of influence, Mussolini hurried to be the one annihilating the Greeks.[42] He wrote Cavallero on 1 January 1941: "After sixty days of anvil we must become the hammer; a decisive offensive will eliminate every possible speculation in the world regarding Italian prestige of which I am the most jealous defender.... My desire, my certainty, is that thanks to your engagement and the valor of the troops, the *direct* aid of Germany on the Albanian front will be rendered superfluous."[43] General Messe warned him by passing on the chief of the Wehrmacht General Wilhelm Keitel's aim to intervene against Greece in order to seize Salonica, thus gaining an outlet on the Mediterranean. Mussolini had recently stated: "The Medi-

---

40. Cited in Cervi, *The Hollow Legions*, p. 190. Geloso and Mario Vercellino were army commanders in Albania, Perugi and Trionfi divisional commanders.
41. Cited in Montanelli & Cervi, *L'Italia della disfatta*, p. 59.
42. NAW, T-821, 129, 000065, Mussolini to Cavallero, 16 January 1941; Also see Montanari, *Grecia*, p. 506.
43. Montanari, *Grecia*, p. 434.

terranean is for us life itself, for England, only a passageway." Did Germany, wondered Messe, aim to replace England by taking possession of such a passageway?[44] But Cavallero, instead of launching an offensive, was the discomfited witness to the Greek capture of the important town Klisura.

Mussolini, Hitler, and their respective generals assembled at the Berghof for meetings on 19–20 January 1941. The two sides fenced over the matter of German military assistance. Hitler was ready to make a troop contribution in Albania, but the Italians, humiliated by the prospect of a large Wehrmacht force in "their" Albania, spelled out obstacles, such as ongoing port bottlenecks, which rendered a quick German deployment of more than one light division impossible.[45] Hitler soon tired of the subject and the matter was dropped. But the growing ascendancy of the Führer over Mussolini was unmistakable. Alfieri captured the change: "Hitler seemed to be saying: 'See how strong I am and how well I have done. You are weak; you have suffered misfortunes and defeats. It doesn't matter: I will help you, and if you leave things to me and have confidence in me there will be a place in the sun for you too.'"[46] Too long had Hitler deluded others, as he deluded himself, as to the strength and capacity of Mussolini to inculcate his nation with the warrior's spirit.

To divert attention from Italy's failings in Albania and North Africa, Mussolini in late January impetuously mobilized all high Fascist officials to do a stint at the front. He, Mussolini, would run the Italian state assisted by a committee of experts. During the Ethiopian war, many Fascist leaders had volunteered to participate in the campaign to revel in the experience of victory. But the war against Greece was a different matter—far harsher and more dangerous, implying punishment rather than adventure. The *gerarchi* this time were decidedly not happy. Bottai told Ciano that it was a coup d'état on the part of the Duce against Fascism.[47] The much-hated Ciano expressed dismay. Grandi, bypassed as Ciano's replacement, bridled over his send-off to intemperate Albanian weather as a "reborn" Alpino. Among the high Fascist officials sent to the war zone were portly middle-aged men pitched into craggy mountains and muddy mule tracks to share the discomforts of the troops. Mussolini sternly ordered that they be denied any privileged treatment at the front: "no servants or suitcases."[48] But those sent to Albania soon returned to their cushy former jobs. Since nothing had really changed, the public fell back into skepticism and indifference. For

---

44. NAW, T-821, 129, 000066–72, Messe to Rome, 4 January 1941.
45. DDI, 9, VI, 472, Conversation between Guzzoni and Keitel, 19 January 1941.
46. Alfieri, *Dictators Face to Face*, p. 94; DGFP, D, XI, 672, Conversation between Mussolini and Hitler, 21 January 1941.
47. *The Ciano Diaries*, 17 January 1941.
48. Cavallero, *Diario*, 23 January 1941.

Mussolini, however, there would be long-term damage. Many Fascists, outraged at having to slog through Albanian mud paddies, nourished a bitterness toward him that ultimately found expression in the Fascist Grand Council meeting on 25 July 1943 when they stripped him of power.

By the end of February, disturbing reports from Germany flooded Rome. The Wehrmacht had just thrown bridges across the Danube into Bulgaria, indicating that Operation Marita was in full swing. The Italians knew that if they took their time in finishing off the Greeks, Wehrmacht soldiers would not simply cool their heels in Bulgaria. Worse still, the OKW was believed to be inducing the Greeks to sign an armistice before the troops crossed over the Bulgarian frontier, an arrangement that would involve Greek concessions in return for avoiding war with Germany. Greece had already promised Berlin in January 1941 that it would renounce British assistance and request German arbitration in the conflict with Italy.[49] Aghast, the Italians moved quickly to squelch the idea. Anfuso informed Berlin that any effort to deal with Athens "did not interest us"; Guzzoni warned that it was inadmissible for German troops to occupy Greece peacefully while Italian troops fight and die. Distrustful of Hitler, Mussolini ordered Marras "to make [Berlin] understand that Italy intends to defeat Greece....it is a question of prestige and nobody should understand this better than the German military."[50] "Seldom," noted Lanza, "has the atmosphere between Rome and Berlin been so cold."[51] Although Hitler, without Italian urging, had actually spared his Axis ally deep embarrassment by ignoring Greek overtures for a negotiated settlement, Operation Marita would proceed apace.

To beat the stubborn Greeks before the Germans arrived in the lower Balkans, Mussolini piloted a three-engine S 79 to Albania escorted by cronies to goad generals into applying a decisive blow. He landed in Albania on 2 March. There was reason for optimism, for after Herculean efforts the Italians had finally achieved numerical superiority on the ground to match their domination in the air. This was due in no small measure to Cavallero's reorganization of the ports. Ten new divisions disembarked during the period January-April 1941 to join the eleven already in place.[52] Having inherited a difficult state of affairs, Cavallero was able to stave off more setbacks by putting the finishing touches on his "wall" of defense. Mussolini, anxious to achieve a crushing victory, wanted to rush in more of everything. Cavallero countered by pointing out that the already overburdened ports could not withstand a fresh infusion of troops and supplies.

---

49. *Germany and the Second World War*, III: 468.
50. NAW, T-821, 129, 000014, Guzzoni to Marras, 28 February 1941.
51. Simoni, *Berlino ambasciata d'Italia*, p. 212.
52. De Felice, *Mussolini l'alleato*, I: 315.

Although Cavallero carried around an array of offensive plans, he was not yet ready to pull one out. The troops were still hampered by inadequate training for infiltration tactics, and all too many officers had received little more than sketchy training. These problems had to be resolved, one would have thought, before a new offensive could be unfurled. But nothing would deter the Duce from ordering a major attack.

To keep in step with Mussolini, the generals, who knew better, put on a sycophantic display of confidence in victory. The irrepressible General Gastone Gambara urged an ambitious offensive. The weathervane Cavallero buoyed the Duce's spirits with upbeat chatter, but concocted a defensive battle plan that precluded defeat. Among the Italians, only General Guzzoni, "with his tightly stretched paunch and his little dyed wig,"[53] had the good sense to eschew offensives till the soldiers were better prepared, but he was not listened to. Rintelen's advice was ignored too: "Your counterattacks in Albania, made with troops just landed in unknown territory, are most difficult, and, without adequate preparation, more damaging to you than for the enemy."[54]

The Italians launched an offensive on the central part of the front on 9 March after a violent artillery barrage accompanied by ineffective bombing raids. When no breach was made in the Greek lines, an agitated Mussolini told General Geloso on the 12th: "Before Germany's intervention it is indispensable to obtain a military success since otherwise the Germans would have every reason to say that the Greeks yielded by their [German] merits alone. Therefore the action must continue."[55] General Pricolo provides the following exchange. Mussolini asked: "What do you think?" Pricolo replied: "I think we're doing all right." "No, no, the attack has failed," replied Mussolini.[56] By the 15th, unaffected by troops wiped out in useless attacks, Mussolini issued the order: "Hold Tepeleni at whatever cost; reach Klisura at whatever cost," which supposedly would bring about the collapse of Greek resistance.[57] As Mussolini prepared to leave Albania, he opined: "the Italian people will rebel at the idea that its army was incapable of beating the Greeks."[58]

The Italian March offensive was planned and waged in the style of 1915–18. Yet up-to-date mobile weapons might not have fared much better in the jagged and mountainous terrain. One cannot blame the Italian troops for the string of failures and disappointments in the military campaign against Greece. They

53. *The Ciano Diaries*, 21 January 1941.
54. NAW, T-821, 129, 000032, Rintelen to General Gandin, 1 February 1941.
55. Montanari, *Grecia*, p. 620.
56. Francisco Pricolo, *La regia aeronautica nella seconda guerra mondiale* (Milan: Longanesi, 1971), p. 344.
57. Montanari, *Grecia*, p. 627.
58. Ibid., p. 635.

arrived in Albania bewildered and harried, berated by an aloof officer class, and constantly subjected to improvised deployment. Armed with worn and outdated weapons, thrown into battle after hasty and incomplete training, unprotected in abominable weather, and fed substandard rations, the Italian soldiers suffered constant hardship. The insufficient numbers of mules, which forced dog-tired troops to take their turn as bearers of arms, munitions and food while slogging through mud and rain, was not exactly a morale booster. The soldiers could only be pushed so far.[59] But they doggedly fought, bled, and died.

General Cavallero came to his job flaunting optimism, a quality not ill placed when faith and hope needed to be restored. His was not an easy task. Routinely Mussolini had to be bridled and frequently the sluggish military apparatus had to be badgered to pick up the pace. Cavallero did excellent work in constructing his "wall," but that was small change when compared to launching a counter-offensive to alter the course of the war. Here, according to Montanari, he made a serious strategic mistake in ignoring a military offensive as outlined in memo-randum number 6, which called for the reconquest of Corçano in the first in-stance and, successively, the envelopment of the major Greek force with action along the Korça-Ersekë-Kalibaki line.[60]

Although not the victory he would have liked in Greece, Mussolini made the best of an irretrievable setback: "When one does not withdraw, the soldier must always consider himself victorious."[61] The Italian generals strove to salvage honor and reap titles from an embarrassing military stalemate. Cavallero schemed to be anointed as "Duke of Tepeleni," a place principally known as the locale of a heroic Italian defense.[62] Not to be left out, Badoglio squelched the notion that he had been plotting a coup d'état by offering on 17 March to engineer the conquest of Greece himself. In this unreal atmosphere Pirelli ex-horted Mussolini to prevail on the Germans to cease their "interference" in the Balkans.[63]

The flip side of triumphalism was derision, sophistry, and cynicism. On his way back home from Albania, Mussolini told Pricolo: "I am disgusted by this environment. We have not advanced one step. They have been deceiving me to this very day. I feel deep contempt for all these people."[64] He returned to the Palazzo Venezia in a grim mood and insisted on "finding those responsible for

---

59. Ibid., p. 572.
60. Ibid., p. 775.
61. Cited in Lucio Ceva, *Guerra mondiale: Strategie e industria bellica 1939–1945* (Milan: FrancoAngeli, 2000), p. 85.
62. Cavallero, *Diario*, p. XX, Bucciante preface.
63. Alberto Pirelli, *Taccuini 1942/1943* (Bologna: Il Mulino, 1984), pp. 291, 294.
64. Pricolo, *La regia aeronautica*, p. 345.

his loss of face."[65] Defiantly he wrote Ciano that the Italian war on Greece was logical and providential for the Axis in cleaning out residual Franco-British influence. This would never have happened had Italy not gone to war against Greece, whose liquidation would open up large horizons for Italy on land and on sea.[66] Ciano confided to Mussolini soon after the end of the Greek campaign that "a compromise peace should be welcomed by us, especially now that we have acquired our share of the booty."[67] Roatta added his view: "In the first instance the idea prevailed of concentrating efforts in Albania, whose situation for reasons of distance was the most felt. The question of prestige had to be faced: the lack of success caused by England was bearable. Insupportable were defeats inflicted on us by Greece."[68]

By 23 April 1941 Italy had deployed 29 divisions in the Albanian theater. At the middle of the month there were 20,813 Italian officers and 470,918 NCOs and men there, plus 487 officers and 11,231 NCOs and combatants of Albanian origin.[69] Quite forgotten by Mussolini and his cohort were the approximately 20,000 fallen and missing troops, 50,874 wounded, and 64,476 frostbitten and sick. All these losses were incurred in a war against a country, which, in Mussolini's contemptuous words, was not worth the life of a single Sardinian grenadier, which made a mockery of the motto "Book and rifle—perfect Fascist."[70] "The revolution against Fascism," wrote Grandi, "started in the bloody trenches of Albania."[71]

At the end of March 1941 Mussolini had not much to brag about. Humiliated on the battlefront in France in an abortive campaign, he suffered further disgrace in a campaign in Libya that was going from bad to worse. Large capital ships lay at the bottom of the sea or listed heavily damaged at port, and Italy had been chased from two-thirds of its colonies while the Negus returned triumphantly to his throne. The bars of the Mediterranean prison still stood to mock "the Italian sea." The Greeks at one point had wrested a fourth of Albania from the beleaguered Italian army, and Italy had fallen from a dubious equal in the Axis to an unmistakable subaltern at a time when Germany was consolidating hegemony over Europe. From now on Mussolini could expect his imperial appetite to be slaked only by a Hitlerian *beau geste*. But since most of Italy's ruling classes led by the king still firmly believed in a German victory, the

---

65. Cited in Cervi, *The Hollow Legions*, p. 265.
66. DDI, 9, VI, 759, Mussolini to Ciano, 21 March 1941.
67. *The Ciano Diaries*, 6 May 1941.
68. Ceva, *Guerra mondiale*, p. 95; ACS, Graziani Papers, lettere Roatta, 1941, 13 gennaio 1941.
69. Figures in *Germany and the Second World War*, III: 448, and Montanari, *Grecia*, pp. 805, 938–43.
70. Cervi, *The Hollow Legions*, p. 241.
71. Cited in Innocenti, *L'Italia del 1940*, p. 159.

hope of imperial prizes continued to beguile the Italian *classe dirigente*, which made Mussolini's continued hold on power unshakable until well into 1942.

Indeed, Mussolini himself declared before the Chamber on 23 February 1941 the "mathematical" certainty of a German victory.[72] This buoyancy was not entirely misplaced, for the immediate future was to bring tangible gains. German general Erwin Rommel, launching a counterattack, advanced toward the Egyptian-Libyan border and placed Tobruk under siege; in April the Axis Powers wiped out Yugoslavia in a fortnight; the following month German paratroopers broke British resistance on Crete. Italy, it was expected, would somehow "fall on its feet" and collect its spoils as had happened when, after battlefield defeats in 1866, peacemakers handed valuable provinces to Piedmont. Similarly, the great Italian rout in October 1917 administered by the Habsburg Empire at Caporetto did not deny Italy rich territorial gain after the end of World War I. But there were differences. Following that disaster, liberal Italy, coming together as a nation, found redemption at the Vittorio Veneto with some degree of aid from Britain and France, whereas in 1941 Fascist Italy was in no position to extricate itself from the Greek imbroglio without decisive German intervention. The Germans had not envisaged a costly involvement in Greece, and the Italians did not want them there. But since for Italy there was no deliverance in sight without Operation Marita, Mussolini had to live with the German *fait accompli*.

---

72. *OO*, XXX: 49–58.

The Balkans under the Axis: occupation and political boundaries.

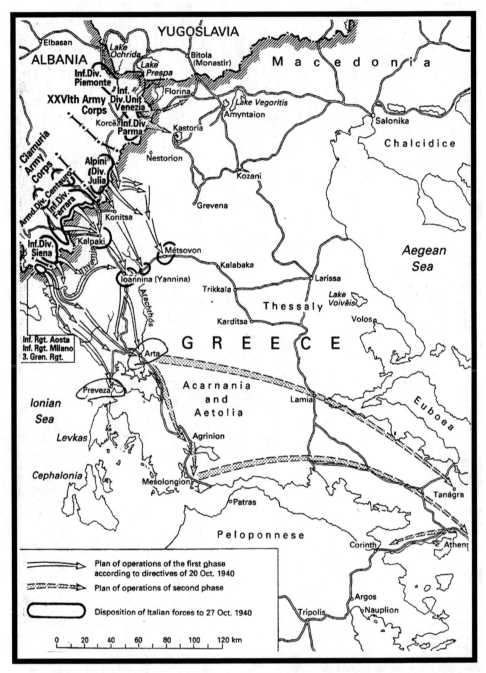

Italian invasion plans for Greece in October 1940.

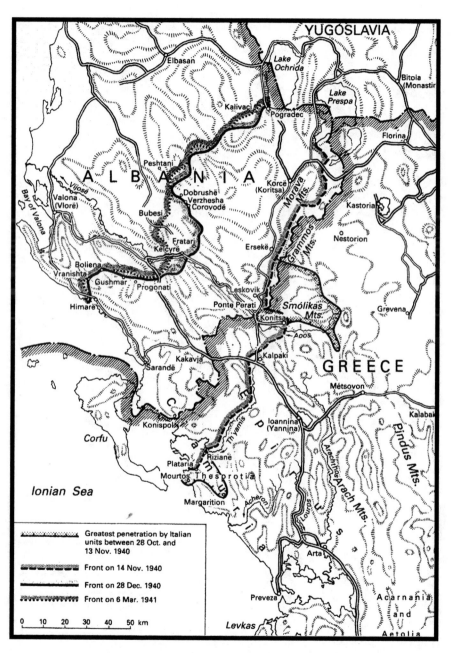

Italian positions on the Greek-Albanian front October 1940-March 1941.

Chapter IV

False Glory

Invasion of Yugoslavia

Mussolini made no secret that he held the Yugoslav peoples in contempt for being nothing more than an agglomeration of primitive tribes unworthy of nationhood. The Yugoslavs replied by belittling Fascists as spoiled Italian children pretending to be virile warriors. Thanks to this mutual disdain, war loomed as a premeditated act, preemptive strike, or as the result of miscalculation caused by a dangerous game of Russian roulette.

After heavy pressure from Berlin, Yugoslavia signed the Tripartite Pact with Germany on 25 March 1941. The government in Belgrade had made a momentous decision in abandoning the historical ties with Britain and France in favor of alignment with the Axis Powers. But two days later, out of the blue, Belgrade was shaken by a coup d'état, encouraged by the British and engineered by military officers and politicians unhappy with this move. The changing of the guard in Belgrade caught the two dictators by surprise. In Berlin an enraged Hitler promised to exact revenge against a country that he felt had double-crossed him. A punishing invasion would also satisfy important strategic imperatives by rendering safe the movement of a German army across Bulgaria to the Greek frontier and by quieting down the Balkans on the eve of Operation Barbarossa, Hitler's planned invasion of the Soviet Union.

In Rome pandemonium ensued. Michele Lanza, the second secretary at the Italian embassy in Berlin, reported: "What are they saying in Berlin? What should we do? What if the Yugoslavs attack us? We're not ready."[1] Mussolini was ambivalent. He welcomed the turn of events that would enable the Axis to sweep away this last artificial state created at Versailles under Woodrow Wilson's sponsorship. Avenging the *vittoria mutilata* had always been an urgent Fascist priority. At the same time Mussolini wondered how Dalmatia and Croatia could be saved from Germany's clutches. He also feared a catastrophe for his troops in Albania if the Yugoslavs joined the Greeks. As usual, the Duce kept his Axis chin up when addressing the Germans: "I have already personally ordered General Cavallero to call off the offensive which was about to be launched [against Greece]," he assured Hitler. Troops would be moved to the Yugoslav frontier in the north and Pavelić was summoned to Rome "in a war that would be popular in Italy."[2] Mussolini could not allow a German attack to proceed without Italian participation for fear of being left out of the division of spoils. Hitler wrote: "Above all, Duce, I consider *one* thing important: *Your front must in no case give way in Albania*."[3] His words emboldened Mussolini to call for a rush to arms.

Without warning, on 6 April—the day that the Yugoslavs signed a non-aggression treaty with the Soviet Union—German Stukas rained bombs down on a defenseless Belgrade, followed by a swift and deadly invasion. On the 17th, routed and outflanked, the demoralized Yugoslav army bent to the inevitable and signed an unconditional surrender. Without pause German forces hurried down the Balkans and easily crushed the Greeks by the end of April. Southeastern Europe, supposedly Italy's province, lay at Hitler's feet. The Italians did their part by invading Yugoslavia at three points, encountering little resistance from an army that suffered from defections on the part of the Croats and had been annihilated and broken up by the Wehrmacht.

The dizzying speed of the Axis victory caught Mussolini without a plan either for the ultimate disposition of Yugoslav territory or for the establishment

1. Simoni, *Berlino ambasciata d'Italia*, p. 216.
2. DGFP, D, XII, 226, Mackensen to Berlin, 28 March 1941.
3. Ibid., 281, Hitler to Mussolini, 5 April 1941.

of a new Croatian regime, as opposed to the Germans, who invaded the Soviet Union with elaborate colonization schemes. Who would serve as the Italian puppet in Zagreb? The moderate Croatian separatists, whose chief spokesman was Vladko Maček, would not do, for the peasant leader had irked Mussolini in 1939 by joining the Yugoslav cabinet instead of intriguing with him for a Croatian uprising. Only the minuscule radical fringe—the Croatian Ustaša— found credibility in Rome. Thus did Mussolini's eye fall on Ante Pavelić, whose major skill lay in the employment of knives and bombs.

Since Germany's military setbacks in the Soviet Union were still to come, and America was slumbering in neutrality, Mussolini crafted an Italian policy regarding Yugoslavia expecting a German victory as he did in the other Italian war theaters in North Africa and the Soviet Union. Germany's conquest of Yugoslavia in April 1941 gave him and his empire-builders a rare opportunity to realize long-standing irredentist claims along the Adriatic coast. No less enticing was the prospect of occupying Balkan lands as Italy's rightful "living spaces."

But the Germans stepped in to hamper Italy's Balkan ambitions. During a meeting 21–23 April, Ribbentrop unveiled a ploy to win Zagreb's allegiance: the creation of an elephantine Croatian state that would include Bosnia-Herzegovina and large tracts of the Dalmatian coast. Furthermore, he announced that Berlin had decided to maintain an occupation force in a strip of Croatia running from northwest to southeast in order to safeguard railroad lines with Serbia bearing a large traffic of raw materials from the lower Balkans. Hence the origin of the demarcation line that would supposedly separate the Italian and German forces occupying Croatia. Instead of an Italian *spazio vitale* over the entire country, it had been divided into two Axis spheres of influence, but with German economic domination assured in the area assigned to Italy.

In looking to the branch of the renegade Croatians surrounding Pavelić, Mussolini was clutching a weak reed, for they were no more than an outlaw minority that had arrived in Zagreb in the baggage of the enemy Italians. When the Axis turned over Bosnia and Herzegovina with their large Serb population to Croatia, it was almost certain that Zagreb would have to govern by strong-arm methods, but the Ustaša, whose political consciousness derived from irrational mistrust and hatred of Serbs, immediately went far beyond that, employing un-restrained terror in attempting to create a "pure" Croatian state. The new gov-ernment was staffed with inefficient and corrupt personnel—or none at all—but the Ustaša squads were surprisingly unified and prompt in launching extermina-tion programs against the Serbs, as well as Jews and gypsies.

Under the command of General Vittorio Ambrosio, the Italian 2nd Army moved through the annexed areas to bivouac on Croatian territory in the demilitarized zone near the Adriatic coast. Facing no competition from Italian civilian functionaries in supervising the public order, the 2nd Army initially had a free hand.[4] The military leaders were not bashful in propagating the view that Italy was a proud military conqueror and that Dalmatia was merely the first step. In late April, speaking for the Duce from his new headquarters in Sušak, Ambrosio laid down the indispensable preconditions for the Italian New Order: a roundup of weapons, taking of hostages, disarmament of the native population, arrest of all undesirable elements, suspension of nationalist organizations, mandatory flying of the Italian flag, prominent public display of images of the king and Duce, posting of popular Fascist dictums, and the death penalty for threats on the lives of Italian military and civilian personnel.[5]

By these measures the Duce placed the 2nd Army and the Fascist commissars who were to take up command posts in Slovenia, Dalmatia, and Montenegro on the same page. Their mandate was to create a tyrannical Italian *imperium* over the Slav population in Italian-annexed territories in Yugoslavia. But not all was harmonious between Sušak, command headquarters of the occupying 2nd Army, and Rome. General Ambrosio in his initial reports made the following points: the *italianità* of Dalmatia was a distant memory preserved only in monuments. The Croats living there, believing that Italian rule was an unfortunate but transitory necessity, were ostentatiously hostile. The NDH (Croatian State) spread anti-Italian propaganda and appointed vocal irredentists to important administrative posts, while the Ustaša, without an Italian warrant, seized the arms stockpiled by the defeated Yugoslav armies.[6] From the moment he assumed command, Ambrosio felt offended by the Pavelić regime that Mussolini had set up. Eventually, differences of opinion between the 2nd Army and the warlords in Rome about his rule would evolve into distinctly conflicting policies in Italian-occupied Yugoslavia.

In Croatia's demilitarized zones, the Italian commissioners, who had exercised power in a number of towns, were instructed to relinquish their authority to Zagreb's representatives as a concession to Pavelić. This was followed up by a directive from Mussolini on 20 May instructing the troops to behave like guests of a friendly and sovereign country.[7] Accordingly, the Carabinieri and the customs guards (*guardia di finanza*) withdrew, and the 2nd Army dismantled its checkpoints, but left garrisons in their fortified positions. The Italian soldiers were ordered to take no part in local politics.[8] But local

4. NAW, T-821, 127, 001025, Mussolini to Ambrosio, 23 April 1941.
5. Mario Dassovich, *Fronte Jugoslavo 1941-'42* (Udine: Del Bianco, 1999), pp. 15–16.
6. NAW, T-821, 128, 000389-94, Ambrosio to the War Ministry, 23 April 1941, 000226–229, Ambrosio to the War Ministry, 16 May 1941.
7. Oddone Talpo, *Dalmazia: Una cronaca per la storia (1941)* (Rome: SME US, 1995), p. 406.
8. Salvatore Loi, *Le operazioni delle unità italiane in Jugoslavia 1941–1943* (Rome: SME US, 1978), p. 144.

politics would not leave them alone. Outraged ethnic Croats who refused to accept the Pact of Rome fled Italian Dalmatia for refuge in the NDH. Those who remained were sullen and alienated, or flocked to the Ustaša. Orthodox Serbs and Jews hounded by Ustaša persecution scrambled out of the Croatian towns handed by Italy to Zagreb's authority and tried to cross over into the Italian-annexed areas. Some were able to slip through the porous borders, while others were caught and deported.

Stripped of authority by the Duce's order, the Italian soldiers, engulfed in murderous ethnic strife, were helpless bystanders as Croatia turned into a slaughterhouse. Troops stationed behind the Dinaric Alps (with the exception of Knin) were withdrawn to Dalmatia, which opened the way for the Ustaša to fall on undefended Serbs. Instead of disengaging Italy from the maelstrom of Croatian politics, the Duce's "declaration of neutrality" did precisely the opposite. The Croats, angered by the loss of Dalmatia, instigated fights with Italians. Under this barrage the 2nd Army thirsted to avenge itself against the Duce's ally, the Pavelić regime, but could not openly defy Mussolini's non-intervention orders. The Italian occupation of Croatia had certainly gotten off on a bad foot.

If the Italian troops and their civilian collaborators encountered hazardous byways as they wended their way through Croatia, even more perilous journeys awaited them in the annexed territories of Slovenia and Dalmatia and in the Montenegrin protectorate. To exercise authority over these unfamiliar lands, Mussolini appointed Fascists of high standing as civilian commissioners who stood at the apex of a centralized system of local power. Anxious to prove their mettle as imperial lords, these newly-arrived rulers unleashed a torrent of ordinances and laws aimed at inculcating the Fascist spirit of mainland Italy in the annexed provinces. Through domination of the cultural domain—education, literature, the arts and social sciences—they were determined to establish a Fascist presence in the daily life of the conquered Slav peoples. Mandatory use of the Italian language in the schools, press, and radio was considered to be key in shaping the minds of future generations. Bent on denationalization, the Fascist commissars moved to break the spiritual and national consciousness of the Slavs by suppressing local newspapers, native cultural organizations, and sports clubs. They requisitioned arms, petroleum, and radios. Fascist squads swaggered about singing Mussolini's praises and Italy's military exploits, somehow imagining that the local residents would believe all the hyperbole. The occupied Slavs did not oblige. Instead of showing deference, they derided the conquerors and their Italianization programs. Eventually, they would resort to insurgency.

Dalmatia was supposed to have been the feather in the Fascist cap. After the humiliations of Libya and Greece, Italians, who had been dazed by the myth of the mutilated victory and who sang *"Dalmazia, Dalmazia, cosa importa se si muore,"*

(Dalmatia, Dalmatia, it's not important if we die)[9] could hold their heads high. But the settlement actually provided Italy with territory not much greater than that granted by the Pact of London in 1915. The cities of Zara, Sebenico, and Cattaro became provinces of the motherland with groups of islands tacked on; the territory of Fiume was enlarged. The remainder of Dalmatia, with a broad strip of its hinterland, was divided into three occupation zones in which the Italians exercised a control that diminished by degrees from the coast to the interior. Required to relinquish areas occupied in anticipation of annexation below Spalato and the Croat Littoral from the Bay of Bakar to Senj, Italy was left holding slips of territory not much wider than a few kilometers in some places. The status of Spalato was left unclear. A disfigured Italian Dalmatia emerged, marked by a broken railroad line from Fiume to Spalato and loss of important hydroelectric plants to Croatia—essential factors to the life and economy of the Italian towns on the coast. Italian Dalmatia would function as an economically backward territory filled with nearly a half-million alienated Croats whose numbers dwarfed the ethnic Italians.

The Italians approached Montenegro with the same frivolity and lack of preparation they displayed elsewhere in the Balkans. In the haggling that followed between the Germans, Bulgarians, and Italians, Montenegro was turned into an Italian protectorate but stood to lose substantial territory. The ex-Yugoslav province of Kosovo was handed over to Ciano's satrapy, Albania, giving the majority Muslim population, which had been persecuted by Serbs ever since the collapse of the Ottoman Empire, a chance to strike back. Five thousand terrorized Montenegrins fled from Kosovo to their homeland where compatriots fleeing the Ustaša from the borderland areas with Croatia in the Sandžak joined them.[10] The atmosphere crackled with ethnic rage. The Italian 9th Army command in Albania, responsible for garrisoning Montenegro, assumed the functions of civilian commissariats. As the troops set about the task of provisioning the towns and countryside, however, they found themselves the object of hatred for trampling on the independence and territorial aspirations of the country. The Montenegrin pot was about to boil over.

In Slovenia, Emilio Grazioli, who had been federale of Trieste in 1938, confidently stepped into office as Italian high commissioner. Although only 458 Italians lived there, the territory was annexed to the mother country. Rome was unwilling to create a puppet state out of fear that it would give a boost to

9. Raoul Pupo, "Slovenia e Dalmazia fra Italia e Terzo Reich 1940–1945," *Qualestoria* XXX, no. 1 (June 2002), p. 132.
10. Giacomo Scotti and Luciano Viazzi, *Occupazione e guerra italiana in Montenegro: Le aquile delle montagne nere* (Milan: Mursia, 1987), p. 64.

Slovene irredentism in Italy, while an annexation would, at least theoretically, eliminate that possibility. There was a peculiar Fascist logic to this. The Fascists had long experienced great difficulty in suppressing the local Slovene minority in the Venezia Giulia, whose rebellious spirit was kept alive by propaganda and weaponry emanating from the safe haven in Slovenian Yugoslavia. By annexing the "Province of Ljubljana," overly confident Fascist authorities thought they could quite easily stamp out Communist and nationalist cells on both sides that would leave the anti-Fascist resistance in the Venezia Giulia to wither and die. No longer would there be a "Slovenian question," because Slovenia would have simply ceased to exist. Ciano boasted that the Province of Ljubljana would rest on "liberal principles,"[11] which for him meant Italianization and the granting of a miserly autonomy.

Among Italian imperialists, an old revisionist ambition was reawakened: expansion of Italian interests in the Balkans and Danube, a central feature of Mussolini's policy during the twenties. No matter that the major obstacle was no longer posed by a debilitated France presiding over an emaciated Little Entente but by an aggressive Third Reich assisted by Quisling states. Mussolini could show Hitler that Italy, too, knew how to encroach on territory held dear by an Axis partner that strove to create a neo-Habsburg entity consisting of Germany, Hungary, and Croatia. To overcome the Italian fiasco in Greece, he hoped to revive Rome's *spirito conquistatore*. There were defensive reasons too. With Slovenia as an appendage of Italy in the heart of Mitteleuropa, the *italianitá* of the acquired irredentist lands would be a buffer against the expansionism of both Germany and Croatia. But the Italians were almost defeated before they got started. By "irrevocable" boundary delineation of the luckless Slovenia, Hitler grabbed the rich mineral deposits and industrial sectors in the north and left Italy the rest: pastoral lands and an overpopulated capitol. The province therefore ended up a poor choice for Italy: a poverty-stricken region on the periphery, simmering in discontent. Slovenia was not Dalmatia, which evoked old irredentist passion or even Montenegro, which was tied to the Savoyard dynasty. It was a foreign entity that for reason of state had been grafted on to the "healthy body" of the mainland.

The divvying up of the Yugoslav carcass was a farce; a kaleidoscope of annexations, partitions, and divisions destined to founder in ethnic strife and general chaos. Italy had not the military force, administrative capability, or political know-how to establish anything more than a transient occupation.

---

11. *The Ciano Diaries*, 29 April 1941.

"Victory" Over Greece

After smashing the Yugoslavs, the Wehrmacht motored into Greece encountering only minor resistance by out-manned Greeks, and a contingent of British soldiers hastily assembled to support them. The American historian Gerhard Weinberg wittily describes the situation: "In a play on the names of three countries, a joke of the time had suggested that when Hitler got hungry, he would have turkey with plenty of grease."[12] On 16 April General Alexandros Papagos urged the British to withdraw from Greece to save his country from further devastation; two days later, Prime Minister Alexandros Koryzis committed suicide. The British needed no urging; on 14 April they began to plan for another Dunkirk—this time from Greek ports.

Prepared to turn over his sword to the Germans as a prelude to an armistice, the Greek commandant General Georgios Tsolakoglou sought out the notorious Sepp Dietrich, commander of the SS "Adolf Hitler." Anxious to take sole credit for the victory, General Dietrich offered Tsolakoglou generous terms in a ceasefire that was to take place on 20 April. The next day Greece surrendered unconditionally to the Wehrmacht command. In ten days their soldiers were to be demobilized, to stockpile their weapons, and return home. The Germans would take no war prisoners and would allow the officers to keep their arms and decorations.

This was much too lenient for Hitler, who instructed Field Marshal Wilhelm List, commander-in-chief of the 12th Army, to reopen negotiations with Tsolakoglou without informing the Italians. Bent on superseding Dietrich's lenient terms, List compelled the unfortunate Greek general to sign a second and much less generous accord the next day. The Greek troops were to be considered prisoners of war rather than set free. As a sop to Tsolakoglou, List allowed the Greeks a safe withdrawal from the Italian front to permit their surrender and disarmament by the Wehrmacht.[13] By positioning his troops on the Albanian boundary, List meant to prevent the Italian army from crossing into Greece. Cavallero, he said bluntly, should make himself scarce at the German-Greek armistice discussions. Though humiliated, Tsolakoglou had avoided the bitter cup of surrendering to the Italians, whom he thought his armies had defeated. This outcome did not displease Hitler, who begrudged

12. Gerhard L. Weinberg, *A World at Arms: A Global History of World War II* (Cambridge: Cambridge University Press, 1994), p. 216.
13. *Germany and the Second World War*, III: 512.

Mussolini for plunging into the war against Greece without obtaining clearance from Berlin.[14]

On hearing this news, Mussolini fumed.[15] He held that the Wehrmacht had committed an "act of perfidy" in instructing General Dietrich to accept the Greek surrender in the absence of the Italians. Cavallero, too, was staggered by this "unpardonable insult" to the honor of Italy.[16] For his country, the war was simply not over. To prevent the Greeks from handing victory to the Wehrmacht, Mussolini bulldozed his troops deep into Greek territory, a mindless act that resulted in more casualties and more dead. Tension with the Wehrmacht reached fever pitch when Italian soldiers ran into German roadblocks in their pursuit of the exhausted Greek enemy.

Mussolini's actions placed Hitler in a quandary. He wanted to salve the Duce's pride but would not be party to the myth that the Italians had forced the Greeks to surrender.[17] In the end, the Duce won out. Much to General List's embarrassment, Hitler dispatched General Alfred Jodl to Salonica to override the agreement he had signed. Another one, more respectful, was drawn up and placed before the Greeks who resented Italy's participation. Although Tsolakoglou protested, he inked this final agreement early on the 23rd. No one was happy. The SMG sent Rintelen a memo reminding the Germans that they had promised Italy "all the Greek war booty not necessary for the German troops," but General Jodl had already told them that such war materiel would be reserved for Italy only west of the Pindus Mountains.[18] Both Italians and Greeks felt deceived by the Germans, and the German military felt their reputation had been sullied by a maneuver that conceded parity to Italy in the Axis victory over Greece.

Mussolini and Cavallero crowed to each other over the heroism of Italian arms in "shattering" the Greek army's will to resist in places "bathed in the blood of the combatants and in the hearts of the Italian people."[19] General Geloso added that the few losses suffered by the Germans proved that Italy had beaten the Greeks.[20] The Germans, in turn, disported themselves as the real victors, taking no notice that it was the Italian soldiers who spilled the blood. Here is the verdict of Giovanni Ansaldo, Ciano's newspaper man: "We delude

---

14. Gerhard Schreiber, "'Due popoli, una vittoria?' Gli italiani nei Balcani nel giudizio dell'alleato germanico," *L'Italia in guerra 1940–1943*, P. P. Poggio and B. Micheletti ed. (Brescia: Fondazione "Luigi Micheletti," 1992), p. 108.

15. NAW, T-821, 129, 001056, Guzzoni to Rintelen, 18 April 1941.

16. Cervi, *The Hollow Legions*, p. 294.

17. *The Halder Diaries*, 21 April 1941.

18. NAW, T-821, 129, 000047, Appunto for General von Rintelen, 26 April 1941.

19. Cited in Cervi, *The Hollow Legions*, pp. 301–2.

20. AUSSME, DS, 631, Allegato 19, 19 October 1941.

ourselves in believing that we have carried out an advance analogous to that of the Germans, who were the ones assaulting the Pindus massif. Not true. The Germans took the Pindus; we did nothing. They have arrived at Larissa; we did nothing; they have arrived at Metzovo and Janina; we did nothing....the Government's major concern....is to demonstrate that the Greeks had capitulated under Italian pressure."[21]

Mussolini passed on to the king what Hitler had told him at Klessheim in April 1942: "Another sign of Providence's benevolence has been your campaign in Greece, because if the Balkan swollen lymph node had not been cauterized, one would not have been able to foresee what complications and dangers there might have been."[22] But later, out of Mussolini's earshot, Hitler angrily remarked that Mussolini's Greek folly, by delaying the attack on the Soviet Union, had cost him victory on the Eastern Front.[23]

Despite Hitler's histrionics, Germany's setbacks in Russia were not primarily occasioned by any presumed delay in the timetable of attack caused by Operation Marita. Rather, the launching of Barbarossa was held up mainly by equipment shortages and incomplete training, which, added to severe flooding in Eastern Europe caused by a late spring thaw, prevented important military movements before the middle of June. Although Operation Marita did deprive the OKW of time to prepare reserves for transportation of the troops eastward,[24] it opened up opportunities and closed off dangers. By exploiting the Balkans, Germany would be able to satisfy half its needs in cereals and livestock, forty-five percent in bauxite, ninety percent in tin, forty percent in lead, and ten percent in copper. There would be no British landing at Salonica as in 1916, and Britain would be denied airbases in Greece from which to strike vital oil fields in Romania.

Winston Churchill had the last word: "I dare say you have read in the newspapers that by a special proclamation the Italian dictator has congratulated the Italian army in Albania on the glorious laurels they have gained by their victories over the Greeks. Here surely is the world record in the domain of the ridiculous and the contemptible. This whipped jackal Mussolini, who to save his skin has made of Italy a vassal state of Hitler's empire, goes frisking up to the side of the German tiger with yelps not only of appetite—that could be understood—but even of triumph. Different things strike different people in different ways, but I am sure a great many millions in the British Empire and the United States will

21. Giovanni Ansaldo, *Il giornalista di Ciano: diari 1932–1943* (Bologna: Il Mulino, 2000), p. 298.
22. DDI, 9, VIII, 492, Conversation between Mussolini and Hitler, 29 April 1942.
23. *Testament of Adolf Hitler: The Hitler-Bormann Documents, February–April 1945*, ed. François Genoud (London: Cassell, 1961), pp. 72–73.
24. Creveld, *Hitler's Strategy 1940–1941: The Balkan Clue*, p. 153.

find a new object in life in making sure that when we come to the final reckoning this absurd impostor will be abandoned to public justice and universal scorn."[25]

A big victory parade before a stunned people took place in Athens on 4 May. After much bickering, General List included an Italian unit in the celebration. Not only were the Greeks disheartened by the sight of arrogant conquerors trespassing on their lands; they were appalled by the dismemberment of their country. The Bulgarians appropriated territory in Macedonia and Thrace, which they began immediately to plunder and cleanse ethnically. The Germans retained a few strategically important zones—the periphery of Athens, Crete, Piraeus, Salonica, and its Macedonian hinterland, the border strip with Turkey, and the islands Lemnos, Lesbos and Chios. Relieved of heavy occupation duty, the bulk of the German army withdrew northwards, while leaving the major garrison work to Italy's *regio esercito*: the rest of the mainland, the Ionian Islands, and the Cyclades. Italy annexed islands of the Ionian Sea—Corfu, Cefalu, and Zante— while handing Ciamuria (Epirus) up to Prevesa to the Albanian satrapy.

Since Barbarossa was pending, the Germans moved quickly to set up General Tsolakoglou on 26 April as ruler in Athens. As with Pavelić and Croatia, so it was with Tsolakoglou and Greece: the Germans would dominate at the smallest cost to themselves and avoid the annoying task of serving as the intermediary between the two satellites and the Italian junior partner, which was saddled with the major costs of occupation. Aware of "how deeply the Greeks hate the Italians," the Germans counted on Tsolakoglou to be their loyal puppet.[26] The ruse was effective. Tsolakoglou gave Rome no end of trouble by working behind the scenes to preserve national and ethnic unity against Italian claims.[27] Instead of having a pro-German figurehead, the Italians would have preferred a "pure and simple" military occupation.[28] Not surprisingly, the ruling class and the majority of the Greek population had no faith in their marionette government, which followed the dictates of the two Axis plenipotentiaries. The Germans wrapped up the last chapter of this campaign with an invasion of Crete: Operation Mercury (*Merkur*), initiated on 20 May.

The Italian soldiers moved slowly into Greek territory earmarked for their occupation, which consisted of poor upland villages linked by mule tracks and snowbound paths. Many of these outlying areas were not reached until October. The troops met a sullen reception by a people whose lands had been devastated by war and who were humiliated by defeat. Fighting a patriotic war, the Greeks

25. Cited in Cervi, *The Hollow Legions*, p. 303.
26. Mark Mazower, *Hitler's Empire: How the Nazis Ruled Europe* (New York: The Penguin Press, 2008), p. 19.
27. *The Ciano Diaries*, 28 April 1941.
28. DDI, 9, VII, 17, Anfuso to Ciano, 24 April 1941.

felt they had beaten the Italians in Epirus but found themselves betrayed and occupied by an angry enemy whom they considered had been lifted half-dead from Albanian ditches by Wehrmacht tank drivers who gave them a free ride into Athens. But whatever preference the Tsolakoglou government held for its German wirepullers quickly dissipated. Within a few days after the arrival of the Wehrmacht in Athens, German soldiers looted factories, private houses and hospitals, requisitioned livestock, plundered food reserves, sank hospital ships in ports, and threw wounded Greek soldiers out of their hospital beds.[29] For their part, the Italians intended to exploit the Greek economy, but had not devised any clear-cut occupation policy save the ball and chain with which to jail dissidents. The country had become a wasteland of suffering people, with only the monuments of antiquity to remind them of their glorious past. On the eighth week of Greece's occupation the Italian flag appeared on the hill of the Acropolis next to the swastika. Observing a smaller Greek banner flying between the two, the Greeks recognized the symbolism: "The Crucified One between the two thieves."[30]

Desert Offensive

The end of Italy's "parallel war" effectively occurred on 20 December 1940 when General Guzzoni formally asked Germany to send men and equipment for the Libyan campaign. One week later General Efisio Marras, the Italian military attaché in Berlin, made an urgent appeal in Berlin for German help to save Cyrenaica. General Roatta ignored this Italian subservience by imagining that Germany and Italy would together undertake profitable operations in the Mediterranean theater.[31]

Hitler agreed to a rescue of the Italian troops in Libya because he was concerned that an Italian loss of Tripolitania might bring about the demise of Fascism, the disgrace of Mussolini, and the end of the Axis, which would besmirch Germany's reputation. Preoccupied by Barbarossa, however, Hitler would do no more than guarantee a stalemate in North Africa to buy time until the war was won on the Eastern Front. Once the Soviet Union had collapsed, the German army would set out from the Caucasus, pass through the Middle East, and capture a defenseless Cairo, thus avoiding a nightmarish Axis march from the west across thousands of kilometers of desert.

---

29. Gabriella Etmektsoglou-Koehn, "Axis Exploitation of Wartime Greece, 1941–1943," Ph.D. diss., Emory University, 1995, p. 111.
30. Laird Archer, *Balkan Journal* (New York: W. W. Norton, 1944), p. 233.
31. Lucio Ceva, *La condotta italiana della guerra. Cavallero e il Comando Supremo 1941–1942* (Milan: Feltrinelli, 1975), p. 49.

To shore up Italian defenses in North Africa, Luftwaffe X Air Corps was transferred from Norway to Sicily on 10 December 1940. The Luftwaffe would subject Malta to heavy bombardment, protect convoys to Tripoli, harass British convoys out of Alexandria and Gibraltar, and attack the ports and unloading harbors on the coasts of Egypt and Cyrenaica.[32] General Albert Kesselring, whom Hitler appointed as field marshal commander-in-chief south, emerged wearing two additional hats: one as chief of the 2nd Air Fleet answerable to Göring as commander-in-chief, the other as subordinate to Mussolini for guidelines relayed to him by the SMG.

To accomplish the limited end of defending Tripolitania, Hitler, on 9 January 1941, ordered the dispatch of an armored blocking force composed of anti-tank units.[33] In agreeing to provide troops, the Wehrmacht insisted on exerting a powerful influence on the Italian conduct of the war in the Mediterranean. On New Year's Day 1941 Admiral Eberhard Weichold complained about the supine attitude of the Italian navy and insisted that Malta was the key to Britain's supremacy in the Mediterranean. Having long given up the hope of goading the Italians into action, he suggested that the Mediterranean theater be placed under German command.[34] Hans-Georg von Mackensen, the German ambassador in Rome—a party member and SS-Gruppenführer—supported this view. However, since Libya was an Italian territory, there was no way it could be placed under German command. General Ettore Bastico was designated theater commander, an appointment to which Hitler agreed so that Mussolini could maintain an Italian face on operations. But the Führer contrived a wide loophole. "Should German troops be given an order whose execution could only, *in the view of their commanding* officer, result in serious failure, and thus injure the reputation of those German troops, the German commander is entitled *and obliged to seek my decision* via C.-in-C. Army by notifying the German general at the Italian High Command in Rome."[35] Behind the scenes Hitler endeavored to control operations by making General Rintelen in Rome an über officer, empowering him to act as liaison between the two general staffs and as a third party between Hitler and Mussolini. General Kesselring ably assisted Rintelen in funneling reinforcements and supplies to the Italian armies reeling before British attacks.

Since the Italians wanted to secure a steady flow of German military assistance, they put up with further sleights-of-hand. In a familiar Axis arrangement, Keitel and Guzzoni on 4 February agreed that if Germans were to be placed

---

32. *Germany and the Second World War*, III: 654.
33. Ibid.
34. Martin Kitchen, *Rommel's Desert War* (Cambridge: Cambridge University Press, 2009), p. 41.
35. Cited in *Germany and the Second World War*, VI: 635.

formally under an Italian general in North Africa, they would still enjoy a privileged status.[36] Cavallero acknowledged this by allowing Kesselring to be Rome's back-seat driver in the North African war theater. The Italians were handcuffed. General Roatta commented acidly: "An entity like the OKW can disinterest itself in the operations of an ally, but if at a certain point it decides to become engaged it does so not to collaborate but to dictate."[37]

Though Mussolini could not avoid the humiliating transition from equal ally to Hitler's first subaltern, he had at least partially learned a lesson from his harmful meddling in combat decision-making in the Greek theater. He would leave battlefield decisions to the generals. Such unwonted restraint held until he arrived at loggerheads with his original favorite, German General Erwin Rommel, during the Axis retreat in the desert in 1942. Mussolini's move from the eye of combat to the fringes of Italy's military command was smoothed by the ease with which he settled in with Cavallero. But when Cavallero just as easily obliged the Germans once they had landed in North Africa, Italy lost control of strategy and Mussolini his position of Italian warlord.

In an address to his armed forces, Hitler went out of his way to make the Italians feel wanted. "The German troops that fight in the Mediterranean shoulder to shoulder with our allies must be conscious of the high military and political task that has been assigned to them. They are required to give considerable psychological and military support to our allies who fight in all war theaters against a strongly superior enemy and who do not possess a sufficient number of modern arms due to the limited industrial potential of the country. They [the German troops] can be justly proud of their valor and results achieved, but they must avoid whatever arrogance that could be offensive. They must earn the esteem and approval of their allies solely through their work, discipline, exemplary audacity, and military professionalism."[38]

On 3 February General Rommel was named commander of the German army troops in Libya under the Italian high command of the North African front. The Luftwaffe, however, stayed under firm German control. Upon their arrival, the Germans quickly realized that use of their troops made sense "only if *by its strength and by its composition* it is really capable of bringing about a turn of fate." And since *"the defense itself must be carried on offensively,"* an additional complete German armored division would have to be added to the blocking force.[39] Together with the previously designated 5th Light Motorized Division, the 15th

---

36. Giorgio Rochat, *Le guerre italiane 1935-1943* (Turin: Einaudi, 2005), p. 303.
37. Roatta, *Otto milioni di baionette*, p. 149.
38. Cited in Petersen, "L'Afrika-Korps," p. 392.
39. DGFP, D, XII, 17, Hitler to Mussolini, 5 February 1941.

Armored Division was to constitute the German African Corps (DAK). Göring, Keitel, and Jodl submitted to Hitler the outlines of Operation Sunflower, "without which England would hold a pistol to Italy's head and oblige it to make peace and cede everything or be bombed into smithereens."[40] "Sunflower" was to become, much to Rommel's discomfort, a perfect symbol: a huge and showy flower at the end of a long and rather fragile stem.[41]

The Germans found General Graziani a beaten man who was not willing to go beyond rallying the remnants of his defeated army for a dug-in defense. His losses, indeed, had been heavy. In early February 1941 the Italians had at most only six divisions with which to defend Tripoli, supported by a mere 100 aircraft, 400 having been lost in the preceding few weeks. Of the 244,500 men, 150,000 had fallen and half their vehicles disabled.[42]

Prospects of checking a further British advance into Tripolitania brightened when General Guzzoni ordered the dispatch of contingents of the armored *Ariete* and *Trento* divisions equipped with vehicles that had been denied him earlier. But Graziani, having requested to be relieved of his command on the 8th, was not to be the beneficiary of these reinforcements. Replaced by General Italo Gariboldi, he left for Rome on the 11th, one day before Rommel landed in North Africa. Mussolini consoled him: "I could not occupy myself with Libya. Between it and Greece I had to choose the latter because Italians could resign themselves to be beaten by the English but not by Greeks."[43]

The Desert Fox arrived to campaign with an ally against whom he had formerly won distinction in the Alpine regions of World War I. In implementing novel infiltration tactics that led to the major Italian defeat at Caporetto in October 1917, Rommel had made his first mark in German military annals.

Impatient over finding Italy's reinforced divisions entrenched in a fortified camp around Tripoli waiting for the British to attack,[44] the OKW urged the Italians to advance about 200 kilometers eastward to establish a more defensible line at Buerat between Sirte and Misurata, with Italian infantry manning the front and armored units under Rommel's command behind the open right flank.[45] Mussolini concurred on 9 February. In defiance of the OKW, Rommel, bent on an offensive, switched alignments by placing his mobile reserve in front of the Italian infantry screen to engage the British straightaway.[46] Mussolini accommo-

---

40. Cited in Bocca, *Storia d'Italia nella guerra fascista*, p. 271.
41. Wolf Heckmann, *Rommel's War in Africa* (Garden City, New York: Doubleday, 1981).
42. Kitchen, *Rommel's Desert War*, p. 49.
43. Cited in Messe, *La mia armata in Tunisia*, p. 57.
44. DGFP, D, XII, 24, Ritter memorandum, 6 February 1941; 35, Rintelen to Berlin, 9 February 1941.
45. Rintelen, *Mussolini l'alleato*, p. 122.
46. Kitchen, *Rommel's Desert War*, p. 57.

dated Rommel by placing the armored *Ariete* and the partially motorized *Brescia* under his command.[47]

After a quick reconnaissance, Rommel unleashed an offensive. By the end of February, assisted by a rapid Italian striking force,[48] the Axis had pushed the Commonwealth troops back 700 kilometers from Tripoli. The Luftwaffe X Air Corps, consisting of dive-bombers and twin-engine fighters transferred from Sicily to North Africa, lent him much-needed support. Rommel looked to begin an attack on Tobruk on 8 May.

Churchill had provided Rommel the opportunity to strike out boldly by making the decision to pull beleaguered Greece from the clutches of the invading Axis Powers. In compliance with Churchill's instructions, British general Archibald Wavell reluctantly sent off the Australian 6th division, jaunty conquerors of Bardia and Tobruk, to eventual defeat in Greece along with an untested New Zealand division. A victory over the Axis in Greece, Churchill argued, would eclipse victory in North Africa. His was mainly a political decision to help a friend, Greece, in distress as proof that Britain would support neutrals threatened by the Axis. After the transfer of troops in March, General Richard O'Connor took command of British troops in Egypt, and Lieutenant-General Sir Philip Neame was appointed head of the Cirenaica command as military governor. They took charge of many untrained and under-equipped soldiers in the stripped-down Commonwealth forces.

Hitler and the OKW supported Rommel's thrust eastward as a means of securing a defensive line to protect the outer edges of Tripolitania. But that was all. Rommel would have to wait until autumn before launching an attack on Tobruk, located in Cyrenaica. In the meantime he was advised to proceed cautiously and expect no reinforcements.[49] Rommel, however, was not familiar with the word restraint. Aware of the confusion in British ranks, he pawed the ground ready to spring. On 19 March he flew to Germany bearing offensive plans to be implemented once the German 15th Panzer Division and the motorized *Trento* had reached the lines, somewhere near the end of May. Confident that his panzers could move swiftly against a disorganized enemy, Rommel had far loftier ambitions: Alexandria and the Suez Canal. This was not exactly what Hitler and the OKW had in mind. Hitler curtly reminded Rommel that once the 15th Panzer Division had arrived, he could mount probing attacks, but should limit himself to the defense of Tripolitania.[50]

---

47. DGFP, D, XII, 76, Mussolini to Hitler, 22 February 1941.
48. *La prima controffensiva Italo-Tedesca in Africa Settentrionale* (Rome: SME US, 1974), p. 19, n. 2.
49. *Germany and the Second World War*, III: 674.
50. *Prima controffensiva*, p. 44; *Germany and the Second World War*, III: 674.

The Italian command was thankful that Rommel had been bridled. The heat was excessive in summertime, the newly arrived troops not fully equipped and trained, and the ports still clogged with ships bearing unloaded cargo. Memories of the thoughtless offensives against the Greeks taught them to observe caution in North Africa. Reconquest of Cyrenaica would have to wait until mid-September.[51]

Rommel, however, "feverish for action," struck out on 31 March with only his 5th Light Division on what was supposed to be a reconnaissance mission. He made some largely uncontested gains, which elicited praise from Mussolini on 2 April, accompanied by a warning: "Because of upcoming events on the Julian and Albanian fronts, dispatch of other divisions and trucks must be delayed."[52] To make sure that Rommel would suspend his offensive, General Gariboldi met with him on 3 April. Citing a shaky supply system and delays in transport, and fearing a powerful counterattack, Gariboldi demanded in the name of the SMG that Rommel desist from further offensives, which elicited the sharp retort that he would obey only the shifting fortunes on the battlefield. In spite of his former restraining orders, Hitler crowed over Rommel's advance and laughed at British propaganda. Mussolini, favoring Rommel's daring over Gariboldi's caution, swung behind the Führer: "It would be a very serious error not to profit from a favorable moment to defy the odds"[53] Undercut by Mussolini, Gariboldi had also been trampled by his formally subordinate Rommel, who had wrested from him the actual field command of the Axis forces in North Africa.[54]

In a rapid advance Rommel caught the British napping. They abandoned Benghazi hardly firing a shot and fell back in confusion on the fortified town of Tobruk on 8 April. A week later Axis reconnaissance ranged as far as the Libyan-Egyptian frontier. British generals O'Connor and Neame, having lost their way in the desert, fell into German hands as prisoners.[55] The repercussions of Rommel's attack, carried out by an advance guard of the lightly armed 5th Division and supported by the *Ariete*, coupled with the surrender of Yugoslavia and Greece in latter April, considerably bolstered Italian morale. The usually cautious Guzzoni told his military colleagues on 11 April that it was necessary to "wipe out Tobruk before the English can receive reinforcements."[56]

---

51. Mario Montanari, *Le operazioni in Africa settentrionale:* Vol. II: *Tobruk (Marzo 1941–Gennaio 1942)* (Rome: SME US, 1993), p. 31.
52. Ibid.: 92.
53. Ibid.: 94.
54. *Germany and the Second World War*, III: 676.
55. *Operazioni*, II: 116.
56. USSME, Verbali delle riunioni tenute dal capo di SME, vol. II, p. 30.

On 11 April Rommel pressed on by storming the heavily fortified Tobruk, which Churchill ordered to be defended to the last man. But in his haste to prevent a consolidation of the enemy forces, Rommel rushed into the attack precipitously in a series of impulsive and improvised movements that counted too few forces—the German 5th Light Division and incomplete units of *Brescia*, *Trento*, and *Ariete*. Encountering furious British air attacks and naval gunfire, Rommel was checked with heavy losses and dispersed forces. On the 13th Mussolini ordered a halt for reorganization and resupply, a judgment to which Gariboldi and the OKW fully agreed. Hitler was not opposed to a standstill either—until the arrival of the German 15th Panzer Division.[57]

Believing the adversary exhausted and about to evacuate, a defiant Rommel renewed the offensive on 16 and 17 April but was once again repulsed. Unfazed, he secured the approval of General Guzzoni on 30 April for yet another assault strengthened by units of the 15th Panzer Division that were filing into the lines at last. When faced with a serious breakdown in his supply system, Rommel finally broke off. The British had held. The Italians sized up his mania for attack as an unwholesome obsession with Tobruk. But Rommel was not yet through. After circling around the besieged enclave to pursue fleeing British troops outside the Tobruk box, he took the Halfaya Pass, the gateway to Egypt. Excepting Tobruk, he had regained Cyrenaica.

While the attacks on Tobruk played out, the major Axis military strategists ordered Rommel to pause for reorganization of the supply lines and arrival of reinforcements.[58] Pained by the Tobruk failure and intractable logistical tie-ups, Rommel reluctantly obeyed orders, though he felt that jealous and unimaginative staff officers should be held to account. But no one in Germany, not Hitler, and not the OKW, had informed him that Operation Barbarossa was in the works, which, swallowing up the bulk of available supplies rendered North Africa a sideshow.[59]

In spite of many mishaps, Rommel had achieved much by reconquering Cyrenaica in defiance of both Berlin and Rome. This accomplishment made him feel invulnerable to censure by his superiors in Germany who, he was certain, would comprehend that criticism of his legendary persona would damage the esteem in which the German soldier was held.

The Italians hardly knew what hit them when Rommel arrived in North Africa. There was no one like him in the Italian army. Uninterested in supply problems, and unwilling to acknowledge that the Italians were responsible for his

57. *Prima controffensiva*, pp. 126–27.
58. *Operazaioni*, II: 115–16; *Prima controffensiva*, p. 126, for Mussolini note.
59. Kitchen, *Rommel's Desert War*, p. 72.

rear, flanks, and lifeline, Rommel acted cavalierly toward them. Some of this was justified, for Rommel, better than they, had the uncanny ability of instantly reading a battlefield and in exploiting his opponent's psychological weakness. Possessing infinite trust in his own ability, Rommel would brook no contrary opinions. No Italian general could stop him; neither could the existing Byzantine command structure constrain him. Rommel demanded and obtained complete freedom of action.

Rommel raked the Italians with criticisms. "It made one's hair stand on end to see the sort of equipment with which the Duce had sent his troops into battle."[60] On the 17th he noted: "We cannot completely trust our allies in combat."[61] More damaging still, Rommel wrote the Italian field commanders on 23 April: "If therefore I would have to repeat analogous cases of a lack of combative will, I will be constrained to advise the Duce through the Italian High Command that he place such commanders, officers and troops before the Military Tribunal in Rome."[62] Rommel might have been on more solid ground by admonishing his ally for having originally created a formidable network of strong points around Tobruk interconnected by concealed passageways and fronted by a deep anti-tank ditch. For behind these mainly Italian-constructed defenses, the British were able to thwart the Axis attack. Other German generals were more charitable toward the Italians. Colonel Maximilian von Herff wrote Rommel on 25 May about the magnificent comportment of Colonel Ugo Monte-murro's troops and proposed that he receive the iron cross first class; this was the first German award for valor conceded to an Italian in Northern Africa.[63]

Unknown to the Italians, Rommel did not spare his own soldiers. Those officers showing weak leadership and urging caution, he thought, deserved to be court-marshaled for cowardice.[64] Major-General Johannes Streich, he charged, had disobeyed his attack orders: "You were far too concerned with the well-being of your troops." Streich replied: "I can imagine no greater words of praise for a division commander."[65]

General Gariboldi owned up to many of Rommel's broadsides. The Italian troops were unwilling to fight to the last man, they were too predisposed to surrender, and they frequently abandoned their trenches under heavy artillery fire.[66] But it was difficult for the Italians to feel confident when they compared

---

60. Cited in *Germany and the Second World War*, III: 683.
61. *Prima controffensiva*, p. 124.
62. *Operazioni*, II: 146.
63. Ibid.: 109.
64. Kitchen, *Rommel's Desert War*, p. 88.
65. Cited in *Germany and the Second World War*, III: 693.
66. *Operazioni*, II: 147.

their antiquated equipment with the fancy gear employed by the Wehrmacht. As foot soldiers negotiating endless sand dunes in scorching heat, they waved enviously at German motorized columns plying back and forth on the Via Balbia. Fascist rhetoric might have exalted the Italian infantry as the "Queen of Battle," but the troops felt more like unwilling performers in a military *opera buffa*.

On 19 May Cavallero returned from Albania. The first order of business was to remove his biggest rival, General Guzzoni, by suppressing the post of deputy head of the SMG (now denominated the Supreme Command: *Comando Supremo*, hereafter designated as CS). Tired of presiding over military chiefs who engaged in endless discussions, Cavallero composed a memo that aimed to tighten up bureaucratic discipline. A top priority was to deny the direct access to Mussolini that they had freely enjoyed in their capacity as civilian undersecretaries. But the final version of the ordinance that emerged on 27 June 1941 left many ties unaltered; the service chiefs' dependency on the CS, therefore, remained as fuzzy as ever.[67]

Thanks to the chaos in the Italian military command, war planning remained disjointed and surreal. A far-fetched idea of an *armata d'Africa*, or an *armata coloniale* (clearly the work of Mussolini), was launched in April/May 1941. After securing the defense of Tripolitania, Italian troops were expected to surge across Egypt, the Suez Canal, and into Palestine and Trans Jordan. In the west, the troops would burst into Tunisia and Algeria and bear down on the Atlantic coast. The reconquest of Ethiopia would be accompanied by a drive toward French Equatorial Africa. Germans would not be needed since Italy had manpower and resources to spare: ten divisions to conquer Egypt, five to recover the lost empire, and five to take over French North Africa along the way to the Atlantic Ocean. The historian Lucio Ceva tabulates the figures: 100,000 men with 14,000 motor vehicles and 850 cannon that involved tripling the armored units and doubling the infantry divisions.[68] Such brainstorming was taking place while the war against Greece was raging, modernized armor non-existent, and the severe transport and supply problems in North Africa unresolved. The official Italian narrative characterized these outlandish goals as a *velleitarismo intenzionale*.[69]

Only after Mussolini decided to commit sizeable armed forces to the Russian front in June were these plans taken off the table, but only temporarily. Carried away by the mirage of a *grande armée*, Mussolini wrote Cavallero and the king in latter July 1941, the contents of which were reported by Paolo Puntoni:

67. Ceva, *La condotta italiana della guerra*, pp. 27–32.
68. *Operazioni*, II: 306; *Prima controffensiva*, p. 167.
69. *Prima controffensiva*, p. 167; *Operazioni*, II: 216–22.

"The Duce thinks that by spring 1942 Italy could have under arms no less than eighty divisions, which would allow for far-reaching maneuvers by twenty of them. A part of the new divisions must be motorized and armored."[70] This idea was purely utopian since at the end of July the Italian Army had only sixty-four serviceable divisions, sixteen short of Mussolini's goal of eighty.[71]

As Mussolini engaged in expansionist reveries, he, together with the rest of the world, was floundering in guesswork over Germany's next big military offensive. After the Wehrmacht had devoured Greece, no one knew where it would strike next. Since Hitler distrusted Italy's ability to keep a secret, he was careful to keep his ally speculating, which underscored the lack of military collaboration between the two Axis Powers. Regarding North Africa the Italians had only a dim awareness of the wide contrasts in strategy between Rommel and the OKW. Although they had picked up scraps of information that Hitler was preparing an attack against the Soviet Union, they had no clue that Germany, in view of Barbarossa, would be sending just enough men and equipment to North Africa to keep the wobbly Italian ally in the war.

General Wavell responded to Rommel's overextended thrust with Operation Brevity, launched on 15 May, followed by Operation Battleaxe in mid-June aimed at lifting the siege of Tobruk. Both were costly failures that needlessly chewed up tanks and planes. The British ended up back on their side of the Egyptian frontier. The Italian *Bersaglieri* did their part by blunting the enemy attack at the Halfaya Pass, putting out of action seven Matildas. This was an Italian first in inflicting serious damage to Britain's much feared, if lumbering, heavy tanks.[72]

The string of the Wehrmacht's breathtaking Blitzkrieg victories had been broken; tank offensives were no longer irresistible. As Tobruk, "Brevity" and "Battleaxe" proved, an innovative and skillful defense, even in open country like the North African desert, could halt a rapid tank-led offensive in its tracks.[73]

In eliminating the British threat to Libya for the foreseeable future, Hitler promoted Rommel to full general and made him commander of Armored Group Africa (Panzerguppe Afrika). To tighten the screws on operations in North Africa, the OKW moved to impose a Wehrmacht general directly over General Gariboldi, the nominal commander-in-chief of the Axis forces in North Africa. In spite of Cavallero's readiness to yield, Gariboldi on 10 June 1941 refused to abide the German ruse. The army brass in Rome rewarded Gariboldi's unwonted

---

70. Puntoni, *Parla Vittorio Emanuele III*, p. 64.
71. Pier Paolo Battistelli, "The Road to Defeat: The Reorganization of the Italian Army After the Winter 1940–1941," unpublished manuscript, p. 10.
72. Ceva, *Guerra mondiale 1939–1945*, p. 41.
73. B. H. Liddell Hart, *History of the Second World War* (Old Saybrook, CT: Konecky & Konecky, 1970), p. 180.

boldness by sacking him on 12 July 1941. Army chief-of-staff General Roatta stealthily engineered his replacement by appointing General Ettore Bastico, who would receive the title Commander of the Armed Forces in North Africa. Cavallero fell into line on 16 July. Although happy to see Gariboldi go, the OKW greeted the Italian changes skeptically. But what really counted was Hitler's adamant refusal to allow anyone to control Rommel except himself. Since Hitler had left him free to pass over both the OKW and General Bastico at his own discretion, the Desert Fox emerged the winner in all these machinations.

By the end of May 1941 the Axis had gained the upper hand in the war. In North Africa the British had been chased out of Cyrenaica with the exception of the pocket of Tobruk. They held important naval depots at Gibraltar, Malta, Crete and Alexandria, but with the exception of Gibraltar they were held hostage by Axis planes. In the Balkans the Axis Powers had annihilated Yugoslavia and Greece. Together with Hungary, Romania, and Bulgaria, Germany dominated a compact territorial block from the Baltic to the Aegean. Hitler beamed with pleasure over the timeliness of Rommel's feat in securing the Libyan flank on the eve of Barbarossa. In spite of certain zigzags, the Führer's evolving "Orient" strategy was proceeding on course. Defeat of the Soviet Union was projected for the autumn, after which a strong armored corps would be sent southward through Persia, and ten divisions would proceed to the Suez Canal to join hands with a victorious Rommel.[74] Left out of these exciting prospects were the Italians. Pushed around in North Africa and mauled in Greece, they had been reduced by Germany to bit players in arenas they viewed as their own.

---

74. Rintelen, *Mussolini l'alleato*, p. 143.

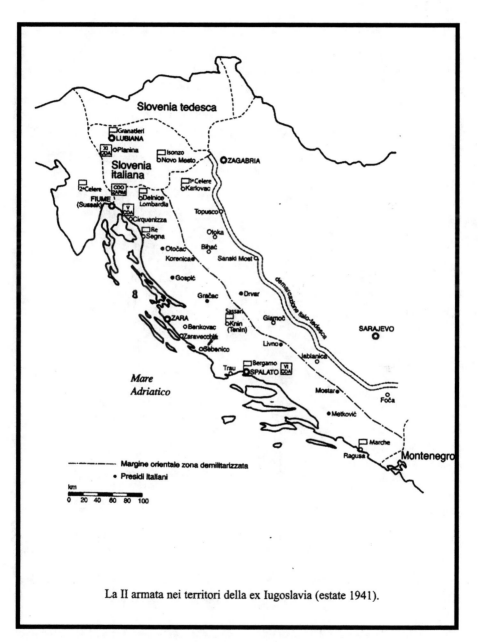

La II armata nei territori della ex Iugoslavia (estate 1941).

Italian Second Army zone of occupation in Yugoslavia. Summer 1941.

German and Italian invasion of Southern Yugoslavia and Greece in April 1941.

Chapter V

The Sword of Islam

Middle Eastern Setbacks
Fallback in the Desert

Middle Eastern Setbacks

Owing to a legacy of wrongdoing, the Italians faced an uphill battle in gaining political traction in the Arab world. Arabs did not easily forget the hanging in 1931 in Libya of Omar al-Mukhtar, followed by Italian atrocities during and after the war in Ethiopia. (Nor did Arabs forget the behavior of the other European colonial powers, which behaved no less brutally against local leaders who rejected their rule.) In June 1940, asked by Ciano to outline Italy's war aims along the southern Mediterranean shore, Pietromarchi got straight to the point. Tunisia would be Italian and England was to be ousted from Egypt. So long as Egypt, as well as Algeria, Syria, Lebanon, Iraq, and Transjordan, accorded Italy exclusively mutual assistance pacts and allowed military garrisons on their territory, they would enjoy "independence." As for Palestine, the Italian king, designated to be the trustee over the Holy Places, would set up an Italian regime that would empower Hadj Amin el-Husseini, the Grand Mufti of Jerusalem, to block the further immigration of Jews and eliminate "communist communities," e.g., the Kibbutzim and Moshavim. To disarm Arab suspicions, Mussolini concealed the imperialist contents of this internal memorandum and claimed that he was not interested in further Italian expansion in the Middle East.

In utilizing "Arab independence" as a ruse to conceal naked imperialism, the Italians broke no new ground. The Western Powers had hardly acted differently at the Paris Peace Conference when they contrived "mandates" as cover for their resolve to dominate Middle Eastern resources. Giving no thought to maintaining the integrity of the Ottoman Empire, the Western Powers, in drawing new boundaries, ignored ethnic and religious differences and disregarded the claims of Arab leaders. With the exception of Egypt and Iran, whose histories covered a millennium, the countries that emerged were an arbitrarily conceived patchwork of land that grew out of the imperial horse-trading between Britain and France. By placing mandates under their stewardship, the Western Powers, followed by the United States in Saudi Arabia, moved quickly to exploit vast oil reserves and secure strategic interests.

Iraq was a case in point. Sunnis, Shiites, and Kurds, whose hatred of each other was long-standing, grimly resisted the challenge of common nationhood. But they were knit together by a common aversion to the West. To express dissatisfaction over the many broken promises of independence proffered by Western statesmen, Iraqi leaders inspired an uprising against British "indirect government" in the early 1920s and were ruthlessly crushed. The British troops, using white phosphorus bombs to suppress the revolt in Baghdad, killed and wounded thousands of Iraqis. On 30 June 1930 the British offered Iraq de jure sovereignty by means of a mutual assistance pact and membership in the League of Nations in 1932. But imperial shackles remained. Baghdad was obliged to help Britain in the event of war by making available transport land routes, ports, and airfields. Iraqi nationalists regarded this arrangement as a fraud. A score of coups, massacres, and rebellions followed, spurred on by British partiality toward the Sunnis. Iraqis vigorously protested the use of British warplanes to suppress tribal uprisings. So much had they grown to abhor British imperialism and its manifest hypocrisy that, to facilitate a nationalist uprising, they were prepared to seek the help of the Third Reich.

The co-founder of the Muslim Brotherhood, Rashid Ali al-Gaylani, emerged as the Iraqi leader to challenge British military control of his country. To broaden his appeal, he spoke passionately in support of the Arab cause against Zionism, a tried-and-true rallying cry throughout the Arab world. By spring 1941, the combination of Arab nationalism among Iraqi officers, the Grand Mufti's broadcasts calling for a Muslim jihad against the foes of Islam, and the anti-imperialist and anti-western sentiment of the country's intellectual elite provided Gaylani an opening to stage a bloodless coup on the night of 1-2 April

1941 assisted by the army. Fearing British retaliation, he appealed to the Axis Powers for air support, weapons, and munitions deliveries.

The Germans split over how to react. In accordance with Hitler's views, the Wilhelmstrasse was content to take a back seat to Italy in the Middle East, but this had not stopped the Führer from approving a statement released by Weizsäcker that stated: "Germany recognizes the complete independence of the Arab states, or, where independence has not yet been achieved, the right to achieve it."[1] But Weizsäcker proceeded no further, apart from the observation on 1 May that Germans and Arabs had common enemies in people hoisting the Union Jack and those bearing the Yellow Star.[2] Behind this tepid support lay the belief that the Iraqi rebellion would not succeed. Faced by far greater logistical problems, Rome, too, chose risk-free platitudes to deeds.[3]

The British instantly moved to forestall perceived threats to the land route between India and Egypt and the vital oil supply from northern Iraqi oilfields. An Arab nationalist success in Iraq, it was feared, might trigger similar uprisings across the Arab world. Goaded into action by Churchill, a reluctant General Wavell, who thought his lines were already stretched too thin, landed a brigade at Basra on 30 April. Gaylani retaliated by marshalling an armed force to eliminate the British air base at Habbaniya, located near Baghdad, before it could be reinforced.

On 2 May the Gaylani government in Baghdad gave the order for military operations against the British troops and asked for German assistance. A few days later the Grand Mufti helped out by a call for a jihad in a fatwa aimed at the invading British. Gaylani did not wait for German guns and troops before acting, which left the Wehrmacht wondering where to find weapons and how to get them to Baghdad. The area in closest proximity with stockpiled supplies was Syria. On 5 May the Germans secured the permission of the Vichy government to utilize Syrian airports for flights to Baghdad. The Italian Armistice Control Commission lent assistance by releasing French arms stored under its control for use by the Iraqi insurgents. Vichy France, therefore, was complicit in their decision to ship weapons to Iraq.[4]

Since the Vichy government was determined to defend the Levant against a possible British attack, Deputy Prime Minister Admiral Darlan was prepared to give the Germans use of Syrian airports in exchange for help in preparing French

---

1. Cited in Klaus-Michael Mallmann and Martin Cüppers, *Nazi Palestine* (New York: Enigma Books, 2009), p. 73.
2. *Germany in World War II*, III: 593.
3. DGFP, D, XII, 372, Bismarck to the Foreign Ministry, 19 April 1941; 413, Ribbentrop to Rome, 27 April 1941.
4. Ibid., 442, Woermann memorandum, 3 May 1941; 459, Abetz to Foreign Ministry, 5 May 1941.

defenses. On 9 May German planes began to refuel in Syria on their way to Mosul in northern Iraq. The RAF retaliated on the 15th and 18th by bombing Syrian airfields.[5]

From 5-16 May 1941 German aircraft intervened in the fighting, but on the whole the operation was inadequately prepared and produced disappointing results. There were insurmountable logistical problems, and the invasion of Crete (on 20 May General Student's paratroopers dropped from the sky) drew off a large part of Germany's airborne strength. Hitler provided only moderate support since for him every measure taken in the Middle East was a stopgap measure until after the defeat of the Soviet Union. Gaylani had overestimated Germany's willingness to provide him military assistance, and Berlin had over-estimated the ability of the Iraqi army to withstand a British attack. Since Gaylani had done little to foster popular support, his precipitous seizure of power looked like an old-fashioned coup.

While the Axis Powers moved tardily, Churchill sped forward. By mid-May the British had occupied Basra and lifted the siege of Habbaniya, which effec-tively closed off Axis intervention. Gaylani left hastily for exile in Germany.

The Italians, far too weak to be much more than onlookers, still maneuvered to enhance their position in the Middle East. Unhappy over continued German poaching on their presumed sphere of influence in the Eastern Mediterranean, they had since the beginning of April pondered reaching Iraq first with an arms delivery via Syria by a "corsair operation" at sea, but that turned out to be quite impractical.

Once hostilities were in full swing, Mussolini felt obliged to support Gaylani with aviation to earn Arab gratitude. Twelve CR 42 planes were dispatched to Mossul. However, when they landed on the 27th, it was too late, for Gaylani's regime was already tottering.[6] On 30 May Ciano owned up to his country's neglect: "Information from Iraq is bad and, what is worse, our planes, a month after the conflict, have not yet gone into action. If there were any need of it, here you have new proof of the lack of preparation of our air force."[7]

To preserve the fiction that Iraq's liberation was due to a popular uprising against Gaylani's regime, the British held back from crossing the Tigris and entering downtown Baghdad. At the end of May, two days of looting and rioting broke out in the capital at the expense of the Jews who were celebrating the festival of Shavuot, which the British troops, having taken up positions in the

5. Vincent P. O'Hara, *Struggle for the Middle Sea: The Great Navies at War in the Mediterranean Theater, 1940–1945* (Annapolis MD: Naval Institute Press, 2009), p. 126.
6. Romain H. Rainero, *La politica araba di Mussolini nella seconda guerra mondiale* (Padova, CEDAM, 2004), p. 117.
7. *The Ciano Diaries*, 30 May 1941.

city, did nothing to stop. This pogrom claimed hundreds of lives and presaged considerable destruction after 1948 of the largest and oldest Jewish community in the Arab Middle East. With the collapse of the Gaylani government on 30 May 1941, the newly installed puppet regime concluded an armistice with Britain.

After the fall of Iraq, Berlin backed off from further military involvement in the Middle East. The Luftwaffe in Syria was commanded to refrain from attacking British troops and German officers were required to wear civilian clothes in the streets of Beirut. The leader in Vichy France, Admiral François Darlan, also retreated from the brink. To avoid provoking the British, he asked the Germans in early June to remove their military personnel streaming back to Syria from Iraq as soon as possible.[8] On 6 June Hitler obliged by giving orders for the withdrawal of German aircraft from Syria. The French high commissioner in Syria, General Henri Dentz, breathed a sigh of relief, believing that once the Germans had left the British would see no point in an invasion.[9] But it was too late, for the damage had already been done by Luftwaffe flights to Iraq using Syria as a stopover. Prompted by Vichy's military cooperation with the Axis, the British struck. In removing the Axis toehold in the Levant, they hoped to ease the immediate threats to Cyprus, the Suez Canal, Egyptian bases, and the oil refineries in the Persian Gulf.

The Free French had somewhat differing views. Their leader, Charles de Gaulle, meant to discredit the Vichyite regime and expunge British influence by incorporating Syria into a Free French empire. To do this he would have to spearhead the attack. On 14 May General Georges Catroux, de Gaulle's deputy in the Levant, issued a call to arms against Vichy authority and the Axis cohort in Syria.[10] But since the Free French could not do the job alone, de Gaulle flew to Cairo in April, where he pressed Wavell to invade Syria and Lebanon, while Catroux was planning to lead his force into Damascus. Catroux disingenuously proclaimed to the Syrians that he was entering the country to proclaim Syrian liberty and independence—promises he knew de Gaulle had no intention of honoring.

On 8 June 1941 General Wilson, British commander in Palestine, launched the invasion of Syria joined by Free French forces in Operation Exporter. Dentz requested Luftwaffe support and demanded reinforcements from France and French North Africa. Enraged by the British invasion, Darlan ordered French ships deployed off Sidon on 9 June to launch salvos against units of the Royal

---

8. DGFP, D, XII, 581, Achenback to Foreign Ministery, 1 June 1941.
9. Stefano Fabei, *Il Fascio, la svastica e la mezzaluna* (Milan: Mursia, 2002), p. 129.
10. Romain Rainero, *Mussolini e Pétain: Storia dei rapporti tra l'Italia e la Francia di Vichy (10 giugno 1940–8 settembre 1943* (Rome: SME US, 1990), Vol. I, *Narrazione*, p. 202.

Navy. A spirited battle commenced. Although General Dentz vigorously opposed the Allied forces on both land and sea, Hitler decided to abandon Syria to its fate. He did not believe that Vichy troops could hold out, and there was little he could do since Germany lacked the sea power to break the British blockade.

Having overcome the stiff resistance put up by the Vichy garrison, the British captured Beirut and Damascus on 11 July. His troops exhausted, General Dentz requested an armistice and got his wish. After the Acre Convention was signed between his forces and the British, Dentz left Syria on the 14th, Bastille Day. In leaving the Gaullists out, which lent credibility to Vichy charges that Free France was merely Perfidious Albion's lackey, the British, by means of the armistice, could claim that they had set Syria and Lebanon on the road to independence. The Levant had fallen from Vichy to the British, bypassing the Free French. The bitterness of the French defeat in Syria impaired Allied camaraderie. De Gaulle steamed over British craftiness, and, as at Dakar, French and British soldiers had shot at and killed one another.

The Italians had done their best to reduce the fighting strength of the Vichy regime in Syria regardless of the ongoing military threat that the British posed. Suspecting a defection of Vichy soldiers to de Gaulle, General Fidele De Giorgis, who headed the Italian control commission, supervised the demobilization and repatriation of units in the French Army of the Levant, which left only about 35,000 French and 14,000 natives to resist a possible British attack.

The Italian post-mortem was filled with both telling observations and colonialist preconceptions. Although the Italians themselves had made practically no military moves, De Giorgis wrote highly critical reports of the regime in France for failing to commit its fleet, sending scant reinforcements, and offering only verbal protests.

But De Giorgis did not doubt the loyalty of the French forces in Syria in carrying out orders by the Vichy government to resist. The villains in his piece were the "cowardly" Arabs, who sat on their hands while waiting to see who would win. "In the crucible of experience in the conflict, the Syrian and Lebanese population have demonstrated again their political immaturity that borders on a lack of dignity…. Syrians and Lebanese have always claimed from the Axis formal promises of liberty and independence. But to ask this, they must enjoy a rebirth, learn how to act decisively in difficult situations, and merit fulfillment of such claims. Now, after this recent experience, I deny such populations these rights and I have finally come to disbelieve Arab hatred of the English because of their pro-Jewish policies. I arrive at the point even to deny that Arab hatred against the English, because of their pro-Hebrew policy, is truly generalized and profound."[11] Like the imperialists in Rome, De Giorgis looked down on the Arab peoples whom Fascist Italy aimed to seize from the British and French. As Mussolini told General Arturo Vacca Maggiolini, president of the Italian armistice commission with France, on 15 August 1941, once the Arabs were under his control, he would let them plaintively muse on their notions of freedom and independence.[12]

When Syria fell, the Germans came out openly in "vigorous" support of Arab demands for political freedom and independence. Notwithstanding the obvious duplicity of these promises, it was not difficult for them to outpace the Italians in winning popularity throughout the Middle East simply because, in this era, German might and violent anti-Semitism made a better impression on the Arabs than feckless Italian posturing.[13]

Fallback in the Desert

On 7 November, "the day of infamy," the Japanese struck Pearl Harbor. The Italians misread or purposely misconstrued this earth-shattering development. Euphoric over Japan's stunning successes in the Pacific and Southeast Asia, official Italy was happy to join Hitler in a declaration of war against the United States on 11 December.[14] The American chargé d'affaires in Rome (the ambassador was absent) could not believe this turn of events. "He thinks I have called him to discuss the arrival of certain newspapermen," Ciano records, "but I disillusion him immediately."[15] Italian overconfidence in handling the United States was not usually so barefaced. If Hitler had always considered war in Europe as a prelude to an eventual global showdown with America, Mussolini in January 1940 had admonished him to avoid a confrontation with the American colossus. Roosevelt, warned Mussolini, would never permit the defeat of Great Britain.[16] But in May 1941, the ever-changeable Mussolini airily dismissed the American president as a statesman. "Never in the course of history," he told Ciano, "has a nation been guided by a paralytic. There have been bald kings, fat kings, handsome and even stupid kings, but never kings who, in order to go to the bathroom or the dinner table, had to be supported by other men."[17] From

11. Rainero, *La politica araba di Mussolini*, pp. 122–23.
12. Ibid., p. 123.
13. DGFP, D, XIII, 132, Ribbentrop to Foreign Minister's Secretariat, 20 July 1941.
14. *The Ciano Diaries*, 8 December 1941.
15. Ibid., 11 December 1941.
16. Ennio Di Nolfo, "Guerra stato e nazione nel secondo dopoguerra," in *Guerra e pace nell'Italia del novecento*, eds. Luigi Goglia, Renato Moro, and Leopoldo Nuti (Bologna: Il Mulino, 2006), p. 236.
17. *The Ciano Diaries*, 28 May 1941.

this, Mussolini drew the conclusion that Uncle Sam would never recover from the blow the Japanese administered at Pearl Harbor.[18]

By declaring war against the United States, Mussolini had misread the mind of the Italian public and put him in opposition to the leading classes, which contributed to the slow but steady estrangement of the country from the regime.[19] Bottai noted a lack of enthusiasm among Italians: "Uninspiring news. A crowded square, but lifeless, which requires explanation.... This crowd is hungry. They don't shout, or shriek, but are languid. Mussolini speaks briefly and in hushed tones. It is not a scintillating and captivating performance that issues from a forced voice. At the final 'we will win,' people rapidly disperse to eat their rationed meals."[20]

For many Fascists, on the other hand, the dazzling exploit by the Rising Sun proved the exquisite temperament of the Yellow Race as compared with the Jewish-dominated and racially polluted United States. The tabloid press poured out attacks. Barbarous Americans enamored of comic books must not be permitted to disseminate their uncouth taste on a people nurtured in Renaissance artistry. Democratic despotism had rendered Americans weak and unwilling to sacrifice. Gangster capitalism, blind faith in technology, depersonalization of the individual, sclerosis of family values, and worship of skyscrapers all were signs of a culturally impoverished country. The Fascist vulgate reads on: Americans were enslaved to the economic Jewish-Communistic plutocracy. Their nation was cleaved between the super-rich and lowly proletariat and characterized by widespread poverty, roving bands of unemployed living in squalor, and vast slums with endemic criminality. The population was obsessed with abortion, divorce, and women's rights. Here El Dorado ruled as the patron saint. Another theme stressed the contrasts between an essentially peace-loving Italian people and a warmongering American political class presided over by a messianic president who, in his sectarian hatred of spiritual Fascism, had flogged his incarcerated country into aggression against Italy.

Many Americans, led by the novelist Sinclair Lewis, agreed with much of Fascism's critique of American society. But in disseminating stock phrases of disdain, Fascist propaganda ignored the huge industrial potential for war production of American industry. The Italian Communist leader Palmiro Togliatti asked probing questions about the relationship between the two countries: "How many Italians regard America as a second home? How many Italian enterprises have

---

18. *OO*, XXX: 57; Nino D'Aroma, *Mussolini segreto* (Bologna: Capelli, 1958), pp. 196, 200, 214.
19. Di Nolfo, "Guerra stato e nazione nel secondo dopoguerra," p. 236.
20. Bottai, *Diario*, p. 292.

their prosperity bound up by exchanges with America? Only a few Italians ever regarded the United States as a true enemy."[21]

Beating up on America could not conceal the mounting problems within Italy itself. People felt pinched, and by September ration cards had been widely distributed. Yet the country did not "feel" the war. German general Albert Kesselring observed: "I never got the impression that the people knew from the start that war was a life-and-death struggle."[22] Desultory efforts were made to mobilize and exact sacrifice of the entire population, including the high and mighty, who would be brought down to the level of the humblest worker. Rationing of the staple food product, bread, was introduced in October 1941.[23] Mussolini said sternly: "Let no one think....that rationing will end after the war. It will stay as long as I want it to."[24] If Italy suffered severe shortages in lead and zinc, its depleted resources would be restored by plunder Germany hauled out of Russia.

Frustrated by his country's indifference and desperate to light up a moribund war effort, Mussolini appointed the boorish and inexperienced Aldo Vidussoni to be party chief on 26 December. In the attempt to rejuvenate the PNF, Vidussoni spoke of "that environment of old whores which [these days] is the Party"[25]—a comment that elicited only mirth and contempt. "From the golf caddies to Count Volpi," noted Ciano, "everybody is commenting on it [the appointment] sarcastically."[26] Other Fascists made efforts to limit private travel by forcing people to seek permits from the local prefecture, which would have overwhelmed the already overburdened bureaucracy. Admonished to abolish sleeping cars, restaurants, first-class train service, and to close the golf clubs because of the war, Italians reacted by rolling their eyes in dismay.

Like Mussolini, young Fascists despised the entire bourgeoisie—the "phony" Fascists. The war was "the pretext....offered by providence" for a "surgical operation" on Fascism, wrote Fidia Gambetti, a young Fascist, in 1942. Once over, "the revolution will recommence its journey with full vigor, with young blood," he added.[27] For youths like Gambetti the war would signal the triumph of the left-wing essence of Fascism—a revolution within, not against Fascism.

---

21. Cited in Pietro Cavallo, *Italiani in guerra*, p. 186.
22. Albert Kesselring, *The Memoirs of Field-Marshal Kesselring* (London: Greenhill Books, 2007), p. 106.
23. Philip Morgan, *The Fall of Mussolini: Italy, the Italians, and the Second World War* (Oxford: Oxford University Press, 2007), p. 67.
24. *The Ciano Diaries*, 27 September 1941.
25. Cited in Richard Bosworth, *Mussolini* (London: Arnold, 2002), p. 383.
26. *The Ciano Diaries*, 27 December 1941.
27. Cited in Farrell, *Mussolini: A New Life*, p. 353, n. 110.

This grumbling and discontent derived from Italy's misfortunes in war. Memories of the useless bloodletting and humiliation in Greece were still strong. A grinding partisan resistance in the Balkans that gathered strength in the fall followed, for which the Italian occupiers had no good answer. In the Mediterranean theater well into November 1941 the British Mediterranean fleet and the RAF aided by submarines deploying from Malta managed to inflict heavy losses on Italian convoys, resulting in a drastic decline in Axis shipments. The Italians began carrying troops and fuel almost exclusively in warships, an expensive practice that at least ensured that they would actually reach Libya. The throttling of Italy's sea lines of communications with North Africa was assisted by the decryption, through ULTRA, of Italian radio traffic, which revealed to the British the departure, nature and route of every convoy down to lone ships.

In the desert things looked equally bleak. Ever since the failure to take Tobruk in April, Rommel had been forced to bide his time until supplies and reinforcements arrived, allowing for another attack on the well-defended fortress. The German invasion of the Soviet Union had deferred this plan momentarily, but with a quick victory in sight the Wehrmacht in the Caucasus was expected to launch a two-pronged attack on the Middle East. Rommel's offensive proclivities undiminished, he set about strengthening the Axis positions at the Halfaya Pass while proceeding with plans for an assault on Tobruk in mid-November, which had Hitler's approval.[28] Bastico expressed opposition to the attack and pointed out the distinct chance that the 8th Army would strike from Egypt, imperiling the Axis as they stormed the British-held fortress.

The Germans resorted to dissimulation to reduce Italian fears. Major General F. W. von Mellenthin writes: "Rommel instructed his staff to adopt a confident tone in all discussions with Italian officers, and in November—as the date of our attack drew nearer—I deliberately minimized the possibilities of a British offensive whenever I spoke to our allies."[29] Cavallero was a victim of the same dissembling: "I asked Rommel whether it was possible that the enemy might make a large-scale enveloping attack. Rommel regarded this possibility as extremely unlikely, as the enemy would be afraid of having his line of withdrawal cut by the Italo-German divisions. He only foresaw an action with small forces that could be stopped by using the air force."[30] Rintelen stated that he had received "tranquilizing reports" from North Africa.[31] In this vein, the German Intelligence Service dismissed Italian warnings of an imminent British offensive

---

28. Battistelli, unpublished manuscript.
29. F. W. Von Mellenthin, *Panzer Battles: A Study of the Employment of Armor in the Second World War* (Old Saybrook, CT: Konecky & Konecky, 1956), p. 59.
30. Cavallero, *Diario*, 4 November 1941.
31. *Operazioni*, II: 507.

as "excessive Latin nervousness." But as General Mellenthin writes, "actually we were very perturbed about the possibility of a British offensive."[32]

Flying back to Africa from holiday just before the British advance had begun, Rommel was beaten to the punch by the Commonwealth forces, which launched Operation Crusader on 18 November 1941 with a long approach march that passed around the German-Italian fortified position near Sollum on the coastal route. The offensive force comprised the equivalent of seven divisions, including the Tobruk garrison, and was opposed by three German and seven Italian divisions—the partially motorized *Bologna, Brescia,* and *Pavia.* Bastico's chief-of-staff, General Gastone Gambara, commanded a further motorized corps, *Corpo d'Armata di Manovra* (CAM), made up of the *Trento, Trieste* divisions, and the armored *Ariete* Division, which had 137 M13/40 tanks that were lightly armed and unreliable, easily caught fire when hit, and had no radios. CAM was not part of the Panzer Group Africa, but Bastico agreed that it would assist should the British attack.

Sallying forth from Egypt, the British smashed into the Italian *Ariete* but, when confronted by a robust resistance, broke off the offensive.[33] Tank losses were heavy on both sides.[34] Simultaneously, the British launched a breakout from Tobruk on 21 November.[35]

In the mayhem and confusion of battle, Rommel failed to keep General Bastico apprised of his intentions, the deployment of the Afrika Korps, and the unfolding mêlée. No wonder Bastico had no influence on the course of the battle.[36] When Rommel came under heavy enemy pressure, he needed reinforcement by Italian armor, but since CAM was not under his own command, Rommel was compelled to ask, not order, that Gambara release his troops. Gambara, however, was only prepared to send parts of the *Ariete*. Rommel hit back at this "insubordination" on the 23rd by demanding that Rome dispense with the "Axis Condominium." "It is necessary to substitute immediately the dual command of the operations by a unitary command of all the units that are located in Marmarica and Cyrenaica. I ask that I be charged with this command, subject to the approval of the Duce, to begin immediately, because of the decisive importance of this battle."[37] The Italian military historian Montanari was taken aback by this discourtesy,[38] but the bewildering chain of command did

32. Von Mellenthin, *Panzer Battles*, pp. 59–60.
33. I. S. O. Playfair, *The Mediterranean and Middle East*, vol. 3, *British Fortunes Reach Their Lowest Ebb (September 1941 to September 1942)* (Uckfield, England: Naval and Military, 2004), p. 40.
34. *Germany and the Second World War*, III: 730.
35. Ibid.: 731.
36. *Operazioni*, II: 507.
37. Ibid.: 507–08.
38. Ibid.: 509.

indeed cry out for a remedy. Mussolini answered Rommel's prayers by anointing him as commander of the Axis troops in Marmarica and placing Gambara's XX Army Corps at his disposal.[39] By allowing Rommel to act as he saw fit, the Duce had slighted his own commander, Bastico.

Since Bastico was a shadowy figure who skulked about well behind the lines, Rommel had a point in turning him into a paper commander. As the one on the spot, he could respond immediately to dramatic or unexpected shifts on the battlefield. But Bastico did have legitimate grievances: Rommel had violated hierarchical etiquette by snubbing him, and Mussolini had thrown him under the German panzers. Moreover, the CS had misled him by describing a full-scale British offensive as a scouting expedition.[40]

The outcome of the battle of "Memorial Sunday," 23 November (*Der Totensonntag*), dedicated to the German fallen of World War I, strengthened Rommel's expectations of victory. He had destroyed the 5th South African brigade as a fighting unit, which gave him the confidence to develop an outlandish plan for a "Dash to the Wire," the Egyptian frontier. The aim was to relieve Axis troops strung along the coast and to deliver the enemy a mortal blow. First Rommel wheeled his main force eastward, but, on encountering stiff resistance on the 26th, abruptly turned his troops around to the original positions facing Tobruk. This disintegrated into a series of uncoordinated actions determined more by Rommel's presence at a given place than by a common plan worked out with the Italians. He was lucky on the Tobruk front, where the British were equally at a loss in pinpointing accurately the positions and movements of the Axis forces opposing them.[41] On the coastline to the Halfaya Pass, matters shaped up differently. In turning back to Tobruk, Rommel left the Axis forces trapped there, which resulted in the eventual loss of irreplaceable troops and equipment.

The Italian navy assembled a large convoy, code-named Beta, loaded with a cargo of fuel, ammunition, and vehicles. In a decisive battle on 9 November 1941, the British Force K sent out to intercept the Italian ships recorded a notable victory by sinking or putting out of action ships bearing Rommel's much-needed supplies and many of their escorts. Both Italian admirals involved in the embarrassing defeat were relieved of duty. The Germans were furious and wanted to force the *regia marina* to accept German officers as advisers. Grand Admiral Erich Raeder reported to Hitler: "Today the enemy has complete naval and air supremacy in the area of the German transport routes…. [T]he Italians are not able to bring about any major improvements in the situation, due to the

39. Ibid.: 509–10.
40. Cavallero, *Diario*, 21 November 1941.
41. *Operazioni*, II: 561–62; Playfair, *The Mediterranean and Middle East*, III: 59.

oil shortages and their own operational and tactical impotence."[42] Already the *Kriegsmarine* had dispatched six submarines and an S-boat flotilla to the Mediterranean to interdict traffic between Tobruk and Alexandria from a base at Salamis in the Aegean.[43]

No surprise then that Rommel would nag the Italians for supplies and complain about their inability to break the British maritime blockade. He further grumbled over the indiscipline and ill will of CAM.[44] "Where is Gambara?" cried his men.[45] But Rommel could not deny that the *Ariete* had distinguished itself in the fighting. Shortly after the war General Sir Claude Auchinleck wrote: "The Italian M-13 tanks which, as a result of the previous campaign, we had inclined to dismiss as valueless, fought well, and had an appreciable effect on the battle."[46] There were other problems that begged solution: the crushing superiority of the British air force and the wear and tear of the overused German armor. The many slip-ups that these shortcomings produced gave the British time to save themselves from their own errors and regroup.[47]

Between 28 November and 4 December fighting continued to rage around Tobruk; both German and Italian units fought well and bravely. But upon learning that no more military supplies or reinforcements would be forthcoming to make up for the losses in the recent fighting,[48] Rommel realized that his offensive was over. Fearing that British frogmen were about to land behind him, he unexpectedly ordered a withdrawal to the Gazala line about fifty miles west of Tobruk.[49] This startling announcement rocked the Italians. Without transport, their infantry and equipment would not be able to keep up with German panzers moving at a fast clip rearward. The CS swallowed its doubts by agreeing to give up the siege of Tobruk, which had lasted 242 days.[50]

Beset by serious setbacks and troop surrenders, Rommel gloomily predicted that the Axis forces would not be able to hold Cyrenaica.[51] He took out his frustration on General Bastico by suggesting that he was prepared for a flight to Tunisia and internment with his German divisions.[52] Without hesitation Bastico

42. Cited in O'Hara, *Struggle for the Middle Sea*, p. 147.
43. Ibid., p. 142.
44. *Seconda offensiva britannica in Africa Settentrionale e Ripiegamento Italo-Tedesco nella Sirtica Orientale (18 november 1941–17 gennaio 1942)* (Rome: SME US, 1949), p. 83.
45. *The Rommel Papers*, p. 171.
46. Cited in Lucio Ceva, "The North African Campaign 1940–1943: A Reconsideration," in *Decisive Campaigns of the Second World War*, ed. John Gooch (London: F. Cass, 1990), p. 92.
47. *Seconda offensiva*, pp. 89-90.
48. *The Rommel Papers*, p. 171.
49. *Germany and the Second World War*, III: 746.
50. Playfair, *The Mediterranean and Middle East*, III: 79; *Seconda offensiva*, pp. 79–80.
51. *Germany and the Second World War*, III: 747.
52. Ibid.: p. 739; Douglas Porch, *The Path to Victory: The Mediterranean Theater in World War II* (New York: Farrar, Straus and Giroux, 2004), p. 253.

refused any retreat and threatened to take the Italian divisions under Rommel's command for repositioning at his own discretion. Rommel replied: "I would have no option but to make the retreat through Cyrenaica with the German forces alone, leaving the Italians to their fate."[53]

Tempers continued to flare. The Italians thought that Rommel was excessively jumpy over imminent enemy encirclement and deaf to their assurances that reinforcements were on their way.[54] Bastico held that every idea of further retreat must be dismissed.[55] Since Rommel had already informed Hitler of his decision, he paid the Italian general no attention.[56]

Against the background of another heavy loss of Italian supply ships inflicted by the Royal Navy at the battle of Cape Bon on 13 December, both Italians and Germans closed in on the Desert Fox in a dramatic meeting held three days later. To spare the Duce damaging political repercussions, there would be no retreat. Gambara was ready to fall on his sword: "Resist to the end, die at your post." But Rommel was unyielding.[57] Cavallero brought the firebrand Gambara and the proud Bastico to order, for Rommel, he knew, held the whip hand. So his decision stood: a fall back from Tobruk and even Benghazi but in an orderly manner to save equipment and stores.[58] Did the Italian generals forget that the Axis air forces in Libya on 15 December had fuel for just one day's operations?[59]

Whenever Rommel pondered retreat, the Italians feared that it would be precipitous. The Germans could usually manage to extricate themselves from untenable positions because they were motorized, whereas the immobile Italian infantry, shackled to a ponderous supply service, would be exposed to capture, huge losses of equipment, or worse. But the Italian commanders were more worried about salvaging equipment than saving soldiers, whereas Rommel did not want to stand accused of sacrificing Italian lives to save his panzers. Lost equipment could be made up.[60] Rommel won the war of words; there would be no delay in the retreat to Agedabia.

Worse was to come. On 22 December Rommel informed the Italians that he would only have time to leave his calling card at Agedabia on his way westward to Agheila at the border of Tripolitania and blamed them for the hasty retreat. The Italians, he said, were unable to hold their positions at Agedabia, and they

53. *The Rommel Papers*, p. 173.
54. *Seconda offensiva britannica*, p. 102.
55. Ibid., p. 104.
56. Ibid., p. 108.
57. Cited in *The Rommel Papers*, pp. 173–75.
58. Cavallero, *Diario*, p. 287.
59. O'Hara, *Struggle for the Middle Sea*, p. 155.
60. *Seconda offensiva britannica*, p. 159.

were responsible for the breakdowns in the supply system. Down to the last drop of fuel, planes would be grounded and the panzers immobilized.[61]

Rommel's headlong retreat across Cyrenaica left Axis troops pinned against the Mediterranean to the east of Tobruk assailed by a crushing enemy force. They were desperately short of munitions, on the verge of starvation, reduced to sips of water, and without any hope of relief. On 19 December Rommel requested the evacuation of the garrisons on Italian warships, but received no meaningful reply. There was nothing left for him to do but allow surrender for troops who could no longer endure.[62] By mid-January, with no objection from the CS, the white flag was run up. Approximately 11,000 Italians and Germans laid down their arms.[63]

During Operation Crusader, the squabbling and mistrust between Rommel and the Italian ally grew progressively worse. When Rommel strained at the leash for an offensive, he lied to them about his assessments of the enemy's strengths. When on the retreat, he left them uninformed. Martin Kitchen singles out Rommel's "dash to the wire" before Tobruk as a colossal blunder. The German historian Bernd Stegemann delivers a no less scathing critique of Rommel's performance: "When he [Rommel] encountered unexpected obstacles, he improvised in such a scatter-brained way that bore little resemblance to a carefully planned military operation. German operations disintegrated into a series of uncoordinated actions determined more by Rommel's presence at a given place than by a common plan. His erratic movements led to senseless losses of irreplaceable troops and equipment."[64]

The criticisms of Stegemann and Kitchen might not be far off the mark, but results are results. In spite of his madcap improvisation, the bad blood he created with the Italians—and the blistering criticism of his own commanders—Rommel succeeded in orchestrating a successful move back across Cyrenaica, having saved the main body of the Axis troops. He was not wrong in waving off the exhortations of Cavallero and Bastico to stay put and fight, for the odds were stacked heavily against him. The enemy outnumbered the Axis forces in every category and, if lumbering, pressed on doggedly. Had Rommel tarried too long, he might well have been forced into a head-on fight he could not win. Retreat was inevitable. The costs were, however, great. In the precipitous and herky-jerky moves during the long trek from the Egyptian frontier, the Axis forces

---

61. Ibid., p. 130.
62. Ibid.
63. *Operazioni*, II: 735–37. According to Greene and Massignani, *The Naval War*, 13,800 surrendered.
64. *Germany and the Second World War*, III: 742.

blew up equipment and supplies that they could not carry or, if not given the time, simply abandoned them.

It appeared in January 1942 that the Commonwealth forces had achieved a victory in Operation Crusader. Enjoying superiority in numbers and assisted by information gleaned from Ultra, they succeeded in recovering lost ground by driving the Axis back from the gates of Egypt to the edges of Tripolitania. The siege of Tobruk had been lifted and the Axis swept out of Cyrenaica. But given their sizeable advantage in tanks, the Commonwealth armies stumbled and faltered in an effort that sputtered out well short of a decisive victory. The Axis forces, in spite of Rommel's mishaps, had put the enemy in the shade; only a vast superiority in equipment had enabled the Commonwealth forces to gobble up huge tracks of desert, but Tripoli and the frontier between Libya and Tunisia had not been reached. Now it was the enemy's turn to suffer long supply-lines in holding Cyrenaica. Little did they know what was in store for them, for Hitler in December had ordered an entire air wing transferred from the Russian front to Italy and North Africa to pound Malta and regain control over the sea routes to Tripoli. This was bound to stiffen the resolve of the Axis forces fighting in the desert.

Chapter VI

Illusions of Victory

On the Russian Front
Fencing with France
The Canal Denied
A Last Look at Malta
Desert Battlefield Performance

On the Russian Front

The Fascist regime was borne into power in 1922 on a wave of anti-Communism, which formed a leitmotiv of Mussolini's foreign policy. But two years later, at a time when Realpolitik was vying with restless revisionism, Mussolini normalized relations with the Soviet Union and, in 1933, he signed a treaty of friendship with Moscow. In spite of the substantial differences between them, the two regimes did share certain ideological preconceptions in that both were anti-democratic and anti-bourgeois, and they hated the capitalist, plutocratic imperialist powers whose global reach dominated the four continents.

The Spanish Civil War, which broke out in 1936, changed things around. Nationalist leader General Francisco Franco launched an uprising against the legitimate Republican government in Madrid. The French Popular Front under the premiership of the Socialist Léon Blum responded by opening the frontier for assistance to the besieged Spanish Republicans. The threat to Fascist Italy was palpable. Both emphatically anti-Fascist, these leftist regimes, if permitted to act together, would pose as a stumbling block to Mussolini's endeavor of dominating the Mediterranean. After a brief delay, he reacted by pouring in troops to assist his fellow would-be dictator. Only a few steps behind, Stalin established a foothold in Spain by means of equipment, troops, and political commissars. A race ensued between the totalitarian powers—Germany, Italy, and the Soviet Union—in providing sustenance to their respective ideological favorites. In the dynamics of the Spanish Civil War, a budding, if ill-coordinated, Axis alignment gave Franco the victory over the Republicans and thwarted Stalin's effort to Bolshevize Spain. By cultivating the image of standard-bearer in the crusade against Communism, Mussolini connected ideology and Realpolitik, but not to the point of no return. From the withdrawal of Italian troops from Spain in 1939 to the outbreak of World War II, the Duce conducted a "double track" policy, acting at once as a stern anti-Bolshevik and as a promoter of workable, if not particularly profitable, economic exchanges with Moscow.[1]

In the run-up to Hitler's Operation Barbarossa, relations between Rome and Berlin were burdened by strung-out negotiations over trade agreements. Dependent on German largess to spur industrial production, Italy constantly clamored for raw materials. In return, having an insatiable appetite for laborers, the Germans demanded Italian workers, who, when delivered, were subjected to rough treatment. The obvious German preference for labor over soldiers carried the unkind suggestion that Italians could work but not fight. Meanwhile, Hitler was putting the finishing touches on Operation Barbarossa, typically keeping the Italians in the dark.

To wean Germany from the Nazi-Soviet Pact, Mussolini wrote a letter to Hitler focused on the Führer's hatred of Jews and Communists. "You cannot abandon the anti-Semitic and anti-Bolshevik banner that you have unfurled over these twenty years and for which many of your comrades have died; and you cannot deny your gospel in which the German people have blindly believed. I have the imperative duty of adding that any further step in your relations with Moscow would have disastrous repercussions in Italy, where there is a unanimous anti-Bolshevism, especially among the Fascist masses, which is absolute, stone solid, indivisible….the day in which we will have demolished Bolshevism, we will have kept faith in our two revolutions." Mussolini then revealed what really motivated him: hatred of the Western Powers. "It will be then the turn of

1. Lucio Ceva, "La campagna di Russia nel quadro strategico della guerra fascista," in Ceva, *Guerra Mondiale*, pp. 102–3.

the grand democracies, which cannot survive the cancer eating away at them, that shows up in their demographics, politics, and morality."[2]

But when confronted by the prospect that the Führer sought to cut a deal with Britain for a division of the world, Mussolini tested the ground with Russia for a coordination of their common interests in the Balkans, the Turkish Straits, and the Mediterranean. By soft-pedaling ideological differences and dwelling on common interests, Mussolini hoped to arrive at a rapprochement with Russia that would head off an Anglo-German peace and counterbalance the influence of an overbearing Axis ally. While Rome and Moscow set out to define their respective spheres of influence in those areas, Ciano told German ambassador in Rome Hans Georg Mackensen that Italy acknowledged Russia's special position in the Black Sea and vowed to support demilitarization of the Straits.[3] But since the idea of an Italian agreement with Moscow did not sit well in Berlin,[4] Ciano, in September, instantly drew back, which severed the independent Italian line to Moscow.[5]

From the end of 1940, having been provided information by secret agents and Italian military attachés in Berlin, Moscow, and Bucharest, Mussolini had more than an inkling of what was afoot in Hitler's plans to invade the Soviet Union. On 30 May he ordered Cavallero to prepare three divisions for an operation on the Eastern Front: "We cannot be absent in a struggle against Communism."[6] The Fascist regime would salvage its worth as an ally by becoming part of the anti-Communist crusade. Germany and Russia were headed for an apocalyptic denouement, Mussolini prophesized, and Italy would join the attack by moving armored and motorized divisions assembled between Ljubljana and Zagreb northward.[7] The continued silence in Berlin gave rise to speculation in Rome. On 2 June 1941 Ciano wrote: "The general impression is that for the moment Hitler has no precise plan of action."[8] But, according to Göbbels, Hitler had told Mussolini during their meeting at the Brenner that a German attack was coming,[9] although he did not specify the exact timing.[10]

On the fateful day of 22 June, when the German panzers clattered into the Soviet Union virtually unopposed, Mussolini was vacationing in Riccione. He

2. Hitler-Mussolini, *Lettere e documenti* (Milan: Rizzoli, 1948), pp. 33–38.

3. DGFP, D, X, 290, Mackensen to the Foreign Ministry, 6 August 1940.

4. Ibid., 348, Ribbentrop to the Embassy in Italy, 16 August 1940; DDI, 9, V, 431, Alfieri to Ciano, 17 August 1940; *The Ciano Diaries*, 6 September 1940.

5. DGFP, D, XI, 42, Mackensen to the Foreign Ministry, 10 September 1940.

6. Cavallero, *Diario*, 30 May 1941.

7. Ibid.

8. DDI, 9, VII, 200, Conversation between Ciano and Ribbentrop, 2 June 1941.

9. Schlemmer interview, 18 September 2009.

10. Gerhard Schreiber, 'La participazione italiana alla guerra contro l'URSS. Motivi, fatti, conseguenze," in *Italia contemporanea*, 191 (1993), p. 248.

needed no persuasion to tap into the received opinion expressed in conservative Allied circles that the Stalinist regime, weakened by recent purges, would fall like a house of cards; "Asiatic hordes" and non-Russian ethnic minorities would migrate to the Germans at the first shot. Indeed, Hitler was not entirely delusional, or alone, in thinking that his legions would wipe out the Soviet armies by autumn.

Mussolini therefore confidently offered Germany an army corps for the Russian front. Dogged by the fear of arriving too late to take his rightful place on the victor's podium, he was determined to move quickly. There would be no repeat of the debacle following the defeat of France when a tardy Italian intervention had prevented fulfillment of Italy's claims on the loser's empire, the "*occasione mancata*" of June 1940. How humiliating it would be to be absent when an Axis New Order was taking shape and a paltry country like Slovakia was fighting shoulder to shoulder with the Third Reich! Mussolini railed to General Giovanni Messe, "I must be at the side of Hitler in Russia as he was at mine in the war against Greece, and is henceforward in Africa. The destiny of Italy is intimately bound up with that of Germany."[11]

The stark contrast, visible by winter 1940–41, between what Germany had achieved on the battlefield and the setbacks experienced by Italian arms was deeply upsetting. Before the Council of Ministers on 5 July, Mussolini vowed to eliminate this imbalance by sending Italian forces to the Russian front.[12] Unless Italy obtained war trophies, he told his ministers, a victorious Germany would "dictate its law to us as well as to the vanquished."[13] Wanted or not, the Italian troops would soon be on their way.

In these heady days of Hitler's invasion, Mussolini seems to have forgotten the "clash of civilizations" between Fascism and Communism when he told Ciano on 1 July: "It is false to speak of an anti-Bolshevik struggle. Hitler knows that Bolshevism has been non-existent for some time. No code protects private property like the Russian Civil Code. Let him say rather that he wants to vanquish a great continental power with tanks of fifty-two tons with which he intends to settle accounts."[14]

More than ideological imperatives, strategic arguments swayed Mussolini. If the Italian armies were on hand while Hitler was ringing up victories, Italy would

---

11. Giovanni Messe, *La guerra al fronte russo* (Milan: Mursia, 2005), pp. 215–16.

12. Giuseppe Gorla, *L'Italia nella seconda guerra mondiale: memorie di un Milanese, ministro del re nel governo di Mussolini* (Milan: Baldini and Castoldi, 1959), pp. 217–18.

13. Cavallero *Diario*, 24 July 1941; Bottai, *Vent'anni e un giorno*, 25 September, 14 October 1941, 7 February 1942; *The Ciano Diaries*, 30 June 1941; Alfieri, *Due dittatori di fronte*, p. 199; Gorla, *L'Italia nella seconda guerra mondiale*, pp. 216–19.

14. *The Ciano Diaries*, 1 July 1941.

be in a better position to check Germany's surge into the Balkans, which would add strength to its own lien on British and French possessions in the Mediterranean. Already Mussolini was looking beyond the defeat of the USSR: "Once having liquidated Russia, the fate of Great Britain will hardly be delayed and will be decisive, especially if we succeed in bringing Turkey into our camp, which will enable us to attack Egypt from two sides."[15]

Besides Realpolitik and the hubristic desire to earn Germany's acceptance of Italy's parity in the Axis, Mussolini angled for economic advantages. Italy must make a convincing contribution to victory to render credible its bid for a substantial share of Russian raw materials. In a meeting on 9 July 1941 with German economic experts, Admiral Riccardi made this clear.[16] Mussolini set his sights on the huge Soviet oil fields at Maikop, the only viable solution to his country's great need of fuel.[17] Since Italy was also running dangerously low in coal, grain, and metals, Rome reveled in the prospect of replenishing a dwindling supply of raw materials from Russian-occupied territory that Germany was loath to provide from its own resources.[18]

The ageless Russian push toward the Straits was another factor inducing Mussolini to rush troops eastward. Should the Soviets link the Black Sea with the Mediterranean, they would poach on "Italy's sea" in a no less serious way than the British had done at the eastern extremity. Soviet penetration of the Balkans, having grown by leaps and bounds after the Nazi-Soviet Pact, imperiled Italy's *spazio vitale*.

Mussolini was plagued by other discomfiting thoughts. Beyond the many vague promises to Italy of territorial spoils, Hitler had committed to nothing definite in writing. Equally disturbing was the thought that Hitler, after victory over the Soviet Union, would engage in a separate peace with the British facilitated by a sacrifice of Italy's imperialist claims.

Such a frightening prospect prompted the vengeful hope that Germany be put in its place by a strung-out war of attrition on the Eastern Front that would give Italy time to recover its lost prestige.[19] On a different tack Mussolini held that the Germans would welcome a compromise peace that would "save the balance of Europe."[20]

---

15. DDI, 9, VII, 346, Mussolini to Hitler, 2 July 1941.
16. ADAP, E, III, 97, Undated memorandum, without signature, 15 July 1942.
17. Cavallero, *Diario*, 11 October 1942.
18. Thomas Schlemmer, *Invasori, non vittime: La campagna italiana di Russia 1941–1943* (Rome-Bari: Laterza, 2009), pp. 30–31.
19. *The Ciano Diaries*, 6 June 1941.
20. Ibid., 30 June 1941.

None of this suggests that Mussolini actually considered changing course, or that he looked forward to playing high steward at Hitler's coronation as master of Europe in another "Munich." But it does illustrate how little he understood Hitler's *Lebensraum* mania or, as Ciano put it, "Oh, his eternal illusions!"[21] On balance, Mussolini's "crusade against Communism" stemmed from a warped understanding of Realpolitik and pivoted on his determination to showcase his country in Berlin as an indispensable ally that could not be abandoned in the war that really mattered to Italy: the fight to the finish against Britain for its colonial possessions in Africa and the Middle East. Whatever Germany's fate might be, or whatever actions Hitler took, Mussolini was locked into the Axis.

There was one serious problem: Hitler was not happy in having Italian troops sent to the Eastern Front—troops who, in his view, were no better than "harvest hands."[22] Rather, they would be more gainfully employed in North Africa (a view shared by the OKW) and in keeping France under guard from the Eastern Alps to North Africa.[23] This disdain for Italian fighting abilities was shared by Keitel, who described overage officers leading "half-soldiers" incapable of standing up to the Red Army.[24] Invariably such remarks reached Mussolini. "I hope for only one thing," he told Ciano on 1 July, "that in this war in the East the Germans lose many feathers."[25] Such outbursts took place well out of German earshot.

In a display of derring-do, Mussolini flew his own plane to Verona where his troops were assembling for the long trip to Russia. After an inspection of arms, he moved about the crowds without an escort. He took his leave with a terse challenge: "Live dangerously!"[26] But the elderly General Francesco Zingales, commander of the CSIR (Corpo di Spedizione in Russia), was not destined to carry out the Duce's exhortation. An aide whispered: "Good God! The commander has suffered a heart attack, and we have to secure a gurney to take him to the hospital."[27] General Messe replaced him on 13 July as the commander of a force made up of 62,000 men, 4,600 horses and mules, 5,500 motor vehicles, 220 artillery pieces, 94 anti-tank weapons, 60 light tanks, and 83 planes.[28] This was a drop in the bucket when measured against the 3,050,000 Germans and 4,700,000 Russians squaring off against each other. Although the

---

21. Ibid.
22. David Stahel, *Operation Barbarossa and Germany's Defeat in the East* (Cambridge: Cambridge University Press, 2009), p. 357.
23. DDI, 9, VII, 288, Hitler to Mussolini, 21 June 1941.
24. Stahel, *Operation Barbarossa and Germany's Defeat in the East*, pp. 356–57.
25. *The Ciano Diaries*, 1 July 1941.
26. Rintelen, *Mussolini e l'alleato*, p. 138.
27. Cited in Santi Corvaja, *Hitler and Mussolini: The Secret Meetings* (New York: Enigma Books, 2001), p. 225.
28. Schreiber, "La partecipazione italiana," p. 253, n. 33.

Italian expeditionary force was put together hastily, many were veteran and élite troops who arrived with Italy's best equipment.[29] Yet there were problems. Planes were launched into sub-zero temperatures without de-icing equipment. Although "motorized" divisions were sent—*Pasubio, Torino*, and *Principe Amedeo Duca d'Aosta*—they were essentially normal infantry. Baggage trains were actually motorized, and artillery dragged by tractors. Foot soldiers left on 10 July without transport and filed stoically across thousands of miles of barren countryside.[30] (Many German infantry units also plodded on foot, using mules and horses to carry equipment.[31]) The Italians arrived in Russia on 5 August, taking positions assigned to them by their German superiors.

Settling in at the front was not easy. The Wehrmacht wondered why it had to be weighed down by small numbers of Italian soldiers who, although fairly well supplied from Italy, were still dependent on Germany for transportation. Positioned at their side were Romanians who still smarted over Italy's having applied pressure on them in the Second Vienna Award to cede Transylvania and lower Dobrudja to the ancient Hungarian foe. No surprise, then, that the Romanian General Antonescu would greet General Messe "with icy courtesy." [32]

Expecting to emulate the autonomy enjoyed by the Afrika Korps, the CS counted on General Messe to be self-reliant and secure quick victories. Rome was in for a rude awakening. Given the paucity of motorized vehicles at his disposal, Messe found himself uncomfortably dependent on the Wehrmacht to secure supply routes and train deliveries over such vast spaces. On 31 July General Keitel dashed Italian hopes of immediate glory by demanding that subalterns button up, obey, and be content with the unglamorous job of cleaning out Soviet pockets of resistance, leaving the grave business of attack to Field Marshal Ewald von Kleist's armored columns. Disgruntled over playing second fiddle, General Messe at the beginning of August implored the CS to send mobile units that would enable him to move promptly into the heat of battle.[33]

After two or three weeks, however, a turnaround occurred when the Germans ordered the *Pasubio* to advance toward the Dnieper River under the command of the 111th German Infantry Division. General Messe was charged with spearheading the assault in a *secondo lancio*.[34] This operation, whose aim was to bar the road to Soviet troops retreating eastward, was successfully completed on 11 and 12 August. At the end of the next month the major force of the CSIR

---

29. Schlemmer Interview, 18 September 2009.
30. Schreiber, "La participazione italiana," p. 253.
31. Schlemmer Interview, 18 September 2009.
32. Bocca, *Storia d'Italia nella guerra fascista*, p. 328.
33. Messe, *La guerra al fronte russo*, p. 82.
34. Schlemmer Interview, 18 September 2009.

undertook a deft maneuver by surrounding Soviet troops and taking 10,000 prisoners.[35] Notwithstanding many serious shortages, the Italians acquitted themselves well during fall 1941 in spite of ongoing wrangling with the Germans over delays in the shipment by rail of supplies for the Italian divisions.[36]

From August 25 to 29 Mussolini made the long and arduous journey to the Rastenburg forest to meet Hitler in his secluded bunker. On one of their frequent air travels together along the front over desolate Russian landscapes, Mussolini unexpectedly seized the throttle of the aircraft from the pilot, an act of bravado that taxed Hitler's patience. In a more leisurely moment, "The Duce informed the Führer of his lively desire for Italian armed forces to take part on a larger scale in the operations against the USSR. Italy—the Duce said—has an abundance of men and can send another six, nine or even more divisions."[37] Little did he heed Messe's warning that given the lack of trucks, the troops faced grave difficulties in keeping up with the German motorized units or in guaranteeing the movement of supplies to the front.[38] In pointing out that the enormous distances involved created irresolvable logistical and transport problems, Hitler eluded the Duce's offer of more troops.[39] Disgruntled, Mussolini vented to his aides that Italian fighting capabilities were superior to the best of the Wehrmacht's crop; a robust *regio esercito* would provide credibility for Italy's vast claims on Russian resources.[40] The parallel war concept having suffered a terminal illness on the Greek battlefields in late 1940, the mandarins in Rome hoped to create "a war of the Axis" out of joint cooperation on the Eastern Front. For this to work, Italy would have to devote enough military manpower to hold its own in the alliance.

Focused on his ability to send large reinforcements, Mussolini gave little thought to their equipment and preparation. Italy could send six new divisions and provide the men if Germany provided the means, he stated. General Keitel on 25 August repeated: Italy should not count on German transport. "Nor would it be prudent to utilize for this second Italian corps motor vehicles destined for Libya."[41] Cavallero, who knew that Italy was in no condition to deliver the 4,600 vehicles required, was not one to impress this unpalatable reality on Mussolini. Hence, what Keitel had delivered as a wake-up call met with a glassy stare in Rome.

---

35. Schlemmer, *Invasori, non vittime*, pp. 21–23.

36. Schreiber, "La participazione italiana," p. 258.

37. Ciano, *Diplomatic Papers*, August 1941, pp. 449–52.

38. Messe, *La guerra al fronte russo*, p. 71.

39. DDI, 9, VII, 511, Conversation between Mussolini and Hitler, 25 August 1941.

40. *The Ciano Diaries*, 30 June 1941; Filippo Anfuso, *Dal Palazzo Venezia al Lago di Garda* (Bologna: Cappelli, 1957), p. 205.

41. *The Ciano Diaries*, 25 August 1941; Messe, *La guerra al fronte russo*, p. 44.

Driven by overweening ambition, Mussolini overlooked the harmful dynamics of the Axis alliance and the full destructive fury of the Nazi regime, let alone Hitler's Holocaust mania and extermination policy. Visceral anger frequently bested his judgment. Whenever there was the slightest hint that his alliance partner held Italy in low esteem, Mussolini was galvanized to provide Hitler irrefutable proof of the Italian army's military prowess. "In Russia our [troops] are fighting 'like lions' and are equipped better than the Germans," he told Bottai; "Messe is 'an exceptional' general. In the spring we will send an army. Thus our participation will be considerable. The very undisciplined Spanish contingent is disintegrating. The Frenchman, Doriot said at Vel[odrome] d'Hiver, were not more than 1,400 and have had forty dead."[42]

On 7 February, reacting to the Soviet arrest of the German advance during the winter months, Mussolini told the council of ministers: "Perhaps it is not altogether a bad thing that German pride has been wounded by the sudden resumption of the Russian offensive. This pride has patently swelled up and threatens to become intolerable." But the Duce quickly revealed that he knew on which side his bread was buttered: "However, now that Germany has received the lesson it deserved, it is time for the Wehrmacht to resume the path of victory. Otherwise, too many disagreeable events will happen, also for us."[43] No matter how great Mussolini's resentment and desire for revenge, a split from Hitler was never an option.[44]

Whenever Hitler crowed over victories yet to come, Mussolini listened raptly, his spirits restored.[45] This was the case in October when he was informed that Russia was as good as defeated. Off went a band of Italian journalists to report on the march into Moscow. Over the objections of the German high command, Mussolini insisted on sending "another twenty divisions" to the Russian front, downsized to "fifteen" a few days later.[46] Cavallero had the nerve to remark that increasing the infantry's pace from eighteen to forty kilometers a day would solve the motorization shortage; a bit later, he lowered his sights. Six divisions could be readied—if the Germans supplied the transportation.[47]

Undertaking a trip to Rastenberg in latter October to see Hitler, Ciano conveyed the offer of more Italian troops to the Germans. Because the Wehrmacht had bogged down in the East—a fact that Hitler covered up—he "in principle, showed himself to be in favor of this, and particularly when operations move

42. Bottai, *Diario*, 25 September 1941, 14 October 1941, pp. 286–87, 296–97.
43. Cited in Gorla, *L'Italia nella seconda guerra mondiale*, p. 285.
44. *The Ciano Diaries*, 13 October 1941.
45. Ibid., 10 October 1941.
46. Ibid., 22 October 1941.
47. Schreiber, "La participazione italiana," p. 257; *The Ciano Diaries*, 22 October 1941.

towards Caucasus and beyond." The Alpine divisions, Hitler remarked, were "the best" for fighting in those mountainous regions.[48] Still, Mussolini chafed over the straitjacket in which the Germans had placed him regarding Italy's contribution to the battles that loomed.[49] Germany should not lay down the law "as if we were a defeated nation," nor dictate to us "as it will to the conquered peoples."[50]

Having only a few anti-tank and anti-aircraft guns to spare for Russia, Cavallero, in a chastened mood, admitted to Ciano that he had "boasted too much" and had "to pour some water in his wine, and so slip out of his previous statements." There was much else for him to think about: more troops for Northern Africa, a possible seizure of Tunisian ports, and reorganization of the CSIR. "'It's true,' et cetera, et cetera, he said, 'we can't send to Russia more than six new divisions, and only on condition that the motorized equipment be furnished by Germany.'"[51]

On 6 November Mussolini shared with Hitler the geopolitical thinking that underlay his determination to send additional Italian troops quickly to the Eastern Front. America would soon intervene in the war, he correctly prophesied (Pearl Harbor occurred the next day) and was preparing to land an expeditionary corps to Egypt to reinforce the British. Since "Bolshevism was in tatters" and incapable of revival—notwithstanding a last-gasp effort to constitute a line of resistance at the Urals—the Americans and British would not be able to avert the pending annihilation of their Bolshevik ally. Now it was time, he advised Hitler, to induce the Turks to join the Axis, thus facilitating a march across the Middle East before American reinforcements could arrive.[52]

Mussolini's conduct turned downright erratic when he deputized Ciano in latter November to impose armored divisions on Hitler that Italy did not have.[53] Ciano listened while Hitler once again lampooned Mussolini's judgment. Italian armored divisions on the Russian front were neither necessary nor advisable. "If Italy is in a position to furnish new armored divisions, she might usefully station them in Tripolitania, where a French threat cannot be altogether excluded." On the other hand, Hitler hastened to add, he would welcome a contingent of *Alpini* for "an attack on the Caucasus and the beginning of a grand march to the Orient through Iran, Iraq, Syria and Palestine, which should lead to the conquest of one

---

48. DDI, 9, VII, 682, Ciano to Mussolini, 25 October 1941; 686, Ciano to Mussolini, 26 October 1941.
49. Schreiber, "La participazione italiana," p. 257.
50. *The Ciano Diaries*, 10 October 1941.
51. Ibid., 23 October 1941.
52. DDI, 9, VII, 722, Mussolini to Hitler, 6 November 1941.
53. Ceva, *La condotta italiana della guerra*, pp. 90–91.

of the key positions in the British Empire: Egypt."[54] This was exactly what the Italians wanted to hear—a linkup of Axis forces somewhere between the Caucasus and North Africa. Mussolini wrote Hitler on 3 December that he was ready to triple the number of troops operating on the Eastern Front.[55] Together Cavallero and Mussolini offered to dispatch twenty divisions, then nine, and ultimately settled on seven, not counting the phantom armored division.[56]

Mussolini immediately sent out orders to prepare an Alpine army corps for the Caucasus.[57] At the same time, he received news that German troops were staggering back from the Red Army's counteroffensive in December—proof to him that Italian soldiers were not second-rate,[58] and that Hitler needed him as much as he needed Hitler. "The war will be long, very long,"[59] the Duce told the industrial luminary Alberto Pirelli, one of his closest confidants from the business world. He confided to Ciano that it would last "at least four or five years."[60] Behind the careless thought of a war without end and the pleasure of getting even with Hitler lay a blatant callousness toward his own soldiers, whose fate was inextricably linked to the fortunes of the Wehrmacht. General Messe, who was more sensitive to the condition of the Italian troops, informed him that after the rigorous fall campaigning they needed to be called home.[61]

In December, due to the slowdown of the German offensive in the East occasioned by stiff Soviet resistance, Hitler stated that he would be "very grateful" to have six more Italian divisions on the Russian front.[62] This request quite flattered the Duce. But would the Germans finally offer equipment and supplies? The answer was not long in coming. On 27 January 1942 General Walter Warlimont informed General Marras that German help would not be forthcoming. At about the same time General Keitel wrote Cavallero that Germany was in no position to supply heavy equipment; two months later he told him that Italy was well supplied because neither of the Axis armies was well supplied![63]

Reeling from huge losses of equipment, the Germans could not possibly undertake the prodigious task of providing the Italian divisions with up-to-date weaponry. Their top priority had to be resupply of their own troops. Mussolini

54. DDI, 9,VII, 786, Ciano to Mussolini, 24–27 November 1941.
55. *Le Operazioni delle unità italiane al fronte russo* (Rome: SME US, 2000), p. 183 and D. 50.
56. Lucio Ceva, *Africa Settentrionale 1940–1943* (Rome: Bonacci, 1982), p. 169.
57. Schreiber, "La participazione italiana," p. 259.
58. *The Ciano Diaries*, 20 December 1941.
59. Pirelli, *Taccuini*, p. 315.
60. *The Ciano Diaries*, 27 December 1941.
61. Messe, *La guerra al fronte russo*, pp. 159–94.
62. DDI, 9, VIII, 80, Hitler to Mussolini, 29 December 1941.
63. Ibid., 194, Mussolini to Hitler, 23 January 1942; Schlemmer, *Invasori, non vittime*, pp. 32–36; Schreiber, "La participazione italiana," p. 261; Messe, *La guerra al fronte russo*, p. 44.

ignored this reality, telling Ciano: "Among the cemeteries, I shall someday build the most important of all, one in which to bury German promises. They have delivered nothing, or almost nothing, of what they promised. For this reason it is better not to insist. I persuaded Cavallero not to ask for the anti-tank guns and the anti-aircraft guns for our divisions going to Russia. I prefer to take the risk of taking twelve batteries from the Rome defenses."[64] Thus Mussolini was prepared to strip the Italian peninsula and the war theaters in the Balkans and Libya to equip distant armies fighting at the side of the Wehrmacht at the expense of homeland defense and the Italian empire. As for "German promises," aside from an offer of anti-tank guns,[65] none had been made.

The conservative generals, who were more in tune with the king, looked with skepticism on diverting so many resources to the Eastern Front. They preferred to consolidate positions already conquered and to keep a certain distance from the German ally—a stance more in keeping with Italy's "parallel war," which, in their deluded minds, was still operative. However, their chieftain Cavallero predictably caved in to Mussolini by sending troops and equipment desperately needed in Italy and North Africa to feed the meat-grinder in Russia.

General Messe claims that he told Mussolini: "It's a grave error to send an entire army to the Russian front. Had I been consulted, I would have advised against this, as I did the dispatch of the second army corps last year."[66] If Messe's bold statement is accurate, he was one of the few high-ranking Italian officers who did not flinch from telling Mussolini what was on his mind.

On the assumption that the British losses of Singapore and Hong Kong would draw off forces in the Mediterranean, and that the United States would be indefinitely tied down in the Pacific, Mussolini staked the future of his regime on the outcome of the Axis war in the Soviet Union. In this, he was not alone. Count Volpi di Misurata, voicing the Duce's view, told Pietromarchi: "The reality is that for Europe the stakes being played out in Russia are high; our fate depends on the result of the struggle between Russians and Germans."[67]

On the war front, Mussolini told General Messe on 2 July 1942 that General Italo Gariboldi would replace him as the commander of the newly formed 8th Army (Armata Italiana in Russia, designated ARMIR). The next day, after twelve months of collaboration with General Ewald von Kleist's army, the CSIR passed under the authority of the German XVII Army and assumed the denomination of the XXXV Army Corps. Messe stayed on as its commander.

64. *The Ciano Diaries*, 20 February 1942.
65. Schlemmer interview, 18 September 2009.
66. Messe, *La guerra al fronte russo*, p. 215.
67. PP, *Diario*, 17 February 1942.

Messe was furious over having been replaced as 8th Army commander by the mediocre Gariboldi, whose most recent gaffe had been a switch of divisions: his *Sforzesca* for Messe's *Torino*. For having broken the unity of the XXXV Army Corps troops under his command, Gariboldi had, in Messe's view, committed an unpardonable mistake.[68] Ciano reported: "I saw Messe on his return from Russia. He sees red because Cavallero made the old and stupid Gariboldi commander of the Army over his head, in spite of Messe's excellent record. Like everybody else who has had anything to do with the Germans, he detests them, and says that the only way of dealing with them would be to punch them in the stomach. He thinks the Russian Army is still strong and well armed, and that any idea of a complete collapse of the Soviets is an absolute Utopia."[69]

Tongues wagged in Rome that Gariboldi was Cavallero's choice "to block the road to Messe, who was beginning to grow too much in the eyes of the Duce and the country. Cavallero is a faithful follower of the theory that instructs the decapitation of those too big for their britches."[70] Cavallero told Messe: "The decisions have been taken by Mussolini on the basis of political considerations and it is futile to discuss the matter further."[71] More relevant perhaps in the switch of commanders was Mussolini's surprising respect for time in service, and Cavallero's belief that the Germans welcomed the shuffle of the Italian commanders.[72]

Bad blood and recrimination made for a lot of titillating talk in Rome. Bottai on Messe: "Around his neck hangs the German iron cross; and one sees in his face the joy of that pendant. It takes a pinch of the female to make a good soldier. Immediately he manifests his disappointment over the nomination of Gariboldi as commander of our army in Russia. He senses in the lack of his own validation the hostility of Cavallero; fiery words against him and Farinacci, two men….that the army and country detest."[73]

Giusto Tolloy, an officer attached to the army command by the CS, colorfully sketches Gariboldi's character: "The commander of the army Gariboldi reminds one of Kitchener, Pétain, and [Kaiser] Wilhelm II: austere, taciturn, of haughty demeanor and military moustache; of the first, a vacuous silence, of the second, weakness, of the third, vanity."[74] Ciano added: "I have known him

68. Messe, *La guerra al fronte russo*, p. 222.
69. *The Ciano Diaries*, 4 June 1942.
70. Cited in Bocca, *Storia d'Italia nella guerra fascista*, p. 443.
71. Messe, *La guerra al fronte russo*, pp. 214–16.
72. Rosita Orlandi, "Giovanni Messe: da volontario a Maresciallo d'Italia," in *Il Maresciallo d'Italia Giovanni Messe* (Mesagne: Congedo, 2003), p. 100.
73. Bottai, *Diario*, 26 May 1942, p. 307.
74. Giusto Tolloy, *Con l'armata italiana in Russia* (Milan: Mursia, 1968), p. 16. Also see Orlandi, "Giovanni Messe," p. 100.

[Gariboldi] for many years, from the time of the capture of Addis Ababa. I have never had a very favorable opinion of him. Just now he seems even more tired and aged, notwithstanding the bleached-blondness of his heavy mustache, trimmed *á la fin de siècle*."[75] General Francesco Saverio Grazioli observed that Gariboldi was a "hard and irritable man, who nevertheless was a professional: conscientious, and diligent and had a strong character. But no stroke of genius. A second-rate man."[76]

By the middle of July 1942, ARMIR had begun to take up positions about fifty kilometers west of the XXXV Army Corps. It included approximately 230,000 men, 16,700 motor vehicles, 25,000 horses and mules, 1,150 artillery tractors, 960 antiquated canon, 380 1.8 inch antitank guns, 19 self-propelled light guns, and 55 light tanks deployed in static positions along the Don to guard the northern flank of the German drive on Stalingrad.[77]

On 12 August the first formations of General Messe's XXXV Army Corps arrived at the Don. Between 20 and 25 August the Soviets undertook a massive attack, forcing the Axis command to divert troops from the Stalingrad front to shore up the lines along the Don. The Soviet attack succeeded in penetrating the lines of the *Sforzesca* and threatened to encircle the Italian left wing. To avoid a rout, and after asking vainly for the intervention of the XVII German Corps, Messe on the 25th ordered a retreat of fifteen kilometers. This immediately raised objections at the German command. It was not the retreat as such, but the hole in the center of the Italian front that the retreat created, for this widening gap in the front lines endangered the supply road to Stalingrad that the Germans perceived to be so threatening. To make sure the line held, according to Messe, the Wehrmacht arbitrarily "tore" troops from his command and placed them directly under the German II Corps (*Sforzesca*, *Celere*, and the 179th German Infantry Regiment), which had the order to block any retreat by the *Sforzesca* whatever the cost and at the risk of serious sanctions.[78]

The situation, however, was a bit more complicated than Messe implied. The Germans wanted to create a unified command in the threatened sector, a measure they often adopted in similar crises.[79] Having not taken this into consideration, Messe drew the conclusion that he was viewed as a coward afraid to fight. Only proud Wehrmacht warriors had the stuff to thwart any retreat "of our divisions." In writing Gariboldi on 26 August that "troops who, at my

75. *The Ciano Diaries*, 17 May 1942.
76. Luigi Emilio Longo, "Profili di capi militari tratteggianti da uno di loro," in *Studi Storico-Militari* 1994 (Rome: USSME, 1996), p. 566.
77. Schlemmer compiles the figure 229,000 men. *Invasori, non vittime*, p. 35.
78. Luigi Emilio Longo, Giovanni Messe: *L'ultimo maresciallo d'Italia* (Rome: SME US, 2006), pp. 171–72.
79. Schlemmer interview, 18 September 2009.

orders, have durably, valorously, and bloodily fought an enemy of crushing strength for six days without any help," Messe demanded that honor be served.[80] Gariboldi, however, failed to stand by him, while the Germans made the conciliatory gestures of removing the "incriminating" phrases from the order of the day and by bestowing the Iron Cross on forty soldiers of the XXXV Army Corps in Messe's presence.[81] On the 27th, the German commander of Army Group B disposed that the units of the XXXV Army Corps be returned to Italian command. Still, the touchy Messe simmered.

In spite of the animosity between the two Italian generals, this chapter of the Russian campaign ended on a high note. On 20 August, involved in fierce defensive fighting as ammunition ran out, the Italians of the XXXV Army Corps faced the last Soviet attack with fixed bayonets. *Bersaglieri* reinforcements arrived just in time and the enemy was repelled. During the struggle, the Cavalry Regiment of Messe's XXXV Army Corps—"dashing but no longer up to modern needs"—engaged in one of the last cavalry charges in European war history.[82]

At the end of August Messe had run out of patience with his superior over his failure to face up to the Germans. When the Wehrmacht issued commands that ran contrary to the opinion of both Italian commanders, Gariboldi replied with arguments and protests but invariably fell into line. Messe, however, thought it his duty, in defending the honor of his country, to refuse compliance with orders he judged to be beyond the ability of his troops to carry out.[83] For Messe the Wehrmacht commanders were overbearing and Gariboldi spineless. Unable to cooperate any longer with him, the distraught Italian general asked Mussolini that he be recalled, but assured him: "I have only one ambition: to serve as a soldier of Fascist Italy and you as our esteemed leader."[84] General Zingales replaced him. Taking over the command on 1 November, he hardly had any time to settle in before military disaster struck his troops.

Fencing with France

Ever since Italy signed the Armistice with France at Villa Incisa in June 1940, Mussolini had hoped to scrap it in favor of an imposed peace treaty that would oblige the Vichy regime to hand over the full measure of Italy's claims on both metropolitan France and its colonies in North Africa. However, at con-

---

80. Messe, *La guerra al fronte russo*, pp. 260–61.
81. Orlandi, "Giovanni Messe," pp. 103–4; Schreiber, "La participazione italiana," p. 264; Longo, *Giovanni Messe*, p. 173.
82. *Germany in the Second World War*, VI: 1074.
83. Longo, *Giovanni Messe*, p. 194.
84. Ibid., pp. 182, 184–85.

ferences in October 1940 with Hitler at the Brenner and in Florence, Mussolini once again encountered Hitler's "New Policy" toward France, which forced him once again to live with a postponement of Italy's claims until after the Axis victory in the war.

On 10 February 1941 Admiral Jean-François Darlan became foreign minister of Vichy France. Anticipating the defeat of Britain, he would not mourn the loss of a deadly imperial rival. Darlan was not an admirer of Nazi Germany but believed his floundering country could find a new lease on life in a German New Order. A carefully calibrated appeasement strategy toward Germany would enable France to escape pauper status in a final peace settlement. As France navigated from an onerous armistice to a restored sovereignty based on the ageless principles of the *ancien régime*, Darlan hoped that he would be in a position to persuade the Third Reich to defend the French empire from Italian depredations.

Pleased to have such an accommodating Vichyite in high office, the Axis Powers counted on Darlan for assistance in supplying General Rommel with desperately needed military equipment. Plying the usual Mediterranean routes from Italy to Libyan ports, Axis supply ships suffered heavy losses administered by the British Mediterranean fleet. To trim the number of such perilous journeys, the Axis hoped that Darlan would allow them to draw on the large stocks of French trucks in North Africa so that they could convey overland goods from safe Tunisian ports to the desert battlefronts. Berlin was also interested in supply bases for U-boats on the southern rim of the Mediterranean, use of French merchant vessels on the west coast of Africa, and delivery of French arms stored in Syria to Iraq.

To sort out these logistical questions, the French and Germans sat down on 28-29 May and initialed, but did not sign, the Protocols of Paris.[85] The French offered the Reich substantial concessions: airfields and military supplies stocked in Syria to help Rashid Ali al-Gaylani's rebellion in Iraq; use of the Tunisian port Bizerte to supply Rommel's Afrika Korps; sale of French trucks and heavy artillery in North Africa; access to neutral merchant shipping in French hands for journeys across the Mediterranean; and, eventually, German use of a submarine base at Dakar.[86] In exchange the Germans promised the French a limited rearmament.

The Vichy regime was not averse to discussing Axis use of Tunisian bases, but only if this would lead to a replacement of the Armistice Conventions with a vast political and military accord restoring French rights. As an equal of the Axis,

---

85. *Germany and the Second World War*, III: 582.
86. Robert O. Paxton, *Parades & Politics at Vichy* (Princeton, NJ: Princeton University Press, 1966), p. 233.

a truly collaborating France should be given the right to rearm in North Africa and receive restitution of sovereignty over Axis-occupied and annexed territory save for a scattering of German forts in certain strategic areas along the Atlantic coastline.

Hardly had the ink dried on the Paris Protocols than the French widely expanded their demands by asking for a comprehensive revision of the armistice as well as a sharp reduction in Italian claims on their territory—a stiff price for use of the Tunisian ports. The Germans, too, had second thoughts. If the British learned of the collaboration given them by the Vichy government, they would likely disrupt maritime traffic between North Africa and France. Opposing such moves in the western Mediterranean was simply beyond the *Kriegsmarine*'s reach.

Denied parley in initialing the Paris Protocols, Italy looked on helplessly while Germany, not for the first time, ignored the so-called predominance of the junior partner in matters pertaining to French-held colonies in North Africa. The divergence between the two Axis partners became obvious during a meeting at Friedrichshaften in mid-June. The Germans spelled out their "elastic" approach to Vichy and openly urged the Italians to be more flexible and conciliatory by allowing the French to provide for the defense of their North African territories.[87] The Italians asked themselves: was Berlin really true to its word that their country was "the mistress of the Mediterranean as Germany was of the Baltic"?[88]

To placate the Italians, Hitler engaged in talk that invariably played well in Rome: "The present French Government," he wrote the Duce on 20 July, "sees itself in the role of Talleyrand at the Congress of Vienna, and at the same time forgets that I am neither Metternich nor Hardenberg."[89] Mussolini replied: "At the end of the war France will have to pay dearly for its tenacious and constantly harsh policy toward Germany and Italy."[90]

The Duce's revanchist attitude was matched by the behavior of the Italian occupiers, who expelled the mayor of Menton and Vichy authorities from lesser towns and communes. Newly appointed Fascist commissioners imposed Italian law, introduced Italianization programs, distributed irredentist leaflets, randomly pillaged, and arrogantly hinted at the annexation of the "city of lemons" (cité des citrons). French citizens were subjected to "the Fascist rhythm."[91]

---

87. Massimo Borgogni, *Italia e Francia: Durante la crisi militare dell'asse (1942–1943)* (Siena: Nuova Immagine, 1994), p. 342.
88. *The Ciano Diaries*, 13 October 1941.
89. DGFP, D, X, 134, Hitler to Mussolini, 20 July 1941.
90. Rainero, *Mussolini e Pétain*, I: 251.
91. Jean-Louis Panicacci, *L'Occupation italienne Sud-Est de la France, juin 1940-septembre 1943* (Rennes: Presses Univeritaires de Rennes, 2010), pp. 19–100.

In a memorandum to Mussolini on 13 August 1941, Vacca Maggiolini took stock of radical changes that had taken place since the Armistice. As an Axis victory was no longer imminent, and the war had no end in sight, the armistice clauses that fettered France militarily were no longer viable. German hectoring to ease up on hard-line treatment of France was relentless, which presented Italy with the unavoidable prospect of inserting Vichy in a partnership with the Axis under the rubric "New European Order."[92] Vacca Maggiolini concluded that Italy was faced with a Hobbesian choice: continued pursuit of a tough line toward Vichy that would produce further strains with the Third Reich, or a "French policy" of winks and smiles reminiscent of Otto Abetz, German ambassador in Paris, to bring Italy in line with German "appeasement" as embodied in the Paris Protocols of 28 May 1941.

In mid-August Mussolini showed "flexibility" in adopting, for the short run, an Italian *"politica francese."* Italy would "manage things cleverly" by granting anti-aircraft batteries on the coast of Africa. But there would be no political concessions. For the first time Mussolini seemed to have shown a disposition to accept France as a participant in a "secure" Axis victory on the condition that Vichy ceded Corsica and Nice to Italy. France would be compensated later by colonies taken from the British Empire. In the meantime, "We must sedate the French to keep them quiet."[93] Whatever concessions Mussolini pondered can be directly traced to his military's urgent pleas for use of the Tunisian ports. The leitmotiv remained unchanged, to take vengeance on France for the "mutilated victory."

When the British opened an offensive in the desert on 18 November 1941, they placed the Axis commanders in perilous straits. Cavallero wrote on 7 December that if two additional divisions could not be added to the existing force in Libya, "the game would be up."[94] Tripoli had only limited dock services and, given its closeness to Malta, was continually exposed to British attack. The Italian military believed that enormous advantages would accrue from use of the Tunisian ports. The distance between the mainland and Africa would be sharply reduced: 140 kilometers from Sicily to Cape Bon and 10 navigation hours as opposed to 32 navigation hours to cover the 444 kilometers between Sicily and Tripoli. Italian traffic in men and arms would proceed practically undisturbed while the Sicilian canal to the Royal Navy would be hermetically closed. With its back against the wall in Libya, the Italian military seemed prepared to renounce

---

92. DDI, 9, VIII, 476, Vacca Maggiolini to Mussolini, 13 August 1941; Rainero, *Mussolini e Pétain*, II: D. 32, pp. 205–8.
93. Rainero, *Mussolini e Pétain*, I: 302.
94. Cavallero, *Diario*, 7 December 1941.

important colonial claims. They committed outright heresy by suggesting that the French could keep Nice if they would give up Tunisia and Corsica.

In spite of strong pressure exerted by the Italian military to overcome German resistance,[95] nothing could be done to alter Hitler's strategic thinking that the Mediterranean was a secondary theater. But in the absence of a strong Axis presence in the central Mediterranean, the British were effectively utilizing Malta as a base from which to launch raids on Axis convoys.[96] To reduce shipping losses, Hitler banked on bringing Malta to its knees by air bombardment rather than risking an open breach with the Vichy regime by seizing the Tunisian ports. Ciano put on a brave face: "Hitler is right: Tunisia is 101 percent de Gaullist; any unwelcome pressure would in itself accentuate the separation which is developing between the French Empire and the government of Vichy."[97] Italian hopes for use of the Tunisian ports were dashed.

On 18 November 1941 General Maxime Weygand, who had cleverly slowed deliveries for the Axis troops in North Africa, was sacked as Vichy's proconsul in North Africa. Admiral Darlan, Weygand's great rival, hoped that his removal would break the glacial coldness with Mussolini that had grown out of Italy's colonial claims. But the Duce was not ready for reconciliation. "If the French would not voluntarily concede the use of the harbor of Bizerte," he told Hitler on 2 December, "one would have to take the harbor by force."[98] Having long sought a meeting with Mussolini, thinking to play him off against Hitler, Darlan had to settle for Ciano, whose antagonism toward him was no less than the Duce's.[99]

At that 10 December meeting in Turin, Darlan started off on the wrong foot by declaring that transshipment of Axis supplies through Tunisia was to be excluded *a priori* for fear of British countermeasures. But since the French were reeling from a German refusal to grant them any political concessions, they, at the risk of a rupture with the United States, agreed, in the "Torino Accords" of 24 December, to allow Italy use of its ships for the transport from Marseille to Tunisia or Algeria of Italian trucks and non-war supplies destined for the Axis front in the desert.[100] The Italians enjoyed a rare taste of retaliation against Berlin. Having been shut out of the "Protocols of Paris" by the Germans, they signed the "Torino Accords" without them.

---

95. DGFP, D, XIII, 557, Mackensen to the Foreign Ministry, 7 December 1941.
96. Ibid., 532, Keitel to Rintelen, 4 December 1941; 557, Mackensen to the Foreign Ministry, 7 December 1941.
97. *The Ciano Diaries*, 7 December 1941.
98. DGFP, D, XIII, 532, Rintelen to the General Staff of the Army, 2 December 1941.
99. Ibid., 501, Conversation between Ribbentrop and Ciano, 28 November 1941.
100. Borgogni, *Italia e Francia: Durante la crisi militare dell'asse (1942–1943)*, p. 24.

But this was not nearly enough for Mussolini. On Christmas Day, a holiday that "reminds one only of the birth of a Jew who gave the world debilitating and devitalizing theories,"[101] he told Vacca Maggiolini: "If the French do not accord Italy full use of the Tunisian ports, and the English succeed to advance on Tripolitania, Italy would be constrained to take possession of Tunisia itself by landing divisions."[102] More bellicosity followed in a letter to Hitler on the 29th: "If the French reject every accord, even the most generous, I declare to you, Führer, that I would rather take my divisions to Tunisia rather than see them sent to the bottom of the sea on route to Tripoli."[103]

Mussolini was infuriated by a certain Vichyite Cartesian logic that denied Italy's victory and Fascism's primacy. This logic held that the French were not defeated because they did not fight; they did not fight because they were not prepared, and they were not prepared because their government was composed of leftist traitors. According to this peculiar logic, Europe had need of a conservative France for its reconstruction.[104]

The Italian "deciders" in Rome arrived at the belief that Vacca Maggiolini, in his frantic search for a solution to the imperiled Italian sea routes, was out of his depth. It was foolish of him to suggest that the French were looking to Italy for support in overcoming Germany's opposition to a modification in armistice orthodoxy; sillier still was his suggestion that the French would accept the loss of Tunisia and Corsica provided that Italy gave up Nice.[105] Obviously Vacca Maggiolini was modifying Mussolini's imperial agenda. "With good reason," Pietromarchi observed, "Germany is opposed to this kind of maneuver."[106] Ciano declared: "Mussolini told me that Vacca Maggiolini is an imbecile who should not concern himself with politics."[107] In Pietromarchi's view, he was "a man of tact but weak, without diplomatic negotiating experience, without precise ideas, without prestige."[108]

At the end of December Rome removed diplomatic responsibility from the CIAF in favor of the newly appointed representative in Vichy, political plenipotentiary Gino Buti.[109] But Mussolini tied his hands: "He should try to stimulate economic and commercial exchanges; not do very much in the cultural

---

101. Cited in Arnold, *The Illusion of Victory*, p. 153.
102. Rainero, *Mussolini e Pétain*, II: Conversation between the Duce and Vacca Maggiolini, 25 December 1941, p. 240.
103. DDI, 9, VIII, 79, Mussolini to Hitler, 29 December 1941.
104. DDI, 9, VIII, 211, Conversation between Mussolini and Göring, 28 January 1942.
105. PP, *Diario*, 21 December 1941.
106. Ibid.
107. *The Ciano Diaries*, 26 December 1941.
108. PP, *Diario*, 21 December 1941.
109. *The Ciano Diaries*, 12 December 1941.

field except to send to France some of our products, such as books, plays, films, and not to take anything from the French."[110]

On 13 January 1942 the French sent a *Memento* to the Axis Powers repeating Vichy's desire for a political agreement that would allow France space in an Axis-dominated Europe. Irritated that the French had described territory claimed by Italy in the *Memento* as "territorial amputations," Mussolini dwelled on the restitution of lands that had been severed from the Italian nation: "Everyone knows in fact how and why Nice had been taken from us in 1860 and we demand nothing more than what was taken from us then. With respect to Savoy, we have already renounced the part that lies beyond the Alpine crest. Corsica is an Italian land as explicitly acknowledged by the great French geographer Elisée Reclus. And in 1870 Clemenceau wanted to cede Corsica to Italy for a symbolic payment of one lira! Regarding Tunis we will always find some accommodation: once the war is won, there shall be more than enough of England's colonial spoils to go around!! Likewise for Corsica and Nice we can offer compensations: the province of Vallonie in Belgium, which is worth much more by its size, population, and wealth than the territories that we demand."[111] On one question Mussolini would not budge: "Today Tunisia is indispensable and we must obtain it from France. Without Tunisia, we cannot be secure in holding Libya. Without Tunisia and Libya we cannot conquer Egypt, and without Egypt we cannot reconquer Ethiopia."[112]

If Mussolini was momentarily willing to relieve France of the stigma of defeat, he insisted that it behooved Germany, not Italy, to pay the price: restoration of French sovereignty symbolized by a return of its capital to Paris, limitation of German military control to a strip on the Atlantic coastline, reduction of occupation expenses, and release of war prisoners.[113]

In Berlin, Mussolini's idea of wringing territorial handovers from France through substantial German concessions was, naturally, quite unthinkable.[114] At the same time, in Vichy France, compromise turned into intransigence toward the Axis Powers. Bending to the pressure of the Americans (who blew the cover on the trickle of supplies conveyed to the Axis armies in the desert), the French on 11 February 1942 suspended indefinitely the movement of transports from Marseille to Libya through Tunisian ports.[115] Between June 1941 and May 1942,

---

110. Ibid., 13 January 1942.
111. DDI, 9, VIII, 160, Lanza d'Ajeta to Ciano, 16 January 1942, Allegato II, Conversation between Mussolini and Vacca Maggiolini, 14 January 1942.
112. Ibid.
113. DDI, 9, VII, 823, Pietromarchi to Ciano, 6 December 1941.
114. Borgogni, *Mussolini e La Francia di Vichy*, p. 315.
115. Rainero, *L'Italia in guerra*, p. 331; DDI, 9, VIII, 264, Liberati to Ciano, 13 February 1942; 268, Liberati to Ciano, 14 February 1942; Allegato 1, Vacco Maggiolini to Cavallero, 13 February 1942.

France had provided the Axis Powers with about 1,700 vehicles, a small quantity of arms, and about 3,600 tons of fuel.[116] This brought to an end the "French policy" sponsored by Abetz and certain German generals. Mussolini would no longer be pressured to make further concessions to Vichy France.

The Canal Denied

There was as yet no Italian capture of Cairo and the Canal, which had been among Mussolini's foremost war aims. The island of Malta appeared to the Italians as the major barrier to this. For the British, Malta had become a "Verdun of the Naval War," a symbol of their will to resist. Located in the narrow channel separating Tunisia from Sicily, the island provided the Royal Navy with an essential fueling station for long-range operations in the Mediterranean as well as a base for flank attacks on the Italian routes to Libya. It linked the British supply line from Gibraltar to Egypt and provided a central base from which the RAF could strike out at Axis shipping.

In fall 1941 Hitler decided to take on Malta by transferring a large number of U-boats and minesweepers to the Mediterranean. For their part the Italians on 16-17 December 1941 made a supreme effort to provision the troops in North Africa by sending four battleships, three light cruisers, and twenty destroyers to escort a convoy to Libya. In this First Battle of Sirte, the Italians could legitimately claim success. The route to Libya, which had been red with the blood of Italian sailors, could now be considered open again.[117] The Kriegsmarine's Admiral Weichold acknowledged: "The convoy reached its destinations without losses. The task has been completed and the critical supply situation in North Africa has improved considerably."[118] A daring mission undertaken by the Xth Flottiglia Mas on the 18th punctuated the newly established Italian predominance in the central Mediterranean. Piloting a SLC (*siluro a lenta corsa*) midget submarine nicknamed *maiale*, or pig, frogmen slowly approached their target and launched torpedoes that put the British battleships *Valiant* and *Queen Elizabeth* out of action, leaving the Mediterranean fleet without aircraft carriers, battleships, or heavy cruisers. Thanks to tightened Italian protection of their convoys, the British in that month sank only eighteen percent of all tonnage bound for Libya. These striking Italian victories had broken the British stranglehold over the Axis line of communication in the central Mediterranean.

---

116. Jackson, *France the Dark Years 1940–1944*, p. 183; Robert O. Paxton, *Vichy France: Old Guard and New Order 1940–1944* (New York: W. W. Norton, 1972), pp. 127–28.
117. O'Hara, *Struggle for the Middle Sea*, p. 59.
118. Cited in *Germany in the Second World War*, III: 723.

Cavallero still had a major supply problem on his hands since the ports of Tripoli and Benghazi lacked the landing facilities to allow docking space for more than a handful of cargo ships at a time. Thwarted by Hitler, who would not prevail on Vichy France to grant Italy use of Tunisian ports, Cavallero had to seek out other avenues to choke off British forays into the Mediterranean. For long the Italians had contemplated an invasion of Malta, but existing plans were sketchy and no implementation was underway. In September Cavallero wrote: "Occupation of Malta! If the Axis wishes, it can do it! This is also the opinion of Roatta."[119] On 14 October, Cavallero once again: "I send Roatta the order to study an undertaking for the occupation of Malta: Operation C3. Given the possibility of making use of Biserta, such action has become inevitable."[120] Cavallero was fully aware that the British could launch an attack on Pantelleria, Sicily, or Sardinia using Malta as a base. Finally he tackled his *istrice* (porcupine) on 6–7 January 1942 by speeding up plans for the capture of Malta by means of a combined airborne and amphibious attack targeted for July-August.[121] Malta had become Italy's "Delenda Carthago."

Under Mussolini's favorable eye, Italian and German generals and admirals assembled at Garmisch on 14-15 January. The going was tough. The Italians were themselves at odds, and the two Axis partners saw matters from different perspectives.[122] Italian attention was riveted on the middle Mediterranean to secure the traffic to North Africa and to ward off any possible British invasion of Pantelleria, Sicily or Sardinia,[123] while Admiral Raeder, taking a broader view, counted on Italian participation in securing the communication lines linking together Corfu, Salonica, and Crete. Agreement was reached on the need to neutralize Malta but hardly a word was voiced favoring its capture. To compensate for the slow progress in the Malta talks, Mussolini on the 18th ordered the Axis air forces to attack Malta "day and night."[124]

In planning the invasion, the Italians had to overcome serious shortcomings. Having no experience in amphibious operations, they had to hone skills in night-time fighting and radar technology. Saddled with a weak CS, the military branches were obliged to find a way to coordinate their efforts. Given the desultory contact between the Axis Powers, it behooved the Italians to draw up an integrated command structure and win German adherence.

---

119. Cavallero, *Diario*, 13 September 1941.
120. Cited in Mario Montanari, *Le operazioi in Africa settentrionale*, Vol. III: *El Alamein (gennaio-novembre 1942)* (Rome: SME US, 1993), p. 120.
121. Mario Montanari, "Dalle battaglie della Cirenaica allo sbarco alleato in Marocco," in *L'Italia in guerra: Il terzo anno—1942*, p. 310; *The Ciano Diaries,* 7 December 1941.
122. Mariano Gabriele, *Operazione C 3: Malta* (Rome: Stato Maggiore della Marina US, 1965), pp. 129–32.
123. Cavallero, *Diario*, 31 October 1941.
124. Cited in Battistelli's unpublished manuscript.

The auspices for an invasion of Malta brightened when Admiral Raeder became a convert. On 13 February he pointed out to Hitler the imperative need of establishing an Axis sway over the Mediterranean. The Japanese attack on America, he said, had occasioned the need of a revamped global strategy. In a guarded response, Hitler agreed in principle but insisted on time to reflect. In the meantime an invasion of Malta would be postponed *sine die* and brought to the table only as a last resort if air attacks alone did not force the island to capitulate.[125]

Rommel was provided another chance for an offensive in January 1942 when the Italian navy successfully docked at Tripoli with a battleship convoy of six vessels carrying fifty-four powerful panzer III tanks, nineteen armored cars, anti-tank guns, and a large quantity of fuel and other supplies. Rommel's task was further eased when the British sent seasoned desert troops and RAF squadrons to the Far East to meet the Japanese threat. A sly hand in SIM made life smoother by pilfering the "Black Code," which contained top-secret American military reports. Using this code, Colonel Bonner Fellers, the American military attaché in Cairo, regularly sent home detailed reports that described British military deployments, sinking morale, and equipment shortages. Tipped off by Axis decryptions of Fellers' messages, Rommel had less reason to keep Kesselring, Bastico, and Cavallero apprised of his plans for attack. Since Rommel feared Italian leaks, he informed only Gambara—since he supplied trucks and fuel to the Germans—by word of mouth on 19 January that his jump-off date had been set for the 21st.

Because of the ongoing precarious supply line and fuel shortages, Mussolini frowned on the idea of an offensive and sent a directive to hold Tripolitania against a British counterattack.[126] In reading Mussolini's order literally, Bastico, without informing Rommel, promptly halted movement by the Italian infantry with the exception of the *Sabratha* Division. Rommel replied that he meant to attack come what may.

The Italian generals were dogged by the fear that, like Graziani before them, their infantry would be caught in the open by British armor and destroyed, or forced to surrender. Lacking trucks and equipped with obsolete weapons, the Italian troops were easy prey for the pursuing British. In a view shared by Kesselring and Rintelen, Cavallero, given the transport shortage, cautioned against any precipitous advance into Cyrenaica.[127] Rommel, however, was bound

---

125. Montanari, "Dalle battaglie," pp. 134–38.
126. USSME, DS, IV, D. 10, Allegato I: Directive of the Duce, pp. 33–34; *Operazioni*, III: pp. 50–51.
127. *Seconda offensiva britannica*, pp. 32, 42, 49.

to prevail since at any time he could leapfrog the opposition by going directly to Hitler.

On 22 January 1942 "Panzergruppe Afrika" was renamed "Panzerarmee Afrika," consisting of all the Italian troops at the front: XX Corps, *Ariete* armored and *Trieste* motorized; XXI Corps, *Pavia, Trento,* and *Sabratha* infantry; and X Corps, *Bologna* and *Brescia* infantry.

The maverick Rommel was a thorn in the side of the OKW, and his cockiness and daredevil style—for instance, spurring on his troops from a tank cockpit—were beyond the comprehension of the Italian commanders, who sat rooted at desks far from the din of battle. Mussolini told Bottai that, as opposed to "our *pazzo furioso*," he held Rommel in highest esteem as a general who "'throws himself into battle standing upright in his tank. He is a genius.'"[128]

In the final reckoning, Mussolini's 23 January order was anything but categorical, for he had given Rommel's mobile forces license to pursue the enemy within a limited range.[129] It was not difficult for the Desert Fox to reconcile Mussolini's concern about the eastern bastion of Tripolitania with reconnaissance toward Benghazi. The wily German commander was careful not to tell the Duce that he was bound for Tobruk.

While the battle raged in the desert, Göring, during a visit to Rome on 28 January, told Mussolini that Germany was about to wrap up the campaigning against Russia, which left Italy with the unenviable task of "cleansing" the Mediterranean of British warships.[130] Mussolini replied that the battle in Africa had already been won. In a meeting with Rintelen, Göring pushed for an immediate attack on Tobruk, which elicited his observation that Rommel should be braked rather than unleashed. Göring replied that Mussolini would be "reinvigorated by two years if Tobruk was reconquered." In another venue, upon taking his leave of a group of Italians, he shouted at Ciano, "Tobruk!"[131] Annoyed by the servility of Italy's leading military men to this "paunchy individual," Ciano noted: "Following the example of that perfect clown, Cavallero, who would even go so far as to bow to the public lavatories if this would be helpful to him, the three heads of our military staff acted today in the presence of that German as if he were their master."[132]

At the end of January, in a lightning strike Rommel took the Commonwealth forces, which had pooh-poohed the likelihood of an Axis offensive, completely by surprise. Their resistance broke up almost instantly, which left both Italian

---

128. Cited in Bottai, *Diario*, p. 297.
129. *Operazioni*, III: 58.
130. DDI, 9, VIII, 211, Conversation between Mussolini and Goering, 28 January 1942.
131. Rentelen, *Mussolini e l'alleato*, p. 152.
132. *The Ciano Diaries*, 2 February 1942.

and German generals gasping. As Rommel cruised eastward, Bastico had no choice but to release his motorized units. The Axis armies stormed Benghazi on the 29th, capturing large booty from a befogged enemy. Mussolini's permission for advancing on Benghazi reached Rommel as he was riding into the city.[133]

Allowing his troops no respite, Rommel, by 6 February, had cleared the British out of Cyrenaica save the Marmarica district in the east. The Desert Fox displayed masterly generalship against an enemy burdened by poor leadership and overextended lines. With unseemly haste, Bastico hurried to congratulate him for the victory. Rommel was further placated when Mussolini on 14 February finally allowed two infantry divisions to move up for the advance on Tobruk. The Duce, who was given to making invidious comparisons between the audacious German condottiere and his own lackluster generals, would never be bothered by Rommel's deviousness so long as the Wehrmacht won important battles and seemed always to be on the move.[134] Still, under heavy pressure from his own military commanders, Mussolini was not ready to grant Rommel a free hand. The Duce confirmed the importance of holding the current positions at el-Agheila until the Axis armies were fully prepared to resume the initiative, at which time they should push relentlessly on to the Canal.[135] Hitler backed him up by informing Rommel on 17 February that under no circumstances was he to undertake a major effort to reach the Nile.[136]

As the two sides glared at each other across the Gazala Line, which covered the port of Tobruk, the Axis leadership stumbled toward a plan for the invasion of Malta. On 17 March Cavallero told Kesselring that Operation Hercules, the German code word for the Italian 3C, would be ready by the end of July.[137] Kesselring had other ideas. Aware that the German aircraft based on Sardinia would be sent to the Russian front after mid-April, he suggested that he lead a surprise attack (*colpo di mano*) paratroop drop from the air, with large-scale German participation. Since Malta had already been flattened, Kesselring argued, it would be easy for a small landing party to round up the dazed defenders at a cost in resources less dear than a full-fledged amphibious operation.[138]

On the 27th, General Jodl limited the Wehrmacht's contribution to 1-2 paratroop regiments plus torpedo boats and minesweepers. "No army units are available." Without a strong German crutch, Italian hopes sank.[139] Cavallero noted:

---

133. Mellenthin, *Panzer Battles*, p. 91.
134. Ibid., p. 110.
135. Ibid., p. 104.
136. Ibid., p. 110.
137. Cavallero, *Diario*, 17 March 1942.
138. Gabriele, *Operazione C 3: Malta*, pp. 155–59.
139. *Germany in World War II*, III: 658.

"Has the initiative so far given such satisfactory results to allow for a la. one would wish? I doubt it…. Our parachutists are not ready."[140] Sir. would not be set to go till the full moon in July, he told the Germans on 21. March: "One cannot speak of a *colpo di mano*."[141] The naval people were le. sanguine still: no "sudden attack" between 15 April and 15 May; perhaps after 1 August.[142] General Roatta, supported by the Italian naval historian Mariano Gabrielle, depicts this as foot-dragging; in their view a "sudden attack" could have been launched on schedule with a reasonable chance of success.[143]

Although British submarines had taken a heavy toll on Italian shipping, the losses they inflicted did not impede the delivery of a great quantity of supplies. By late March the Italian convoys reached record levels in delivering equipment and armor. The upper hand in the Mediterranean seemed to be passing to the Axis, which held Malta in a vise-like grip. To relieve the beleaguered island, the British undertook a major expedition to replenish dwindling supplies. On 22 March the opposing fleets clashed in the Second Battle of Sirte. Much to the chagrin of Rome and Berlin, whose expectations of a decisive victory were high, a standoff ensued. The British, albeit with great difficulty, still managed to drop anchor at Malta. Following this somewhat inconclusive battle, Admiral Raeder told Hitler that Britain could only be swept from the Mediterranean by the conquest of Malta.[144] On 20 April Axis planes unfurled a punishing attack on Malta that left only seven Spitfires serviceable at the end of the month. Unimpeded from the air, Italian cargo deliveries reached their highest figures for the year in April and May.[145]

Aware that departure of the German aircraft from the Mediterranean was imminent, Mussolini on 11-12 April, in an order reminiscent of Kesselring's "surprise attack," ordained that the invasion of Malta be set for any time after the end of May. On learning that Malta seemed ready for the taking, Cavallero expressed renewed interest in a *colpo di mano*. Such an early date did not trouble General Hermann Ramcke, the German officer who helped in the training of the Italian paratroops.[146]

On 21 April Kesselring communicated to Cavallero at Fiumicino airport that Hitler was in principle favorably disposed to Hercules and would supply gliders, 88 cannon, and tanks—weapons "that can dominate a battlefield."[147] Still, Hitler

---

140. Cavallero, *Diario*, 23 March 1942.
141. Gabriele, *Operazione 3 C: Malta*, pp. 158–61.
142. Ibid., pp. 175–76.
143. Roatta, *Baionette*, p. 210.
144. *Operazioni*, III: 130.
145. *Germany in World War II*, VI: 836.
146. Gabriele, *Operazione C 3: Malta*, p.172.
147. *Operazioni*, III: 131.

...dge a set date in the hope that the air raids in progress
...ond repair. In spite of his inner reservations, he sent
... Rome on 21 April to participate in the invasion
...er judgment, the OKW limped along.[149]

... players assembled at Klessheim castle on the 29th in one of
...,or efforts to work out a common strategy. Cavallero informed Keitel
...at an invasion of Malta "should be undertaken as soon as possible," but under-
lined the need of ample German military hardware and troops: a parachute division, panzers, anti-tank guns, 150 landing craft, 200 Junker transports, 50 gliders,
naval support, 400 tons of fuel oil, and 40,000 tons of gasoline.[150] Keitel gave
Cavallero's demands short shrift and talked up Tobruk.[151] Abruptly Kesselring
abandoned "sudden attack" for "desert offensive."[152] Like Rommel, he argued
that the British should be caught before they received reinforcement, after which
the invasion of Malta "could not go awry."[153] They had all begun to read Hitler's
mind.

In a meeting with Mussolini at Berchtesgaden on 30 April, Hitler stated that
Malta must "be taken from the English" and promised gliders and tanks.[154] In
the next breath he noted that any delay in Libya would allow the enemy to
reinforce its position, ergo, Rommel should be given the go-ahead to attack the
British in late May or early June and seize Tobruk. This spelled death to a "*colpo
di mano*" that in reality he had never seriously considered.

Behind a benevolent façade lay Hitler's belief that the Italians would fumble
an amphibious operation. The Führer unburdened himself in May to General
Student: "With the arrival of the first warnings [that the British were on their
way], everyone [Italians] will turn around, including the navy and transports.
Then you will land alone with your parachutists on the island!"[155] Above all
Hitler had already had his fill of airdrops following the heavy losses incurred on
Crete. In any event his attention was riveted on the pending mammoth offensive
in Russia that would suck up every drop of German oil and consume countless
soldiers and planes, leaving little to spare for a Malta expedition. The Axis should
let the British bleed in defending their island from their attacks.[156]

---

148. *Germany in World War II*, VI: 659.
149. Rintelen, *Mussolini e l'alleato*, p. 156.
150. DDI, 9, VIII, 493, Conversation between Cavallero and Keitel, 29 April 1942; Montanari, "Dalle battaglie," p. 318.
151. Ibid.
152. *Operazioni*, III: 33–34.
153. Kesselring, *Memoirs*, p. 124.
154. DDI, 9, VIII, 495, Conversation between Mussolini and Hitler, 30 April 1942.
155. Cited in *Operazioni*, III: 358.
156. Rintelen, *Mussolini e l'alleato*, p. 157.

Cavallero, deprived of his main pillar of support in Kesselring, was putty in Hitler's hands. Not able to live with improvisation, sudden decisions, and a small invasion force, he needed no persuasion to remand the invasion of Malta to mid-July while Rommel proceeded with his offensive. Gone was Cavallero's preference for a standstill in the desert to avoid further wear and tear on his troops and equipment, and gone was his fear of exposure to dangerous counter-attacks by British armor.[157] Mussolini, forever mesmerized by the Suez Canal, was also easily manipulated. The Führer had worked the room well.

While Hitler ruminated on the Nazi mystique during the lengthy meetings, his listeners struggled to keep awake.[158] "Hitler talks, talks, talks, talks," Ciano recorded. "Mussolini automatically looked at his wrist watch, I had my mind on my own business, and only Cavallero, who is a phenomenon of servility, pretended he was listening in ecstasy, continually nodding his head in approval.... General Jodl, after an epic struggle, finally went to sleep on the divan. Keitel was reeling, but he succeeded in keeping his head up."[159]

During a period of relative calm in May, when Malta received heavy reinforcements of Spitfires (since the German air force was moved to support the land war in North Africa), Rommel struck on the 26th. The Battle of Gazala was joined. Rommel was drawn forward to the attack on Tobruk by intelligence based on Fellers' decrypts that spoke of plummeting British morale and a massive destruction of tanks. The 8th Army seemed on the ropes. These reports were misleading, for that army actually outnumbered the Axis forces in tank strength and had laid out a strong defense in a series of "boxes" surrounded by deep minefields.

Still, Rommel enjoyed important advantages that transcended current battlefield deployments. Germany could bring a tank into the desert in less than a month after leaving its workshop in Europe while the British needed approximately ninety days lead-time. In a heartbeat Axis aircraft could swarm over North Africa.[160] Since Rommel believed that the balance of forces had begun to shift against Germany, he could hear the clock ticking. Summer 1942 was the last chance for victory in North Africa. Rommel counted on his own military genius, the superiority of the German soldier, the panzers, and the 88 anti-tank weapon to carry the day in a Blitzkrieg offensive. His tremendous drive and faith in his ability to surmount the worst odds was infectious. A charismatic motivator, he

---

157. *Seconda controffensiva Italo-Tedesca in Africa Settentrionale da El Agheila a El Alamein, gennaio-settembre 1942* (Rome: SME US, 1951), p. 352.
158. Rintelen, *Mussolini e l'alleato*, p. 157.
159. *The Ciano Diaries*, 30 April 1942.
160. Bocca, *Storia d'Italia nella guerra fascista*, p. 354.

galvanized troops to endure insufferable hardships—anything to earn his approval.

A turning point occurred when the 8th Army launched an attack on 4-5 June against well-prepared Italians supported by powerful anti-tank guns. British tank strength was broken and the Allied offensive waned quickly. Still, there was disarray in the ranks of the Axis armies. Bastico, having no idea of what Rommel was up to, enjoined him not to work his troops to total exhaustion.[161] But there was no letup in the Italian supply service, whose contribution to DAK contributed greatly to the Axis victory at Gazala.[162]

While British troops were floundering in the desert under inexpert leadership enduring assaults by Rommel's units, a large battle took place on the high seas on 14 and 15 June. The British undertook a rescue mission that converged on Malta from two directions. In Operation Harpoon, H Force sallied forth from Gibraltar, while Operation Vigorous sailed from Alexandria. The Italian navy dished out major damage. Only two out of the six convoy ships in Harpoon and two out of the seventeen in Vigorous reached Malta. In addition, German U-boats and the Luftwaffe sank five Royal Navy escort ships. Battered by such severe losses, the British temporarily suspended convoys to Malta.

The battle that raged back and forth in the desert put Cavallero on edge. With the Malta operation having been sidetracked, and exasperated by Rommel's insistent pleas for fuel, he would not suffer further postponement in the invasion date.[163] Admiral Riccardi agreed: "We are not in the position to guarantee a regular provisioning at Tobruk unless we subdue Malta."[164] Planning proceeded apace. General Student would command the parachutists while General Carlo Vecchiarelli would be in charge of the landing troops. The 3C plan was finally falling in place and the troops were ready to go. The invasion force consisting of three army corps and one German airborne unit totaling some 62,000 men; the air wing would deploy 1,506 planes, 666 of which would be German.[165] The Italians involved numbered 100,000, along with 104 tanks, 276 canon 47/32, and 326 artillery pieces.[166] But major glitches remained: a debilitating shortage of fuel for both ships and planes and a dearth of transports and landing gear. There were many naysayers in the Italian military, particularly among those generals who, perhaps influenced by their hatred and fear of Cavallero, did not share his

161. Kitchen, *Rommel's Desert War*, p. 232.
162. Green and Massignani, *The Naval War in the Mediterranean*, p. 160.
163. Cavallero, *Diario*, 10 June; Gabriele, *Operazioni 3 C: Malta*, p. 265.
164. *Operazioni*, III: 320.
165. Gabriele, *3C: Malta*, pp. 203–60; Cavallero, *Diario*, 12 April 1942. According to Green and Massignani, *The Naval War in the Mediterranean*, p. 229, the invasion force consisted of 96,000 men, 754 guns, 850 motocycles, 270 81mm mortars, and 170 tractors for heavy guns.
166. Figures drawn from Battistelli's unpublished manuscript.

"easy enthusiasm" for an attack on Malta.[167] General Giacomo Carboni, a commander of an assault division designated the C3 operations, was convinced that the operation would end in disaster. "Preparations have been childish, equipment is lacking and inadequate."[168] Joint planning with the German ally was not smooth either. The two sides differed over the idea of a glider expedition and the most appropriate places to stage a sea landing.

Riding along with Cavallero, Mussolini informed Hitler by letter on 20 June that the rapid build-up of Spitfires on Malta demanded an invasion without further delay; operations in Marmarica should be deferred till August.[169] But there was the usual catch that the Germans would have to supply 40,000 tons of fuel oil before the Italian navy could weigh anchor and carry over the troops.

The next day the British raised the white flag over Tobruk. In the investment of the port city, the Italian *Ariete* and *Trieste* divisions performed with distinction. The sudden collapse of the citadel and the surrender of 33,000 men erased a symbol of British resistance in the Mediterranean, a humiliation equal to the fall of Singapore on 15 February to a lesser number of Japanese. "Defeat is one thing," commented Churchill; "disgrace is another." The situation on Malta was almost as bad; its governor announced on the radio that edible rations were being cut to four ounces a day.

To give the impression that the capture of Tobruk was primarily an Italian success, Mussolini proclaimed that the English had offered to capitulate to the commandant of the XXI Italian Army Corps. Hitler replied by promoting Rommel to field marshal, which spoke to his belief that Germans, not Italians, had carried the day. In a game of one-upmanship, Mussolini induced the king to grant Cavallero a marshal's baton, then promoted Bastico. Ciano observed: "Bastico's promotion will make people laugh; Cavallero's will make them indignant."[170]

Rommel was hardly humble in victory: "We will not stop until we have destroyed the entire British army. In the next days I will ask you again for great services to enable us to achieve our objectives."[171] He took little notice of logistics and supply, whose resolution, no less important than front-line combat, consisted of grinding tasks tailor-made, in his view, for Italians. The huge haul from Tobruk would provide the wherewithal to finish off the undeniably disorganized, broken, and withdrawing enemy.

---

167. *The Ciano Diaries*, 13 and 31 May 1942.
168. Ibid., 31 May and 20 June 1942.
169. *Germany in the Second World War*, VI: 706.
170. *The Ciano Diaries*, 26 June 1942.
171. *Operazioni*, III: 331.

Rommel's confidence had soared because he held in his hand a slew of Fellers' reports that detailed British recriminations, low morale, crippling losses, and the 8th Army's battle deployment. Fellers' *pièce de résistance*: "If Rommel intends to take the Delta, now is the time." The Desert Fox accepted these reports by an American as unvarnished truth, having no idea that Fellers, who was basically anti-British, was prone to increasingly criticizing the struggling 8th Army and their British commanders. Loftily, Rommel told Bastico: "I know only the supreme directives of the Führer and the directives of the Führer in this case are identical to mine... I am going. If you Italians want to follow us come along; otherwise stop where you are. It makes no difference to me! When all is over, I'll invite you for lunch in Cairo."[172]

At first, it seemed that Rommel stood alone in his desire to reach the Delta. Cavallero wrote on the 22nd, the day after the capture of Tobruk: "It is now indispensable to realize Operation C3."[173] Kesselring, supported by Rintelen and Raeder, expected to activate the invasion of Malta too.[174] There was no time to lose since Malta was slowly getting back on its feet.[175] The Japanese advisors, too, had no trouble in signing off on the invasion plan.[176]

Mussolini saved the day for Rommel by going back on what he had written Hitler on the 20th. Beguiled by the fall of Tobruk, he removed C3 from center stage. In a decrypt of one of Fellers' telegrams, Mussolini read: "The English have been beaten....if Rommel continues his action he has a good chance of getting as far as the Canal Zone." This report induced Mussolini to pursue the attack.[177]

Since Hitler was convinced that his panzers were invincible, he was a setup for Rommel's arguments. Just as the Führer had mesmerized millions of Germans, so he was spellbound by Rommel's dazzling battlefield victories and thus easily gave way when the desert condottiere promised him the Canal. He wrote Mussolini on 23 June: "The English 8th Army is practically destroyed.... If now our forces do not continue to the utmost limit of what is possible into the heart of Egypt itself....the situation will alter for us unfavorably.... This time Egypt can be, under certain conditions, wrenched from England. The consequences of such a strike will be of world importance!.... If, Duce, in this historic hour, which will never be repeated, I can give you some advice straight from my eager heart, it is this: order the continuation of the operation until the complete

172. Ibid.: 360–61.
173. Cavallero, *Diario*, 22 June 1942.
174. Rintelen, *Mussolini e l'alleato*, p. 159.
175. Kesselring, *Memoirs*, p. 128.
176. Gabriele, *Operazioni C 3: Malta*, pp. 428–29.
177. *The Ciano Diaries*, 23 June 1942.

annihilation of the British forces. The Goddess of Fortune passes only once to warriors in battle. Anyone who does not grasp her at that moment can very often never touch her again."[178] With these words, the Führer was preaching to the converted.

Rintelen described Mussolini's reaction to Hitler's letter: "He looked at me with pride and burned passion for an immediate attack against Egypt and the capture of Cairo and Alessandria. The faith in Hitler's strategy remained unchanged."[179] In the Duce's eagerness to take possession of the Suez Canal,[180] Rommel could do no wrong.[181] Cavallero glumly remarked: "The problem of transport is not Rommel's, but ours."[182]

The Axis generals gathered at Derna on 25 June to work on strategy. Cavallero revealed that he could not rest in peace as long as Malta "lived" in the middle of the Mediterranean,[183] while Kesselring lectured the assembled generals on the perils of any precipitous move on the Canal.[184] But since Mussolini and Hitler had imbibed Rommel's heady brew, Cavallero retreated to Kesselring's fallback position. El Alamein should be taken, followed by a fresh look at Operation Hercules, before allowing the Desert Fox to proceed toward the Delta.[185] Rommel strove to placate the Italians by promising them not to incorporate their infantry in his advance.[186]

The more Rommel was bewitched by conquest, the more he succumbed to hubris, which inured him to danger and the pain of his troops: "I have little fuel and very little water, but in this climate of success my soldiers don't ask to drink and not even to eat. They solely want to advance.... The ultimate objective is the Nile—to capture Alexandria and reach Cairo."[187] Rommel had words for the spiritless Cavallero: "For now I will arrive at el-Alamein, but there are other objectives: Alexandria, Cairo, and the Nile. If the army succeeds in overcoming the obstacle of el-Alamein, on what I believe will be 30 June (that is, as Montanari notes, four days later!), I will be in Cairo.... I will wait for you there. Then we will be able to speak at our leisure."[188]

Sensing victory and dreaming of a march of conquerors down the boulevards of Cairo, Mussolini departed for Libya on 29 June. Two hundred drums of

---

178. *Operazioni*, III: 359–60.
179. Rintelen, *Mussolini e l'alleato*, p. 160.
180. *Seconda controffensiva*, p. 151 and Allegato n. 48.
181. *The Ciano Diaries*, 22 June 1942.
182. Cavellero, *Diario*, 23 June 1942; Gabriele, *L'operazione 3 C: Malta*, p. 272.
183. Cavellero, *Diario*, 25 June 1942; Montanari, "Dalle battaglie," p. 322.
184. *Seconda controffensiva*, pp. 141, 149; De Felice, *Mussolini l'alleato*, I: 651.
185. *Operazioni*, III: 371–72.
186. *Seconda controffensiva*, p. 151.
187. *Operazioni*, III: 375.
188. Cited in Montanari, "Dalle battaglie," p. 323.

black shoe polish were brought along to burnish the boots of the Italian soldiery for the occasion.[189] Mussolini's entourage took up twelve planeloads that included his clerical staff and cook. His barber was unfortunately killed in a plane crash.[190]

At Berta, where Mussolini stayed, he set about the creation of an Arab legion to further his popularity among the Egyptian people. He predicted that they would shout "Avanti Rommel" in the hope that the Axis armies would finally free them from the yoke of British imperialism. Panicked by the Axis advance, the British burned documents and prepared to evacuate citizens and their Arab supporters to the Sudan.[191]

If the Italians had ever reached the Delta, they would have encountered difficulties from the Egyptian government in Cairo, for the wire pullers of British imperialism had done their work well. In February 1942 they had choreographed a coup by forcing King Farouk, who secretly favored the Axis, to replace the incompetent cabinet staffed with a claque of pashas by one filled with the Wafd party, which enjoyed a certain popular support. This was a shrewd move, for the party had favored a treaty with Britain in 1936 and was therefore basically anti-Italian. Disconcerted by this changing of the guard, the Italians put pressure on Berlin to join them in taking a position against the Wafd, but did not meet with much success. Still, the Germans made concessions by agreeing to support two archetypal Italian slogans: "The Mediterranean Sea for the Mediterranean peoples" and "Egypt for the Egyptians."

On 3 July Mussolini issued a declaration promising that Egypt, once "liberated from the fetters shackling her to Great Britain," would take its place among the independent and sovereign nations of the Mediterranean world. By this ploy the Italians hoped to stimulate a rebellion in Cairo against British rule as the Axis armies pounded eastward. To prevent the Germans from fleecing the Egyptian peoples beyond requisitions needed to provision troops, the Italians urged Berlin to participate in an Axis commission as a hedge against the kind of economic ruin brought about by the despoliation of Greece.

Mussolini roughed out plans for governing Egypt without discussion with Berlin. Rommel would be the military commander-in-chief in tandem with an Italian civilian high commissioner, Minister Plenipotentiary Serafino Mazzolini, serving as the Axis political delegate. Ciano believed that this proposal ceded Rommel too much power.[192] But Mussolini was prepared: if the Desert Fox were

---

189. John Bierman and Colin Smith, *War without Hate: The Desert Campaign of 1940–1943* (New York: Penguin Books, 2004), p. 200.

190. Paolo Monelli, *Mussolini an Intimate Life* (London: Thomas and Hudson, 1953), pp. 9–10.

191. Anwar Sadat, *In Search of an Identity* (Glasgow: Collins, 1978), p. 46.

192. *The Ciano Diaries*, 2 July 1942.

to emulate a conqueror atop his tank turret, he would pose as Napoleon mounted on his white charger.

Mussolini paid one visit to Tobruk accompanied by Rintelen, but Rommel never invited him to his headquarters at the front 800 kilometers away. Nor would Rommel come to Berta to pay his respects to Mussolini. Pietromarchi noted: "The Duce will not forgive him [Rommel] for having drawn him to Libya giving the assurance that the troops would shortly enter Alexandria. Instead, not only was there the lack of success, but Rommel, scandalously, refused to meet with the Duce…. Rommel [it was said] did not want to meet him because 'he [Rommel] was making war and not cinematography'…. For a man like the Duce, who has put into play his popularity, the regime, and the future of the country on the alliance with Germany, the humiliation could not have been greater."[193]

After the panzers roared to the outskirts of El Alamein on 30 June, Cavallero on 7 July quietly took Malta off the table and the expeditionary force was broken up.[194] Operation C3 was replaced by C4, the occupation of Tunisia, possibly combined with a seizure of Corsica and a move beyond the Italian bridgehead in France. With the conquest of Malta fading from view, use of Tunisian ports loomed of vital importance as supply depots for the Axis troops. Far ahead of the Germans in anticipating an Allied landing in French North Africa, Cavallero was hoping that Mussolini would divert forces destined for the Russian front to Tunisia.[195] But to no avail. Pressed by stiff Soviet resistance on the Eastern Front, Hitler wanted no flare-up with the French caused by precipitous Italian action vis-à-vis Tunisian ports. Although longing to punch out France once and for all, Mussolini, lacking the resources to swoop down on Tunisia on his own, bent to Hitler's will. The Italian troops assembling for the long trip to Russia left on schedule.

Instead of a month crowned by Axis conquest, July recorded serious reverses during this first battle of Al Alamein. As Kesselring had anticipated, Rommel had outrun his air support and pushed his troops to exhaustion. He lost sight of the pursued when the Fellers' reports dried up on 29 June. Instead of collapsing, as foretold by Fellers, the British scrambled together reinforcements from throughout the Middle East. They waited for Rommel behind an imposing array of barbed wire fencing and minefields protected by swarms of newly arrived aircraft.

The Italians in particular suffered from Rommel's impetuosity and lack of adequate preparation. Their infantry, especially the raw troops thrown into

---

193. PP, *Diario*, 6 February 1943.
194. *Operazioni*, III: 850
195. *The Ciano Diaries*, 7 July 1942.

battle, were targets of attacks on the part of the enemy that stayed away from German armor. The *Ariete* was severely battered and barely hung together, but received no sympathy from Rommel.[196] On 10 July the newly arrived *Sabratha* Infantry Division buckled under an intense barrage, lost artillery, and melted into captivity. The turn of the *Bersaglieri* and *Trieste* came next, overrun during nighttime fighting. With the help of Ultra, New Zealand and Indian units on 15 July virtually destroyed *Brescia* and *Pavia,* which belonged to the Italian X Corps. Worn down by ceaseless fighting and constant movement, Rommel's panzers took a bad beating too. In combat that was often messy, confused, and seemingly random, Rommel devised new tactics whereby German infantry were interspersed among Italian formations to hold them together.

The British were assisted greatly by the capture of Rommel's radio intercept unit, which denied him his main sources of signals intelligence on Allied strengths, dispositions and intentions. Having already been deprived of the reports of General Fellers at the end of June, Rommel was thrown back completely on his own devices.

Rommel did not hesitate to protect himself by foisting blame on others. As for supplies, he melodramatically chastised Rintelen for failing to stand up for Germany against "devious" Italians who sent over shabbily outfitted units.[197] Worse still, the Italian troops had "several times lately....deserted their positions under the effect of artillery fire"; their officers had not persuaded them "to stand up to the enemy." And the British were quick to exploit this weakness. Italian officers should have been "summarily and with the utmost severity" urged to bring any soldier who "cravenly deserted the battlefield without fighting" before Italian court martial. Rommel wound up by saying that the Italians should not "shrink from [imposing] the death penalty."[198]

In messages to the OKH, Bastico took exception to Rommel's constant complaints about the performance of the Italian troops. His men were utterly exhausted by unceasing orders to attack without regard to troop and equipment replenishment.[199] This time Mussolini backed up his general. After reading Rommel's report on the retreat of the *Sabratha* on 10 July, he vowed never to forgive his former idol.[200] In quite a different mode Mussolini apologized to Hitler over the lamentable performance of his troops. But he did point out that

196. Rommel unfairly commented: "The battle worthiness of the Italian troops is so insignificant that on 3 July 360 men from the Ariete Division surrendered to a small number of tanks, without offering the slightest resistance." Cited in Kitchen, *Rommel's Desert War*, p. 262.

197. Ibid., p. 294.

198. *Germany in World War II*, VI: 746.

199. Kitchen, *Rommel's Desert War*. p. 267.

200. *The Ciano Diaries*, 22 July 1942.

the Italian infantry had been in action for 30–40 months; they had "marched hundreds of kilometers through the desert, always on foot" in the hottest of summer temperatures.[201]

The strain of battle, the numbing fear of running out of fuel, and the arrival of American tanks that pointed to overwhelming Allied superiority gave Rommel pause. Was the tide of battle turning against the Axis? In mid-July, he made oblique reference to this idea with Cavallero and Bastico. Owing to mounting enemy strength, Rommel told them, he should think of abandoning positions at El Alamein in order to conduct an orderly retreat toward the Libyan frontier, bringing him in closer proximity to his supply depots.[202] Kesselring perceived danger in retreat for imperiling Axis aviation located in forward camps. Cavallero agreed, noting that reinforcements were already on the way to brace up Rommel's existing defenses. In fact, three groups of artillery arrived on the 18th with more still to come, while the *Folgore* and units of the *Giovani Fascisti* were on schedule to arrive imminently.[203] Limited German reinforcements were preparing to disembark too. Buoyed by this news, Mussolini stepped in to disrupt any thought of retreat with a directive issued on 19 July: "The battle of Tobruk is over; tomorrow's battle will be for the Delta." The present line should be held as a jumping-off position for an impending future attack; there would be no other option.[204]

After waiting three weeks in vain for the decisive blow, Mussolini returned to Rome on 20 July. Still, as Ciano notes, he was upbeat: "He is so certain of it [the decisive blow] that he has left his personal baggage in Libya as guarantee of a quick return."[205] A nasty tongue wagged: "Mussolini left in his baggage the sword of Islam that he intends to grasp for the victory march in Cairo."[206] But Mussolini was indignant that his generals should have repeated their Albanian blunder of 1941 by summoning him to celebrate a victory before it was won.

The CS supported Mussolini's endeavor of putting to rest Rommel's *tendenza al ripiegamento*; the troops would stand firm come what may.[207] In a dramatic role reversal, the usually stolid Bastico replied that he would not budge from his fixed positions. For his part, Cavallero expressed himself ready to combat "the momentary depression" enveloping Rommel's headquarters.[208]

201. DDI, 9, IX, 4, Mussolini to Hitler, 22 July 1942.
202. Cavallero, *Diario*, 22 July 1942; *Germany in the Second World War*, VI: 747.
203. *Seconda controffensiva*, pp. 187–88.
204. *Operazioni*, III, Allegato 27, Mussolini's considerations on the military situation, pp. 952–53.
205. *The Ciano Diaries*, 21 July 1942.
206. Bocca, *Storia d'Italia nella guerra fascista*, p. 365.
207. *Operazioni*, III: 858.
208. Cavallero, *Diario*, 22 and 27 July 1942; *Germany in the Second World War*, VI: 747.

To clip Rommel's wings, Cavallero implemented a reorganization plan first outlined on 24 May. The new "Order of Battle" stipulated that the Libyan command would be detached from the Egyptian theater. Bastico, who held the position of superior command armed forces in North Africa (Comando Superiore della Forze Armate of Africa settentionale italiana), was given a new title as commander of the armed forces, confined to Libya. For all other matters—logistical and administrative duties in Libya—the Italian troops were placed under the delegation of the supreme command in North Africa (Delegazione del Comando Supremo in Africa Settentrionale—DELEASE) under Bastico. The Panzer Army Africa (designated on 18 September the Armata Corazzata Italo-Tedesca ACIT) under Rommel's command passed directly to the CS, which assumed direction of field operations.

Rommel was not displeased by these changes. As commander of the Panzer Army Africa, he no longer had to answer to General Bastico in Egypt, only to the far-off CS in Rome whose directives he was used to flouting. Bastico's sway as the commander-in-chief of the armed forces of Libya (Comando Superiore FF. AA della Libia—Superlibia) was limited to that territory. These changes neither streamlined the chain of command nor facilitated Axis cooperation. The continued lack of a unified authority in the African theater allowed interferences, lacunae, and confusion to remain the order of the day.[209] Cavallero acidly commented: "That's it for Bastico,"[210] while Rommel, fighting in Egypt, was glad to see the Italian commander shackled.

Pressured by Kesselring, Rommel dutifully renewed preparations to attack the Commonwealth forces before they could build up a crushing superiority of men and weapons. Mussolini gave his approval to Cavallero for an offensive set for the 30th.[211] But there were problems. Supplies and equipment piled up in Italian ports awaiting shipment; whatever cargo arrived safely docked at congested ports; and trucks burnt up much precious fuel on the long and lonely trip eastward in barren desert to the El Alamein front.

In spite of Rommel's complaints, the Italians satisfied many of his demands, particularly in tanks and ammunition. The Luftwaffe, too, flew in reinforcements. When added to the captured equipment taken at Tobruk, Rommel had supplies with which to get by, if barely, with one notable exception—fuel.

In playing down problems, musing on defense, and talking up Alexandria, Cairo, and the Suez Canal at the same time, Cavallero was all things to all

---

209. *Terza offensiva britannica in Africa* (Rome: SME US, 1961), pp. 14–15.
210. Cited in *Germany in the Second World War*, VI: 747, n. 125.
211. Kitchen, *Rommel's Desert War*, p. 196.

people.[212] But in his defense, he could contrive no plausible solution, for there was none. It was beyond Italy's power to overcome the nagging fuel shortages and clogged ports to ease Rommel's logistical problems or reverse the odds stacked against the Axis armies no matter how heroically Italian seamen and troops put their shoulders to the wheel in provisioning the troops under Rommel's command. Kesselring tried to intensify Axis bombardment of Malta but had not nearly enough aircraft to slow down British attacks on Axis convoys. As luck and bad timing would have it, on 27 and 28 August the enemy was able to sink three Italian submarines bearing 730 tons of fuel and 170 vehicles.[213] On the night of 3 September, unchallenged British planes and submarines sent three more fuel-bearing ships to the bottom of the sea. Ultra came into great use in tracking down and sinking unescorted Italian tankers.

The Desert Fox clearly saw the writing on the wall. Since his campaign coincided with the launching of the German drive on the Russian Caucasian oilfields, he stood little chance of obtaining much-needed reinforcements. Haunted by defeat, he knew there was no turning back. The decision to attack was, Rommel averred, the hardest he had ever taken. "Either we succeed in pushing forward to Grozny and, here in Africa, in reaching the Suez Canal, or...and he made a dismissive gesture."[214] Running on adrenalin alone could not sustain him against an enemy vastly replenished by American supplies: 300 tanks and 100 self-propelled guns. In mid-August British strength was greatly enhanced owing to the success of Operation Pedestal that shipped in much needed aviation fuel and supplies. The Royal Navy had put Malta back on its feet. Newly arrived planes proceeded to pound Axis convoys and troops in the field. But the cost to the Royal Navy was dear. As one recent writer noted, "The Pedestal battle was the largest aero-naval victory won by Axis forces during the Mediterranean war," Italian ships having inflicted the bulk of the damage.[215]

On the morning of 30 August, Rommel unleashed what was to be his last Egyptian offensive at Alam Halfa, the second battle of El Alamein. Tracked by Ultra, Rommel's "surge" in the summer heat, after initially breaching the enemy line, was checked by lack of fuel, massed British armor, a huge array of mine fields, and Allied air superiority. The great number of tankers that were sunk destroyed Rommel's objective of breaking through to the Nile. After his offensive stalled, he conducted a masterly withdrawal, preserved a coherent front, and kept his forces largely intact.

---

212. Cavallero, *Diario*, entries for August, and *Germany in the Second World War*, VI: 750.
213. *Seconda controffensiva*, p. 232.
214. *Germany in the Second World War*, VI: 755.
215. O'Hara, *Struggle for the Middle Sea*, p. 185.

Before leaving for Europe to consult with Mussolini and Hitler, Rommel told the Italian command on 22 September: "Capital importance lies in the mastery of the Mediterranean. At this point the army has not received enough on which to live. We are all animated to proceed toward Egypt, but at this time we cannot risk a new offensive... For now we will hold the line."[216]

This is not what the Italians wanted to hear. They contended that Rommel suffered from a loss of nerve, overestimated his fuel shortages, exaggerated the enemy's offensive ability, and blamed them unfairly for the breakdown in supply; they interpreted his orders to dig in as a loss of faith in reaching the Canal, which was deadly to the morale of the Italian troops.[217] Their expectation had been that Rommel would pull himself together to throw the 8th Army aside and resume the advance toward the Canal.[218] This was a pipe dream, for by this time British general Bernard Montgomery had amassed a crushing superiority in weaponry. Admiral Weichold on 15 October made the realistic assessment that the obstacles put up by the British to prevent Italy from ferrying supplies across the Mediterranean had the makings of a catastrophe in North Africa.[219]

Finally, on 24 September 1942 Mussolini began to face reality. He told a haggard Rommel: "We have temporarily lost the battle in the Mediterranean. Italy no longer possessed sufficient shipping space," and, during the next year, "a landing in North Africa by the United States must be expected."[220] No matter what the obstacles were, he urged Rommel to capture the Nile Delta before the Americans arrived.[221] While Bottai noted that Mussolini appeared "tired, mortified, wilted," the Duce observed that Rommel was "physically and morally shaken."[222]

The summer had produced quite a turnabout. In June both Germans and Italians had listened rapturously as Rommel preached an onward push by the Axis forces to the Delta. Now, surrounded by his own converts, Rommel was faced with a tough sell in seeking retreat. His brusque manner, tactless behavior, and obvious impatience with the Italians had cost him plenty. And many were disillusioned with him. For Cavallero, he was an alarmist, for Kesselring, a pessimist, for Göring, a defeatist, for Barbasetti, uncommunicative, for Bastico, arrogant. Nobody wanted to hear him out, least of all Hitler, who was opposed to any voluntary abandonment of conquered territory, as was Mussolini, who, in

216. *Operazioni*, III, Allegato 38, Rommel report, pp. 977–79.
217. *Seconda controffensiva*, pp. 250–51.
218. *Operazioni*, III: 859.
219. *La terza offensiva britannica*, pp. 30–31.
220. Cited in *Germany in World War II*, p. 766, n. 235; *La terza offensiva britannica*, p. 21; Cavallero, *Diario*, 24 September 1942.
221. Kitchen, *Rommel's Desert War*, p. 313.
222. *The Ciano Diaries*, 27 September 1942.

any case, dared not override the Führer's will. Ignoring the facts on the ground—that 80,000 Axis troops faced 230,000 soldiers under British command—Mussolini counted on a miracle in Egypt to salvage his reputation, while Cavallero, as usual when pondering attack or retreat, wavered between "'yes' and 'no.'"[223] In advocating retreat, Rommel was right.

On the eve of General Montgomery's great offensive, the third battle of El Alamein, Mussolini admitted: "You know, everything considered, I have arrived at the conclusion that instead of advancing on Marsa Matruh it would have been better to undertake the operation on Malta."[224] On 1 October he excused Berlin of any bad faith for failure in carrying out what they had promised.[225] But in captivity, in August 1943, Mussolini would say: "The wheel of fortune....turned on 28 June 1942, when we halted before El Alamein.... The Germans have never grasped the importance of the Mediterranean, never."[226] Rommel would have heartily agreed.

A Last Look at Malta

General Cavallero, who originally conceived the idea of the 3C operation, was not a man who commanded respect or inspired confidence. Though an exemplar of procrastination, he liked to give the impression that he was straining at the leash to implement 3C, which, against the received opinion, would be the crowning achievement of his career. If Cavallero had once warmed up to Kesselring's "sudden attack" against Malta in April, and favored an invasion in June, he shed only crocodile tears when Rommel headed for the Canal, which spelled the demise of 3C. "As is his nature," noted Ciano, "he digs himself in behind a great quantity of ifs and buts."[227] General Rino Corso Fougier remarked that he was "a dangerous clown, ready to follow every German whim without dignity."[228]

Did the Axis miss a golden opportunity by failing to seize Malta? Kesselring, supported by the naval historians Jack Green and Alessandro Massignani, thought that the starving island would most likely have put up twenty-four hours of resistance and then surrendered.[229] They argue that the invasion forces, consisting of 96,000 men, 754 guns, and 850 motorcycles, would have overwhelmed

---

223. Ibid., 31 August 1942.
224. Cavallero, *Diario*, 20 October 1942.
225. *Terza offensiva britannica*, p. 36.
226. Benito Mussolini, *Memoirs 1942–1943 with documents relating to the period* (London: Weidenfeld and Nicolson, 1949), p. 220.
227. *The Ciano Diaries*, 28 April 1942.
228. Ibid., 16 May 1942.
229. Green and Massignani, *The Naval War in the Mediterranean*, p. 230.

the scattered half-starved British and Maltese defenders opposing them.[230] An American expert on Italian military affairs, Brian Sullivan, suggests that Italian central Mediterranean naval superiority in mid-1942, Malta's starvation for fuel and food, and the good training of the invasion forces augured well for success.[231] But the rocky nature of the island rendered invasion chancy. British historian Martin Kitchen points out that in spite of the heavy bombing, Malta's infrastructure was virtually unharmed. Power plants, communications, hangars and workshops had been dug deep underground where they could escape damage.[232]

If the Axis powers had been able to capture Malta, they would have reduced British submarine attacks and air firepower. Furthermore, the burden of the Axis forces to protect convoys would have been considerably eased. But Malta's aerial threat to Axis North Africa, which was limited to the central Mediterranean, left out of account enemy submarines and planes utilizing depots and ports in Egypt and the Middle East. Therefore Axis occupation of Malta would have relieved but not resolved the supply problem.

If 3C had been undertaken, Rommel would have been the biggest immediate loser. Stripped of vital air cover provided by planes shifted to Malta, his forces would have been left at the mercy of a rapidly reinforced RAF, backed up by American long-range bombers. Any delay would have cost him dearly, for the British would have used the breathing room to reinforce their pummeled troops for a powerful stand at Alam Halfa rather than at El Alamein.

In advocating an amphibious landing in Malta, the Italians had only themselves to blame for failing to bring it off owing to a decade of neglect. In the years leading up to the war, there was no study or preparation for the conquest of Malta, which closed off the possibility of a swift attack in April or June 1942 when the British were decidedly under-strength.[233]

In late 1941, when 3C was conceived, the Italians were forced to start from scratch. MacGregor Knox delivers a scathing critique of the Italian invasion potential: "The navy's landing flotilla was a bizarre patchwork of minesweepers, small merchant ships and tankers, tugs, self-propelled barges, armored motor launches, motor sailors, and ferries from as far away as Venice. Experience was lacking to handle the inevitable complexity of an amphibious landing, extensive night movement under radio silence, coordination and support of two main landing sites and several subsidiary ones. The likelihood that the air forces would

230. Ibid., p. 229.
231. Brian R. Sullivan, "The German-Italian Alliance, 1939–1943," in *Hitler and His Allies in World War II*, Jonathan R. Adelman, ed. (New York and London: Routledge, 2007), p. 133.
232. Kitchen, *Rommel's Desert War*, p. 205.
233. Montanari, "Dalle battaglie," p. 319.

deliver the paratroops far from their designated drop zones, the pervasiveness and strength of the British fortifications, and the central uncertainty about the reaction of the British Gibraltar squadron, suggest an Axis Dieppe in the making."[234]

Desert Battlefield Performance

By 1942, in view of German dominance on the North African battlefield, the Italians could no longer pretend that they were fighting a "parallel" war. Still, out of pride and dumb persistence, they contrived to uphold the centrality of the CS in battlefield strategy. Hitler played along with this ruse since he wanted to salve Italian pride to keep his ally in the war. But no one could doubt that in North Africa the Germans were in charge. The Italians served as grumpy chauffeurs of the Axis war chariot while Kesselring and Rommel barked directions.

As in the first phase of battle under Graziani, the Italian troops on the whole consisted of infantry that suffered from the usual chronic problems growing out of Mussolini's frivolous war preparations and a modernity-fearful general staff. There were many intractable problems, notably, a superannuated officer corps and commanders inexpert in conducting mobile warfare. The troops possessed only a handful of armor-piercing weapons and lived on insufficient rations. Field kitchens were practically non-existent. Freshly arrived troops were thrown into battle and rarely rotated for rest and rehabilitation. When trapped in hot sands with no hope of reinforcement or rescue, the soldiers' only option frequently was surrender to avoid dehydration and certain death.

The organization of the Italian support services (Intendenza) left much to be desired. A quartermaster general well behind the lines allocated equipment and supplies down to the last bullet at his own pace. Neither regiments, nor divisions, nor army corps had logistical units of their own. Few stocks could be built up at the front since the Intendenza was supposed to offer its warriors a daily ration. The strict and undependable supply regimen condemned the frontline soldiers to fixed positions, for any movement might interrupt the flow of ammunition, food, and water.[235] Presiding over such an unwieldy and inflexible logistical system, the CS was understandably loath to allow Rommel to move the Italian infantry and its Intendenza backward more than a few paces at a time.

---

234. MacGregor Knox, *Hitler's Italian Allies: Royal Armed Forces, Fascist Regime, and the War of 1940–1943* (Cambridge: Cambridge University Press, 2000), p. 136.
235. Knox, *Hitler's Italian Allies*, p. 127.

Finally, the Italian command was not unaware of shortcomings. Following the July disasters, General Benvenuto Gioda wrote division commanders that the behavior of the troops had cast discredit on the pride of the army, citing the scarce will to defend tenaciously when under heavy fire and an excessive readiness to throw down arms and surrender. Those responsible for poor performance, he suggested, should be referred to the War Tribunal.[236] Was his a lonely voice, or did his fellow commanders, who were well aware of the many shortcomings, join together by observing an *omertà* to avoid criticism and disgrace?

No question, the caliber of the Italian high command in North Africa was mediocre by any standard. Political connections affected promotions and the generals lacked imagination. Better as a staff officer than field commander, Bastico owed his position to Ciano. His philosophy was spelled out in 1937: "The tank is a powerful tool but let us not idolize it; let us reserve our reverence for the infantryman and the mule."[237] Bastico continued to regard Germans scurrying about the battlefield as undignified and productive of "excesses the consequences of which I believe [Rommel] himself does not understand."[238] Not a few Italian officers criticized Bastico and his successor Barbasetti of the great distance they kept between themselves and the front. This gave the impression that as absentees from battle they had forfeited the conduct of operations to Rommel.[239]

In spite of all the disadvantages and shortcomings, the Italian troops in this phase of the campaign began to surmount the harsh memories of defeat and humiliation suffered by Graziani at the hands of the British in the first year of desert warfare. Although they still continued to arrive in North Africa sketchily prepared, the most blatant failings were slowly overcome by tough training in pauses on the battlefield. Some Italian commanders turned out to be forward-looking taskmasters who could rally morale and instill discipline.[240] As they picked up experience, the troops gained greater confidence and elasticity of movement. Occasionally they achieved a workable coordination between infantry, artillery, and armored vehicles. The Italian artillerymen, though largely equipped with captured Austrian models and their own World War I leftovers,

---

236. *Operazioni*, III, Allegato 26, Commanding General Benvenuto Gioda to the command of the X Army Corps, pp. 950–51.
237. Cited in Knox, *Hitler's Italian Allies*, p. 55. However, as Brian Sullivan reminds us, Bastico was one of the few Italian generals who understood the necessity for vigorous and effective instruction. See his "The Italian Soldier in Combat, June 1940–September 1943: Myths, Realities and Explanations," in Paul Addison and Angus Cronin eds. *Time to Kill: The Soldiers Experience of War in the West 1939–1945* (London: Pimlico Press, 1997), p. 192.
238. Cited in Knox, *Hitler's Italian Allies*, p. 116.
239. *Operazioni*, III: 875.
240. Rochat, *Le guerre italiane*, p. 351.

fought with great tenacity, and not a few died on their guns. Doubtless the Italians learned much from the exacting standard of panzer battlefield expertise. But if the Wehrmacht won most of the laurels, Rommel could not have done anything without the *regio esercito* at his shoulder and in the rear zones managing the supply lines.

The *Ariete* was the pride of Italian armor. Still, the M13/40 tank that provided its backbone was mediocre and obsolete on arrival. Its successor, the P40 heavy tank equipped with a 75mm gun, only emerged from the blueprints shortly before Italy's war was over. Slow, underpowered, poorly protected and armed with a 47mm gun, the M13 "steel coffin" was regularly outgunned by the 75mm-equipped Grant and Sherman tanks that the British proceeded to put into the field in ever larger numbers. The *Ariete* eventually replied with improved anti-tank guns and the self-propelled 75/18-assault canon that provided greater firepower but was poorly armored. Another tank force, the *Littorio*, joined the *Ariete* in midyear 1942, taking part in the hectic pursuit to El Alamein.

Despite what Bastico rightly described as the "brutal qualitative and quantitative inferiority" of its equipment, the *Ariete* learned important lessons. It developed an imperfect ability to move at night, find and attack enemy flanks, and use deception by feinting withdrawal. The commander of the *Ariete* in its final desperate stand at El Alamein could plausibly claim that Italian artillery, with its emphasis on centralized direction, had cooperated with other branches more effectively than had the decentralized German gunners.[241]

The *Folgore* stands out as an elite paratroop unit that exuded a high esprit de corps and camaraderie between ranks born from a shared life in the trenches and mess halls. Officers were expected to lead out in front. As one *Folgore* recruit noted: "If we have to jump off a four meter wall, the senior ranks jump first, and then we jump."[242] All were volunteers. After the invasion of Malta had been postponed indefinitely, it was sent to the El Alamein front in July. Although out of place serving as lightly armed infantry in the desert, the *Folgore* earned the enemy's respect for its thorough training and bravery. Inculcated with shock trooper spirit, the division staged several successful lightning strikes before being destroyed by overwhelming enemy armor.

The much-maligned Italian navy actually made a substantial contribution in upholding the African maritime supply-line. Convoy protection, to which the heaviest warships were also assigned, became the Italian navy's principal function as time went by. Many ships were lost to British submarines, which were

---

241. Knox, *Common Destiny*, p. 178; NAW, T-821, 31, 000008, Generale Francesco Antonio Arena, 13 December 1942.
242. Cited in Knox, *Common Destiny*, p. 173.

irregularly aided by Ultra. Between June 1940 and January 1943 the shipments that reached Africa safely amounted to 80 percent of vehicles, 88 percent of weapons and equipment, 81 percent of the other dry cargo, and 82 percent of the fuel.[243] From December 1941 to July 1942, only 7% cargo and 4% fuel oil were lost. Troops were mainly carried over by air.

General Rommel repeatedly claimed that many Italian navy officers committed sabotage.[244] By this irresponsible charge he overlooked the complicated nature of the supply system, the hard work expended by Italian seamen, and the patent reality that in the matter of planning sea traffic Kesselring sat with Admiral Arturo Riccardi on a high-level Axis commission that met almost daily. The historians Martin Creveld and John Ellis argue that Rommel's supply problems were due less to convoy losses at sea and fuel shortages for ships than to limited discharging capacity of the North African ports and the difficulty of transporting supplies overland. Far more than Malta-based air and sea interdiction, Rommel's defeat was caused by a general shortage of trucks, sporadic coastal shipping, a lack of fuel, and wear-and-tear on vehicles and drivers forced to cover long distances between the ports and the front lines along the Via Balbia.[245]

Moreover, insufficient cargo space made worse by an increasingly reduced number of serviceable transport ships multiplied breakdowns. Vast quantities of supplies destined for North Africa therefore piled up in Italian ports, never to be ferried across to Libya.[246] But since the overwhelming majority of maritime shipments sent from Italy actually reached North Africa, neither the losses the Axis incurred in the convoy battles fought out in the central Mediterranean, nor the survival of Malta, sealed the fate of the Axis powers. The growing power of the 8th Army did.

---

243. *Germany and the Second World War*, VI: 838.
244. This is a common thread running through Rommel's memoirs.
245. Martin Creveld, *Supplying War: Logistics from Wallenstein to Partition* (Cambridge: Cambridge University Press, 2007), p. 186.
246. *Germany in the Second World War*, VI: 838–39.

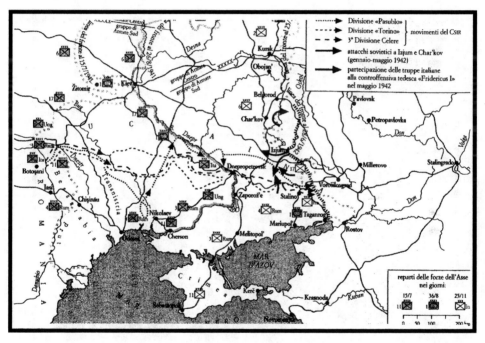

Initial Italian operations in Russia by the CSIR August 1941 - Spring 1942.

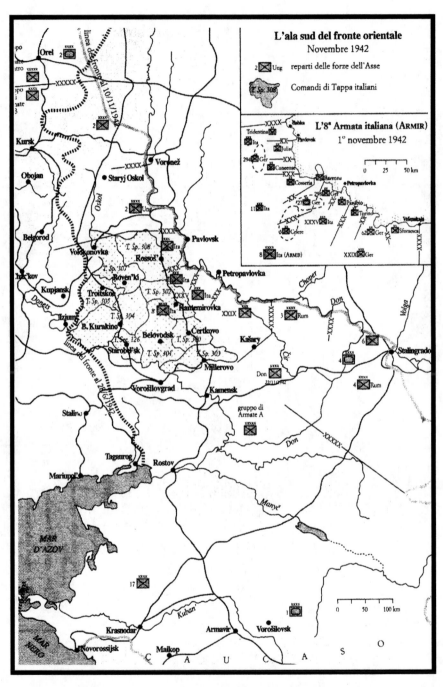

Positions held by the Italian Eighth Army ARMIR in November 1942 near Stalingrad.

Chapter VII

Counterinsurgency in the Balkans

Carnage in Yugoslavia
"Model" Fascist Rule in Albania
Messy Occupation of Greece

Carnage in Yugoslavia

At the outset of the Italian occupation of Yugoslavia, the troops filed into the country expecting easy duty in comfortable barracks and plenty of time off for merriment in cafes and drinking haunts. But in July 1941 their leisure was brought to an end by outbreaks of insurgency. Under the leadership of Josip Broz Tito, Communist partisans struck unprepared and bewildered troops by use of unorthodox guerrilla tactics—his guerrilla attacks coinciding with the German invasion of the USSR. Dispersed throughout the countryside in isolated pockets, the Italians were killed singly and in groups. Without the benefit of effective reconnaissance, their regiments, trained for conventional warfare, frequently fought ghost battles. When confronted by superior numbers or firepower, the guerrillas took to the hills or retreated to their villages, hid their weapons, and blended in with civilians till the occupying forces left for their barracks. On 6 January 1942 Ciano noted: "Our public relations officer with the second army in Croatia sends bad news on the situation and on the morale of the troops. Some units permitted them-selves to be captured without firing a shot."[1]

On an inspection tour, just before taking charge of the 2nd Army on 19 January 1942, General Mario Roatta was appalled by Italy's untidy occupa-tion in Yugoslavia. Feuds between Italian civilian authorities and 2nd Army commanders were raging without letup in Slovenia and Dalmatia. In Croatia a hodge-podge of ethnic groups and diverse religions defied uniform treat-ment. Ustaša violence and the NDH authorities obstructed the 2nd Army at every turn. An endless train of representatives from Rome, Berlin, and Zagreb crowded into army headquarters at Sušak dispensing advice, lodging complaints, and competing for power and influence.

Nor did order prevail in the strictly military spheres. Troops huddled in forts in the craggy mountains of the Lika region were under siege by partisan forces; Tito was roaming freely in eastern Bosnia; the Italian army had un-leashed a major crackdown in Ljubljana against dissenters to Italian rule; and no one could predict when or where the partisans would strike next. Confu-sion also reigned in the command centers. There were no Axis joint chiefs-of-staff in the Anglo-American mold to provide a framework for systematic planning and oversight of agreed-upon strategy. Meetings between the Axis generals were ad hoc and irregular, every detail being subject to haggling. Each Axis partner fought its own anti-insurgent war and negotiated behind the others' backs with both friend and foe. The suspicion and uncertainty that dominated life between the two Axis Powers gave the Croats and Serbs enough space to conduct their own deadly struggle.

Roatta believed that a thorough and efficient suppression of rebellion could not proceed until unity of command had been achieved by placing the civilian public security forces at the disposal of the 2nd Army.[2] But he had to make his way carefully. Sudden and sweeping moves against the Fascist over-lords might inspire Mussolini to extra vigilance in protecting their preroga-tives against military encroachment. In the long run, however, nothing would stop Roatta from usurping the police functions of the Fascist Italian civilian authority in the annexed territories. Moreover, in his determination to estab-lish untrammeled military domination in areas declared "zones of military operation," Roatta would not hesitate to infringe upon the sovereignty of the NDH in Italian-occupied Croatia. Mussolini, he gambled, would support

---

1. *The Ciano Diaries*, 6 January 1942.
2. Zbornik dokumenata i podataka o Narodnooslobodilačkom ratu naroda Jugoslavije (hereafter cited as Zbornik), XIII, bk. 2, D. 80, Roatta memorandum, 23 July 1942.

strong-armed and decisive military leadership over less competent Fascist underlings and intractable allies in Zagreb.

Communist insurgency, Roatta pointed out, fed on Ustaša violence and Croatian corruption. The 2nd Army should therefore sweep out the untrained Fascist commissars and administrators—imported Italians as well as local Slavs—in favor of an outright Italian occupation. To restore military initiative and breathe new life into Italian imperialism, Roatta hoped that he could gain an ally among Serbians alienated by Ustaša violence. A group of disbanded Yugoslav officers under the leadership of the Serb military commander Dragoljub-Draža Mihailović set up a clandestine military organization in the Ravna Gora area deep in the mountains of western Serbia. Under his titular leadership, Četnik bands sprang into existence to defend themselves and exact revenge against the Ustaša. Since as rabid nationalists they hated the Communist partisans, they were, for Roatta, an excellent recruiting ground for a joint crusade against Communism.

Roatta therefore proceeded to change Italian practice—if not official policy—from friendship toward the Zagreb regime to support of their hereditary enemy, the Orthodox Serbs, as the most effective means of defeating the hated partisans. This was not inconsistent with Mussolini's long-range goal of placing the entire region under an Italian protectorate. It was a question of means.

For Roatta, befriending the Četniks was no do-gooder's gesture but an exercise in Realpolitik, for they could be used against the partisans. They would occupy territory liberated by Axis *rastrellamenti* instead of the pro-German Croatians. Like his fellow commanders, Roatta feared that the Wehrmacht generals who sought release from Hitler's repeated oral pledges to respect Italy's long-standing claims in Yugoslavia would never honor this. These fears were not misplaced, for Italian agents had already gathered irrefutable proof that the Third Reich, in complete contempt of Italian interests, was recharging the engine of *Drang nach Südosten*.

To reduce wear and tear on his own troops, Roatta without scruple pitted Četniks against Tito's partisans. Why not enjoy the sport of the two rival insurgent movements "slaughtering each other?" In fighting to the last Četnik, he was sure, the 2nd Army would be left with an easy chore of "mopping up" exhausted partisans; afterwards there would be no problem in disarming and breaking up a Četnik movement thought to be the stalking horse of the enemy British. But there was a catch. In return for their cooperation, the Četniks expected that Italy would look away while they avenged themselves against Muslims and carried out retaliatory raids on Croatian communities. Roatta did not condone such vengeance because of the dismay this caused in Zagreb and Rome. But the warnings he occasionally issued the Četniks to exercise restraint had little effect.

Roatta went out of his way to point out that Italy was involved in "abnormal" warfare with insurgents, where the traditional rules of engagement had given way to lawlessness. The entire Italian-occupied territory, he declared, was a battlefield; the soldiers faced not only criminal "bandits," but also malevolent bystanders anxious to waylay unsuspecting troops at every turn. Save for a handful of collaborators, the enemy was everyone and the front everywhere. All civilians were potential "rebels." In this climate, civilian and insurgent, male and female, parent and child, were indistinguishable as potential killers of Italian troops. This was no job for untrained and squeamish civilian Italian functionaries, Roatta maintained; the military should have a free hand to crush any sign of rebelliousness and crack down on disrespectful behavior on the part of the indigenous population.

To turn these notions into fixed policy, Roatta wrote a detailed pamphlet under the rubric of 3C that was distributed to the field commanders on 1 March 1942. The pamphlet focused on counterinsurgency strategy and measures to be taken for the security of the troops against civilian sabotage. His list of punishments for a multitude of transgressions was exhaustive. In locations deemed "abnormal" (imminent or actual war zones), males between sixteen and sixty were liable to internment. To intimidate the population, hostages in territories of operation would be rounded up among social and professional groups deemed "dangerous." "Treacherous aggressions" against Italian military and civilians justified the taking of hostages, who would be shot in reprisal if the "bandits" who had escaped refused to come forward and admit their "crimes" within forty-eight hours. In areas declared war zones, Roatta gave his commanders a free hand. They need not worry about the consequences, he wrote: "Let it be understood that excessive reactions, undertaken in good faith, will never be prosecuted." In this environment of hate, there would be no taking of prisoners. "The treatment dealt the rebels ought not to be expressed by the formula 'tooth for a tooth' but by a 'head for a tooth.'"[3] Roatta reserved his greatest fury for the partisans who were disrupting life in the annexed areas. To uproot rebellion, he ordered: intern family members, sympathizers, and all males absent from their homes without a clear motive; reduce ration cards of all those suspected

---

3. Institute of Military History, Belgrade, Serbia (hereafter cited as AVII), b. 93, f. 1, Roatta's 3C Circular, 1 March 1942.

of collaboration with the "rebels."[4] The brutality evidenced in Roatta's writings on repression exposes a blatant denial of justice and respect for the occupied peoples of Yugoslavia.

Mussolini found little to criticize in the 2nd Army's ruthless counterinsurgency programs. He certainly favored them over the assimilation ideas of his Fascist governors. But he seemed in the main to be a passive spectator in Rome who only directly intervened in Yugoslavia on the spur of the moment to posture or grab headlines, as in his 31 July 1942 speech, when he hurled invective at the Slavs. Counterinsurgency was not a program Mussolini worked out in Rome and delivered to Sušak for implementation. He merely rubber-stamped Roatta's codification and expansion of the 2nd Army's ongoing repression of the Yugoslav peoples.

In Slovenia, where for Roatta "it was a question of national territory," he had no need to convince his military commanders and civilian Fascist overlords to be merciless.[5] General Mario Robotti, commander of the 11th Army Corps, had already established a formidable reputation as a pioneer of repression against partisans, who, although not numerous, brazenly spread propaganda in the capital, sniped at Italian troops on patrol duty, conducted raids in the countryside, and disrupted railroads and supply convoys.[6] Robotti retaliated by overkill, which alienated even more the essentially anti-Communist majority of the Slovene population, which was left in a no-man's-land between collaboration and Communism. Robotti was ably assisted by the Slovene anti-Communist militia, which did its share of indiscriminate killing of innocent persons.

The preeminent figure carrying out atrocities in the annexed Italian territory of Fiume was the prefect and squadrista Temistocle Testa. He left behind a true "chamber of horrors," visiting terror on the Slav population and brazenly exploiting commercial enterprises, fully earning his reputation as "the protagonist of a colossal contraband of the state." Mussolini rewarded Testa's exuberance by appointing him head of the Intendenza dei servizi di guerra in Rome in 1943.[7]

Under the 2nd Army's watch, internments and concentration camps represent the single most frightening abuse of human life and violation of civilized

---

4. AUSSME, N I-II, b. 724, Roatta to the Governor of Dalmatia, the High Commissioner of Ljubljana, and the Prefect of Carnaro, 5 March 1942. Roatta inserted new punitive clauses in the original 3C pamphlet by means of Order 7000, issued on 7 April 1942. NAW, T-821, 218, 000152-57; 000410, 001040-47, Roatta memorandum and appendix "A" to 3C Circular, 7 April 1942. As Italy's efforts to suppress the partisans flagged in December 1942, Roatta broadened his punitive measures to include "the upper classes" along with other new draconian measures. AVII, b. 93, f.2, Roatta's Circular 3CL, 1 December 1942.

5. NAW, T-821, 55, 000622–24, Roatta to Robotti, 4 April 1942.

6. AUSSME, N I–II, b.724, A note on "rebel bands" by Francesco Delfino, Colonel of the Royal Carabinieri attached to the 2nd Army, 20 November 1941.

7. Teodoro Sala, "Guerra e amministrazione in Jugoslavia 1941–1943," in Sala, *Il fascismo italiano e gli Slavi del sud*, pp. 302–3.

norms in Italy's campaign against the partisans, as well as the worst blemish on the Italian war record in Yugoslavia. Involving many officers and men led by General Roatta, these war crimes have been so comprehensively documented as to be irrefutable.[8] In spite of strapped finances and limited space, the Italians, according to the International Red Cross, managed to arrest and intern close to 100,000 Slav citizens.[9] Slovenes and Croats constituted the overwhelming majority in the concentration camps run by the military and the interior department. For these actions, Roatta won the well-deserved sobriquet, "the black beast."[10] One is left to ponder what the final tally of the Italians might have been had they managed to build concentration camps fast enough to absorb the military's projected roundups—let alone what Mussolini had in mind.

Can one pin the charge of ethnic cleansing on Mussolini and the 2nd Army? Certainly massive transfer of Slovenes to internment camps and their replacement by Italian settlers was much talked about among the Italian occupiers. Mussolini on 10 June 1941 spoke of 30,000 Slovenes to be rounded up, held as hostages, or interned, and he lowered the bar to forced population exchanges by affirming that "when ethnicity does not accord with geography, it is the ethnic group that must be moved. . .population exchanges and forced exodus of people are providential, because such transfers result in political frontiers that coincide with racial groups."[11] At about the same time General Roatta toyed with a somewhat smaller figure of 20,000 Slovenes to be interned, women and children included; destitute families of fallen Italian soldiers, as in Napoleonic days, would move in to occupy their lands.[12] Three months later he gave expression to the same idea.[13]

To divert public attention from possible war crimes they had committed in Yugoslavia, the Italian generals in the postwar era depicted the partisans as the ones who introduced atrocities in the fighting. An officer like Taddeo Orlando, commander of the *Granatieri* Division, who had committed horrible crimes, strove to whitewash his actions by pointing out the enemy's barbaric behavior and uncivilized manner, conveniently forgetting that the Italians through inva-

---

8. The latest richly documented book on this subject is by Alessandra Kersevan, *Lager italiani: Pulizia etnica e campi di concentramento fascisti per civili jugoslavi 1941–1943* (Rome: Nutrimenti, 2008).

9. Carlo Spartico Capogreco, *I Campi del duce: L'internamento civile nell'Italia fascista (1940–1943)* (Turin: Einaudi, 2004), pp. 77–78. The latest Yugoslav study arrives at the following figures. Under Italian occupation, 149,639 persons were interned at one time or another and 92,902 people imprisoned. Dragan S. Nenezić, *Jugoslovenske Oblasti Pod Italijom 1941–1943* (Belgrade: Vojnoistorijski Institut Vojske Jugoslavije, 1999), p. 159.

10. Roy Carroll, *Manchester Guardian Weekly*, 11 July 2001.

11. *OO*, XXX, p. 97; "Il Piccolo di Trieste," 11 June 1941, cited in Ferenc, *La provincia 'italiana' di Lubiana*, p. 286, n. 13.

12. NAW, T-821, 61, 000776, Roatta note, 2 June 1942.

13. He would "transfer a large part of the population, settle them in the Kingdom, and put Italians in their place." ARS, 1788, XII, f. 2, Roatta note on internments, 8 September 1942.

sion of the country and a ruthless occupation were the real provocateurs of brutality and carnage. There is no doubt that the partisans knew how to take the gloves off, but they were the defenders, not the aggressors. As the Italian historian Teodoro Sala reminds us, the ultimate criminality lay with Mussolini and the Fascist regime for undertaking a war of conquest against Yugoslavia without provocation that was no less wicked than Hitler's indiscriminate bombing of Belgrade out of pique over a Yugoslav snub.[14]

Counterinsurgency, originally conceived as an improvised response to a startling and increasingly unmanageable insurrection, had taken on a life of its own. The more unwinnable the war, the more ruthless the repression. Yet, the 2nd Army should not be collectively described as war criminals carrying out dastardly deeds because of a shared hatred of Fascist enemies. When it was all over, a majority of troops could leave Yugoslavia with a clear conscience, save the barbaric few from all ranks who unmistakably committed war crimes. Still, that the Italian troops "faced this war with scarce enthusiasm" does not alter the inescapable truth that one did not have to be a Fascist true believer to have committed a crime against humanity in the "dirty war" in Yugoslavia. And of these crimes, there were all too many.

In the postwar period, the Italian mass media formulated a clear distinction between Italy and Germany with respect to their policies in Yugoslavia. Thus the image of *cattivo tedesco*, a fanatical warrior capable of every wickedness, was contrasted with the so-called *bravo italiano*, the "good guy." Badly outfitted, thrown into a wretched war against his will, and unwilling to commit violence against the unarmed, the Italian soldier supposedly lent succor to the hungry and dispossessed of the invaded countries, saving many lives of innocent and victimized people. Incapable of hate, he in turn was not hated.

A host of recent Italian historians have effectively exposed the notion *bravo italiano* versus *cattivo tedesco* as an absolute fallacy.[15] Thanks to their searching studies, there is no credibility left in the notion that the Balkans were filled with merry, irresistible Latin lovers, who fed children candy in their off-hours or simply slouched around in cafés, as compared with inhumane Germans, who caroused and pillaged in their time off, Nazi to their last breath.

Still, there were differences in the comportment of Italian and German troops vis-à-vis the Yugoslav peoples. The two major areas in which the Germans clearly surpassed the Italians in brutality and barbarism in Yugoslavia were

---

14. Teodoro Sala, "1939–1943. Jugoslavia 'neutrale,' Jugoslavia occupata," in Sala, *Il fascismo italiano e gli Slavi del sud*, pp. 152–53.

15. See the articles by Filippo Focardi: "'Bravo italiano' e 'cattivo Tedesco': riflessioni sulla genesi di due immagini incrociate," in *Storia e Memoria* (1996) 1: 55–83; "La memoria della guerra e il mito del 'bravo italiano'. Origine e affermazione di un autoritratto collettivo," *Italia Contemporanea* (2000): 393–99.

mass hostage killing and the extermination of Jews. While the Italians gave refuge to most of the Jews who sought their protection, the Germans made sure to shoot or send to death camps every male Jew they could lay their hands on— 17,000 in Serbia alone.[16] (Notice that it was not the SS that opened this Serbian chapter of the Holocaust; the Wehrmacht commanders themselves assumed the initiative.[17]) The Italians' protection of the Jews in Yugoslavia, as well as elsewhere in occupied Europe, should not be forgotten no matter the reason: rank opportunism, defiance of the overbearing Germans, or as simple acts of mercy.[18] (In contrast with the Italians, German acts of mercy during World War II were few and far between.) On the other hand, the smoking ruins the 2nd Army left behind in Yugoslavia and the large number of Slav lives broken and lost in the internment camps should give pause to those still focused on a favorable comparison between the *bravo italiano* and the *cattivo tedesco*. No medal need be struck for coming in second in this macabre competition between the two Axis countries in Yugoslavia during World War II.

"Model" Fascist Rule in Albania

"Albania, linchpin of the imperial community of Rome." "Albania, Italy's 5th shore." "Albania, the trampoline for Italy's expansion in the European Orient." Albania, the bulwark of the Balkans." "Whoever holds Albania holds the Balkans." These were aggressive Fascist slogans that clearly indicated Rome's intention of turning Albania into an Italian protectorate.

On 7 April 1939 the time seemed ripe for the Italian imperialists to realize this goal by invasion. In a campaign marred by embarrassing flaws in the landing operations, the Italians suffered little loss of life thanks to negligible Albanian resistance. The Albanian king Zogu I abandoned the country and made haste for Greece.

To broaden popular support, the invaders, in search of collaborators, made a pitch to Albanian nationalists who aspired to independence, self-government, and irredentist goals, but with the reservation that they be colonial subjects integrated into a "model" government prescribed by the Fascist regime. In a decidedly strange setup, Rome decreed a personal union of Italy and Albania.

---

16. Walter Manoschek, "'Coming Along to Shoot Some Jews?', The Destruction of the Jews in Serbia," in *War of Extermination: The German Military in World War II, 1941–1944*, eds. Hannes Heer and Klaus Naumann (New York and Oxford: Berghahn Books, 2000), pp. 39–51.

17. Lutz Klinkhammer, "La politica di occupazione nazista in europa. Un tentativo di analisi strutturale," in *Crimini e memorie di guerra*, eds. Luca Baldissara e Paolo Pezzino (Naples: L'ancora del mediterraneo, 2004), p. 77.

18. A recent analysis of Italy's protection of the Jews in Yugoslavia can be found in H. James Burgwyn, *Empire on the Adriatic: Mussolini's Conquest of Yugoslavia 1941–1943* (New York: Enigma Books, 2005), pp. 185–95.

Annexation was forgone to preserve the illusion that Albania continued to exist as an "independent" country; in its place would be a protectorate. Power would formally be vouchsafed in the hands of King Victor Emmanuel III, who would have the authority to declare war and peace, command the Albanian armed forces, issue administrative ordinances, and appoint a lieutenant-general. But the king was destined to be only a figurehead, for Mussolini exercised the power behind the throne to interfere at will in making all the important decisions. Ciano ended up the major stage-manager, imparting political directives to the lieutenant-general. To complete this rather confusing chain of command, Ciano created an under-secretariat for Albanian affairs in the foreign ministry.

Francesco Jacomoni di San Savino was chosen to occupy the office of lieutenant-general of the king. He immediately set about the formation of a collaborationist government whose members would be supervised by Italian counselors. The Albanian armed forces were amalgamated with the Italian, and the country's gendarmerie and border guards were incorporated into the Italian military. The concept of nationhood for the Albanian peoples was nothing more than lip service, for what the Italians gave them amounted to servitude in the Fascist imperial community.

Jacomoni found no shortage of collaborators, calling on those disgruntled politicians who had been marginalized by the departed King Zogu and who had long-standing contacts with Italy. A new government was formed under the prominent landowner and ardent foe of Zogu, Shefqet Vërlaçi, as prime minister. Ciano remarked: "The operation to emasculate Albania without making the patient scream—the annexation—is now practically realized."[19] Despite the veneer of constitutional monarchy, the Italians had created an authoritarian, hierarchical, and antidemocratic regime.

This absolutist dictatorship was grafted onto an Albanian feudal aristocracy made up of landowners in the central and southern regions and leading clansmen in the north. Since the Fascists in charge introduced no radical social revolution in the Bolshevik style, they banked on feudal chieftains for major support. The invasion, therefore, had produced little change in Albania's social structure. Internal rivalries and struggles among the clans continued. Vengeance remained the favorite method of resolving disputes rather than deliberation in formal political and social structures. The result was a decentralized rule superimposed on a fragmented Albanian society that baffled Fascist reformers. In Rome competing pressure groups and lobbyists trying to gain a foothold in Albania worked out a similarly chaotic series of compromises. Foisted on a hapless country, the

19. *The Ciano Diaries*, 3 June 1939.

Fascist government in Albania hardly pretended to answer the needs of restive and discontented native peoples. Rather, a system was created that featured corruption and official banditry, which deferred a true Fascist *civiltà* to a remote future.

At the outset of occupation, to avoid the impression that they had arrived as haughty conquerors, the Italians showed a conciliatory disposition. Ciano personally gave orders that Albanian soldiers, particularly officers, should be well treated. To earn good will, he planned a program of public works. "Only in this way will we definitely link the people to us and destroy the authority of their chiefs, showing that only we are capable of doing what they have not been able or did not want to do."[20] The Italians could afford such restraint because the Albanians greeted them, if not with overt hostility, with indifference and apathy. As long as the Axis marched from victory to victory, those nursing aggrieved nationalist sentiments would suppress them.[21]

In spite of general Albanian resignation, the Italian light hand rapidly gave way to severity: Albanians would be taught to become good Fascists obedient to Rome. Indoctrination through schooling in the Italian language received special attention; the Dante Alighieri Society propagated culture.[22] The Albanian Fascist party, the only party permitted, was organized by Rome and placed under the direction of Giovanni Giro, a personal friend of Mussolini, whose purpose was to acquaint Albanian recruits with the niceties of Fascist ideology. Ciano noted how Albanians were learning civilized manners under the paternal Fascist regime: "There is no question that the mass of the people is now won over by Italy. The Albanian people are grateful to us for having taught them to eat twice a day, for this rarely happened before. Even in the physical appearance of the people greater well-being can be noted."[23]

On the religious front the Italians, in a Muslim-dominated country, nursed the development of Catholicism by funneling in priests, sending children to seminaries, and subsidizing the Albanian Catholic Church. As for the Jews, Jacomoni in 1940 had ordered that "Jews of foreign citizenship [in Albania] must be returned to their countries of origin as soon as possible." But since "not a single Jew was apparently expelled," his efforts seemed half-hearted, and he received no cooperation from the Albanians. Jacomoni fell back on the exclusion of all Albanian Jews from cultural, social and political activity. The fate of the Kosovar

---

20. Ibid., 13 April 1939.
21. Ministero Interno Direzione Generale Pubblica Securezza 1943, b. 11. Reports of 22 October 1940 and 6 September 1941.
22. Bernd J. Fischer, *Albania at War 1939–1945* (West Lafayette, Indiana: Purdue University Press, 1999), pp. 44–45.
23. *The Ciano Papers*, 23 May 1940.

Jews was considerably worse, for the Italians, complying with German demands, compiled lists of Jews who were required to wear white armbands with the word "Jid" written in black letters and to have their identity cards stamped with a red "J." Worse still, the Italian authorities turned over fifty-one Jews of Pristina to the Germans, fully apprised of their ultimate destiny.[24] On the other hand, on the suggestion of local Muslim authorities, the Italian army saved many Kosovar Jews by moving them to Albania under the pretext that they had typhus and needed hospitalization in Albania.[25]

Apropos the economy, the Banca di Napoli and the Banca di Lavoro expanded aggressively in Albania and a customs and currency union was established. Raw materials like copper and chrome, important for the production of steel, constituted Albania's most significant mineral resources that were used to feed Italian industry. Electric power, oil production, and fisheries were placed under Italian control. To facilitate the exploitation of the economy, the Italians invested in a vast public works program that actually benefited many Albanians, particularly merchants and sectors of the lower classes. Ostentatious new public buildings, road construction, and land reclamation projects brought in large amounts of capital and employed many Albanians. Most of the firms handling the contracts were Italian as were most of the foremen.[26] The sudden influx of Italians proved to be a mixed blessing. If, as Ciano reported, "Italian laborers mix well with the Albanians," problems were created by the "Italian middle classes, who treat the natives badly and who have a colonial mentality. Unfortunately, this is also true of military officers, and, according to Jacomoni, especially their wives."[27]

On 29 June 1939 General Badoglio described the real purpose behind the conquest of Albania: the exploitation of Albanian irredentism to open up Fascist imperial expansion in the lower Balkans. In spearheading such a movement, Italy expected to earn the gratitude of Albanians hankering after an enlarged country. Having thus achieved popularity, the Italians could impose their minted *stile fascista* to suppress general dissent against their rule.[28] Albanian irredentism excited Bottai too, who compared the country to Piedmont and spoke of its

---

24. My thanks to Filippo Focardi for bringing to my attention this Italian turnover of Pristina Jews to the Germans.

25. The Italian policy toward Jews is taken from Bernd J. Fischer, "The Jews of Albania during the Zogist and Second World War Periods," in http://www.ipfw.edu/news/resourses/speakers/bios/f/fischer.shtml.

26. Fischer, *Albania at War*, p. 67.

27. *The Ciano Diaries*, 24 May 1940.

28. *Le truppe italiane in Albania (1914–1920 e 1939)* (Rome: SME US, 1978), relazione sull'ispezione compiuta in Albania tra il 19 e il 26 giugno 1939, Ufficio del Capo di Stato Maggiore Generale 29 giugno 1939, n. protocollo 4533.

enlargement in two or three years.[29] The two greatest driving forces were Ciano and Mussolini. "The Duce and I have brought up the problem of the irredentism of Kossovo and of Ciamuria," wrote Ciano; "The Duce defines this irredentism: 'The little light in the tunnel.' That is, the ideal spiritual motive that we must stimulate in the future to keep the Albanian national spirit high and united."[30] Mussolini emphasized this objective by telling Jacomoni to encourage Albanian irredentism "as a guarantee of the fidelity of Albanian patriots in the union of their country to Italy."[31] A year later, on 22 May 1940, Ciano stated: "They [the Albanians] want Kossovo and Ciamuria. It is easy for us to increase our popularity by becoming champions of Albanian nationalism."[32] The idea was to divert the attention of the Albanians from the Italian occupation by employing them to foment uprisings among their brothers in the Yugoslav and Greek border provinces.

During the outset of the Italian invasion of Greece in late October 1940, Vërlaçi commented: "I expect that a great power like yours will act like a thunderbolt."[33] Jacomoni supported this optimism by reporting on the "magnificent spirit" of the Albanian Fascist militia and their desire "to fight for the expansion of their country and the Italian empire."[34] But when the Italian offensive bogged down, the dispirited Albanian units, believing that the war against Greece was entirely an Italian affair, began to fall away. They also noticed that under cover of war the Italians were involved in shady transactions intended to penetrate and monopolize markets.[35] Rome, in turn, felt betrayed by the Albanians. But the fault lay with Ciano, who obviously had exaggerated the popularity of irredentism in the country. Mussolini admitted that there had appeared no sign of revolt on the part of the population of Ciamuria behind the advancing Greek troops.[36]

In spite of this *tradimento albanese*, the Italians, after the Greek collapse in April 1941, reactivated their irredentist plans for Albania. On the 24th Ciano was able to talk Ribbentrop into allocation of a large chunk of Kosovo, the Debar (Dibra in Italian) region in western Macedonia, and a small strip of Montenegro for his satrapy. Cavallero sent Bottai on a special mission to assemble a combina-

29. Fischer, *Albania at War*, p. 71.
30. *The Ciano Diaries*, 3 June 1939.
31. Francesco Jacomoni di San Savino, *La politica italiana nell'Albania* (Rocca San Casciano: Cappelli, 1965), p. 144.
32. *The Ciano Diaries*, 22 May 1940.
33. Cited in Federico Eichberg, *Il fascio littorio e l'aquila di Skanderbeg: Italia e Albania 1939–1945* (Rome: Apes, 1997), p. 82.
34. DDI, 9, V, 139, Jacomoni to Benini, 29 June 1940, 443, Jacomoni to Ciano, and 642, Jacomoni to Benini, 17 August 1940 and 25 September 1940.
35. DDI, 9., VI, 318, Jacomoni to Rome, 18 December 1940.
36. Ibid., 71, Meeting between Mussolini, Badoglio, Cavagnari, and Pricolo 10 November 1940.

tion of patriots and brigands as irregular forces to stir up Albanians against ethnic Serbs in the country's provinces facing Yugoslavia.[37]

Carlo Umiltà arrived as civil commissioner for Kosovo and Debar on 25
May 1941. Landing in a territory where "racial hatred had destroyed everything,
where Slavs and Albanians burned each others' houses and slaughtered as many
people as they could," he was immediately struck by the intention of the new
Albanian masters to rid the land of its Serb civil servants.[38] They arrived with
"Albanization" on their minds—payback on the part of a poor and pastoral
people who, under the Yugoslav regime, had suffered discrimination and hardship at the hands of their Serb masters. After tough negotiations, Umiltà was
able to persuade the warring ethnic peoples to recognize a truce and form mixed
municipal councils. Units of the Italian military, however, did not swing behind
these efforts. According to Umiltà, the troops, by showing a decided preference
for lively and emancipated Slav women over veiled and supervised Albanian
females, impeded orders from Rome to treat the ethnic groups impartially.[39] To
reconcile Serbs and Albanians in Kosovo was a tall order, which to this day has
defied the most gifted and even-handed of disinterested parties. In Debar, where
Umiltà found the majority population to be Macedonian, he learned that, if
unable to create their own state, Macedonians would prefer to be part of Greece.
If annexed by Albania, they would rebel.[40] When the Albanian nationalist
Mustafa Kruja was appointed president of the Albanian Council in late 1941, he
created a special ministry for the "redeemed" lands of Debar and Kosovo, which
enabled mixed battalions of Italian and Albanian Blackshirts in these territories
to end Umiltà's work of conciliation by engaging in a vigorous repression of the
Serb and Montenegrin populations.

At the same time Ciano hoped to annex much of Ciamuria to Albania.
Greeks and Albanian members of the Orthodox Church, which was placed
under High Commissioner Xhemil Dino, predominantly inhabited this area.
According to Umiltà, the Muslims living there, while desiring better treatment by
the Greeks, were far from enthusiastic over the idea of incorporation into
Albania. The Germans, who were also opposed to annexation, thwarted Ciano
from gathering in Ciamuria,[41] which continued formally as part of Greece,
though the province remained under control of the Italian military command in
Athens.

---

37. Bottai, *Diario*, p. 261.
38. Carlo Umiltà, *Jugoslavia e Albania. Memorie di un diplomatico* (Cernusco sul Naviglio: Garzanti, 1947), p. 112.
39. Ibid., pp. 136, 140–41.
40. Ibid., p. 129.
41. Fisher, *Albania at War*, p. 85.

After an initial burst of activity, the Italian occupation of Albania began to deteriorate rapidly into disorganization, lack of direction, and preference for form over content. With a large secret fund at his disposal for miscellaneous expenses in Albania, Ciano initiated a widespread network of corruption. The vast sums that Rome spent on roads and public buildings provided a unique opportunity for Italian contractors and suppliers to rake in kickbacks. A considerable bureaucracy was built up to administer the funds. Fascists secured jobs for friends and contracts for firms in which they had a personal interest. Although Ciano was the one ultimately responsible for the corruption, he saw no contradiction when dressing down a personal rival such as Cavallero for his involvement in the same kind of *affarismo*.[42]

Bitter rivalries between the various levels of Italian authority in Albania precluded efficient government too. Jacomoni tangled with General Guzzoni within a month of the invasion; Giro, who mimicked Ciano's *tono fascista*, stepped on toes wherever he trod.

To arrest declining support, the Italians switched around leaders and promised them more autonomy to broaden the base of government by bringing in new faces closer to the intellectual elites and the people. But the constant shuffles at the top did not include any radical change in the existing feudal social order. Support of the beys remained fundamental. Vërlaçi was replaced by his hated rival Mustafa Kruja, who released anti-Fascists from jail, offered amnesty for bands operating against Italians, and resurrected an independent Albanian gendarmerie. But his success was both superficial and temporary, and inner fighting between Albanian factions grouped around Vërlaçi and Kruja remained as bitter as ever.

Throughout 1941-42, the Italians made only tepid efforts to puzzle through solutions to the miasma they had created in Albania. Jacomoni wrote bland reports, and Ciano saw only an untroubled rule. When Albanian opposition began to stir, the Italians initially seemed genuinely surprised, given their belief that they had bought Albanian good will by the vast sums of money plowed into public works and land reclamation. On 19 October 1941 Jacomoni reassured

---

42. *The Ciano Diaries*, 8 October 1941. "When I was in Albania Vërlaçi, in the presence of Jacomoni, talked to me about the Albanian Government's intention to offer Cavallero some Albanian soil. At the time I thought that it had to do with the customary urn filled with earth, as with the earth of the Grappa or the water from the Piave, and I made no objection. But when I learned that the offer was not symbolical, since it had to do with a grant of almost twenty-five hundred acres of land in Fieri, I definitely opposed it. This did not please the interested parties, who are now trying to twist things around with a letter from Vërlaçi announcing the accomplished fact. I spoke to Cavallero about the matter and I will stop it. But Cavallero is not grateful to me. Just the contrary. He cannot realize that for a man like himself, on whose fame as a strategist people disagree, but on whose reputation as a swindler all agree, the acceptance of such a gift would spell his doom. When bread is being rationed and the people are hungry is not the time to announce that Cavallero is celebrating a very dubious Greek victory by accepting a present of a few millions."

Ciano that "the critical period is now over, and that, with some gesture of force against the rebels, it may be possible to bring order and quiet back to the country."[43] A couple of months later Ciano noted: "Jacomoni is not pessimistic and believes that, with good steering, we can set our ship on its course again. So far he has never been mistaken."[44] Whenever Jacomoni reiterated that all was well, Ciano took at face value that autonomy meant reform.[45] In April he reported that the only problem was a shortage of materiel that prevented the Italians from continuing with their public works.[46] By September, as rumbles of discontent continued, Jacomoni told Ciano that a bit of force against the rebels would quickly restore quiet. In this "oasis of peace in all the Balkans,"[47] Ciano concerned himself mostly over the lack of troops—four divisions in name only—a total of 11,000, to meet threats from outside the borders.[48] As late as January 1943 General Lorenzo Dalmazzo, commander of the 9th Army in Albania, viewed "the Albanian situation with remarkable tranquility."[49]

There were some grounds for Italian nonchalance. Although Albanians grumbled over food shortages and the rising cost of living, a truly national resistance movement was slow in the making. In the cities and towns, Albanian opposition came mainly from professional classes, intellectuals, and students, where budding nationalists began to protest against life in an Italian plantation economy. Insurgency leaders, however, gradually emerged in the countryside primarily among tribal chieftains. But they were still mainly caught up in clan feuds over territorial rights rather than setting out forthrightly to assault Italians or their own puppet functionaries.[50] A small nucleus of hardy Communists was, however, quietly organizing for future serious insurgency.

Before any real hint of rebellion, Ciano had already created a police state. After noting that "twenty or so persons will immediately be sent to concentration camps" to quell "a bit of a storm in the intellectual spheres of Albania," he affirmed: "There must not be the least sign of weakness; justice and force must be the characteristics of the new regime."[51] In June 1939 decrees were issued demanding the arrest and deportation of persons deemed dangerous to public law and order and the surrender of arms and ammunition. Crimes "against the personality of the state" were issued in January 1940, followed a few months

43. *The Ciano Diaries*, 19 October 1941.
44. Ibid., 19 December 1941.
45. Ibid., 2 March 1942.
46. Fischer, *Albania at War*, p. 137.
47. *The Ciano Diaries*, 1 September 1942.
48. Ibid., 9 September 1942.
49. Ibid., 7 January 1943.
50. Fischer, *Albania at War*, pp. 92–97,
51. *The Ciano Diaries*, 12 May 1939.

later by a ban on demonstrations, rallies, processions, and meetings, with severe penalties, including death, for those who defied the decrees.[52]

With the help of a strong police force sent from Italy, Jacomoni in the following months imposed curfews and prohibitions on use of bicycles, motorcycles, and closed vehicles. Military and Blackshirt patrols were given the mandate to fire on all those who, upon being so commanded, refused to halt. Those possessing firearms could expect severe punishment and the death penalty if caught with explosives. Parents were placed under an obligation to denounce their children to the police if they took part in patriotic demonstrations or provoked disturbances. On 29 August Jacomoni decreed that persons who propagated new ideas with the intention of sowing disorder, or who made mocking gestures with the object of ridiculing the occupation forces, would be liable to imprisonment from three to ten years.[53]

Mussolini emerges from this period as a quixotic optimist. Was he, like Jacomoni, in denial in his refusal to believe that Fascist imperialism was turning Albanians into enemies rather than deferential subjects? Regarding Jacomoni, noted Ciano, Mussolini, in a new directive, advocated a greater autonomy without eliminating the beys, who still count in the country, and for the government to recruit new elements "which are closer to the intellectual classes and to the people."[54] Echoing Jacomoni's upbeat reports, Mussolini told Ciano on 17 February 1942 that Albanians deserved a more liberal and autonomous local regime. "This is the only policy possible that bears good fruit."[55] On September 29th, he issued an order to the Italian military that contained a novel interpretation of "liberal reforms": "The armed forces in Italy are not to be considered as troops of occupation. They safeguard an interest at once imperial and Albanian. Therefore while the use of the armed forces takes place according to the orders and instructions of the Supreme Command, it is necessary that the Superior Command, in resolving questions that can affect Albanian interests, as well as our political action in Albania, holds always uppermost the general political direction, whose responsibility is entrusted in the lieutenant-general of the king.

"This line of conduct must inspire the behavior of the troops with regard to the Albanians in whatever circumstances—public demonstrations, public order, and the population's welfare.

---

52. Fischer, *Albania at War*, p. 113.
53. Ibid., pp. 113–14.
54. *The Ciano Diaries*, 13 June 1941.
55. Ibid., 17 February 1942.

"It is also necessary that in daily contacts, officers and soldiers impart the precise notion that we consider the Albanians not as an inferior people held under strict vigilance, but as a proud and friendly people who have freely wished to unite their destiny with the Italian nation, and who therefore merit our full consideration and support.

"Acting in a different matter will gravely compromise the juridical rapport and those spiritual qualities that today bind the two peoples together.

"As a matter of principle, the armed forces that are under the orders of the Superior Commandant provide for the defense of the territory. The Albanian government, which is granted the means at its disposition, that is, forces of the police and Albanian fascist militia, superintend to the safeguarding of public order. Units of the CC.RR and GG.FF deployed in Albania are likewise at the disposition of the government. All these forces are placed under orders of an Italian general.

"Of course as long as the actual state of disquiet lasts in the Balkans, which is having repercussions in Albanian territory, the use of the Italian armed forces for the safeguarding of internal order will be rendered somewhat necessary. In such cases, the Superior Command FF.AA. will concert together with the lieutenant-general on the use of the dependent forces. In the case of important operations, it [the Superior Command FF.AA.] will undertake them, in agreement with the aforementioned authority, and will assume the responsibility and direction.

"Finally, with regard to assistance afforded the population, the Superior Command will bear in mind that every act of our armed forces is intended to impress on the government and Albanian people our solidarity and our moral support—and materiel when necessary and possible—which concurs with the cementing of the ties that must link the Albanian nation to ours and to make Albania the solid pillar of our military and political situation in the Balkans."[56]

This order gives one pause. It appears that on the Albanian question Mussolini and Italians were one day suspicious, on another complacent, and reacted accordingly, with rough and unpredictable repression on some occasions, and conciliation on others

Did Mussolini actually imagine that he could at once bring civilization to so-called underlings and reap glory from Italian imperial conquest? Or was the former simply a sham to disguise the latter? One need not ask such questions regarding Hitler, who never spoke of uplifting the quality of life of Poles or

56. ASMAE, Gabinetto Albania, 1931–1945, Anno 1943, b. 195/1, NORME E DIRETTIVE GENERALI CIRCA LA FUNZIONE ED IL COMPORTAMENTO DELLE FF.AA. IN ALBANIA. Mussolini, 29 September 1942.

Russians to the German level; his motive stemmed directly from the search for Lebensraum galvanized by the unabashed determination to crush "inferior races."

As opposed to the blank check that Mussolini gave General Robotti in superseding the authority of the bumbling Grazioli in Slovenia, the Duce counted on Ciano's favorite, Jacomoni, for straightening out the disorder in Albania. He saw this task much as he had envisioned the role of the solidly Fascist Bastianini, who was charged with upholding Fascist rule in Dalmatia. Whereas Jacomoni sought to implement "liberal" reforms mixed with harsh law-and-order measures, Bastianini did not refrain from all-out repression. Neither provided the right answers.

Messy Occupation of Greece

At the beginning of the Italian occupation of Greece, Rome was tempted to win the loyalty of important minorities by partitioning the country beyond what the Axis Powers had already done as conquerors in the peace treaty imposed on the hapless General Tsolakoglu. Areas in northwest Greece occupied by "Ciamurioti," of Albanian tongue and Muslim religion, would go to Albania, and a "reserved zone" set up in the Pindus mountain chain, where the Aromanians, a minority people, lived in scattered villages. The influential Jacomoni lobbied hard to engorge Albania with additional Greek territory inhabited by Muslims. But General Geloso wanted no part of Jacomoni's plans. In his view Greek anger would surge if Italy swung behind Ciamuriota hirelings and Aromanian separatists, who were deemed unworthy of guerrilla warfare and better suited for menial tasks.[57] Carlo Umiltà, in noting the preferences of the people living in the localities claimed by Jacomoni, concluded that the majority preferred Greece and would rebel if handed over to Albania.[58]

Rome was persuaded. They would not repeat the mistake made in Montenegro where, in dismembering the country, they earned Montenegrin hatred. By deciding to shelve further territorial amputations of Greece, Rome relieved Geloso's anxieties and drew limits on Jacomoni's empire-building.

During 1941, Italian troops filed into a country overpowered but hardly cowed. Having left the battlefield feeling triumphant against Mussolini's legions, the Greeks stewed over their "victory denied" and bitterly resented the Italian

---

57. AUSSME, N I-II, DS, b. 1070, 28 December 1942; L 15 (27) R/28; DS, 839, Geloso memorandum, Annex 5, 17 September 1941; L13, b. 105; N I-II, DS, b. 554, 8 September 1942.
58. Umiltà, *Jugoslavia e Albania*, pp. 130–31.

annexation of the Ionian Islands. Their anger grew as the Italian occupation forces took up quarters in the urban areas and along transportation arteries.

Thanks to a lack of mobility and rutted roads, the Italian troops moved haltingly and were unable to blanket the countryside and mountainous areas, which left a vast no man's land. The discharged Greek soldiers, who took away weapons and equipment from the battlefield, were therefore able to hide them. Since the writ of the skeleton collaborationist government in Athens hardly reached the hinterland, the Italians stepped into a void created by the collapse of local municipalities. "In essence," concludes a military report, "Greece exists no longer; only in old and glorious monuments."[59] But this was a premature judgment. If Greece had been defeated, its people remained unbowed.[60]

General Geloso set up headquarters in Athens. The army intendancy office, which had the responsibility for provisioning the troops, immediately had its hands full in coping with major supply problems caused by a serious shortage of shipping space at the ports and increasingly unsafe sea routes to the Italian mainland. To make up for the shortfall, the office exploited local markets and resources, hardly taking notice of the already impoverished population. The Italian occupiers did not help their cause by dismissing civil servants and gendarmes, which paralyzed the public services. A thinned-out local administration was left to struggle on with a paucity of trained personnel. The Orthodox clergy, many of whom were impassioned nationalists, disseminated hatred of Italy. Most bankers and business people had fled the country, and those who stayed were pro-German. To restore some semblance of order in the public administration, a handful of former functionaries was reinstated, but only after signing a declaration of loyalty, obedience, and demonstrating "absolute, unquestioning and totalitarian" subservience to their Italian masters.[61]

From the moment of his arrival, General Geloso did not hesitate to remind his soldiers that they represented a great and victorious nation. As Roman conquerors, their authority should never be abused by the sheer display of power. But, he warned, do not fall victim to the fatal flaws in national character and compromise Italy's political destiny in Greece by becoming overly generous and friendly. To command awe and respect, proud conquerors should be imperious and distant. Repressive measures for upholding security and order should be carried out in a lordly manner, not by crass bullying. "The moral conquest of a country is no less important than territorial conquest," Geloso wrote. "Respect

59. AUSSME, L-15, r. 23, F. 9.
60. A perceptive analysis of the first year of Italy's occupation of Greece can be found in Lidia Santarelli, "Fra coabitazione e conflitto: invasione italiana e popolazione civile nella Grecia occupata (primavera-estate 1941)," in *Qualestoria*, no. 1 (June 2002), pp. 143-55.
61. AUSSME, L 15, b. 23, 10 August 1941; L 13, b. 106, Geloso report, 1 November 1941.

on the part of the enemy must issue from spontaneous and reasoned admiration and esteem rather than from fear of sanctions."[62]

In the first year, the calm in the countryside was broken only sporadically by small resistance groups (andartes). But criminal elements and rural brigands roamed at will to rob and plunder defenseless farmers, which underscored the precarious safety of the rural population and the inability of the soldiers to defend them from depredation. To expect secure protection from the demoralized, grossly underpaid, and "deceitful" gendarmerie was totally unrealistic.

Demonstrations in the urban centers, featuring anti-Axis pamphlets, newspapers, and wall graffiti, were only an annoyance. As time went on, however, the troops began to be harried by isolated acts of sabotage: cut telephone wires, stolen fuel, ignited munitions dumps, destroyed factory machines, dynamited rail lines, ambushed transport convoys, and beaten up collaborating Greek gendarmes. Still, when compared to Croatia, where the Italians stepped into a whirlpool of Ustaša terror against Orthodox Serbs, Greek turbulence, in the absence of a parochial Communist leadership and with the flight abroad of many Greek officers, remained minor and under control.

In this preliminary period preceding the emergence of organized armed insurgency, General Geloso took steps to ease the food crisis by providing social welfare and health services, distributing seeds for high-quality spring wheat, improving the railway transportation of food, and making available credit facilities for public utilities. Deteriorating sanitary conditions featuring endemic malaria also faced the Italian commander. Not absent from his calculations was to earn Greek gratitude by contrasting Italian good will with German ruthlessness. But whatever the public relations stunts, the Italian occupier did not arrive as a do-gooder but as a predator not much better than the local bandits or inchoate insurgent groups ready and willing to requisition food and stock. Hardly anything was done to ease galloping inflation, control rampant malaria, and provide foodstuffs for the cities caused by the loss of English trade.

Although there was talk by both Axis Powers of treating Greeks gently like Norwegians rather than *Untermenshen* Jews and Slavs, they immediately engaged in a spirited race to seize Greece's assets. Chilled by their shabby treatment elsewhere at the hands of the Third Reich, the Italians braced for the worst, which was not long in coming. When the Germans swooped down to corner the Greek market, Ciano warned that "this 'buying up' by certain private German parties of the principal economic enterprises of the country we have conquered is certainly not in harmony with the cooperation....so vital to each country,

---

62. AUSSME, N I-II, DS, b. 502, Allegato 4, 19 May 1941, Geloso to his commanders, 19 May 1941.

which ought to exist between Rome and Berlin."[63] Geloso's task of patrolling the countryside was greatly hampered by the German company Telefunken's purchase of Greece's airwaves, which provided the Wehrmacht with a monopoly over radio communications in the country.[64]

Count Giuseppe Volpi di Misurata, a financial kingpin linked to Fascist hierarchs, arrived in Athens in early May to prevail on Greek industrialists and business interests to favor them over the German agents swarming throughout the country with pockets lined with money and lucrative contracts. The Italians lost before the competition began. When Volpi's associates visited the National Bank in Athens to acquire shares in Greek electricity corporations and buy out important plants, they found that most Greek companies had already closed deals with Krupp.[65] In obtaining deposits of chrome, iron, pyrites, nickel, manganese, and bauxite, German agents easily squeezed out Italian entrepreneurs.[66] Germans also quickly confiscated or bought at rock-bottom prices stocks of tobacco, leather, and cotton. During the first weeks following the armistice, before the Italians could bat an eye, the Reich had appropriated around ninety-five percent of Greek raw materials and industrial output.[67] Momentarily relaxing their grip, the Germans allowed an Italian firm to buy up shares in the Lokris mines containing nickel, important for the production of armor plate. Shipments of cotton, resin, and other goods useful to the Italian war effort sporadically arrived in Italy.

As 1941 turned, to make matters worse, the Axis armies imposed a new currency and vouchers on the oppressed Greeks, which enabled the armies to make profligate purchases at bargain-basement prices. Ultimately, the Greek government was compelled to redeem huge occupation expenses in drachmas, whose exchange rates were manipulated to assure Axis exploitation.

After the Germans turned the plundered country over to the Italians, Ralph Kent, the Principal of Athens College, wrote in August 1941: "It is one of the nastiest tricks they [the Germans] have yet played on the beam end of the Axis, and one suspects that the Italians know it."[68] Just as in Croatia, where the Germans moved quickly to snap up economic resources in the Italian "living space,"

---

63. DDI, 9, V1, 92, Ciano to Alfieri, 12 May 1941.
64. Lisa Bregantin, "Fronte greco-albanese," in *Gli Italiani in guerra*, vol. IV, Tomo 2: *Il Ventennio fascista: la Seconda guerra mondiale* (Turin: UTET, 2008), p. 193.
65. Etmektsoglou-Koehn, *Axis Exploitation of Wartime Greece, 1941–1943*, p. 288.
66. ASMAE, AP, 52, Ciano to GABAP, N. 6098, 1 May 1941.
67. Davide Rodogno, *Fascism's European Empire: Italian Occupation During the Second World War* (Cambridge: Cambridge University Press, 2006), p. 236.
68. Cited in Ralph Kent, "I Saw Greece Looted," in Homer W. Davis, *Greece Fights. The People Behind the Front* (New York City: American Friends of Greece, 1942), p. 65.

so in Greece did they present Italy, the "privileged" occupier, with an already fleeced country.

Widespread hunger in Greece, which greeted the 11th Army as it took up positions, turned into outright famine as 1941 came to an end. A tight British blockade contributed to food shortages, and Bulgaria seized the most fertile agricultural regions to deny Greece its breadbasket. In addition to the 11th Army's depredations, the Wehrmacht deepened Greek misery by commandeering agricultural products at will. Mussolini caustically replied: "The Germans have taken from the Greeks even their shoelaces, and now they pretend to place the blame for the economic situation on our shoulders. We can take the responsibility but only on condition that they clear out of Athens and the entire country."[69] Ciano began to worry: "Anything is possible, from epidemics to ferocious revolts on the part of a people who know they have nothing to lose."[70] He pleaded that Italy had little food to spare for Greek relief; the Italian merchant fleet had not a single ship to spare.[71] To ease the threat of starvation, the Italians worked on the Germans in January and March 1942 to arrive at a final agreement that would establish limits on Greece's occupation costs. But the OKW could not be stopped from the practice of levying forced loans to sustain the war effort. Invoking Italian "humanitarianism," both Ghigi and Geloso deplored the Wehrmacht's unrestrained pillage.[72]

On 20 July 1942 on his way back to Italy from his junket in North Africa, Mussolini flew into Athens where he was greeted by currency breakdown and dead and dying Greeks scattered about the streets of the city. The Italians once again brought up the dangers of imposing exorbitant expenses on Greece. Communism feeds on starvation, which, in turn, reinforces alienation of Greek public figures from the Axis, Mussolini told Altenburg, the Reich Plenipotentiary.[73]

Back in Rome, deprecating Germany's "systematic impoverishment of Greece,"[74] Mussolini wrote Hitler, quoting Sotirios Gotzamanis, the prime minister: "Greece is on the brink of financial—and therefore economic and political—catastrophe.... Hunger is a bad counselor." The Duce followed up: "It was the interest of the Axis that Greece should be orderly and tranquil."[75] Caring

---

69. *The Ciano Diaries*, 4 October 1941.
70. Ibid., 11 October 1941.
71. Ibid., 26 January 1942.
72. Mark Mazower, *Inside Hitler's Greece: The Experience of Occupation* (New Haven and London: Yale University Press, 1993), pp. 31–32; Etmiktsoglou-Koehn, *Axis Exploitation of Wartime Greece, 1941–1943*, pp. 498–99.
73. Etmiktsoglou-Koehn, *Axis Exploitation of Wartime Greece, 1941–1943*, p. 499, n. 134.
74. *The Ciano Papers*, 22 July 1942.
75. DDI, 9, IX, 4, Mussolini to Hitler, 22 July 1942.

nothing about Greek suffering, Hitler had little to say.[76] Between 15 August and 30 September the Italians sent 93,000 quintals of grain, mostly to the Ionian Islands, Epiros and the Cyclades. The Germans sent a trifling 50,170 quintals while informing Rome that "for the future the Italian government must take the responsibility for provisioning Greece, since Greece lies in Italy's sphere of influence."[77]

Ghigi was appalled by German heartlessness. Mussolini, too, was "very much disturbed by the attitude of the Germans" and their absurd claims on the Greeks, which, according to Ciano, meant that "the Germans are trying to create disorder and complications at all costs."[78] Aware that bankruptcy was imminent, Ciano commented: "Today the middle class is already obliged to give up its jewels, its beds, at times its daughters, in order to live. Hence, we are facing uprisings and disorders, the proportions of which it is impossible to estimate accurately at this time. But nothing can make the Germans change their absurd and idiotic attitude, and the worst of it is that we Italians must stand for 80 percent of the consequences."[79] Negotiations with them were "Tough going!" With utter obtuseness, the Germans "insist on demanding a crazy sum, which in the space of a few months would cause the total collapse of the drachma. Even before this we shall have a political crisis, because the Greek government will resign, and then we can hold the country only by force of arms. The Duce agrees with me, and expresses himself in harsh terms against the Germans. He goes so far as to say that 'the only way to explain such a bestial attitude on the part of the Germans is that they are convinced that they are lost, and since they have to die, they want to create general confusion.'"[80]

To placate the Greeks, Mussolini, if reluctantly, allowed the International Red Cross to organize the distribution of relief goods. In September 1942 the first supplies arrived from Montreal.[81] Mussolini also asked Bulgaria to deliver Greece 100,000 tons of wheat or maize, but that was like asking Hitler to feed starving peoples in Nazi concentration camps. While the Axis Powers engaged in acid exchanges over how to handle hunger, starving men were left with little alternative but revolt, to kill, or be killed. Although humanitarian concerns were not absent, Mussolini's attempt to soften the severe image of the Italian conquistador was due mainly to a feeling of helplessness over Italy's inability to compete with the Axis ally for domination of Greece. Germany had tossed Italy

76. DDI, 9, IX, 21, Hitler to Mussolini, 4 August 1942; Mazower, *Inside Hitler's Greece*, p. 67
77. Cited in Mazower, *Inside Hitler's Greece*, p. 31.
78. *The Ciano Diaries,* 8 October 1942.
79. Ibid., 10 October 1942.
80. Ibid., 17 October 1942.
81. Etmektsoglou-Koehn, *Axis Exploitation of Wartime Greece 1941–1943*, p. 454.

aside in the competition over Greek resources, managed two-thirds of Greece's export trade, and controlled the country's exchange relations. Lacking the strength to challenge the Germans, Mussolini's only hope was to persuade Greeks that a close liaison with Italy, a kindred Mediterranean power,[82] was a better deal than life under untrammeled German oppression. But if the Duce had been able to put up a tough fight against the Germans over control of Pavelić in Croatia, he stood no chance of loosening the German iron grip on Greece.

Finally on 16 August 1942 the two Axis Powers took small steps to deal with Greek famine. Hermann Neubacher, named special plenipotentiary of the Reich for financial and economic questions in Greece, met several times with Alberto d'Agostino, the president of the Italian Banca Commerciale. They were not able to agree on meaningful remedies beyond stopgap measures to ease the famine.

The Italian occupation of Greece had not paid off in any economic dividends. Imperialism, which was supposed to advantage the conqueror by bringing in a steady inflow of resources, instead brought about a hemorrhaging of funds spent in provisioning the Italian army and the famished colonial peoples. At the same time the Axis ally whisked away the bulk of the country's movable assets. Ghigi might have been truly moved by Greek famine, but any concern Mussolini had for the country's suffering vanished when General Geloso set in motion a vicious counterinsurgency at the end of the year.

During 1942 armed resistance in Greece slowly spread to the countryside and mountains. Initially it was fragmented, divided into rival groups. At times the various leaders tolerated each other, but eventually, due to conflicting post-war aims, mutual suspicion and even abhorrence, open conflict flared, hampering the common purpose of expelling the invaders. Because the king and his government-in-exile were unable to coordinate and support insurrection, the Communist party, ELAS, was able to step into the leadership vacuum in spring 1942.[83] Capitalizing on urban hostility to the Axis and their collaborators, they won popularity before launching partisan warfare.[84] The nationalist officer Napoleon Zervas formed a second resistance movement in early summer 1942. Urged by the British, he took to the mountains as head of EDES, the National Republican Greek League. Brigandage did not cease, however, and both the local population and Italian occupiers were not always able to distinguish between insurgent and predator. This is not surprising, for sometimes the ideologically

---

82. DDI, 9, VII, 264, Ciano to Ghigi, 17 June 1941.
83. John Hondros, *Occupation and Resistance: The Greek Agony, 1941–1944* (New York: Pella, 1983), p. 101.
84. Etmektsoglou-Koehn, *Axis Exploitation of Wartime Greece, 1941–1943*, p. 222; Hondros, *Occupation and Resistance*, p. 111.

oriented guerrillas pillaged the uncommitted with as much savagery as brigands who, in turn, sometimes moved seamlessly into the political insurgency.

The Italian response was quick in word and slow in deed. In late summer 1941 General Profundi ordered his field commanders to repress rebels in a "totalitarian manner." The Greeks are astute, he wrote, but Italians must be more astute still and act like victors.[85] This was only the beginning. On 4 March 1942 the order went out "to shoot all those who give hospitality and assistance to English parachutists and Greek soldiers still at large."[86]

Already in this early phase of the Greek resistance Geloso worried about the ability of his troops to stamp it out. To disarm the population, he ordered his troops to proceed with roundups with tightened organization, improved reconnaissance, and inflexible will.[87] Suffering from what he called "a peacetime mentality," his soldiers needed constant reminding that they lived in an ambiance of war.[88] The Blackshirt battalions stood at the ready. As opposed to the cumbersome regular army units, they were able to move rapidly and engage the "bandits" fiercely in a task for which they were particularly well suited.[89]

Overall, the army, suffering from sickness, malaria, poor food, and insufficient leave time, produced scarce results. Thanks to faulty preparation and scattered deployment, many "rebels" slipped through the dragnets. Geloso raged against the "stereotypical training" of his troops and their "mental laziness."[90] In areas infested with rebels, the troops set up posts as if preparing for a family picnic in a peaceful Italian countryside. Geloso was concerned that his troops, dulled into *quietismo* by boring garrison duty, were loitering in dangerous places and frequenting local public places awash in "bandits" and enemies,[91] thereby ignoring the reality of guerrilla warfare.[92] The officers behaved no better. They were stolid and frivolous, and wrote superficial reports. "Gentlemen," Geloso reminded, Italy is at war and in a conquered country infested with enemies. Don't ever camp in villages, but always in elevated places easily defended; don't go out in small columns.[93] "Those captured with arms must be eliminated on the spot,"[94] he implored. To meet the challenge of insurgent warfare, Geloso, like Roatta, threw out the old rigid military handbook in favor of new tactics that

---

85. AUSSME, L 15, R/28, 26 August 1941.
86. Ibid., N I-II, DS, b. 736, 4 March 1942.
87. Ibid., Geloso report, 20 April 1942.
88. Ibid., Geloso to his commanders, 20 March 1942.
89. Ibid., 27 April 1942.
90. Ibid., b. 966, Geloso directive, 19 August 1942.
91. Ibid., b. 1064, Geloso report, 16 September 1942.
92. Ibid., b. 1098, Geloso report, 30 November 1942.
93. Ibid., b. 632, Geloso report, 24 September 1942.
94. Ibid., b. 966, A 10, Geloso report, 19 September 1942.

stressed quick responses and greater initiative in the conduct of counter-insurgency.

At the same time Geloso anxiously watched his troops engage in overkill. On 30 August 1942 he wrote: "Before undertaking a raid, commanders must take stock of the brigandage they face before taking excessive measures; and they must avoid useless pursuit of the vanishing enemy." Most irritating were the many field reports proclaiming the capture of isolated knots of innocent by-standers as stunning achievements.[95]

The ill-prepared officers and troops frequently panicked and struck back heavy-handedly. Throughout July and August Geloso admonished them to use force judiciously. Conduct reprisals with "extreme foresight" and care, he counseled. "Firmness and inexhaustible energy against the guilty....must not degenerate into a blind brutality inconsistent with our tradition of justice in the Italian army, for such responses are deleterious to our prestige and contrary to our interests..... During a *rastrellamento* only torch houses proven to be bandit dwellings or belonging to sympathizers. Shoot outright only bandits and rebels who are armed...and take into custody suspects who will be subjected to regular judicial procedures"[96]

Pietromarchi noted that Ghigi and Geloso—as well as Ciano—had cautioned against large-scale reprisals, such as the shooting of hostages and other barbarities, as over-the-top measures in dealing with Greek dissidence. According to Pietromarchi, Geloso claimed that he had received such draconian directives directly from the Führer.[97]

When guerrilla attacks surged in early autumn 1942, however, Geloso became less vigilant in avoiding excesses and more prone to issuing robust responses. Since it was hard to find "rebels" among a hostile people, and since the population openly supported them, Geloso imparted sharply worded memoranda to his field commanders starting in mid-September. The commanders have to promulgate stringent curfews and arrest those suspected of giving sympathy and help, he ordered. They must impose fines, sequestrations, and carry out comprehensive house searches. If family members are missing, they are to be considered as "bandits." There should be no hesitation in interning as hostages all males older than eighteen belonging to these families. "Bandits" and "rebels" captured with arms must be shot on the spot at the moment of their capture.[98]

---

95. Ibid., b. 632, Geloso directive, 30 August 1942.
96. Ibid., b. 966, 22 July 1942.
97. PP, *Diario*, 24 June 1942.
98. AUSSME, L 13, Undated Geloso memorandum [probably mid-September 1942]; N I-II, b. 1054, Allegato 7, Geloso to field commanders, 8 October 1942.

On 23 September Geloso instructed the troops to break the rebellion, segregate the andartes from the civilian population, and remove the male adult population from built-up areas for internment in "provisional concentration camps." For mopping-up operations in areas infested by "bandits," "exercise no pity." In the event of armed aggression, "evacuate villages to a radius of ten kilometers and then destroy them." No living soul should remain in the hands of the enemy.[99] An order on 29 September called for the arrest and internment of suspected local heads and community notables, and collective penalties were levied on villages to be paid in drachmas, foodstuffs, farm animals, and moveable materials. The local populations were to be held responsible and punished.[100]

Frustrated over the meager results of the expeditions against the partisans, Geloso told his troops to burn houses of those who have flown to the mountains—houses that obviously serve as outposts and collection points. Exercise severe and inexorable firmness toward the population and show no pity toward the "bandits" and their fellow travelers. Shoot everyone bearing arms save for leaders who, if possible, can be bribed into providing information. Since the population at large is often in complicity with the "bandits," do not trust village leaders or Greek gendarmes. Execute leaders in public squares as a salutary message to the population to stop peasants from giving food to the rebels. Fire on all illegally armed people who attempt to flee and all those who entered prohibited zones around railroads and military instillations.[101] On 29 December 1942 Geloso ordered the troops to deny rebels desperately needed food and to undertake reprisals on the population to deter them from provisioning the "bandits."[102]

When Greek insurgency began to overpower the Italian occupiers during latter 1942, General Geloso summoned ethnic minorities to afford military assistance.[103] The Italian historian Davide Conti indicates that during this period the Italians encouraged the formation of a Legione Valacca made up of Armenians under the direction of the Carabinieri, which was responsible for numerous homicides and outrages.[104]

---

99. Ibid., Geloso memorandum.
100. AUSSME, N I-II, DS, b. 1064, 29 September 1942, Allegato no. 3:
101. Ibid., b. 1064, Allegato 7, Geloso to his field commanders, 8 October 1942.
102. Ibid., b. 1098, Geloso to army commanders, and Allegato 4, 29 December 1942.
103. Ibid., b. 1122, Geloso memorandum, 30 November 1942.
104. On the Legione Valacca see NAW, T-821, 354, 000786-8, 000824-26; Conti, *L'occupazione italiana dei balcani*, p. 174. Apparently the Italians did little in utilizing the Aromeni in breaking up Greece by forming a "Latin" bastion in the lower Balkans. A foreign ministry document of early January 1943 talks of missed opportunities and proposes that the full weight of Italy should be thrown behind the Aromeni yearning for autonomy or independence—a little late in the day. USSME, DS, IV, D. 13, Memorandum of the foreign ministry, The "Aromeni" of the Balkans, 4 January 1943.

Having dismissed any distinction between bystander and insurgent, Geloso concluded correctly that practically every Greek hated the Italian occupiers. At every opportunity they rallied around the resistance—offering sympathy, sheltering guerrillas on the run, providing them food and weapons, and participating in hit-and-run operations. To keep an entire population subdued as his own army floundered in futility, Geloso struck back blindly in what was tantamount to a war on civilians no less brutal than the one waged by General Roatta in Yugoslavia. But his severe counterinsurgency measures boomeranged. By escalating Greek hatred of Italy, Geloso inadvertently provided the partisans a boon for mass recruitment.

The defection of the gendarmes was vitally important in bringing men and arms into the resistance. Their loss contributed to the surge in the guerrilla movement, signaling the breakdown of Geloso's policing methods and forcing him to rely solely on Italian military resources. As autumn progressed, the guerrillas, to isolate the Italian troops, conducted attacks on public officials, Axis sympathizers, and army informers.[105] The Italians struck back by arresting large numbers of suspects in their ceaseless efforts to track down EAM/ELAS insurgents. As attacks on Italian troops increased over the winter, many former Greek officers were seized as hostages and executed in reprisal killings. Worse was to come in 1943 when the demoralized Italians fought back desperately against a tidal wave of insurgency.

---

105. AUSSME, N I-II, DS, b. 1070, 31 October 1942.

Chapter VIII

The Vortex of Defeat

Adieu Libya
Desert Wrap-up

Adieu Libya

On 23 October 1942 General Bernard Montgomery launched his carefully prepared offensive with a strong and well-trained force of 230,000 men, a truly cosmopolitan army that included British, Free French, Indian, Australian, South African, and New Zealanders. They faced a worn-down enemy consisting of about 54,000 Italians and 50,000 Germans. The Axis faced daunting supply problems. As opposed to the British, who had depots in Egypt a short distance from the front lines, the Axis had to cover 2,000 kilometers from Tripoli and 500 kilometers from Tobruk, pounded by constant air attacks. Montgomery's advantages in tanks, 1,440 to 540, and in planes, 1,500 to 350, gave him such a big edge that he could hardly fail to win. In a barrage reminiscent of World War I, 900 heavy guns and bombers unleashed their fury on the Axis forces deprived of Rommel, who was home in Germany on sick leave.

In a few days of fierce fighting, the Axis infantry and artillery (l'Armata Corazzata Italo-Tedesca—ACIT) were down to a third of their opening battle strength; only thirty tanks remained operational. General Curio Barbasetti Di Prun informed Cavallero that his troops were headed for total collapse.[1] On his return to the battlefield, Rommel intuited correctly that Montgomery was gearing up for a *coup de grace*. He saw no other choice but to order a retreat toward Fuka on 2 November using the Axis armor, including *Ariete*, as a screen to enable the non-motorized Italian infantry to withdraw.[2] In spite of Montgomery's thundering artillery, the Axis forces resisted stubbornly, and their carefully laid mines took a heavy toll on the advancing enemy. Instead of a speedy *tour de force* promised by heavy superiority in equipment and men, Montgomery moved forward cautiously.

At this point the dictators courted catastrophe. Mussolini instructed Cavallero to advise Rommel that he should "hold fast at the actual front at whatever the cost."[3] Hitler was just as obstinate: "In the situation in which you find yourself there can be no other thought but to stand fast, yield not a yard of ground and throw every gun and every man into battle.... It would not be the first time in history that a strong will has triumphed over the bigger battalions. As to your troops, you can show them no other road than that to victory or death."[4]

Rommel was dumbfounded. What nonsense for Hitler to suggest that the enemy was reaching "the end of his strength."[5] But since a Führer order invited no disobedience, Rommel instructed his already retreating men to about-face, which wrought havoc on the non-motorized Italian infantry, his "ball and chain," caught in the open desert with no transport or air cover. An outraged Rommel met with Kesselring, who, after some heated words, conceded the mindlessness of "stand or die" and renewed the order for retreat. The hard-hit *Ariete* gallantly held out long enough to stymie Montgomery's plan to encircle and destroy the main body of armored forces, including DAK and the 90th Light, which were able to withdraw westwards largely unimpeded.[6]

Many Italian foot soldiers were lost in the mayhem. Contingents of the XXI Corps, without trucks to transport the infantry, were destroyed after stiff resistance against the overwhelmingly superior British; the rest were abandoned in the desert to be captured or die of hunger and thirst. The XX Motorized Corps had been practically wiped out.[7] In this disaster Rommel admitted that the

---

1. Cavallero, *Diario*, 30 October 1942.
2. *The Rommel Papers*, p. 314.
3. Cavallero, *Diario*, 3 November 1942; *Terza offensiva britannica*, pp. 157–58.
4. Cited in *The Rommel Papers*, p. 321, n. 1.
5. *Germany in the Second World War*, VI: 784.
6. Ian W. Walker, *Iron Hulls Iron Hearts* (Ramsbury: Crowood Press, 2006), p. 174.
7. *The Rommel Papers*, p. 325.

Italians had fought "with exemplary courage." Doubtless, the twenty-four hours lost because of Hitler's unfortunate order had been crucial. But for that, "we would probably have been able to escape to Fuka with the bulk of our infantry."[8]

Ciano acknowledged that "our forces are wearing out and supplies are arriving as if delivered through an eyedropper." On 6 November he recorded: "Even the Duce thinks that as matters stand Libya will probably be lost." Other high-level Italian military "see the morrow in dark colors."[9] The Italians were at one in faulting Rommel for the heavy losses sustained by their infantry. General Barbasetti remarked: "The sacrifice of the XX Motorized Corps abandoned in the desert has been very painful." Rommel retorted: "Is this a reproach? From the Führer there has arrived no word of disapproval." Barbasetti replied that he had seen many Wehrmacht trucks in retreat filled with useless materiel or only German troops and wondered why there was no effort to take on board Italians who were under his supervision. Rommel rejoined that he needed the transport for his own troops.[10]

From the comforts of Rome, on 6 November 1942 Mussolini conveyed to Rommel his belief that the retreat should be halted at the Sollum-Halfaya-Sidi Omar line, the gateway to Egypt. Rommel, deep in the fury of battle, retorted that his position could not be held. In addition to the heavy Italian losses suffered earlier, the celebrated *Folgore* paratroopers and the motorized *Ariete* had been decimated. Thirsty soldiers were milling around helplessly, and much German heavy equipment had been captured or destroyed. Still, many Italian units made it to Capuzzo, on the Libyan side of the wire, where Lieutenant-General Giuseppe de Stefani, commander of the practically defunct XX Motorized Corps, rallied the survivors for a new combat group.[11]

Consistent with Mussolini's orders to hold the Sollum line, the Italians moved elements of the *Pistoia* and some battalions up to the Libya-Egyptian frontier, ready to be placed under Rommel's command. "I was forced to decline," wrote Rommel, "as I no longer had the necessary equipment for their communications, transport or supply."[12]

After negotiating a terrible traffic pile-up at the Halfaya Pass on the frontier, the Axis forces finally passed through to the Libyan side on the 10th. Egypt was lost. Italian military historians claim that Rommel abandoned Halfaya without

---

8. Ibid., p. 329.

9. *The Ciano Diaries*, 3, 6 November 1942.

10. Mario Montanari, *Le Operazioni in Africa settentrionale*, Vol IV: *Enfidaville* (Rome: SME US, 1993), p. 30, and Allegato 1, Conversation between Barbasetti and Rommel, 9 November 1942, p. 585; *Terza offensiva britannica*, pp. 228, 236.

11. *The Rommel Papers*, pp. 399–400; *Terza offensiva britannica*, p. 215; Samuel Mitchem, *Rommel's Desert War* (Mechanicsburg, PA: Stackpole Books, 2007), p. 179.

12. *The Rommel Papers*, p. 347.

contesting the eminently defensible pass, which gave Montgomery an easy drive-through the next day.[13] Would Rommel scuttle Cyrenaica next? Mussolini, supported by Rintelen, recommended that he draw a line in the sand at the border to allow reinforcement of positions to the rear, but leave the door open for further retreat.[14]

Although Rommel can be fairly criticized for obstinacy and a bias against Italians, it must be noted that he was a chivalrous commander. On 8 November 1942 ACIT headquarters finally received Hitler's chilling order of 18 October 1942, which stated that even if in uniform, allied soldiers "in Europe or Africa" were to be "slaughtered to a man, either in combat or while escaping." General Siegfried Westphal burned this directive with Rommel's consent.[15]

The Allies in Operation Torch knocked the Axis off balance on 8 November by a dramatic landing along the coasts of French Morocco and Algeria. Weakly opposed by the Vichy military, they pressed straightaway toward Tunisia where they hoped to catch Rommel in a pincers movement. But the Axis moved swiftly by undertaking a crash defense of Tunisia, which meant that even fewer supplies would be available for Rommel's beleaguered forces in Egypt.

With only diminishing resources to stop the mammoth enemy plodding inexorably toward him, Rommel was unable to prevent him from gashing holes in the Axis lines during a rush on Tobruk in the middle of November. This startling turn of events caused him to ponder not only an evacuation of Cyrenaica, but also a brisk pullback to Tunisia where the remnants of his forces could be added to the Axis build-up in hilly terrain far more suitable for defense than the endless deserts in Libya. One Italian intelligence officer concluded that Rommel was considering an honorable surrender.[16] The general's superiors in Rome concluded that their audacious warrior had turned into a naysayer.

To disabuse Rommel of these negative thoughts, Cavallero flew to Tripoli, where he handed Bastico Mussolini's order to defend Tripolitania "to the bitter end....with such acts and heroism that make for a true epic!" Simply ignore the Allied landings in Morocco, the embattled Italian general was told: "You, Bastico, don't have a western front."[17]

Matters took a bizarre turn when Rommel and Cavallero did not meet in Benghazi on the 13th.[18] Rommel concluded that Cavallero avoided him because, as a weak office-chair soldier who lacked the will to win, he did not relish facing

---

13. *Operazioni*. IV: 31; *Terza offensiva britannica*, pp. 364–65.
14. Ibid.: 32; *Terza offensiva britannica*, p. 229.
15. *Germany and the Second World War*, VI: 808.
16. *Operazioni*, IV: 40.
17. Ibid.
18. *The Rommel Papers*, p. 352.

an indomitable warrior.[19] The official Italian military historian Mario Montanari provides a different version, claiming that Cavallero had gone out of his way to meet with Rommel, who discourteously evaded him. More upsetting still, Rommel had unilaterally ordered the abandonment of positions at Ain el Gazala before experiencing serious pressure from the enemy.[20] Finally, when the meeting of the Axis generals finally assembled, the Italians Cavallero, Barbasetti, and Navarini resolved on risking everything in defending El Agheila. Cavallero departed for Rome on the 15th.

The next day ACIT and all forces operating in Libya, including Rommel's, were placed under the command of General Bastico, who took his orders directly from the CS and ultimately Mussolini. With the Axis chased out of Egypt, the High Command Delegation in North Africa (Delease) passed into history. But nothing had really changed, for there was still no common German-Italian high command, and Rommel's direct access to Hitler was left unimpaired.[21]

Not to be outdone by his fellow dictator, Mussolini talked about will and faith holding the keys to victory. All eyes should fix on him to resolve crises. Since the paltry force facing the Axis was advancing at a snail's pace, it was the enemy, not Italy, that faced disaster in North Africa. To encourage Bastico to hold his ground in Tripolitania, Mussolini wrote on 16 November: "Everything possible will be sent from the mother country to reinforce a stabilized line that must, I repeat must, be held no matter the cost.... I count on you, dear Marshal Bastico, and I am sure that the victor of Santander will as always be at the top of his form."[22]

How Bastico reacted to Mussolini's pep talk is unknown, but he did not refrain from giving Cavallero an earful on the Desert Fox. "I must tell you a few things about Rommel," he wrote. "During the period in which he was my subordinate, not only did he never obey but showed me an attitude that was not always correct from the disciplinary standpoint." [23]

Angered by such treatment, Bastico asked for the second time to be recalled and recommended that General Roatta replace him. Such an idea, however, would never have sat well with Hitler, who said of Roatta: "Clever? He is the Fouché of the Fascist revolution, an unprincipled spy. He is indeed a spy."[24] Bastico was told, once again, to stay at his post.

19. *Operazioni*, IV: 43.
20. Ibid.: 45.
21. *Germany and the Second World War*, VI: 75; *Terza offensiva britannica*, p. 241.
22. *Operazioni*, IV: 48.
23. Ibid.: Allegato no. 4, Bastico to Cavallero, 16 November 1942, pp. 596–97.
24. *Hitler and His Generals: Military Conferences 1942–1945* (New York: Enigma Books, 2004), p. 134.

Mussolini's peremptory order of 16 November, which called for defense to the last man at the Tripolitanian border, was greeted as lunacy by Rommel, who justified his defiance by shifting the fault to the CS for failure to meet the goal of 4,000 tons of gasoline and 4,000 tons of ammunition deemed necessary for holding the Marsa el Brega Line.[25] For Rommel, the real problem was not the question of supply shortages as such, but Italian inefficiency and flagging efforts in carrying them over the Mediterranean to the front lines.[26] Annoyed by Rommel's caution, Mussolini wrote Hitler on 19 November that the Axis armies should hold El Agheila for the defense of Tripolitania,[27] to which Hitler agreed.[28]

In defiance of the two dictators, Rommel, after destroying harbor installations and supply depots, ordered his troops on the 19th to pull out of Benghazi toward new positions near the Tripolitanian border. Rommel justified this fallback to Rome on the heavy losses recently sustained. The Italian X Corps, *Pavia, Brescia,* and *Folgore,* had been taken prisoner "almost to a man"; the Italian XX1 Corps, *Trento* and *Bologna,* had been "wiped out"; and a regiment without tanks was all that remained of the XX Armored Corps, *Trieste* motorized, *Littorio* and *Ariete* armored.[29] Since only a third of his fighting capability was left, and important reserve stocks and supply dumps had been lost, he held out no hope in parrying a British outflanking movement.

Just as the Axis armies settled into the Agedabia position, having traveled 1,000 kilometers in eighteen days, Rommel on 22 November again faced a tough decision. His Afrika Korps was down to one battered German division. To avoid certain defeat, he considered a further withdrawal of infantry to the Buerat line deep in Tripolitania.[30] This was not an easy decision to make, for the El Agheila line was more rock-solid than the one at Buerat thanks to its marshland, vast salt plains, and extensive sandbars. But Rommel reasoned that the enemy, faced with covering another 300 kilometers of Sirta desert, would give ACIT breathing room for at least three weeks to redeploy and integrate Italian reinforcements that had begun to arrive in the lines. Although furnished with old equipment, the freshly arrived troops had not been worn down by the battles of El Alamein.

To break the deadlock in strategy, Rommel met on the 24th with Kesselring, Cavallero and senior Italian officers at Mussolini's triumphal Arco dei Fileni, called by the British "Marble Arch" (located on the boundary between the Libyan provinces of Cyrenaica and Tripolitania). In a bruising meeting, Rommel,

---

25. *Operazioni.* IV: 48.
26. *Operazioni,* IV, Allegato 6, pp. 603–8.
27. DDI, 9, IX, 325, Mussolini to Hitler, 19 November 1942.
28. Ibid., 331, Hitler to Mussolini, 20 November 1942.
29. *Germany and the Second World War,* VI: 811; Deakin, *The Brutal Friendship,* p. 82.
30. *Germany and the Second World War,* VI: 812.

concerned solely with his strategic position, declared his intention of holding off the enemy at Mersa el Brega long enough for the Axis to evacuate this last toe-hold in Africa, thus saving both troops and equipment in an orderly evacuation that would spare the Axis the agony of Dunkirk, or worse, mass surrender.

Taking a more global perspective, Cavallero argued that the mainland would be placed in immediate peril if Italy withdrew immediately from North Africa. Delaying the loss of Libya as long as possible was imperative to ward off this danger and to buy time for widening the bridgehead at Tunisia.

As far as Kesselring was concerned, Rommel's task was to stop the British from setting up airfields in western Libya that would enable them to attack the Axis forces forming up in Tunisia. The ubiquitous "Smiling Albert" was quite happy in playing the double-role of Hitler's mouthpiece and Cavallero's front man. In belittling the enemy and magnifying the strength of the Axis armies—even advocating counterattack—Kesselring took Rommel's penchant for retreat as defeatism. From the shadows Cavallero looked on contentedly, believing that the German general was standing up for Italy. But Kesselring saw the matter strictly from the standpoint of the Luftwaffe, whose mission to defend Germany's communications in the Mediterranean would be seriously impaired if the British were to advance on the Axis airfields at Tripoli, Biserta, and Tunis.

On 25 November Mussolini reiterated his demand to stand fast at the Marsa Brega line and urged Rommel to seize the initiative by attacking the enemy with lightning jabs. Rommel ignored these orders and told Bastico that he must deliver 500 vehicles pronto lest the Italian XXI Infantry Corps be left to perish. Montanari lit into Rommel for his rude and disrespectful behavior toward Bastico, his superior.[31] But the Italians were in no position to discipline him.[32]

After the many flair-ups with Bastico, Rommel impulsively flew off to Germany on 28 November to tell Hitler that the Axis game was up in North Africa; the troops should be evacuated while there was still time. Hitler's response: "How dare you leave your command without my permission?" When told by the Führer, "the Panzerarmee had thrown away its weapons," Rommel backed away, "a nervous wreck."[33] Against his better judgment, he had to obey his leader. Rommel would faithfully carry out his unchanged order to hold Tunisia and North Africa as long as possible in the hope of staving off an Allied landing in the lower Balkans, a possibility that gave the Führer many a restless night.

---

31. *Operazioni*, IV: 62.
32. *The Ciano Diaries*, 30 November 1942.
33. *Germany in the Second World War*, VI: 813.

On learning that Rommel had seen Hitler without telling him, Bastico remarked: "His gesture is an act of open indiscipline and a flat-out refusal to acknowledge my authority as supreme commander and governor general. If any Italian general had done this he would be hauled before a war tribunal for abandoning his post before the enemy."[34] Rommel, he felt, had sullied his prestige and flouted his superior rank.[35] The Desert Fox was hounded by criticism from all quarters.

After Rommel's encounter with Hitler, Göring accompanied him to Rome with full powers to negotiate with the Italians. As a strong exponent of a build-up in Tunisia, he promised to send the Göring Division and two SS divisions totaling 45,000 men, an offer accompanied by gratuitous criticisms of Italy's war effort.[36] Rommel, though appalled at Göring's manner, shared certain of his views. "Many Italians," he wrote perceptively, "felt very deeply that the Axis was a sham, and consequently believed that in final victory we would have scant regard for their interest. It was generally felt that, if Tripolitania were lost, Mussolini would be threatened by a political crisis in Italy."[37]

When by the end of November the Axis forces fully settled in at the El Agheila pass on the Mersa el Brega line, they were out of immediate jeopardy. Here they would enjoy an unexpected seventeen-day respite. From their position on the border between Cyrenaica and Tripolitania, Benghazi lay a hundred and fifty miles inside Cyrenaica. Montgomery's caution and the heavy rains that impeded his advance convinced the Axis leaders, excepting Rommel, that they could encamp there indefinitely.

Not concerned that he was a minority of one, Rommel on 6–7 December began a withdrawal from El Agheila on the coast, picked up some reinforcements including a refurbished *Ariete*, and, around the 19th, settled in his new defensive positions at Buerat 230 miles from Tripoli, untroubled by British pursuit.[38] No sooner had he arrived in Buerat that Rommel informed Bastico that if they stayed put the enemy would break through their ragged defenses on the first assault and head on an open road to Tripoli.[39]

This was no longer simply *déja vue* for Bastico; it had finally dawned on him that the sunny promises from Rome of heavy reinforcements for North Africa

---

34. *Operazioni*, IV: 64.
35. Ibid., Allegato 7, Bastico to Cavallero, 28 November 1942, p. 609.
36. *The Ciano Papers,* 1 December 1942.
37. *The Rommel Papers*, p. 369.
38. *Terza offensiva britannica*, p. 298.
39. *Germany and the Second World War*, VI: 815.

amounted to double-talk. Holding existing positions "to the last" began to give way to Rommel's retreat mode.[40]

But Cavallero, looking at the matter from a larger perspective, argued: "If we don't hold Libya, Africa will be lost."[41] Mussolini supported him by imparting this order on 19 December: "Resist to the last. I repeat: Resist to the last with all units of the German-Italian Panzerarmee in the Buerat positions."[42]

Mussolini actually did speak for many Italians who were furious over Rommel's inclination to abandon Buerat without fighting a decisive battle that might have saved Tripolitania. But Rommel answered only to supreme battlefield dictates as he saw them. Sure that the 8th Army was about to spring a trap on 30,000 Italian infantry, he took Mussolini's order as suicidal. Undoubtedly he also resented Bastico's admonition: "It is….absolutely necessary that the foot soldiers [Italian] not be sacrificed once again."[43] While this charge might have had validity at El Alamein, Rommel had since then taken precautions to salvage Bastico's soldiers as best he could on the many retreats. A shaken Bastico commented: "I exclude the possibility that Rommel can comply with the said [Mussolini's] orders."[44]

In Rome military reality finally hit home. On 20 December Cavallero handed the Axis armies another Duce order, which indicated a softening from "resistance to the last" to "holding on as long as possible." Time must be bought for the consolidation of the Tunisian defenses.[45] This change was rendered unnecessary by General Montgomery's pedantic, by-the-book tactics. While Bastico had joined Rommel in expecting a major British attack, Montgomery, satisfied over having effortlessly captured El Agheila, called for a stand-down to reorganize and regroup. Rommel was therefore allowed to assemble his army safely behind the Buerat Line ready for any eventuality.

On 26 December Cavallero charged Paolo Puntoni, the king's aide-de-camp, with the task of telling him that, given the impossibility of provisioning the Libyan sector, the CS was prepared to evacuate Tripolitania for a final stand in Tunisia. Since the military cupboard was bare, Italy was reduced to reliance on Germany for reinforcements, munitions, and primary resources. Having no leverage, Cavallero fawned before Kesselring in the hope that the Third Reich would answer the Italian call. Such total dependency allowed the Germans to

---

40. *Operazioni*, IV: 137.
41. DDI, 9, IX, 422, Cavallero to Mussolini, 18–19 December 1942.
42. Cited in *Germany and the Second World War*, VI: 815.
43. *Operazioni*, IV: 139.
44. Ibid.: 138.
45. Ibid.: 141.

offer supplies, break promises, and boss their ally around with impunity without fear of betrayal.

In early January the front lapsed into an eerie silence. Luckily for Rommel, Montgomery made no brisk moves against his forces. Taking heart, Mussolini on 2 January instructed ACIT to delay Montgomery's advance for a total of six weeks; this would provide time for the completion of the defenses on the Mareth Line in Tunisia. The CS weighed in for a two-month stand. These orders seem outlandish when measured against ACIT's obvious shortcomings,[46] but Montgomery's super-cautious and dilatory movements gave Rome reason to think Rommel's spine could be stiffened. Still, ever fearful that an Allied drive from the west would beat him to the Mareth Line, Rommel insisted that the decision to move off would be his.[47]

Finally, on 17 January, Montgomery placed ACIT under heavy attack. Rommel instantly ordered a further retreat from Buerat to the Tarhuna-Homs line for a brief stop on a preordained voyage westward. This was the last straw for the Axis army brain trust. Mussolini charged Rommel with insubordination for failing to hold out for "at least three weeks" and for retreating hastily in the absence of any real threat. In a stormy meeting with Cavallero, Rommel said defiantly: "You can either hold on to Tripoli a few more days and lose the army, or lose Tripoli a few days earlier and save the army for Tunis. Make up your mind."[48] Mussolini and Cavallero yielded; it would be up to Rommel when to settle the army in Tunisia.[49] Accordingly, since the 15th Armored had only twenty-three tanks left, Rommel ordered about a third of the *Pistoia, La Spezia,* and *Giovani Fascisti* troops to fall back from the Tarhuna-Homs Line on the 19 January under a sky dominated by Axis planes and in absence of pressure from the enemy.[50] Tripoli was left undefended as Rommel bypassed the city on his way to Tunisia.

In Cavallero's willingness to give up Tripolitania, he had no scruple in exposing the undefended Italian settlers to the wrath of the Arabs, who, it was feared, were poised to strike back for having suffered decades of humiliating exploitation. "All the civilian personnel must remain regularly at their posts in order to give a spectacle of order and organization," he avowed, as he set his sights on Algeria and Morocco.[51]

---

46. Reinhard Stumpf, in *Germany and the Second World War,* VI: 816, calls them wholly unrealistic.
47. *Operazioni,* IV: 150; *The Rommel Papers,* p. 382; *Germany and the Second World War,* VI: 816.
48. *The Rommel Papers,* p. 389; *Germany and the Second World War,* VI: 818.
49. *Operazioni,* IV: 178–79; Cavallero, *Diario,* 6, 19 January 1943; *The Rommel Papers,* p. 389.
50. *Operazioni,* IV: 157.
51. Cavallero, *Diario,* 2 January 1943.

Led by the Pipes of the 1st Gordon Highlanders, Montgomery's army filed down the streets of Tripoli shortly before dawn on 23 January, the day after the Axis troops had vacated the city, which heralded the end of the Fascist empire. The victors had chased them 1,400 miles from El Alamein in a journey that lasted three months. But Rommel had saved his army. By 15 February his forces were ensconced in their Tunisian stronghold at the Mareth Line, a chain of sand-filled pre-war French blockhouses originally built to keep Mussolini at bay. Halting for logistical reorganization after the fall of Tripoli, Montgomery hardly moved to impede Rommel's retreat into Tunisia.

Lunching with Bottai and Farinacci, Ciano noted that his friends were both exasperated. Speaking of the loss of Libya, Bottai said: "At bottom we have achieved another aim: in 1911 [the Socialist] Mussolini declared, 'Let us get out of Libya.' He has kept his word—thirty years too late."[52] On 26 January Rommel was granted sick leave, which paved the way for the Axis powers to engineer changes. On 20 February the Panzerarmee Afrika/ACIT was renamed Italian First Army and placed under the command of General Messe. On his return, Rommel was to take over command of the Heeresgruppe Afrika, which enabled him to stay on until 9 March. On 31 January Mussolini cashiered Cavallero; Bastico laid down his command the same day.

London radio took pleasure in announcing that German troops had abandoned the Italians during the Libyan campaign. "The rearguard action from el-Agheila to Tripoli was fought by Italian soldiers. They had no other task than to protect the German retreat. The Italians had to fight without supplies and water."[53] However one-sided this rendition, it rang true to the Italian military.

Desert Wrap-Up

From El Alamein to Tunis the Italian generals were offended by Rommel's prickly personality and flawed judgments. Repeatedly, they thought, in spite of good cards to play, he missed chances for quick and incisive counterattacks to throw the enemy off balance.[54] Furthermore, he damaged the morale of his Italian troops by precipitously abandoning Tripolitania.[55]

Fortunately for Rommel, the dictators and the Axis generals usually left him safety hatches. After admonishments to hold certain positions, they backed

52. *The Ciano Diaries*, 8 January 1943.
53. Cited in *Operazioni*, IV: 179.
54. Cavallero, *Diario*, 22 December 1942, p. 143.
55. *Operazioni*, IV: 169–70.

down every time and grudgingly allowed him to pick and choose battlefield strategy as he saw fit. There were rebukes, but no dismissal.

It was Bastico's fate to take the brunt of Rommel's defiance since he had the obligation, as Rommel's superior, to carry out Rome's directives in the desert and bring the Desert Fox to heel if he resisted orders. The two constantly squabbled as the Axis armies crossed North Africa. Insufferably arrogant, Bastico was also a hard man to deal with. During the Spanish civil war, as commander of the Blackshirt *23 Marzo*, his condescending behavior caused Franco to demand "his head."[56] Rommel would have been happy to see him go too. But since the Desert Fox held the upper hand in the fragmented Axis command structure through direct access to Hitler, he was able to limit Bastico to a grandstand view of the African campaign.

Confronted by Rommel's high-handedness, Bastico fought back. Having received the directive to "resist to the bitter end" at el-Agheila followed by an "*arresto definitivo*" at Buerat, he dressed Rommel down for ordering a pullout from those defensive positions in the absence of serious enemy pressure—an admonishment that fell on deaf ears. General Messe undoubtedly spoke for Bastico and the rest of the other Italians in rebuking Rommel for besmirching Italian imperial pride by his uncaring attitude toward the Italian settlers in Libya: "The abandonment of the Buerat line, where the troops had looked forward with fiery courage to fighting the decisive battle for the defense of Tripolitania, and the consequent evacuation of our colonists, who stood so dear to the hearts of everyone, had depressed and saddened commanders and soldiers."[57] Libya, containing 50,000 settlers, was for the diehard Italian nationalist not a colony but a borderland of the *patria*—a sentiment that left the German warrior Rommel cold.[58]

Shamed by the thought that Tripolitania might be abandoned with little more than token resistance, Bastico continued to insist that a serious threat of defeat should not deter a commander from engaging in battle, for this was the warrior's gamble. But in late December, realizing that the supply pipeline from Italy had practically dried up, he gradually began to modify his views: don't throw the dice of aggressive combat unless there is a decent chance of winning that is, not until ACIT received sufficient munitions and reinforcements.[59]

Bastico was greatly disadvantaged by the quality of information the CS received in Rome that was passed on to him. The chronicle of the painful retreat

---

56. *Diari e le agende di Luca Pietromarchi (1938–1940)*, p. 136, n. 17.
57. Messe, *La mia armata in Tunisia*, p. 146.
58. *Terza offensiva britannica*, pp. 347–49.
59. Cavallero, *Diario*, 22 December 1942.

from El Alamein to Mareth, comments Paolo Colacicchi, an intelligence officer of the *Granatieri di Sardegna* Division in Tunisia, "was marked by notices that were incomplete and fragmentary, gossip and idle talk that had hardly anything to do with harsh reality."[60]

Despite his changed thinking, Bastico's job was still to follow Rome's dictates, which meant prevailing on Rommel "to stand fast no matter what the cost." Doubtless, the two dictators and the CS complicated Bastico's life by this kind of peremptory and unequivocal order. But if such bravado served to convince the dictators and their followers of their indomitable will, it made no sense to Rommel who, in retreat, carefully calculated strategy based on facts as he perceived them. Since Bastico had begun to see matters the same way, he looked at the Desert Fox's troop deployments with a less jaundiced eye.[61]

Many questions have been raised over priorities set in Rome regarding the provisioning of the troops. During summer and fall of 1942, Rommel groused over the insufficient help ACIT received when the losses in navy ships were around 12.5 percent. In November, when a bridgehead was established in Tunisia, the Axis made far more efforts to send over troops and equipment: 13.302 men, 1,600 vehicles, and 17,000 tons of materiel. These numbers were considerably stepped up the following month. If Rommel had been given the comparatively large contingent of troops and supplies that the Axis started delivering to Tunisia in November, ACIT would have been in a better position to slow down or bring Montgomery's 8th Army to a standstill.

Regardless of the critics in Rome, it is unarguable that Rommel had conducted an epic retreat across difficult terrain under intermittent bombing and the constant threat of encirclement. In transferring much of his support services and about a third of the army's equipment to Tunisia, his front was never breached in spite of Montgomery's vast superiority and the comprehensive information derived from Ultra. Heavy rains played in Rommel's favor by turning the desert into sticky mud that slowed enemy pursuit and grounded Allied aircraft. ACIT further disrupted the enemy's movements by clever sabotage and effectively concealed booby traps. Rommel had done a masterly job of masking his army's decline from an awesome striking force to dog-tired soldiers capable only of ponderous movements and rearguard action. Martin Kitchen, in his

---

60. Paolo Colacicchi, *L'ultimo fronte d'Africa. Tunisia: Novembre 1942–Maggio 1943* (Milan: Mursia, 1977), p. 20.
61. Rommel wrote later: "Marshal Bastico was a fundamentally decent man with a sober military understanding and considerable moral stamina. He saw the position as I did in its true light but had the misfortune to be charged by the Commando Supremo with the task of representing the Duce's point of view to me. As this was usually fallacious he was always on bad ground in the argument that followed. He did, in fact, always take my part, and by his efforts at mediation contributed greatly to the fact that the retreat through Tripolitania, in spite of the senseless obstinacy of our superiors, was a success." *The Rommel Papers*, p. 382.

brilliant study of Rommel's desert campaign, is no apologist. Yet he concludes that Rommel and his staff "showed their true mettle during the retreat to Tunisia, which was one of the most brilliant retreats in the history of warfare."[62]

In dancing away from what should have been assured destruction, Rommel exposed Montgomery as a sluggish pursuer unable to catch a nimble foe. Ironically, it was this trait that enabled Rommel's critics in Rome to chide the Desert Fox for quick and premature retreats. A plodder in World War I style, Montgomery relied for success on a rigid plan anchored in a deliberate infantry advance behind a wall of massive firepower, which gave the CS and Kesselring the impression that his 8th Army was less a juggernaut than a shambling conglomerate of forces vulnerable to quick jabs and counter-blows that would keep it off balance. To pursue the Axis enemy rapidly, he required a level of personal initiative on the part of his subordinate commanders for which they showed scant flair.

Rommel certainly enjoyed advantages. He had at his disposal an army honed on professional skills that the German General Staff had built up during the interwar period. He inherited a mission-based command doctrine that expected junior commanders routinely to show flexibility, initiative, and improvisation. Montgomery, on the other hand, had a lot of spadework to do in breaking down old habits rooted in British military tradition that featured inter-service rivalries, lack of coordination among infantry, armor, and artillery, poor signals equipment, and a top-heavy command structure that precluded battlefield initiative by lower-ranking field officers in the German style. Aware of the existing culture of the army—the methodical predictability in tactics and silo mentality of individual units that hampered rapid change—Montgomery began to provide remedies during the course of the African campaign.

All in Rome and Berlin had come to believe that Rommel's renowned initiative in this last stage of the African desert campaign had been paralyzed by his fatal surrender to the ineluctability of events moving against him. Mussolini and Hitler, who had been such avid cheerleaders when Rommel seized the initiative earlier in the year, thought he was a spent force. They were aghast at the very idea of evacuation and were harshly censorious when Rommel ignored their insistence that he slow down the retreat toward Tunisia. In the weeks to come, Rommel would show his critics a thing or two about waging imaginative offensives.

---

62. Kitchen, *Rommel's Desert War*, p. 420.

Chapter IX

Disaster in Russia

Destruction of an Army
Fascism and the Italian Troops
Italians and Germans
The Warlord at his Worst

Destruction of an Army

Worried that time was working against Germany, Hitler was a man in a hurry. He counted on capturing the Caucasus oil fields by the end of 1942 in a campaign that had already tied down over 200 German and satellite divisions and seventy percent of Germany's armed forces. Having been forced to abandon the drive on Moscow, Hitler fixed his sights on Stalingrad in Operation Blue, a great offensive of forty divisions unleashed on 28 June 1942. By seizing land between the southern Don to the Volga, the Wehrmacht, he thought, would cut off central Russia from the Caucasus and bring into German hands the granaries of the Kuban, the industrial regions of the Donetz Basin, and the Caucasian oilfields, which supplied thirty million tons of oil a year. However, although the Germans advanced toward the Don, they did not succeed in wrapping up the Russian forces. At this point Hitler modified the original plan by dividing the Army Group South into two blocks: Army Group B for a drive on Stalingrad, and Army Group A to move toward the Caucasus. By the middle of August the Wehrmacht in the southern advance had gobbled up the oilfields at Maikop.

To support the German drive on Stalingrad, ARMIR, subordinated to German Army Group B under the command of General Maximilian von Weichs, took up positions on the Don in August, sandwiched between the 2nd Hungarian and 3rd Romanian armies. General Gariboldi's ARMIR consisted of the II Corps (2nd *Sforzesca*, 3rd *Ravenna*, and 5th *Cosseria* infantry divisions), the XXXV Corps (9th *Pasubio* and 52nd *Torino* infantry divisions and the 3rd *Principe Amedeo Duca d'Aosta Celere* Division), the *Alpini* Corps (2nd *Tridentina*, 3rd *Julia*, and 4th *Cuneense Alpini* divisions), and the 156th *Vicenza* Infantry Division. The sector assigned to the Italians covered from 230 to 270 kilometers, far too long a stretch for their nine small binary divisions and the two German divisions assigned to it. But nobody gave this much thought in Berlin, which expected that the Soviets, faced by the threat on Stalingrad, would be in no position to launch a major assault on the thinly held defensive positions along the Don, manned in the main by satellite troops. The Germans had grossly undervalued the endless reserves the Soviets could draw on.

The Italian command was equally complacent. On 6 September General Gariboldi wrote: "The enemy does have forces deployed in rear area zones, but since their numbers are small, they are good only for supporting offensives."[1] In this inattention, he singularly failed to prepare defenses in depth. When the Wehrmacht command did not include his troops in major attacks planned by Army Group B, Gariboldi was offended. To prove Italian mettle, he undertook a series of small jabs beyond the Don.[2] The Soviets replied with counter-thrusts that Gariboldi was able to beat off with inconsequential losses.

On 12 September the German 6th Army under the command of General Friedrich Paulus arrived on the outskirts of Stalingrad. General von Weichs decided to help Paulus for a direct assault on the city by transferring more German troops from rearguard positions. This left a heavy responsibility on the Romanians to cover positions west of Stalingrad.

On the 20th Gariboldi handed down the following order received from his German superiors: defense *à outrance* in occupied positions at the Don to cover the left flank of Paulus' 6th Army advancing on Stalingrad.[3] In the unlikely event of a Soviet attack, the troops were to stay put whatever the consequences until the Wehrmacht could muster a force to relieve them—an imperative under-

---

1. Giorgio Scotoni and Sergej Ivanovich Filonenko, *Retroscena della disfatta in Russia nei documenti inediti dell 8ª Armata,* 2 vols. II: *Documenti della disfatta,* D. 37, Gariboldi memorandum, 6 September 1942.

2. Ibid.: II: pp. 211, 221.

3. Ibid.: D. 51, Gariboldi memorandum.

scored by Hitler on 14 October. Such an edict denied Gariboldi flexibility. Should a fallback be in order, he would have to obtain explicit authorization from the German command of Army Group B. But since at the time ARMIR anticipated a quiet winter, this was not considered a problem, for Soviet armies were assembling 500 kilometers to the south in the crucial battle shaping up at Stalingrad, the epicenter of the struggle. Hence the Italians burrowed in for the long haul. Defensive preparations were, however, slowed by a lack of materiel and labor, much of the latter being composed of drafted Russian citizens and captured prisoners. Mussolini, the CS, and ARMIR, anticipating heroic deeds, resented the covering task assigned them.[4]

But trouble lay ahead. As October slid into November the German armies advancing on Stalingrad, slowed down by increasingly stiff Soviet resistance, were running out of steam. Stymied by the mountainous terrain of the southern Caucasus, their clearly delineated ultimate objectives—the Grozny oilfields and Baku—faded from view. The limit of the southern advance was reached during the first days of November.

In a bold and unexpected move on 19 November, the Soviet command, realizing that the enemy was over-extended with fragile supply lines, seized the strategic initiative against the German and satellite forces of Army Group B by launching a major offensive, Operation Uranus, to relieve Stalingrad. To staunch the Soviet drive, the beleaguered Wehrmacht drew off forces on the Middle Don—22nd and 6th Panzer divisions—in the certainty that, thus reinforced, Paulus would successfully beat off the Soviet attack and proceed with the capture of the city on the Volga. But nothing could stop the Soviets from blasting through the weak Romanian defenses to the north and south of Stalingrad in two armed columns that successfully met at Kalach four days after the operation had begun. More than 300,000 German and Romanian forces were trapped in the Stalingrad cauldron.

The plans of the Russian generals Zhukov and Vasil'evskij to enclose Paulus had worked brilliantly. All the German reserves of Army Group B had been sucked into the black hole of Stalingrad, many having been deployed behind the Italian lines. Without breaking stride, the Soviets moved to shatter the entire Axis alignment from the Don to the Volga.[5]

ARMIR was left breathless. Bereft of German motorized reinforcements, it was about to pay a high price for throwing up only a thin screen along the river. Few trench lines had been dug or effective defensive positions prepared. Heavy snow and severe frost further hampered troop movements.

4. Schlemmer, *Invasori, non vittime*, pp. 122–23; Cavallero, *Diario*. 4 August 1942.
5. Scotoni and Filonenko, *Retroscena della disfatta*, II: 301.

To elevate the spirits of his troops, General Giovanni Zanghieri, the commander of the II Army Corps, sent the following circular to his officers on 6 December: "Today we are in a much better situation than the one in which we achieved the brilliant successes of August and September." In spite of supply problems, "a steely resolve and careful use of the means at hand constitute our most secure weapon." If some units are encircled, "there is no reason to worry: resist to the end and you will surely be liberated. Do not take a step backward, for Italian and allied reserves are assembling behind the lines to guarantee victory."[6] As for Mussolini, distracted by events in North Africa, he did not immediately take in the troubles befalling the Italian troops.[7]

On 11 December 1942, the Soviets, in Operation Saturn (or, in Italian military records, "The Second Defensive Battle of the Don"), began launching multiple attacks with waves of tanks and strafing aircraft toward Rostov to disrupt the anticipated efforts by German forces to relieve the encircled 6th Army. Destruction of the enemy in the great bend of the Don River would cut off Army Group A's withdrawal from the Caucasus region. But since the Soviet forces encountered difficulties in reducing the 6th Army's pocket around Stalingrad, this became a tall order. German Field Marshal Erich von Manstein, who at the end of November had taken command of Army Group Don, undertook a thrust to save the besieged Paulus. The Italians of the II Army Corps did their part by substantially holding their positions in five days of fierce fighting.[8]

Faced by German forces mounting a strong relief column that stretched sixty kilometers from Stalingrad, the Soviet command scaled down Operation Saturn and took on the less ambitious Operation Little Saturn. Instead of a deep thrust in the direction of Rostov, they directed an attack southwestward on the 16th aimed at the annihilation of Army Group Don, which defended positions along the southern banks of the Don and Chir rivers. The Alpine Corps deployed to the north was not to be involved in this round of fighting.

The Russian force totaled 370,000 men, 1,170 tanks, 5,600 canon, and the much-feared Katuscha rocket launchers. They faced 100,000 Italians of ARMIR (minus the *Alpini*), 60,000 Germans, and 50,000 Romanians of Group Hollidt, with an absolute superiority in tanks and crushing advantage in artillery.[9] At first, their artillery hampered by thick fog, the Soviet troops achieved only a few infiltrations, which enabled the Italians to stand firm for two days. Even though Gariboldi had make only sketchy plans for a withdrawal, the Soviets, in their

---

6. Ibid.: D. 91, Zanghieri to his commanders, 6 December 1942, pp. 301–2.
7. See Aldo Valori, *La Campagna di Russia CSIR-ARMIR* (Rome: Grafica Nazionale Editrice, 1950–51), II: 655.
8. Schlemmer, *Invasori, non vittime*, pp. 128–29.
9. Figures taken from Rochat, *Le guerre italiane*, p. 391.

reports, confirmed that the Italians put up a tenacious resistance and often conducted counterattacks.[10] In the initial assault the Russians lost twenty percent of their tanks.[11] But faced by relentless mobile attacks, on the 17th the Italian lines buckled and broke, which led to a helter-skelter and non-authorized flight that also involved German units.[12]

On the 19th ARMIR headquarters ordered the remaining troops to withdraw. Italian soldiers moved westward on foot trying to escape the Soviet tanks in temperatures that dipped from ten to thirty-five degrees centigrade below zero. That same day the command of Army Group B finally ordered the remains of the *Ravenna*, the XXXV Italian Army Corps, and the 298th German Division to retreat. But the lightning Russian advance on the evening of the 19th quickly resulted in a counter-order. The Italian command of the XXXV Army Corps was told to interrupt the movement toward Tikhaja and assemble in the triangle of villages to organize a further resistance "to the last man."

How could the Italian units, already in an advanced state of chaos, implement an order that condemned thousands of soldiers to a terrible "march of death" in the winter steppes? Deprived of the most elementary equipment and reduced to near-starvation, the Italian infantry reached its objective thoroughly weakened after having suffered punishing losses. Finally on 23 December the German command of Army Group B authorized Gariboldi to narrow the alignment of ARMIR in a sector to the north on the Upper Don held by the *Corpo Alpino*, where it was greeted by an imperative: resistance to the last drop of blood.

The terrible fate that befell *Sforzesca*, which was under the command of the German XXIX Army Corps and covered the extreme right wing of the 8th Army, merits further discussion regarding German highhandedness. As the Romanians caved in on its southern flank, *Sforzesca* faced encirclement, but was rooted in place by the existing order to stand fast. The commander of the XXIX German Army Corps, Hans von Obsfelder, abrogated the command to maintain the line of security and resistance on 19 December in favor of a retreat to the Chir River to be concluded the next day. But the rapid Soviet advance constrained him to transmit new orders to *Sforzesca* for a further retreat southward. "Destroy what cannot be carried" (vehicles, weapons, artillery lacking fuel). Easier said than done. Thanks to earlier orders not to move from the trenches, *Sforzesca* had piled up equipment that could hardly be pulled back rapidly. Then,

10. Giorgio Scotoni, *L'Armata Rossa e la disfatta italiana (1942–1943)* (Trento: Panorama, 2007), p. 313.
11. Rochat, *Le guerre italiane*, p. 391.
12. David M. Glantz and Jonathan House, *When Titans Clashed: How the Red Army Stopped Hitler* (Lawrence: University of Kansas Press, 1995), p. 134.

on the 20th, the XXIX Army Corps revoked the directive of the previous day and once again ordered that positions on the Chir be held. The Italians were dismayed by this sudden about-face, which came just at the time when the *Sforzesca*, in preparation for an extended retreat, had already destroyed artillery that could not be moved and most of its vehicles that lacked fuel. The German command did not seem to understand that the *Sforzesca* was no more than a huddled band of demoralized and vulnerable soldiers whom they had carelessly thrown weaponless to the Russian Bear.[13]

General Kurt von Tippelskirch, who was assigned to the Italian 8th Army, remonstrated with Gariboldi: "At the army group, one has the impression from various air and land observations that the Italian 8th Army, above all in zones behind the front in threatened areas, who should be defending themselves, are totally finished." Tippelskirch added: "As for the Germans, in these cases the deserters would be arrested and shot." He would "refer to the Führer that the Italian army no longer fights."[14] But nothing could have prevailed against the audacious and surprisingly swift-moving Red Army which, through overwhelming force, had crushed the weakly defended flanks of the German 6th Army.

Throughout these disasters Rome remained bathed in an eerie complacency. Certain military leaders and regime stalwarts doubted that there could be a further Soviet advance on the front defended by Army Group B. As late as early January 1943 both Cavallero and Gariboldi dismissed the idea of a major new Soviet offensive, convinced that in carrying out "Lesser Saturn" the Red Army had reached the end of its offensive potential on the Don front. When the Germans proposed substituting ARMIR, General Gariboldi refused,[15] believing that the remnants of his force were merely undergoing a circumscribed crisis. The CS sent General Carlo Fassi to inspect the front held by the 8th Army in person. On his return at the beginning of January, Fassi told Cavallero why the Italian lines had broken: they were not deployed deep enough, and the Germans had failed to send the promised reinforcements. Fassi predicted that a new Soviet offensive would be unleashed against the woefully undermanned Italians, who would not be able to count on the Germans since they were heavily engaged elsewhere. The CS dismissed Fassi's report of 7 January 1943 as neither persuasive nor accurate.[16] In this state of denial, Italy's generals took no action and did not wake up until disaster hit the *Alpini* later in the month.

---

13. Schlemmer, *Invasori, non vittime*, pp. 136–37.
14. Schreiber, "La participazione italiana," p. 266.
15. Cavallero, *Diario*, 21 December 1942.
16. Valori, *La Campagna di Russia*, II: 659–60.

Indeed, the fate of the *Alpini* lay in the balance. Originally they were to have joined Army Group A. In a plan dear to Mussolini's heart, the *Alpini* would spearhead an offensive against the positions of the British Empire in the Middle East. These prospects had brightened in the aftermath of Axis victories in North Africa and German successes on the Eastern Front during the summer. But General Gariboldi opposed the idea of splitting the Italian forces between two army groups and repeatedly demanded that his troops be engaged as a compact unit in Army Group B. The German High Command yielded. And so the hooks and rope climbers trained for mountain warfare and therefore best suited for fighting in the Caucasus region were placed north of the main Italian force on the Don front. Three divisions of between 15,000 and 18,000 men with few vehicles but 15,000 mules were deployed in relatively secure positions protected by the Don River, cliffs in the rear, and surrounding hills. Despite a storm of Soviet leaflets encouraging surrender and offering good treatment, there were no deserters and spirits remained high. With the exception of the *Julia*, which fought hard against the Russians on 20 December, the *Alpini* were the only units of ARMIR that had been uninvolved in the mighty Soviet offensives during the last two months of 1942.

Toward the end of October the *Alpini*, reinforced by the *Vicenza*, anticipated only partisan attacks or parachute drops; nothing to fear, therefore, from Soviet heavy armor. Only on 19 December 1942, when a Soviet armored corps captured Kantemirovka, a nearby town, were the *Alpini* spurred into action, throwing up defenses against a tank attack aided by forced labor of Soviet citizens and captured prisoners. Fighting swirled around Rossosh', taken by the Russians, retaken by the *Alpini*, and lost for good on 15 January.

Notwithstanding repeated requests to allow a retreat, Hitler forbade the withdrawal of the Alpine Corps.[17] The Don line had to be held until the last bullet.[18] With the exception of General Gabriele Nasci, the *Alpini* generals at Rossosh' questioned this order. Fearing a large breach opening to the south, they reported ominous enemy movements and contemplated an early withdrawal from the Don to save themselves from their hopelessly exposed positions. To escape the impending Soviet attack, General Emilio Battisti, commander of the *Cuneense*, unable to convince his superior General Nasci, the commander of the Alpine Corps, to undertake an immediate pullback, attempted to bypass him by appealing informally to his superiors in the *regio esercito* to put pressure on

---

17. Alessandro Massignani, *Alpini e Tedeschi sul Don* (Vicenza: Edizioni Gino Rossato, 2010), p. 84.
18. Scotoni, *L'Armata Rossa e la disfatta italiana*, p. 437.

Hitler.[19] But nothing came of this, and the *Corpo Alpino* stayed on the Don to encounter a terrible fate.

Just as the *Alpini* suspected, the Russians unleashed Operation Ostrogozsk-Rossosh' against the Axis armies on 12-13 January, continuing until the end of the month. An avalanche of Russian tanks bearing down on Rossosh' tore holes in the lines of the *Alpini* and the German Armored XXIV Corps. On the 14th General Nasci, finally emerging from his doldrums, asked Gariboldi's permission to retreat, but was reminded that abandonment of the Don was prohibited in an order that had been handed down by Hitler.[20] In an astonishing move, German troops under the Alpine Corps command suddenly pulled out of Rossosh' on the 15th. Why? In early December the German commander had warned that in case of an enemy penetration, "It isn't possible with my company to occupy positions in that I am forbidden by my superior command to participate in the defense of this locality."[21]

On the morning of the 16th the Russians hurled waves of tanks against *Alpini* headquarters.[22] To the left of the Alpine Corps the Hungarians abandoned their positions without informing anyone, thereby leaving the left flank of the *Tridentina* uncovered. The Wehrmacht command sent Garibaldi the following order: "To leave the Don line without orders from army [Group B] is absolutely forbidden. I will make you personally responsible to execute this [order]."[23] In accordance with the German command, Gariboldi told Nasci on the 16th: "To leave the line of the Don without precise orders of the army is absolutely forbidden. I hold you personally responsible for the execution of this order."[24] But the unstoppable Soviet advance severed the Alpine Corps' supply line. Faced with imminent catastrophe, partly due to the impromptu retreat of the Hungarian units, General Gariboldi ordered Nasci on 17 and 18 January to carry out a general fallback from the Don, which gave the Russians a clear path into the city.[25] With fuel having run out, the *Alpini* were required to abandon vehicles and equipment that could not be transported by sledges and mules.[26] In a confusing and fluid situation, different command posts sent out a plethora of contradictory directives—hurry-up retreats, modifications of existing orders, and exhortations to comply with dispositions of the OKW—which never reached

19. Ibid., p. 438, n. 50. See also A. Rasero, *L'eroica Cuneense* (Milan: Mursia, 1985), p. 343.
20. Massignani, *Alpini e Tedeschi sul Don*, p. 84.
21. Cited in Scotoni and Filonenko, *La disfatta*, II: 354.
22. Scotoni, *L'Armata Rossa e la disfatta italiana*, p. 441.
23. Cited in Hope Hamilton, *Sacrifice On The Steppe: The Italian Alpine Corps in the Stalingrad Campaign, 1942-1943* (Philadelphia & Newbury: Casemate, 2011), p. 107.
24. Scotoni, *L'Armata Rossa e la disfatta italiana*, p. 477.
25. Ibid., p. 525.
26. Massignani, *Alpini e Tedeschi sul Don*, p. 85

General Nasci. Communications having broken down under a barrage of fire-power, the *Alpini* could not regain their bearings. In temperatures falling to around forty centigrade below zero at night, many staggered in a stupor on frost-bitten feet into Russian huts, where haggard Hungarians, Romanians and Germans joined them.[27] In a few days the Soviets were able to cut off the major avenues of escape.[28] By 31 January the slaughter had come to an end; ARMIR had ceased to function as a fighting force on the Russian front.

General Nasci's decision to abandon Rossosh', taken in consultation with the Germans of the XXIV Panzer Corps,[29] would create much controversy. Under the threat of imminent encirclement, he saw no other choice save a winter retreat in the open steppes. A victim of the "Stalingrad syndrome," Nasci thus exposed his divisions that were trudging across endless Russian plains to complete destruction. The alternative was to barricade his troops in and around the town where they would be dug in trenches in the hope of a German attack that would liberate them. Nasci's detractors point out that since his *Alpini* had men fit for action, an airport, and warehouses full of supplies, he could have held out for the foreseeable future. His defenders claim that a prolonged stay in Rossosh' offered little hope, for the *Alpini*, like the German army at Stalingrad, were surrounded by Soviet troops and therefore doomed to eventual surrender or annihilation. Since Hitler had already abandoned Paulus to his fate, could one ever have expected the Wehrmacht to go out of its way to save Italians? The Alpine Corps was indeed caught between a rock and a hard place. No matter how seriously the Germans may have intended to relieve Italians under siege, the unanticipated disaster at Stalingrad eliminated the conditions in which they might have been able to honor their word.

On 30 January 1943 the first *Alpini* survivors reached the safety of fixed Axis positions. The *Julia, Cuneense* and *Vicenza* divisions operationally had ceased to exist. Only the *Tridentina*, which had fought bravely, survived as a fighting force.[30] At the beginning of the retreat, the *Alpini* consisted of 70,000 men; only 27,500 reached safety.[31]

On arriving at Udine, a soldier wrote: "The first shock I had was that as soon as we left the cars, a desperate crowd assailed us. They were the relatives of the ARMIR missing. Having photos in their hands, they asked us if we had seen

27. Montanelli and Cervi, *L'Italia della disfatta*, pp. 199–200.
28. Scotoni, *L'Armata Rossa e la disfatta italiana*, p. 443.
29. Interview with Schlemmer, 18 September 2009.
30. Schreiber, "La participazione italiana," p. 268.
31. Massignani, *Alpini e Tedeschi sul Don*, pp. 98–99.

this or that man. I escaped to the barracks because I could not stand so great a despair."[32]

The image evoked by the famous writer Filippo Tommaso Marinetti on his return from the Don illustrates how official Rome looked at the situation of the *Alpini* in Russia. As if the breakdown of December had never occurred, on 11 January the "sansepolcrista poet-combatant," in an introductory speech at the Royal Academy of Italy, compared the magnificent order of the "quadrupedal *Cuneense* Division" to the miserable columns of Soviet prisoners: "Masculinity with the winged sonority of Piedmont's valleys, all of the powerful, traditional energy of our race, walked obediently to its great destiny, increasingly noble, exhausted, solid, and refulgent. Confident and precise, they walked several thousands of kilometers in their granite bones.... On the front line, edged in the Italian style by well-placed minefields along the Don, I compared the Italian military organization with the yellowish stream of Russian prisoners all equally submerged in typical filth and with a marching pace from sad destiny to sad destiny."[33] The absurdity of this quotation gives a good feel for Fascist rhetoric.

On 9 March 1943 Mussolini wrote Hitler: "Italy cannot be absent from the Russian front and therefore the Italian Second Army Corps will stay in Russia.... Permit me to express to you the desire that the Army Corps be engaged not in behind-the-lines duties but in combat."[34] These remarkable comments came after the whole Italian front had collapsed under the weight of the massive Soviet winter offensive.

Predictably Hitler was not interested. Relations between the two countries had taken a turn for the worse following the Don disaster. At a military gathering at Rastenburg, he remarked: "I shall tell the Duce that it makes no sense. We give them weapons and it is the same self-deception.... If we want to equip our twenty-one divisions we need our weapons.... We cannot again equip 200,000 Italians.... I shall tell the Duce that it would be much better to take these units away."[35]

In the final accounting, ARMIR lost ninety-seven percent of its artillery, eighty percent of the horses and mules, and seventy percent of vehicles. Much later have we learned what happened to the soldiers. About 25,000 had died in combat; the other 70,000 were taken prisoner. Of the latter, some 20,000 died on forced marches and train journeys to the Russian concentration camps; about 40,000 died in the camps themselves. In some camps the death rate was around

---

32. Cited in Ciro Paoletti, *A Military History of Italy* (Westport CN, Praeger, 2008), p. 178.
33. Cited in Scotoni, *L'Armata rossa e la disfatta italiana*, pp. 477-78.
34. DDI, 9, X, 95, Mussolini to Hitler, 9 March 1943.
35. Cited in Deakin, *The Brutal Friendship*, p. 204.

500 a day. Cannibalism was rife because of the lack of food. In 1945–46, the Soviets released almost all Italian prisoners of war.[36] Some 10,032 Italian prisoners had survived the horrors of the prison camps for a return to Italy.[37]

The failure of the Italian troops on the Eastern Front was hardly surprising. Giorgio Rochat has described as *disastroso* the conduct of the two top commanders of the hidebound Italian military hierarchy, Generals Gariboldi and Nasci.[38] The logistical services were not able to provide the shattered retreating remnants with motor transport, water, food, and shelter. From top to bottom the army suffered from serious shortcomings in leadership, training, and imagination, starting in Rome. Having failed to learn the lessons of Greece and the campaign in the Alps against France in 1940, the CS sent much materiel to Russia of little value, such as hobnailed boots, described as flimsier than ballerina shoes, which disintegrated in snow and mud and failed to prevent frostbite. The Russians were better outfitted in boots of fur and animal skin. Such an important item as anti-congealing oil was wanting too, in the absence of which vehicles and weapons froze or jammed in the cold weather. In the terrible retreats, the soldiers, suffering from freezing temperatures, lack of proper clothing, and utter exhaustion, were forced to abandon artillery and motor vehicles owing to the lack of fuel. Once the ammunition was exhausted, their military equipment was rendered useless. In the terrible war of giants, the Italian military equipment was no much for what the Soviets were able to hurl against them. For example, the Italian M-13 tanks, the famous "sardine cans," were easily crushed by massive Soviet armor attacks.

As the "First Defensive Battle of the Don" was concluding in latter August 1942, the commander of the *Cuneense* reported on the confusion shown by some Italian troops under fire; they had thrown away rifles and abandoned mortars and machine guns. General Battisti labeled this "a crime of cowardice," and frustrated commanders called on their hard-pressed troops to drag out the artillery if they lacked mobile transit.[39] But blame was hardly a one-way street. In

---

36. In her recent book *Sacrifice on the Steppes*, Hope Hamilton has written a moving story of the sufferings endured by the Alpini during their retreats and provides examples of their heroic resistance in fighting rearguard actions against hopeless odds.

37. Of a total armed force of about 230,000 men, ARMIR lost 84,830 men, with 27,690 more wounded, ill, or suffering from frostbite. By the end of the campaign 114,520 lives were lost, and 95,000 men were missing. As Battistelli notes, the final figures are not clear since they range from the initial 118,000 (from German sources) to 114,520 from the postwar SMRE account to the top fugure of 121,207 given by the SMRE during the war. Losses during the winter, in his estimation, numbered about 121–122,000; the grand total during the Italian campaign on the Eastern Front about 133,000. See also Farrell, *Mussolini*, p. 362; Schlemmer, *Invasori, non vittime*, p. 153; Virgilio Isare, *Storia del Servizio Militare in Italia. Volume Quarto-soldati e partigiani* (1943–1945) (Rome: Rivista Militare, 1991)

38. Rochat, *Le guerre italiane*, pp. 392–93.

39. Scotoni and Filonenko, *La disfatta*, D. 89, Battisti directive, pp. 297–98, 30 August 1942.

foisting responsibility for battlefield failure on the soldiers, who, in fact, often fought well, the officers covered up their own deficiencies.[40]

Fascism and the Italian Troops

After the start of Germany's invasion of the Soviet Union, Alessandro Pavolini, the Italian maestro of propaganda, hastened to align Fascism's party line with Nazism's anti-Bolshevism, anti-plutocracy, and anti-Semitism. The Italian public was required to ascribe responsibility for the war, as well as hardships and frustrations, to "World Jewry." Pavolini arranged for the production of five ten-minute radio programs based on the "Protocols of the Elders of Zion."[41] Radical anti-Semites like Giovanni Preziosi and Roberto Farinacci pressed Mussolini to take more drastic measures against the Jews. This, they believed, would divert discontent away from the regime and strengthen national unity.

Pavolini delivered the same kind of message to the troops on the Eastern Front in the form of pamphlets and comic books redolent with anti-Semitic caricatures.[42] Picture postcards illustrated the enemy as a ferocious Soviet beast bent on the destruction of civilization, religion, and Italian family values.[43]

The Catholic Church applauded the regime for spearheading an anti-Bolshevik crusade against atheistic Communism. Involved in a Christian crusade, the troops were invited to see themselves as defenders rather than aggressors, warriors fighting a just cause. Such a missionary impulse made sense to many troops, the majority of whom were not exactly enamored of Fascism apart from the vague notion that Mussolini as head of the government spoke for the nation-at-arms.[44]

But how much this kind of literature actually influenced the typical semi-literate soldier in the popular culture of the times is anybody's guess and leaves open the question to what extent the soldiers internalized such Fascist doctrine. Since it was impossible to determine how broadly and regularly the Fascist pamphlets and journals were distributed, and since a shortage of radios precluded many messages from reaching the front lines, we should be wary of drawing generalized conclusions. Officers frequently added to the confusion by exhibiting incomprehension, negligence, or indifference in acquainting their

---

40. Rochat, "Lo sforzo bellico 1940–45," p. 229.
41. Arnold, *The Illusion of Victory*, p. 143.
42. *Ministri e giornalisti: La guerra e il Minculpop (1939–1943)*, ed. Nicola Tranfaglia (Turin: Einaudi, 2005), p. 153.
43. Schlemmer, *Invasori, non vittime*, p. 71.
44. Amedeo Osti Guerrazzi and Thomas Schlemmer, "I soldati italiani nella campagna di Russia: Propaganda, esperienza, memoria," *Annali dell'istituto storico italo-germanico in Trento*, 33 (2007), pp. 388, 406.

soldiers with the Fascist vernacular, let alone handling the avalanche of enemy propaganda flyers that reached Italian lines. In this hit-or-miss flow of information, it well might have been that the "community of the trenches" spirit and the fear of speaking out against the political objectives of the regime were equally important in compelling the soldiers to carry out orders. Far from home, they faced frigid weather, lacked warm boots, leave time, decent food, and regular mail service, and received newspapers very late or not at all. These were hardly conditions to turn them into ideological warriors.

Loyalty to each other and family, added to a deep patriotism in a viciously fought war under brutal conditions, could bring about the best, and worst, in the Italian soldier's behavior quite apart from Fascist indoctrination. The unmistakably high spirit of such divisions as the *Alpini* grew out of these allegiances. Soldiers without hesitation would risk their own lives in defending comrades threatened by heavy enemy attacks. But vengeful retaliation in savage conditions not infrequently would accompany such bravery.

Rather than focusing on the Fascist message, Italian commanders were absorbed in figuring out how to win the next battle or survive an imminent attack. Besides planning and executing war maneuvers, they repeatedly implored their troops never to let their guard down and to be forever vigilant against civilians, including women and children, who might take pot-shots at them from houses and alleyways. Don't be hoodwinked by friendly smiles after handouts to starving people, they were warned. This "hate the enemy" prodded troops to undertake appropriate safeguards against sneak attacks and urged them to endure the sacrifices of search-and-destroy missions.

In an instruction to his correspondents dated 18 August 1942, Pavolini delivered a telling insight into the views of veterans returning from the Russian front. He reported that they were irresponsibly spreading tendentious rumors suggesting stiff Russian resistance, German atrocities, and a raging partisan insurgency; worst of all, they were enamored of Bolshevik achievements: industrialization, maternity care, social welfare, and education. Such "astonishingly inaccurate" judgments, in Pavolini's view, were the fruit of a "desolating superficiality" seasoned by a "deplorable and malignant" criticism of Fascist progress. Nonetheless, he continues, the soldiers exercised sound judgment in rejecting a Russian "paradise of workers" for Italy. Among the older officers one still saw (thankfully he implies) a hardy belief that Bolshevism represented a worldwide threat that had to be extinguished no matter the cost. Not so, however, among the younger officers, whose insufferable snobbism was shown in their love of things foreign. They were spoiled bourgeois children who longed for Bolshevism's innovations while deprecating the values of their own country.

Pavolini's conclusion: "Our soldiers going to Russia are simply not spiritually prepared for the trip in such an Amazonian jungle."

Pavolini was equally incensed by the attitude of the Italians on the home front. Scathingly, he described the *piccolo borghese* as still addicted to self-interest, which led them to a deadly defeatism, ergo, a "deformed" impression of a *benessere sovietico*. No matter how absurd, infatuation with Bolshevism, he felt, had also captured the imagination of impressionable workers. In this one long elocution, Pavolini made the startling admission that Fascism ran only skin-deep among both soldiers and the general public. His conclusion is not hard to miss: Minculpop's anti-Bolshevik message had flopped.[45]

As the fount of Fascism, Mussolini never yielded an inch on the ideological purposes driving Italy in the war. His soldiers were expected to be proud standard-bearers of the new Italy animated by a profound faith. At the beginning of 1943 Mussolini proclaimed: "Who will win the war? You say: the people who are better armed. No, that's not enough. All right, you say, then the people who dispose of the most raw materials. But that's not enough. The people with the greatest generals. No, that's not it either. This war will be won by those armed forces permeated by a robust political consciousness. The time is past when a soldier ought not to engage in politics. That's a mistaken idea. In another era when there were ten, fifteen parties, you could find ten, fifteen political propagandas in the barracks. But now there is only one party, one regime. For the armed forces, therefore, there will never be enough politics, never enough Fascism. Without that we will not win. It takes Fascist soldiers who fight for Fascism, because this is a war of religion and ideas."[46]

As opposed to Stalin, who, facing military disaster, downplayed Communist ideology in favor of "Mother Russia" to forge a tighter unity, Mussolini, in a similar fix, took an opposite tack by emboldening Italians to flaunt pride in what the regime stood for. In a monotonous tautology he said: "This is the war of Italy because it is the war of Fascism, and it is the war of Fascism because it is the war of Italy."[47] Mussolini and Fascism had from the inception of the regime proclaimed the need for war and decried pacifism. This was the incredible legacy of World War I: with all that death veterans who filed into the Fascist squads came back lusting for war.

Mussolini's most gifted military man, Giovanni Messe, speaking for the conservative generals, thought that declaring the war as Fascist was a mistake. Since

---

45. *Ministri e giornalisti*, ed. by Tranfaglia, pp. 289–93.
46. *OO*, XXXI, 3 January 1943.
47. Ibid., 11 March 1943.

Italy had the right to dominate the Mediterranean, Messe felt the government should stress the national character of the conflict.[48]

Italians, Germans, and Russians

Upon arriving in Russia, the Italian army was awash in logistical problems. In fact, throughout the campaign in the steppes, the Italian supply services were under a terrible strain in providing the troops adequate provisions. Since goods had to be sent at great distances, and the Italians were dependent on Germany for transshipment, there were often shortages that could only be made up by scouring the surrounding countryside. On 15 June 1942 the General Intendente Carlo Biglino handed down the following order: "Utilize to the maximum local resources of whatever kind or sort, in particular wheat and flour, meat, hay, barley and oats.... One must exploit these resources radically as if nothing from the rear areas arrives, absolutely nothing."[49]

In this spirit many soldiers procured necessities by sacking kitchen gardens and raiding hen houses. Vandalism and corruption were ongoing. Against army regulations, Italians bartered precious supplies of fuel and military clothing for food and drink. The Intendenza did its part by expropriating food. But the areas under Italian occupation, having few inhabitants, offered scarce possibility for living off the land. Not only had the Germans already swept clean most of the portable resources; they required the Italians, in March 1942, to seek authorization for obtaining provisions and supplies.[50] If the troops bartered or engaged in commercial exchanges with the local population, they would face punishment.[51] The more Italians could be prevented from buying or sequestering resources, the more the Germans could squeeze food from the Russian farmers for themselves.

Thanks to Mussolini's follies, the Germans were able to shepherd the Italians into battle where the 8th Army served as a subordinate to Wehrmacht generals. They, not the Italians, arbitrarily fixed occupation policies to which unquestioned obedience on the part of the ally was demanded. Drawn into the net of German repression, the Italians had to keep their peace because they were small in number and depended on the Wehrmacht for transportation and supplies. In what was commonly accepted as a German war theater, the Wehrmacht defined authority in territories held by Italian troops regarding the deployment of the *regio esercito*. They assumed authority in the Italian military zones in

---

48. Messe, *La mia armata in Tunisia*, pp. 25–26.
49. Cited in Schlemmer, *Invasori, non vittime*, p. 53–54, emphasis in the original.
50. Giorgio Scotoni and Sergej Ivanovich Filonenko, *Retroscena della disfatta italiana in Russia nei documenti inediti dell 8a Armata*, vol. I: *Inquadramento*, p. 120.
51. Ibid., p. 121.

areas key to Nazi objectives: control over the local economy; jurisdiction over prisoners and the fate of captured partisans and subjects; management of the concentration camps; and implementation of draconian counterinsurgency measures. In such inescapable dependency on the Wehrmacht, the Italians frequently appeared to be accomplices in some of the worst features of German behavior.

General Messe, however, refutes the notion that the Italian troops followed the German example of violence and insists that they were able to preserve a high standard of moral conduct. His soldiers fought a clean and noble war on the Eastern Front, he avers, and incurred German jealousy because of the friendship they had established among the Russian people. Messe makes the remarkable statement that "no one could ever stop our soldiers from manifesting toward the Russian population Italian good will, innate generosity, and the profound sensibility of its animating spirit....often in open contrast with German directives, in assuring captured prisoners treatment and conditions of life worthy of a civilized people." Always light-handed in their treatment of the population, "the troops refrained from forced and violent requisitions." With galling aplomb, Messe observes: "One has the impression of operating in a friendly country." The very suggestion that Italians committed atrocities or war crimes moves Messe to indignation: "With exemplary severity Italian military accused of crimes against the population were prosecuted." Defiantly, he proclaims, in this harsh war it was the Italian who held high the standard of a superior civilization.[52]

Messe's professed nobility of thought is given the lie by a general command issued to his troops: "In the cases of sabotage that are rather rare and due to Communist elements, above all to Jews, one must not undertake reprisals against the entire population."[53] On 25 July 1941 this self-styled white knight prohibited all contacts with Jews, holding that they threatened the life of the soldiers.[54] Two months later he attributed acts of sabotage against Italian soldiers to Jews and Communists.[55]

As opposed to Messe's claim of Italian exceptionalism, the *regio esercito* did not challenge German orders of repression. On 23 August 1941 the Italian command, in conformity with Wehrmacht orders, informed the troops that they should nip in the bud all partisan-style action and short-circuit passive resistance with the strongest measures. Regarding war prisoners, all Soviet commissars and "undesirable elements" were to be transferred to German collection points or to

52. Messe, *La guerra al fronte russo*, pp. 85–97.
53. Cited in Schlemmer, *Invasori, non vittime*, p. 59, italics in the original.
54. Osti Guerrazzi and Schlemmer, "I soldati italiani nella campagna di Russia," p. 411.
55. Schlemmer, "Esercito italiano in guerra in Unione Sovietica," p. 411.

provisional German prisoner-of-war camps. Subsequently the Intelligence Department of the Expeditionary Corps (Ufficio Informazioni del Corpo di Spedizione) defined the procedure to be followed in a summary of the various dispositions issued by the supreme command of the German army: "Civilian suspects captured behind the lines must be delivered to the command centers and to the security police and the SD" (Sicherheitsdienst); that is, to German death squads.[56]

When at the beginning of August 1942 Italians began to replace Germans along the Don, the Wehrmacht laid out instructions on how to treat the civil population, fight partisans, and handle spies and saboteurs. On 11 August 1942 the XXIX German Army Corps issued order #63,[57] which was passed on by General Gariboldi a few days later to his field commanders, supply services, and the Carabinieri. They were required to impose total obedience on the population, apply grave sanctions for transgressors, shoot or hang civilians in possession of arms, evacuate all populated centers found within five kilometers of the Don, and ruthlessly exploit resources.[58]

Conducted in the main by the Intendenza and assisted by the Carabinieri and Blackshirts, the Italian mission was to guarantee the security of the zones assigned to them, defend railroad and communication lines, and exploit local resources. To assist them in implementing these orders, the Italians appointed starostas (village headmen).[59] In carrying out dragnets to recover military equipment and track down partisans and their sympathizers, villages were destroyed, people indiscriminately shot, hostages taken, and food supplies plundered.[60]

The Carabinieri acted in summer 1942 by issuing orders "to take a census of, watch over, and intern all Jews, Communists, and suspects."[61] At the end of December 1942 General Nasci transmitted orders to the *Cosseria* Division regarding the security of the troops south of Rossosh': "Get in immediate contact with the starostas to engage them, on pain of death, to cooperate in the security and tranquility of the zone. If opportune, and on information provided by the starostas, take hostages to be shot if grave cases of hostility are found in an atmosphere of betrayal and silence."[62] General Nasci on 23 September needed no German persuasion to round up Russian civilians and war prisoners

---

56. Schlemmer, *Invasori, non vittime*, p. 55.

57. Ibid., p. 49.

58. Scotoni and Filonenko, *Retrocsena*, I: 84.

59. Schlemmer, *Invasori, non vittime*, p. 50.

60. Schlemmer has documented many of these Italian terror acts in his "Die Comandi Tappa Der 8. Italienischen Armee Und Die Deutsche Besatzungsherrschaft Im Süden Der Sowjetunion," *Quellen Und Forschungen*, no. 88 (2008).

61. Ibid., p. 522.

62. Schlemmer, *Invasori, non vittime*, p. 51.

in work crews as forced labor for digging defenses and building frontline fortifications.[63] "Without any regard for personal welfare, you must put prisoners of
war and local elements and also women on fixed work projects."[64] Italian
commanders, were, therefore, not particularly benevolent, and their hands were
anything but clean.

Not all Italian soldiers, however, were so cold-hearted. An Alpino captain
complained on 2 October about the three-hour walk it took for prisoners to
reach their forced labor sites and the discrimination they suffered regarding food
rations. "Prisoners returning to camp in the evening certainly talk about these
things and wonder why such harsh treatment occurs; we certainly don't make a
good impression." Documented cases demonstrate that some Italian officers and
troops showed care and responsibility in the treatment of civilians.[65] In one
instance three soldiers were rebuked for robbing potatoes and injuring a peasant
farmer. The Italian command periodically, if not very energetically, threatened
penal sanctions for these illegalities—3–5 years confinement and charges to be
brought before the Military War Tribunal of the 8th Army. But vandalism and
illegal barter were hardly brought under effective control.[66]

If both Axis partners were prone to lash back harshly at any suspected
partisan resistance, ARMIR, at least, had the good fortune in the early days to be
deployed where partisan activity barely existed. The partisans initially kept a low
profile because they lacked areas for concealment, and the local population, out
of fear of reprisal, lapsed into apathy.[67] As time passed the Italian troops, particularly the *Venezia* Division, were increasingly involved in activity against the
partisans.[68] Still, *rastrellamenti* on a large scale needed to be undertaken only infrequently, which eliminated any compelling reason to apply a brutal and comprehensive counterinsurgency program à la Roatta against a burgeoning partisan
movement. ARMIR troops were responsible mainly for punishment of misde-
meanors like thievery and illegal barter.

When the Russians opened large offensives in fall 1942 accompanied by
parachute drops behind the lines, partisan sabotage and attacks on Italian supply
lines spiraled upward. To meet this threat, General Nasci in September ordered
that collaborationist militias be recruited, and propaganda agents were empowered to line up local inhabitants on the Italian side. According to Nasci, it
was necessary to demonstrate the primacy of the conquerors' civilization by

63. Scotoni and Filonenko, *Retroscena*, II: 241.
64. Ibid.: p. 304; SME, *Le operazioni delle unità italiane al fronte russo (1941–1943)*, p. 679.
65. Scotoni and Filonenko, *La disfatta*, Preface to D. 82, p. 285.
66. Ibid., p. 283.
67. Scotoni and Filonenko, *L'occupazione*, II: 149.
68. Massignani, *Alpini e Tedeschi sul Don*, p. 110.

showing correctness, justice, and the safeguarding of life and goods. But woe onto those who would reject the Italian message. In the search for "bandits," Nasci masterminded the creation of local militias (Gruppi Cacciatori), who were expected to eliminate them.[69] Perhaps the most frightening of the Axis ordinances, which illuminates the nature of the Nazi-Fascist "New Order," was the proclamation that: "Every homicide or attempted homicide....of soldiers will be punished with death. Beyond that, for every soldier killed, 100 hostages will be shot and their village burnt to the ground."[70] But no proof has yet emerged that the Italians actually carried out their side of this infamous bargain.

In all fairness it must not be forgotten that, as Ilya Ehrenburg and others have pointed out, the partisans in Russia committed many atrocities against the Axis troops too, thus provoking drastic retaliations against them, a truism that has generally characterized guerrilla warfare in the modern era.

On 20 October 1942, a directive issued by the *Vicenza* compelled the Italians to yield control over the local militias engaged in anti-partisan activity to the zonal German command.[71] ARMIR was further required to turn over captured "bandits" to the Germans, who were in charge of the reprisals to be taken against civilians.[72] But all this penultimate juggling did not stave off a dreadful fate. In the disarray of Italian retreat, the Soviets operating behind the lines managed to kill 4,000 Italian soldiers and officers and take 7,000 prisoners in a period of ten days.[73]

To what extent were the Italian troops involved in the roundup and slaughter of Russian Jews? It seems that some Italians collaborated with the Nazi killing units in the persecution of Jews and other groups in Hitler's black book. In at least one case 60 to 100 Jews were handed over to the German *Sonderkommando* for elimination. In 1942 the Carabinieri in occupied villages not only acted against political enemies but also singled out Jews as part of their mopping-up expeditions against Russian partisans. Hundreds of Communists and Jews, including women and children, were delivered to the tender mercies of the Germans.[74] Much more research is needed, however, to clarify how often and under what circumstances Italian officials and soldiers directly assisted in the killing of Russian Jews. Certainly there is not enough evidence so far to demon-

69. Scotoni and Filonenko, *Retroscena*, I: 159.
70. Scotoni and Filonenko, *L'occupazione*, II: 51.
71. Ibid.: pp. 154, 168.
72. Ibid., I: 149–50.
73. Ibid.: 151.
74. Schlemmer, *Invasori, non vittime*, p. 57

strate general Italian complicity beyond individually known cases of Nazi mass murder.[75]

Any insinuation that the Italians were willing accomplices in the Holocaust certainly also needs further investigation. For one thing, the Italian presence on the Eastern Front was miniscule compared to the specialized German *Einsatz-kommando* squads that carried out organized atrocities. Furthermore, there were no Italian squadrons of killing forces roaming behind the lines in search of prey; the Italians were simply following German orders. Rarely acting on their own initiative, the Italians, with important exceptions, exhibited little enthusiasm in aiding the Germans in the mass killing of innocents. The Jews they rounded up were, as far as is known, simply assumed to be part of the Soviet apparatus: implacable enemies, like commissars.

Elsewhere in joint Axis-occupied Europe, Italians moved to protect Jews in areas under their jurisdiction. Why did they not do so in Russia? First and foremost, no Italian Jewish subjects, whose rights needed protection against expropriation of property and violation of citizenship, lived in Soviet Russia. Furthermore, Italy had no occupation rights in territory defined by written agreement with the Third Reich. This stands in contrast with France and Greece where Italian Jews resided, and where the Italians were in a position to extend their occupation rights to protect them against both Vichy and German roundups. In Yugoslavia the Italians could risk conflict with the Germans over the Jewish question because the *regio esercito* functioned as an independent fighting force on their side of the demarcation line with many more boots on the ground than the Wehrmacht. General Roatta, in asserting Italy's sovereign rights, could use Jews opportunistically as political leverage, as a statement of independence, or as payback to a pushy and disliked ally. Likewise in Greece and France. But not in Russia, where the Italians arrived with comparatively few troops and relied heavily on Germany for supplies and transportation.

Giorgio Rochat rightly concludes that Italian forces played a minor but not negligible role in the Nazi war of terror and extermination in Russia and that they contributed to the barbarization of the war.[76] He does not let Rome off lightly. Mussolini and the CS were apprised of German atrocities committed in the Ukraine by General Marras and others but overlooked his reports.

On the whole the Italians fought as loyal allies in the areas the Germans assigned them and were not discriminated against in battlefield missions. Prior to the Russian offensives of latter November, the Italian troops more or less shared the military purposes and objectives of their German allies. The two armies co-

---

75. Ibid., p. 57.
76. Rochat, *Le guerre italiane*, pp. 387–89; Rochat, preface to Massignani, *Alpini e Tedeschi sul Don.*

existed reasonably well until the Italian troops broke and fled in that month, and again in January 1943, when they were overpowered by punishing Russian attacks. These precipitous Italian retreats produced out-and-out animosity between the two Axis partners.

From the Italian standpoint, the Wehrmacht had imposed impossible tasks on them and deliberately sacrificed the Alpine divisions by using them to cover the German retreat. Moreover, the Germans were, in the Italian view, seriously remiss in denying their ally help and sustenance. For sustaining the common cause, the Italians felt that the Wehrmacht should have provided them all possible support, including, perhaps, assistance in reorganizing the ARMIR units. During the terrible retreat from the Don, having been spat at, denied entry into heated huts, and refused fuel for their vehicles by the Germans, some Italian troops said openly that they would prefer to fight with the Russians—or lose the war—than endure further combat on the side of the Third Reich.

Callousness, to be sure, prevailed. The minute that Italian soldiers no longer proved themselves battle-worthy, they were cast aside. The Germans hogged what food there was, kept valuable medical equipment for themselves, and were impervious to Italian suffering. General Granati spoke the truth in observing: "….in combat, they were marvelous comrades; as soon as combat ceased, ceased also every spirit of brotherhood and camaraderie. The Italians were left on their own, treated coldly, if not contemptuously."[77]

In December 1946, General Gariboldi delivered a blistering bill of particulars against the Germans. Blinded by an unshakable faith in the Wehrmacht's infallibility, they did not foresee strong Soviet resistance. To avoid responsibility for poor battlefield decisions taken, they maliciously foisted blame on the Italian troops.[78] This portrayal was a convincing one for many Italians who smarted from what they imagined to be the proclivity of the Wehrmacht to think of them as an inferior race rather than as "Fascist comrades."

The Germans, in turn, claimed that their ally did not deserve better treatment because the Italian soldiers, by yielding to the advancing enemy without a fight, had contributed to the disaster of winter 1942–43. From the German perspective, Mussolini had pushed Hitler to employ Italians on the Eastern Front, which the Wehrmacht wanted no part of, especially at first. Moreover, the German commanders had much on their minds beyond the fate of the shattered Italian troops; every ounce of energy was needed to stabilize their own front for the inevitable Soviet counterattack. In the German scheme of things, the Italian collapse was a minor episode in the titanic struggle against the Soviets.

77. Cited in Massignani, *Alpini e Tedeschi sul Don*, p. 138; NARS, T-821, 355, 000757, Granati report.
78. *Le operazioni delle unita italiane al fronte russo*, cit., pp. 514–15.

Since the German commanders, on the orders of their Führer, never hesitated to sacrifice their own, one must question whether the Italians were actually singled out for brutal treatment. Witness Stalingrad. If the German units involved in the retreat from the Don (beyond the trapped 6th Army in Stalingrad) got away better than the Italians, it was because, as "motorized descendents of Attila the Hun," they had better equipment. Certainly, Italian transportation when compared to the German was primitive, but this might have been oversold in explaining away failure. Just as the Italians relied on mules and horses for basic transport to haul artillery pieces, carry ammunition, and pull supply carts, so did the Germans. The vast bulk of the Wehrmacht infantry, as always, trudged along on foot.[79]

Italian indignation over German heartlessness shielded the breakdown of solidarity among the troops in the general chaos of retreat. Not infrequently the Italians used their German "comrades" as scapegoats when justifying heavy losses of arms and equipment—let alone cowardly behavior—to their superiors. It was easier for Italian troops to point out that Germans commandeered motor transport, seized weapons, and snatched water and food than to admit having thrown equipment away during panicked retreats.[80]

The Italian military cannot be accused of forging a heartless engine of destruction. But not for a lack of will on the part of the Duce, who seemed untroubled by the horrific Nazi record in the Soviet Union. While holding his military in contempt for remaining at heart monarchist—an army that lacked *squadristi* élan and resisted schooling in the Fascist crusader's spirit—he hoped all along that his legions would follow his example by cheerfully joining the Nazis in the winner-take-all war against Bolsheviks, Jews, and Slavs and establish a stranglehold on Russian raw materials in areas they occupied. Much to his disappointment, events played out much differently.

The Warlord at His Worst

In a war marked by mishaps, miscalculation, and sheer bungling, perhaps the worst episode in *il Duce's* leadership was his decision to send troops to aid Hitler on the Eastern front. Not for the first time did Mussolini make an important political decision to commit troops based on the certainty of a German victory; he had already done so in France, North Africa, and Greece. Since shrewd observers in Italy and in Britain too predicted a short life for the Soviet Union, Mussolini's calculation at the outset of Barbarossa was not totally absurd. But as

---

79. Richard J. Evans, *The Third Reich at War* (New York: The Penguin Press, 2009), pp. 200–1.
80. Schlemmer, *Invasori, non vittime*, p. 149.

the stalemate ensued, the Duce took leave of his senses. By committing the flower of his army to a distant place unrelated to any achievable Italian interest, he defied Realpolitik. Worse still, his decision to send ARMIR involved him in an unmistakable war crime.

Cavallero was of marginal help. Although opposed to the Russian venture,[81] he was not about to challenge Mussolini once his mind was made up. But General Giuseppe Montezemolo, who, according to the Italian military historian Lucio Ceva, was the brains of the Supreme Command, was outraged. Presciently, he wrote on 5 July 1941 that dispatch of the small expeditionary corps to the Eastern Front would have negative consequences by denying desperately needed motor vehicles, anti-tank guns, and anti-aircraft canon in North Africa.[82] The 227,000 soldiers sent to Russia made only a tiny footprint, and the trucks and modern artillery swallowed up in Russia's vast spaces, if not a robust force, would have lent more mobility to the infantry in the African desert.

But have we not already seen the grueling problems on the ground and at sea that Italy faced in provisioning the Axis troops in North Africa? Ceva readily concedes the point, but in a sophisticated analysis shows that the mix should have been different in the tonnage actually carried. Rather than sending additional infantry, which arguably was more a burden than help, the CS should have sent over more armor.[83] Between January and May 1942, when the Axis dominated the Mediterranean, they would have been able to ship to North Africa 10,000 motor vehicles, 124 modern canons of great and medium caliber, and anti-aircraft that ended up in Russia, as well as naval units in the Black Sea and air force formations. Subsequently, between 5 and 15 July 1942, the Italian navy could easily have transported an entire battle group composed of infantry originally ticketed for Malta as well as the armored forces bound for Russia.[84] The Italian military expert Pier Paolo Battistelli points out that Italy, by splitting resources between the two war theaters, lost "liberty of movement" vis-à-vis Germany.[85]

Given the failure of Mussolini's ill-advised Soviet invasion, the military ached for redemption by victory in North Africa. According to General Montezemolo, many officers who verged on anti-Fascism deeply resented Mussolini for ignoring Libya. Worse still, the rumor was out that some Fascists actually took pleasure over losses in the desert for taking down the royalist military a

---

81. Ceva, *La condotta italiana della guerra*, p. 98.
82. Ceva, *Guerra mondiale*, p. 112.
83. Ceva, *La condotta italiana della guerra*, p. 110.
84. Ceva, *Guerra mondiale*, p. 123; Ceva, *La condotta italiana della guerra*, pp. 105–6.
85. Battistelli note to the author.

notch or two.[86] But even if the large force sent to the Eastern Front had fought in North Africa, this would only have lengthened Axis resistance and spared Italy further shame on the battlefield. An Axis conquest of Egypt in 1942 would not have altered the ultimate outcome of the war or staved off further disasters following Montgomery's offensive of 23 October and the Anglo-American landing in Algeria and Morocco on 8 November 1942. Far bigger events loomed on the Eastern Front that would dwarf the North African theater in importance: the Russian counteroffensive of 19 November along the Don River; the surrender of the German 6th Army at Stalingrad; and the smashup of ARMIR. For Italy, the failure to capture El Alamein stands out as the decisive turn in the country's military fortunes. Mussolini's decision to send troops to Russia marks the epitome of his disastrous leadership.

---

86. Ceva, *Guerra mondiale*, p. 112.

Chapter X

Bitter Finale in France

A Tempered Occupation
The Unredeemed Vittoria Mutilata

A Tempered Occupation

On 9 October General Cesare Amé (head of SIM, military intelligence) warned Ciano that the Allies were about to sail for North Africa and, in a message to the CS, foretold a "sprint to Tunisia" as a prelude to an invasion of Italy.[1] In early November, based on information assembled by SIM's network of spies, the CS predicted that a large Allied convoy was about to leave Gibraltar; only the ultimate destination remained unclear.[2] Rome was therefore not surprised when the Allies landed in Algeria and Morocco on 8 November. Many Italians concluded that the imminent demise of the Fascist regime was at hand. Mussolini had no doubt about how Vichy would react to the invasion. Riddled with Gaullists, the French army would put up a mock defense to satisfy honor before raising the white flag and joining the invader:[3] France was ready "to open the door to the enemy."[4]

As far back as October, Cavallero had concluded that Tunisia should be seized at once as a hedge against Vichy turncoats. Since Mussolini had for long pondered such a bold stroke, he needed no further persuasion. The Germans,

---

1. *The Ciano Diaries*, 9 October 1942; Cesare Amè, *Guerra segreta in Italia, 1940–1943* (Rome: Casini, 1954), pp. 114–15.
2. Deakin, *The Brutal Friendship*, I: 66.
3. *OO*, XXXI, pp. 107–10, Conversation between Mussolini with Vacca Maggiolini, 3 October 1942.

however, had a contrary view. In the event of an Allied landing in North Africa, they wanted to postpone a warlike move on Tunisia until the Vichy regime showed its hand. Their expectation was that, as intimidated collaborators, the French would put up resistance against the Allies, thus providing the Axis Powers a soft landing in Tunisia. In case of "treachery," they would force their way in.

This constituted "immobility" in the Italian view, a time-waster that would allow the Allies to land uncontested on the North African coast for a hop, skip, and jump into Tunisia. They were right that German hesitation had left Axis initiative in the western Mediterranean to the unreliable Vichy regime. But lacking petrol, troops, and transportation, the Italians could not have preempted Operation Torch by undertaking C4 on their own.[5] Thanks to the delays, the Axis would be faced with an uphill fight in defending Tunisia against the Allied onslaught.

As the crisis unfolded, the two Axis partners, working largely in the dark, had conflicting views on ultimate Allied objectives. At the height of the drama, they frantically reworked ideas on how to handle Vichy France. On 7 November Mussolini concurred with Ciano that the Allies had their sights set on French North Africa. Hitler, however, believed that the enemy aimed to fall not on North Africa but on Rommel's rear by a landing at Tripoli or Benghazi.[6] Excitement grew as the first fragmentary news on the Torch landing arrived in Rome and Berlin. Hitler declared that he would fight with the French "through thick and thin" if they offered resistance.[7] The next day Mussolini endorsed Hitler's position, but appended a warning: "If France is ready to collaborate loyally, it will receive all possible aid from us; if, on the other hand, it plays hot and cold, we are going to adopt preventive measures: occupation of the free zone and a landing in Corsica."[8] Mussolini had evaluated the situation better than Hitler. He knew instinctively that the enemy aimed to administer a mortal blow to the weakest link of the Axis, thereby setting up the Peninsula for an invasion to knock Italy out of the war and himself from power.[9]

Upon verification of the Allied landing, Cavallero, in accordance with Mussolini's wishes, prepared to activate C2, the invasion of Corsica. Italy must do something quickly to compensate for the imminent loss of Libya, he told

---

4. Cited in Borgogni, *Italia e Francia*, p. 73.
5. ADAP, E, IV, Conversation between Göring with Mussolini, 23 October 1942; Deakin, *The Brutal Friendship* I: 65.
6. *The Ciano Diaries,* 7 November 1942; Cavallero, *Diario*, pp. 543–44, 6 November 1942.
7. *Germany and the Second World War*, VI: 824.
8. *The Ciano Diaries*, 9 November 1942; DDI, 9, IX, 283, Mussolini to Rintelen, 8 November 1942, and n. 4; *Germany and the Second World War*, VI: 824.
9. Borgogni, *Italia e Francia*, pp. 99–100.

Rintelen. "As a soldier I demand the right to do everything to avoid a Gaullist occupation."[10] Since Italy lacked ships, tanks, and soldiers to handle both expeditions simultaneously, Cavallero was far less sanguine regarding C4, the landing on Tunisia.[11]

This anxiety dissipated when Mussolini told Cavallero that French Admiral Darlan had asked air support from Germany. In quite a startling turnaround, the Duce declared his readiness "to make an alliance with France."[12] Cavallero expressed this wishful thought: "The French fleet is ready to weigh anchor from Toulon in an hour. I hardly dare hope, but if this collaboration occurs we will have won the war. I am a convinced advocate of the necessity of collaboration...."[13]

Cavallero's optimism died abruptly when on 10 November Darlan signed a ceasefire with the Americans, ordering the French troops to observe the strictest neutrality, while the Vichy government fell silent regarding the "rebels" in North Africa. Hitler, believing that he had torn away Vichy's mask of collaboration during Laval's visit in Berlin, gave the signal to march. On 9–10 November, under a carefully prearranged plan, the Wehrmacht rumbled unopposed into unoccupied France, and German air formations bearing paratroopers quickly landed in Tunisia on the 10th to prepare the ground for a larger landing of Axis troops in the hope of blocking the Allies moving across Morocco. The first Italian ground units did not arrive until a few days later.

Faced by such a quick turn of events, the Italian military discarded time-consuming and rigid marching orders for unoccupied France, substituting a slapdash walk-in that would easily have fallen apart if confronted by resistance. The Italian 4th Army under the command of General Mario Vercellino, thinking that the French were determined to mount a spirited fight, cautiously moved forward. Arriving "a little late,"[14] his troops clattered along the cobbled streets of provincial towns to take up positions in seven French departments, mainly in Provence, on the southern coast of France along the Rhône River. His force looked formidable on paper—three army corps and several divisions, but a German report read: "The 4th Army has no planes, no naval protection, no heavy artillery, no anti-aircraft."[15] Relieved that the French did not put up a fight, General Vercellino quietly settled in, but soon found himself at odds with CIAF, the Italian

---

10. Cavallero, *Diario*, 8 November 1942.

11. Ibid.

12. Ibid.

13. Ibid.

14. *Operazioni*, IV: 98.

15. Cited in Jonathan Steinberg, *All or Nothing, The Axis and the Holocaust 1941–1943* (London and New York: Routledge, 1991), p. 109.

organization empowered to enforce the Armistice terms. Vercellino suggested that it be abolished but encountered Ambrosio's opposition.[16]

General Cavallero was a lucky man. If the Vichy regime had put up resistance against Italy in unoccupied France, Tunis, and Corsica, he could never have met these dangers simultaneously, or even one at a time. As things turned out, he was able to walk in behind the Wehrmacht in France, land planes and troops in Tunisia, which already had been secured by the Luftwaffe, and easily implement C2 by carrying out the first stage of the occupation of Corsica, an island of 300,000 inhabitants, using a flotilla of cutters.[17] Eventually 85,000 Italian soldiers would be deposited on the island; they might have been put to better use in North Africa in November. For political reasons Mussolini decided not to annex Corsica as he had once vowed to do and ordered his commanders to rule with a light hand lest the Corsican population be provoked to rebel. The occupiers were mainly concerned with defending the island from an Allied attack rather than effecting a Fascist-style regime change. The newly appointed Italian prefects at first applied a relaxed administration that allowed civil life to proceed normally—a leniency, however, that did not result in a true modus vivendi with the native Corsicans. Later the Italians resorted to harsher repressive measures to keep the sullen population under firm control. Commanded by General Mazzerelli, 800 Carabinieri joined by eight battalions of Blackshirts supervised crackdowns and bullied the population.[18]

The timing of the march into unoccupied France was especially bad for the Germans. Embroiled in the titanic struggle before Stalingrad, they had just transferred two armored divisions from France to shore up the Eastern Front. As a consequence of the troop cutback in the West, they encouraged the Italians to occupy French territory to the southeast coast and the Pyrenees, including the port cities of Toulon and Marseille.[19] But the 4th Army, moving at a lumbering pace, was not up to the task of reaching the line Rhône-Lyon-Toulouse-Mediterranean Sea quickly enough to suit the Germans, who were anxious to establish a firm Axis defense to head off an expected Allied invasion of southern France. Taking matters in their own hands, the Wehrmacht charged into Marseille and, on 13 and 14 November, ringed the fortified harbor of Toulon, promising Pétain to stay clear of the naval base out of respect for the neutrality of the French navy.[20]

---

16. Rainero, *Mussolini e Pétain*, I: 427–34.
17. *The Ciano Diaries*, 11 November 1942.
18. Panicacci, *L'Occupation italienne*, p. 118.
19. Domenico Schipsi, *L'occupazione italiana dei territori metropolitani francesi, 1940–1943* (Rome: SME US, 2007), p. 128.
20. Ibid., pp., 128–31; Borgogni, *Italia e Francia*, p. 121.

The Italians had no grounds for complaint. Crumbling fronts in North Africa, Russia, and the Balkans forced Mussolini to avoid a costly and wide-ranging military commitment in France. Because the 4th Army moved sluggishly to take up positions, the Duce had to concede Germany the zones around Toulon and Marseille. In a rare gesture of good will, he ordered the Italian command on the 13th to treat the French military, civilian authority, and people respectfully.[21] For the time being there would be no requisitions or talk of territorial claims.[22] The terms of the Armistice would be respected.

Frustrated over the 4th Army's inability to occupy Toulon, the Italians worried about the French fleet anchored there. General Vacca Maggiolini, the head of CIAF, urged that it be disarmed. But by Germans? With only a few troops in the vicinity of the port, Mussolini had to make do with "a more vigilant attention."[23] He endured a rude shock on the 27th when, without prior notice, German troops, supported by a handful of Italians, swept into the fortified harbor of Toulon to seize the French fleet, fearing that it might suddenly raise anchor and join the Allies. In the nick of time French officers were able to scuttle their ships before SS units could stop them, which dashed Italian hopes of expropriating sorely needed warships. There was one positive result: the absence of a French fleet to rival the Italian for many years to come. During early December the Italians were able to wrest from the Germans an accord for the recovery of what remained of the French fleet—over 235,000 tons, either for scrap metal or salvage for use by the Italian navy.[24]

After these dramatic events, the Italian occupation settled into a dull routine as the French people, cowed by Nazis swarming throughout the country, sullenly went about their business. Under the surface, of course, they fumed: the Italians had not defeated them and the occupation stood as an insult to patriotic sentiment. A SIM officer wrote: "The French population welcomes us in a silent rage, and, visibly, by a sentiment worse that hate: contempt. The French fear and hate everything while admiring the German army; but they do not fear the Italian army."[25] Scorn was joined by fear. In flaunting Fascist superiority over a "decadent and washed-up opponent," Rome was thought to be preparing to seize chunks of metropolitan France and colonial territory in North Africa for the Italian Imperium.

But such did not happen, for many obstacles thwarted the regime in Rome: Hitler's refusal to tear up the Armistice (which took annexation off the books),

21. Panicacci, *L'Occupation italienne*, p. 139.
22. Cavallero, *Diario*, 14 November 1942; Schipsi, *L'occupazione italiana*, p. 142 and n. 207.
23. Schipsi, *L'occupazione italiana*, pp. 170–71.
24. Borgogni, *Italia e Francia*, p. 146.
25. Cited in Panicacci, *L'Occupation italienne*, p. 138.

successful French and German resistance to Italian economic exploitation, and the army's abstention from politics in occupied France.

Indeed, in an atmosphere relatively free of overt hostility, the military could avoid local "politics" and keep to itself. By living in accordance with its own rules—the "Italian Law of War and Neutrality, n. 1415 of 8 July 1938," and the "Military Penal Code of War" of 20 February 1941—the military was able to define a degree of *autolimitazione* of its power. Having implored the soldiers to eschew "imperious acts" and to cooperate with French authority, the commanders hoped to achieve a workable rapport with French citizens.[26] Since their daily chores were limited chiefly to ensuring military security, the soldiers had no need of applying *Squadristi* methods. The Military Tribunal did not hand down one capital punishment and carefully reviewed the harshness of other sentences.[27]

On the whole, therefore, as opposed to the OVRA, Blackshirts, and certain elements of the Carabinieri, the Italian military in France could point to a relatively clean slate on war crimes and repression; they also managed their own affairs without Fascist prodding, interference, or indoctrination. French prefects and officials, in spite of occasional ticklish situations, remarked on the 4th that the Army had acted correctly and courteously.[28] Conceiving its mission as primarily preventive rather than repressive, the military did compile a rather respectable record of occupation that stands in marked contrast with the wicked deeds their comrades committed in the Balkans. Differing circumstances provide an explanation for this discrepancy. In the absence of a large-scale insurrectionary movement in France, there was no need for a vicious Roatta-style counterinsurgency that the military visited on the peoples of Yugoslavia, Albania, and Greece. And in a land already browbeaten into silence by Germans (the resistance movement did not swing into high gear until after the Italians had left the country in September 1943), there was no urgency for an anti-Communist crusade, which took the edge off repression. Moreover, contrary to the Balkans, which abounded in political chaos and ethnic warfare—and had a powerful partisan movement—the military found stability in a Vichy government supervised by the Germans and aligned one way or the other with the Axis whose authority they were constrained to acknowledge.

While the military occupation settled into a disciplined routine, the Fascist regime looked forward to harvesting a vast assortment of French resources. But much to their disappointment, since Berlin declined to denounce the Armistice, the country's claims on French assets and territory were left in limbo. Once again

---

26. Schipsi, *L'occupazione italiana*, pp. 387–402.
27. Ibid.
28. Panicacci, *L'Occupation italienne*, pp. 158–59.

the Germans had forced Rome to accept the fiction of an independent Vichy by granting the regime shards of authority. The French, though relieved that the Germans had not given their alliance partner a free hand to exploit resources, were still on their guard, for the Duce did not hide his vengeful intention to exploit and pillage at will no matter the obstacles.[29] But they took solace in the Italian 4th Army's official subordination to Field Marshal Gerd von Rundstedt, which deprived General Avarna di Gualtieri, the CS representative at Vichy, of leverage to wrest concessions from the Vichy government. Vacca Maggiolini confided to Cavallero his fear that Laval would take advantage of the 4th Army's satellite position in the Axis by canceling Italy "with a stroke of the French pen...from the category of sovereign states."[30]

Mussolini blew off steam on 2 December before the Assembly of Fascists and Corporations (Camera dei Fasci e delle Corporazioni). The Allied landing in North Africa was "nothing glorious" since it occurred "with the complicity of the invaded... Everyone in France is a fence-sitter."[31] But notice Mussolini's un-wonted silence on the annexation of French territory.

Since Mussolini was faced with the task of breathing life into moribund factories, which Allied air attacks had pounded unmercifully, he was prepared to abandon his former moderation by replenishing exhausted stocks of raw materials in Italy at the expense of Vichy France regardless of the risks. But because there was no breakout from the Armistice clauses, the Duce was hemmed in by legal restrictions and French resistance to a general impounding of movable resources and confiscation of military equipment.[32] Undaunted, he ordered the CS at the end of December to end the "garrison regime for the purpose of defense against enemy aggression by transforming the presence of Italian troops on French territory to an occupation of no limits." Italians would occupy factories, confiscate prime materials needed by their war effort, issue coupons of occupation in francs for all the acquisitions made by the military, and abolish the customs barrier between Italy and France.[33]

In this spirit the CS on 15 January 1943 authorized General Avarna to inform the French government that the Italian army was set on exercising "all the rights of an occupying power" for the purpose of acquiring the resources of which the Italian economy had need.[34] Italy would act regardless of French law by abrogating clauses of the Armistice agreements. Mussolini told Vacca Maggio-

29. Paxton, *Parades and Politics at Vichy*, p. 391.
30. DDI, 9, IX, 409, Annex, Vacca Maggiolini to Cavallero, 13 December 1942.
31. *OO*, XXXI, pp. 118–33.
32. Schipsi, *L'occupazione italiana*, pp. 274–75.
33. DDI, 9, IX, Vitetti to Ciano, 28 December 1942.
34. Borgogni, *L'Italia e Francia*, p. 78; Schipsi, *L'occupazione italiana*, p. 346.

lini on 12 February: "Get as much as you can and send it all to Italy."[35] Proceeding with this cupidity, Mussolini was bound to worsen his country's relations with France.

On 17 April Rome decreed that "movable goods, both state and private, located east of the Rhône," would pass under Italian control. By applying the Italian law of war, Italy "could proceed with the acquisition of war materiel essential for its factories....by confiscation of state property and seizure of private property."[36] Encouraged by such an assertive attitude, Italian financiers surged forward to occupy factories, impound stocks of raw materials, and issue occupation vouchers in francs for all purchases made by the military authorities. Such a flurry of activity, however, yielded few results. With too few entrepreneurs and too little money, Italy barely had a chance of becoming involved even in small-scale industrial production. In the eyes of the French, Italian behavior bespoke a reckless effort to supply raw materials to the starving Italian war industry that amounted to outright pillage.[37]

However, it was the Germans who posed as the greatest obstacle to Italian exploitation of French resources. Although the Italians cleverly succeeded in avoiding von Rundstedt's military shackles until Mussolini's fall,[38] they had no answer to Germany's relentless drive for economic predominance. A fleet of profiteers and political agents had previously pounced on industrial production and primary resources in territories under Italian military occupation. The Germans had already established control over nine-tenths of the French aeronautics, steel, and metallurgy industries and had secured exclusive contracts on car and truck manufacture.

Once it dawned on the Italians that they had hardly dented the French economy, they strove to emulate the German method of exploitation. Instead of sending confiscated raw materials directly to the Reich, the Germans submitted purchasing orders for finished products to French firms employing local resources, naturally on outrageously profitable terms. But when Rome tendered such contracts, they obtained no more advantages beyond outright seizure of raw materials.[39] Once again, as in Yugoslavia and Greece, the highly resourceful and deep-pocketed Germans were easily able to outpace their ally.

---

35. Rainero, *Mussolini e Pétain*, I: 424.
36. Cited in Gianni Perona's path breaking work on Italy's attempted exploitation of French resources, "Aspetti economici dell'occupazione italiana in Francia (novembre 1942-settembre 1943)," in *8 settembre, lo sfacelo della IV Armata* (Istituto storico della Resistenza in Piemonte) (Turin: Book Store, 1979), p. 138.
37. ASMAE, AP, Francia, 1939–45, b. 70, Memorandum for the CS, 24 March 1943; Rodogno, *Fascism's Roman Empire*, p. 253.
38. Steinberg, *All or Nothing*, p. 110.
39. Schipsi, *L'occupazione italiana*, p. 365.

While harried by these setbacks in France at the hands of German financiers, Mussolini faced palpable dangers at home, such as the imminent fall of Tunisia, a likely Allied invasion, Italy's destruction, and his own political demise. Since the Duce had made his Fascist regime wholly dependent on the Third Reich—the ignoble second in the Axis—he hastened on 9 March to reassure Hitler of his "unshakable intention to march with Germany to the end of the road."[40]

At an inter-ministerial conference held in Rome on 12 June, the Italian Fascists admitted: "According to the Germans the French economy must be considered a unity forming a part of the general plan for European distribution. Germany intends to function as the collecting and distributing agency."[41] Thus had the powerless Italians yielded Germany prior rights of exploitation in their French-occupied territory.

Thwarted at every turn, it seemed that the Italians had only one weapon for retaliation against a condescending ally and a hated enemy: protection of Jews in their areas of occupation from Nazi and Vichy roundups. By upholding the rights of Jewish citizens residing in France, the Italians hoped to prevent their property from falling into French or German hands. Rome would use the occasion to remind the Vichy regime who was in command, and the point could be made in Berlin that Italy was a superpower of equal standing. Although extensive discrimination against the Jews was on the books in the racial legislation of 1938, there was a noticeable absence of visceral anti-Semitism on the part of those responsible for policies in the occupied territories, whose good will was confirmed by the memory of those Jews on the French Riviera who experienced the Italian occupation.

Nothing was more galling to Vichy officials than having cantankerous Italians lecture them on governance. They did not need any goading from the Nazis to reassert their sovereign rights on Italian-occupied territory. One means of achieving this was to enforce ordinances passed in December 1942 that expelled foreign and stateless Jews from the coast. Rome answered by instructing the 4th Army to block French interference in the administration of property seized from Italian and foreign Jews, and notified Berlin that no measures were to be taken against Italian Jews in the German-occupied zones without Rome's express consent.[42]

Berlin scoffed at that show of strength, and Pietromarchi, for one, saw what was afoot: "Notwithstanding all the misfortunes befalling them, the Germans are

---

40. Cited in Daniel Carpi, *Between Mussolini and Hitler: The Jews and the Italian Authorities in France and Tunisia* (Hanover and London: University Press of New England, 1994), p. 127, n. 76.
41. Perona, "Aspetti economici dell'occupazione italiana in Francia," pp. 136–37.
42. ASMAE, AP, Francia, b. 54, 22 December 1942.

ceaselessly insisting that we should surrender to them all the Jews residing in the areas under our occupation. They confirm that by the end of 1943 not a single Jew should remain alive in Europe. It is clear that they want to implicate us in the brutality of their policy."[43]

Between 20–22 February 1943, Vichy police, prodded by the Germans, began to fasten the noose around foreign Jews by widespread manhunts in the former Unoccupied Zone.[44] When the 4th Army flagged down the Vichy police, Laval testily reminded the Italians that they had no right to stand between the Vichy government and citizens of other countries on French soil.

Regarding Vichy's crackdown on Jews as a breach in the authority of the occupying power, Italian commanders sealed off local police stations to prevent deportation of prisoners and demanded their release. Aghast, Ribbentrop hastened to Rome in late February to put a stop to Italy's errant ways. The Duce told him not to worry; the French were the real troublemakers by spreading false rumors of a passive Italian attitude toward Jews in order to cause friction between Germany and Italy. Since the Jews had already been placed in camps, Mussolini assured Ribbentrop, all was well.[45]

Pietromarchi noted in his diary: "Our military authorities (it may be admitted to their credit), maintained a firm opposition to the brutal measures of the Germans. In France they demanded that the local authorities cancel all the instructions against the Jews, such as the duty to wear 'the star of Solomon,' conscription for forced labor and the like."[46]

With Ribbentrop back in Berlin, Ambrosio at the beginning of March served notice on the French that the internment of all Jews irrespective of nationality "was, and must remain, the exclusive responsibility of the Italian authorities." All French persecution of the Jews must stop by canceling arrests and internments of Jews, who are "residents in the territory of France occupied by our armed forces." A couple of weeks later, the 4th Army sternly warned the French: "Any transfer of Jews from the Italian-occupied zone to the one under German occupation is strictly forbidden." The French government "must revoke arrests and internments effectuated by prefects in said territories and return elements arrested and deported."[47]

Impatient with Italian backsliding, Mackensen on 9 March spelled out three options for the Duce: 1. The CS should give orders to refrain from obstructing the French police. 2. The administration of Jewish matters should be transferred

---

43. PP, *Diario*, 2 February 1943.
44. Carpi, *Between Mussolini and Hitler*, p. 113.
45. Ibid., pp. 117–18.
46. PP, *Diario*, 11 March 1943.
47. Citations in Carpi, *Between Mussolini and Hitler*, pp. 122, 155.

from the military to civilian police. 3. Jurisdiction over these matters should be handed over to the SS and the French police.[48]

Mussolini delayed until the 18th before replying: "The imperative necessity for [taking] radical measures against the Jews....still remaining in the Italian zone of occupation could not be presented more clearly and irrefutably." If the Italian generals opposed the implementation of these measures, they did this because "they had not grasped the full significance of all the measures." Furthermore, the Duce believed that "the behavior of these generals was the result not only of the indicated lack of understanding concerning the significance of the action being taken, but also the consequences of a misguided humanitarian sentimentality, which is inappropriate to our harsh times." He would "that same day issue suitable instructions to the Chief of the General Staff General Ambrosio, so that from then on the French police would have a completely free hand in this operation."[49]

Pietromarchi summarized in his diary what happened next: "He [Bastianini] had just received from Vidau [head of Section IV, Confidential Affairs] the latest news from Berlin of the horrifying massacres perpetrated against the Jews and he brought them to the Duce: 'The real reason for the attitude of our officers was not given by Ambrosio, but I am going to tell you, Duce. Our people know what fate awaits the Jews consigned to the Germans. They will all be gassed without distinction, the old women, babies. And that's why our people will never permit such atrocities to take place with their connivance. And you, Duce, ought not to give your approval. Why do you want to assume a responsibility which will fall on you entirely?' That was Bastianini's courageous speech. The Duce was shaken. 'But I have promised Mackensen that I would give orders to make our military men stop obstructing things,' he said. 'With your permission, I'll talk to Mackensen.' 'Very well.'"[50]

Bastianini immediately cashed in on his pledge by telling the German minister that the Duce would accept the second option and promised to give "the order to our head of police to study the transfer of all those people in hotels and pensions in Savoy."[51] The 4th Army would be relieved of having to deal with the Jewish question by turning over to the Italian police supervision for all Jews

48. ADAP, E, V, 189, Mackensen to the Foreign Office, 9 March 1943.
49. Cited in Carpi, *Between Mussolini and Hitler*, pp. 128–29. Mackensen's summary of the meeting can be found in Poliakov and Sabille, *Jews Under the Italian Occupation*, D. 8, pp. 68–70.
50. PP, *Diario*, 31 March 1943; De Felice, *The Jews in Fascist Italy: a History*, p. 396 and D. 32; Serge Klarsfeld, *Vichy-Auschwitz: la "solution finale" de la question juive en France* (Paris: Fayard, 2001), pp. 45–48 and 235–40; Ortona, *Diplomazia di guerra*, pp. 201, 209.
51. Giuseppe Bastianini, *Volevo fermare Mussolini* (Milan: BUR, 1995), pp. 100–101.; Mackensen's telegram to Berlin can be found in Poliakov and Sabille, *Jews under the Italian Occupation*, pp. 70–72.

living in Italian zones of occupation.[52] The "Old Fox" Mackensen raised no objection.[53] Neither did Himmler, because he expected the Italian police to do his bidding on the Jews better than the foot-dragging army.[54]

The next day, moving with unusual speed, Chief of Police Carmine Senise appointed General Guido Lospinoso as Italian Race Police Inspector. Lospinoso's task was to arrange for the transfer of all Jews living in the Italian Occupation Zone in southern France to new places of residence at least 100 kilometers from the coast. In a masterly display of false naiveté, the new inspector avoided making arrests, kept the French police at arm's length, and evaded agents of the Gestapo sent out to brief him.[55] As part of the subterfuge Lospinoso compiled lists of Jews and undertook roundups for their movement to new quarters. Bastianini, therefore, was able to reassure Mackensen on the 20th that everything had been done "to safeguard the security of the Axis troops along the Côte d'Azur" by concentrating the Jews in Savoy where there were plenty of hotels of every category to house them. Ambrosio did his part by convincing Mussolini that the French police could not be trusted; Lospinoso was the ideal person to take over the roundup and internment of the Jews in France.[56]

On 3 April a notable change took place in the typically bland and officious language characterizing military correspondence. Instead of *internment* of Jews, the Italian military stated explicitly for the first time that its purpose was to *save* those Jews who resided in the French territory occupied by the Italian army, whatever their nationality.[57]

From the end of March to the end of July, the Italian police transferred 4,500 Jewish refugees to guarded but safe quarters.[58] At summer's conclusion 30,000 Jews were crowded along thirty kilometers of coast in the Alpes-Maritimes, according to the prefect's information. But lest we conclude that the Italians were altogether magnanimous, it is well to point out that occasionally Jews were extradited to the Germans. For example, the Italian police on 19 May turned over Theodor Wolff, director of the liberal newspaper *Berliner Tageblatte*, to the Germans, who deported him to Sachsenhausen.[59]

"The Israelites have emigrated and continue to emigrate en masse to that Promised Land which the left bank of the Rhône has become," commented

---

52. Carpi, *Between Mussolini and Hitler*, p. 130, n. 83; p. 131, n. 85.
53. PP, *Diario*, 31 March 1943.
54. Steinberg, *All or Nothing*, p. 125.
55. Klaus Voigt, *Il Rifugio precario: Gli esuli in Italia dal 1933 al 1945* (Florence: La Nuova Italia, 1996), II: 312–22.
56. PP, *Diario*, 31 March 1943.
57. USSME, DS, IV, CS Promemoria, Ebrei dei territori francesi occupati dalle truppe italiane, 3 April 1943; Carpi, *Between Mussolini and Hitler*, p. 133.
58. Carpi, *Between Mussolini and Hitler*, p. 145.
59. Voigt, *Il Rifugio precario*, II: 301.

Giovanni Ansaldo, regional prefect of Lyon, in May 1943.[60] The historian Jonathan Steinberg observes: "Italian soldiers and civil servants could not consciously take part in what they knew to be collective murder." To this, he adds, "Conspiratorial actions have a natural fascination in Italian culture, in which carbonari, freemasons, Jesuits, Mafiosi, nets of clients and patrons have spread webs of intrigue and influence and in which knowing slyness, *furberia*, enjoys prestige." Steinberg points out that in the attempt "to protect the thin outer walls of Italian sovereignty in 1943, Italy strove to prove its ability in helping Jews." In this endeavor he discerns "mixed motive and equivocal action."[61] Clearly, humanitarian impulses were not absent from Italian calculation.

Nonetheless, unsatisfied imperialist ambition set the stage for Italian policy toward the Jews. To strengthen occupation rights and legal entitlement, Rome safeguarded Italian Jews from Vichy interference. *Raison d'état* argued for protection, for "they [the Jews] represent a lively and active force in our communities,"[62] meaning that their lucrative economic and social assets should remain Italian against loss to any foreign power. If Rome allowed confiscation of Jewish property, a dangerous precedent would be set regarding the possessions and rights of other Italian citizens living abroad. In the refusal to be a bit player on the European stage, Fascist Italy, in the stale air of the "parallel war," pursued a policy on the Jewish question that would enable the country to act separately within the framework of the Axis. Still, much of these efforts to "save" the Jews came to naught after the Italian surrender on 8 September. In a scrambling retreat, Jews under Italian safekeeping fell into the hands of the German SS. Few managed to escape.[63]

On the protection of the Jews in France, as in Yugoslavia and Greece, Mussolini emerges with a mixed record. He vacillated and showed a disturbing callousness; above all, to avoid German displeasure, he wanted to shoo the problem away.

During spring 1943, the Italian occupiers experienced a spike in Maquis insurgency. To meet this threat, the regime, presuming that moderation and tolerance encouraged resistance and hostility, prodded the soldiers to strike back hard. The secret intelligence agency OVRA, which featured uninhibited cruelty, was more than willing to discharge this mandate. In setting up torture centers to

60. Quoted in Marrus and Paxton, *Vichy France and the Jews*, p. 315.
61. Steinberg, *All or Nothing*, pp. 128, 134.
62. Carpi, *Between Mussolini and Hitler*, p. 49. Italian policy regarding German Jews in France ended up differently. Michele Sarfatti points out that beyond all doubt during the political crisis of the regime in July 1943 Rome had decided to hand over to the Nazis German Jews in France. See his "Fascist Italy and German Jews in south-eastern France in July 1943," *Journal of Modern Italian Studies* 3 (3) (1998): 318–328.
63. Michael Marrus and Robert O. Paxton, *Vichy France and the Jews* (New York: Basic Books, 1980), p. 319.

welcome captured French insurgents, it kept pace, albeit on a much smaller scale, with the Gestapo.[64] The French historian Jean-Louis Panicacci cites many examples of cooperation between OVRA, assisted by the Carabinieri, and the Gestapo, reinforced by Abwehr detachments, in seizing hostages, rounding up suspected maquis, and detaining "undesirables."[65] The "purge" of Nice on 7 May 1943 involved the internment of 1,000 "Communists" in Cais (Fréjus) and 226 "hostile elements" in Modane, proof that the Italians certainly did not wear velvet gloves in handling an increasingly restive French population.

But Italian violence fell substantially short of German cruelty, exemplified in the Nazi siege of Marseille between 24 January and 7 February 1943. SS officials escorted by the French police destroyed the Old Port quarter of the city, interned around 20,000 people, and arrested approximately 6,000.[66] This repression was an embarrassment to Mussolini, who was not consulted before the brusque German move into a city that had originally been assigned to the 4th Army. Speaking with his top military officers on 28 January, he excused the absence of Italian troops by claiming they would have been exposed to French degeneracy if sent to mingle with the city's denizens: "It is a turbulent and effeminate environment because there is widespread corruption on the part of the rich and degenerate. Therefore whenever the occupation of Marseille had come up, I've been opposed, because I have not wanted to send Italian troops into such a city."[67]

The Unredeemed "Mutilated Victory"

Mussolini showed his true colors by turning on the French in his epitaph to "collaboration" on 3 January 1943: "Only by intentionally wanting to delude ourselves could we have thought that a policy of favor towards France would have achieved results. France has hated us, hates us now, and will hate us until the end of time."[68]

The Duce expressed further frustration in an exposition before the national directorate of the Fascist party on 3 March: "The entire policy of détente toward France has been absolutely sterile of results. They are all opportunists, beginning with Pétain.... Everything changed with the landing; there was an absolutely open connivance carried out by the French with few exceptions.... France no longer has any of its metropolitan territory, no colonies, no gold, no navy, army, or air force. It no longer has anything. The French people don't even have their

---

64. Gil Emprin, "L'esercito italiano in Francia: una occupazione paradossale," in *Crimini di guerra*, p. 84.
65. Panicacci, *L'Occupation italienne*, pp. 229-38.
66. Jaques Delarue, *Trafics et crimes sous l'occupation* (Paris: Fayard, 1993), pp. 237–78.
67. USSME, Verbali delle riunioni tenute dal capo di SME, vol. IV, Verbale 7, 28 January 1943, p. 283.

spirit; and this is perhaps the most serious of losses, which….unerringly demonstrates the decadence of a people."[69]

To the end Mussolini did not waver from his obstinate determination to settle scores with the unbowed French, all of whom he considered to be Gaullists and who refused to accept the lessons of defeat. But this earned him no support from Hitler. Italo-German differences on France were aired at the conference at Klessheim on 29 April 1943. Ribbentrop persisted in prevailing on Italy to work together with Laval, who supposedly was doing his utmost in keeping France at the beck and call of the Axis Powers. Laval proposed to Hitler and Bastianini that their countries outline the creation of a new European order as a fresh approach to win the war, adding that he would be delighted to meet with Mussolini in Rome to stir his interest. Once admitted to the Axis inner circle, Laval felt he would be able to chip away at German domination of his country and eliminate Italian claims on French territory.

Laval had no chance of making his case with the Italians. Unless he had first satisfied Fascist pride by yielding up Nice, Savoy, and Corsica, Bastianini would find no room in his *Carta Europea* for France.[70] Once again Rome had spurned the "Levantine merchant."[71]

On 9 May the spokesman for the Palazzo Chigi in the Senate declared: "Regarding France, the legitimate claims of Italy on French territory would not be abandoned." Ten days later Bastianini proclaimed before the Senate that France "must be ready to make sacrifices not only for the war production of the Axis countries but as a contribution to the settlement of questions still open between France and its conquerors. This is the essential condition for French participation in the new world order."[72] The speech enraged Hitler: "How can he say such a thing! The French say that they were not beaten by the Italians….a very rotten speech and it strengthens my feeling that a crisis of the type which we have discussed can develop there at any moment."[73] The men of the Nice Action Party (*Gruppi di azione nizzarda*), led by General Ezio Garibaldi, differed with the Führer. In the paper *Il Nizzardo*, the editorialists held high the flame of Italian territorial claims, flouting the efforts of CIAF and the 4th Army to muzzle Garibaldi. In demanding immediate annexation of Nice, the *Società Dante Alighieri*, a notorious proponent of Fascism, would not be silenced either.

---

68. *OO.* XXXI, p. 136.
69. Ibid., pp. 136–37.
70. Borgogni, *Italia e Francia*, pp. 299–300.
71. Egidio Ortona, *Diplomazia di guerra: Diari 1937–1943* (Bologna: Il Mulino, 1993), pp. 228–29.
72. Both passages are cited in Borgogni, *Italia e Francia*, pp. 299–300.
73. Cited in Deakin, *The Brutal Friendship*, p. 307.

Although the Fascists in Rome fully shared this outlook, they were quite aware of the dangers involved in moving from words to action by carrying out an outright takeover. First, it was obvious that since the irredentist groups in Savoy were unnatural artifacts having no resonance among the majority of the French living in the region, there was no local platform to stir up support for Italy. More importantly, Mussolini realized that any abrupt effort to annex French territory would raise Hitler's hackles by disrupting Germany's policy of "collaboration."[74] The Duce's resolve to correct the injustices of the "mutilated victory" had drawn to a mortifying close.

After Mussolini's fall, the Italian need to settle old scores persisted. Even though the Badoglio government had distanced itself from Fascism and the Axis, it declined to abandon Italy's territorial claims on France. Nor did requisitions, pillage, and roundups of suspected maquis cease. Panicacci attributes this spiteful behavior to career upper-class monarchist officers bent on the suppression of the *peuple révolutionnaire*.[75] The armistice that Italy signed with the Allied Powers on 8 September 1943 saw little softening in Rome's ill feeling toward the "Latin Sister." The "Legend of the Mutilated Victory" only breathed its last on 22 June 1944—two weeks after D-Day, the landing of the Allied troops in France— when the Bonomi government finally renounced Fascist Italy's demands on France.

One wonders what lay behind such ill feeling that did not subside after the fall of the Fascist regime. Envy played a role, for many Italians suffered an inferiority complex toward the "Latin Sister," in whose shadow the country had lived ever since the Risorgimento. Fascists acted out their deep resentment by describing a "dissolute and enfeebled" France, whose intellectual snobs should pay homage to the "virile" new regime and satisfy the Italian claims embodied in the battle cry "The Mutilated Victory." But whatever the old historical griev- ances, many military officers continued to harbor pleasant memories of French comrades who fought by their side during the Great War—Badoglio among them. The French culture—language, history, and literature—had long been staples of Italian education and likewise contributed to lightening the Italian hand on France. There is no question that, as a rule, the Italians felt more charitable toward their old rival-ally than they did toward the "backward" and "coarse" Balkan peoples.

---

74. Borgogni, *Italia e Francia*, pp. 180–81.
75. Panicacci, *L'Occupation italienne*, pp. 266–67.

Chapter XI

Balkan *Spazio Vitale* Abandoned

Backed Up on the Yugoslav Coast
Last Days in Greece
Meltdown of Ciano's Albanian Fief

Backed Up on the Yugoslav Coast

In January 1942, the 2nd Army seemed to be on the verge of cutting its losses by withdrawing troops from outlying areas in Croatia. Operations in the nether regions of the country had already cost inordinate amounts of blood and energy on the part of underachieving troops. But the Italians insisted that German soldiers should stay on their side of the demarcation line. At the same time Mussolini informed Zagreb that in the areas abandoned by Italy, Croatian-manned forts should be reduced and the Ustăsa withdrawn.[1] But would the Germans agree to these plans?

The Wehrmacht, however, had different ideas. Instead of retreat, it intended to press on. General Keitel wrote Cavallero on 4 February that he would "burn out" the insurgents in Axis-occupied Yugoslavia. There would be no more talk of agreements with Četniks or partisans, only resolve to consolidate the Croatian

---

1. AUSSME, M-3, b. 59, Conversation between Ambrosio and Mussolini, 28 December 1941.

state. Keitel wrote off the Italian endeavor to seek ties with the Četniks as cowardice. This was not happy news for the Italians. The 2nd Army's hope to leave a permanent footprint in Croatia had already been foiled by Germany's domination of the country's economy. Now they were faced with a joint German-Croatian determination to keep them on their side of the demarcation line. If the Germans were allowed to dictate field strategy, domination of Croatia would be theirs thanks to a docile subaltern in Zagreb.[2]

In a tense atmosphere the Italian generals met their German and Croatian counterparts on 2 March 1942 in Abbazia near Fiume to draw up Operation Trio, intended to subdue the partisans. Against the wishes of the Croats and Germans, Ambrosio pushed through a motion that gave the 2nd Army the right to garrison troops and police territory freed of insurgency "for an indeterminate time." Rome, he supposed, would make sure that this "would become a diplomatic effective reality."[3] Italy's allies could reasonably ask: was Italy's top priority defeat of the partisans or seizure of eastern Bosnia?

The Axis military summit reassembled in Zagreb on 28–29 March to plot an attack against all insurgents in the area between Sarajevo and the Drina. Roatta pushed the date of the attack to April. The "oily" Italian general, as the German Plenipotentiary in Zagreb Edmund Glaise von Horstenau depicted him, informed the Germans that he would cooperate with rather than disown the Četniks as promised in the Abbazia agreement three weeks earlier.[4] First take on the Communists, then the Četniks, Roatta reasoned—not both at the same time. The Croats were the fly in the ointment. Of all involved in Yugoslavia, Roatta abided them the least, a feeling fully reciprocated by the Ustaša authorities in Zagreb. On how to conduct the campaign Roatta pulled no punches: all men caught with weapons would be immediately shot and all suspects interned. In tiptoeing around orders from Rome by keeping in touch with the Četnik "enemy," Roatta spun out delays over the launching of Operation Trio that allowed the partisans time to prepare for the Axis offensive.

In the end there would be no real Italian contribution to the first stage of Trio. Before the Italians had manned their battle stations, the commander of the German troops in Serbia, General Paul Bader, annoyed by their dawdling, informed Roatta on 18 April that he had to move quickly to relieve the Croatian garrison under heavy siege in Rogatica.[5] The Wehrmacht surged forward against

2. PP, *Diario*, 4 March 1942.
3. Hehn, *The Struggle Against Yugoslav Guerrillas*, p. 110.
4. Peter Broucek, *General in Zwielicht: Die Lebenserinnerungen Edmund Glaises von Horstenau*, 3 vols. (Vienna: Boehlhaus, 1980, 1983, 1988), II: 142, 434.
5. Oddone Talpo, *Dalmazia: Una cronaca per la storia (1942)* (Rome: SME US, 2000), D. 19, De Blasio to Pietromarchi, 25 April 1942.

the partisans, accompanied by bedraggled units of Croatian troops and undisciplined Ustaša. On 20 April Bader informed his superiors: "Joint German-Italian operation miscarried due to absence of Italians."[6]

So as not to be shut out, the Italians accelerated their movements. The *Taurinense* Division reached Sarajevo near the end of April but was kept on the outskirts of the city by German command. Rogatica was taken without a fight on the 27th, and the combined Axis armies reached the right bank of the Drina River on the 30th, which wound up Trio I. Instead of synchronizing the attacking forces to encircle the partisans, General Bader changed his battle plan in mid-stream to minimize the Italian presence in eastern Bosnia, which allowed the partisans to escape the pincers movement.[7] The Italians blamed the Germans for pursuing political goals at their expense. Mistrust was growing on both sides.

Trio II, launched on 7 May, targeted partisan strongholds at Foča and Kalinovik. Despite the many fissures and mutual recriminations, the Axis armies wound up the last stage of the campaign by taking possession of Foča on 10 May. The Germans and Croats cleared the partisans from eastern Bosnia to the demarcation line, and the Italians, with the help of their Četnik allies, swept the partisans out of Herzegovina, which was not included in Trio. Important roads bearing German supplies to the Wehrmacht in North Africa had been secured against partisan incursions.[8] Still, many partisan units managed to escape to the Sandžak and across the Drina into Montenegro; others blended back into the civil population. During these campaigns much of Eastern Bosnia and Herzegovina were completely devastated. Many villages that had favored the rebels were burnt to the ground and those suspected of favoring the partisans were interned or shot notwithstanding sporadic efforts by Italian troops to lend a helping hand to the haggard population.[9]

Just as the Italian offensive had finally swung into high gear, General Ambrosio concluded during the latter part of April that the 2nd Army, short on manpower and equipment, had better trim its forces in the nether reaches of Croatia and withdraw to the "natural frontier" of Dalmatia along the crest of the Dinaric mountain range, as conceived by Mussolini on 28 December 1941.[10] Roatta accordingly withdrew from most of the 3rd zone by the middle of May,

6. Hehn, *The Struggle Against Yugoslav Guerrillas*, p. 127.

7. NAW, T-821, 398, 000604, Roatta's 4C Circular 1 April 1942.

8. Giacomo Scotti and Luciano Viazzi, *L'inutile vittoria: La tragica esperienza delle truppe italiane in Montenegro* (Milan: Mursia, 1989), p. 331, however, believe that the peremptory German order to break off Operation Trio in mid-May was premature and allowed the partisans to get away.

9. Eric Gobetti, *L'occupazione allegra: Gli italiani in Jugoslavia (1941–1943)* (Rome: Carocci, 2007), p. 178.

10. Talpo, *Dalmazia: Una cronaca per la storia (1942)*, p. 82.

leaving only Karlovac and areas in the 2nd zone heavily defended.[11] The Germans were alarmed over the sudden vacuum created which they had not been forewarned of and which they knew the partisans would be able to exploit, while the Croats were elated over re-establishing a presence south of the demarcation line.

In recognition that the Italian forces were overstretched, Roatta signed a landmark accord with Pavelić on 19 June in which Italy promised to withdraw its garrisons from the 3rd zone and yield civilian and police power to the NDH in the 2nd. This represented the kiss of death to an Italian protectorate over Croatia. While Zagreb celebrated a restoration of its sovereignty in these outlying areas, Roatta expected the Ustaša to undertake "a second edition" of the previous summer's persecutions against Serbs and Jews.[12] More than ever he regarded the NDH as a cancer on the Croatian body politic and the Ustaša as a band of half-witted racists estranged from the rest of the population.[13]

In placing his bets on the NDH "ally," Mussolini was fully au courant of the terrible Ustaša-run Holocaust machinery working overtime in Croatia and the unpopularity of the Pavelić regime among the Croatian people. Still, Rome implored Roatta to "create harmony" with "Ustaša formations" to win over Croatian public opinion,[14] ignoring the obvious reality that Pavelić had already sold himself out to the Germans.

Neither Axis partner was able to devise a viable solution regarding the Croatian government. Both were pulled down by its unpopularity, corruption, and violence. Major responsibility for reform as spelled out by existing treaties lay with Italy. But as Italian power waned, the responsibility fell to the Germans, who agreed with the Italians that without a thorough overhaul of the Croatian state and a clean sweep of the Ustaša, victory over the partisans would be a pipe dream.

Hitler, however, would not listen to his top military advisers in Yugoslavia, let alone the Italian 2nd Army. Unmoved by Ustaša atrocities, he joined Mussolini as Pavelić's guardian angel. By declaring Croatian "sovereignty" untouchable, the Führer ignored every criticism over the Poglavnik's (Pavelić's title: leader) monopoly on power. Since there was also the Duce's ego to stroke, Hitler would not modify the official German pose that Croatia was Italy's business. This was

---

11. General Dalmazzo, for one, was quite critical over the Italian withdrawal from both the 1st and 2nd zones for opening up these areas to the nefarious influence of both the Ustaša and the partisans. Talpo, *Dalmazia: La cronaca per la storia (1942)*, D. 9, Dalmazzo to 2nd Army, 9 June 1942, pp. 515–17.
12. NAW, T-821, 410, 000420-26, Roatta memorandum, 10 May 1942.
13. Talpo, *Dalmazia: Una cronaca per la storia (1942)*, pp. 524–32. General Dalmazzo was no less critical of the NDH. AUSSME, M-3, b. 89, Dalmazzo to the 2nd Army, 24 May 1942.
14. PP, *Diaro*, 12 July 1942.

ridiculous. The Germans had done nothing to lift the demarcation line, originally devised as a temporary measure to keep the Axis armies separated, which prevented Italy from taking over Croatian eastern Bosnia, a situation bitterly resented by the 2nd Army. In fact, German economic predators accompanied by Wehrmacht-trained Croatian troops were already swarming into Italian-occupied western Bosnia and Herzegovina. But Hitler's empty promise to respect Croatia as Italy's sphere sufficed for the Duce and his foreign office.

To protect the mainland from a possible Allied invasion, the CS in early 1943 was poised to call home major units from Yugoslavia while leaving the rest to hold the coastal belt on the Adriatic. Evacuation of the Balkans seemed imminent. But the Italians were loath to sacrifice their *spazio vitale*. And they were aghast at the thought of the Germans taking advantage of their country's declining war fortunes by moving into territory abandoned by the 2nd Army. Hence they allowed themselves to be drawn into the German plan to clear out Yugoslav insurgency. The Italians therefore had fallen between two stools: neither did they cease to participate in the German-masterminded sweeps, nor did they proceed to clear out of the outlying regions. Their reluctance to hand over Italian-occupied territory to German and Croat "allies" slowed the evacuation of the interior to a snail's pace.

More than the Italians, the Germans had a great deal at stake in the Balkans: transportation systems, communication networks, and vital mineral deposits essential to the war effort, which required that transportation routes cutting through the Yugoslav interior be secured against partisan attacks. An even worse danger loomed: an Allied landing in the lower Adriatic that would enable Mihailović to emerge as head of a nationwide uprising in the rear. To facilitate the task of suppressing the partisans, the Germans aimed at gaining control of the NDH forces and subordinating the Italian 2nd Army to their command. In anticipating an Allied invasion, they devised Operation Weiss in December 1942, hoping to inflict a mortal blow on both Communist and Četnik partisans. This brought home to the Italians the danger of their relationship with Četniks. In crushing insurgency, the Germans hoped to achieve a secondary aim: the stabilization of the tottering Croatian state. But if Tito's forces had by this time superseded their bitter rival as the most formidable foe, Hitler, fixated on Mihailović, seemed the last to know. An unspoken German purpose was to wrest Croatia from Italian hands. From Berlin's perspective the 2nd Army was a prickly partner, ineffective, and impudently anti-German. With Italy's military fortunes now in a free fall, Berlin viewed the behavior of the 2nd Army, particularly its continued utilization of the Četniks, as treacherous.

The Italian generals were determined that not one German foot should step into Herzegovina, and that no Italian troops should be employed for garrison duty in areas "pacified" by the Germans. Having set these conditions, Cavallero authorized the inclusion of General Alessandro Pirzio Biroli's "volunteers" from Montenegro for operations in Croatia,[15] and Roatta released the *Lombardia, Re,* and *Sassari* divisions, as well as about 6,000 Četnik auxiliaries from the Lika region and northern Dalmatia for the upcoming campaign against the insurgents.[16] To fend off the Germans, Roatta reiterated his divide-and-rule stratagem: instead of taking on Četniks and partisans at the same time, pit them against each other and dispose of the survivors.[17] History was repeating itself. The same differences between Italian and German purposes and policies that vitiated the planning for Operation Trio would now cripple Operation Weiss. And worse was to come.

General Roatta was removed from his command and replaced on 1 February by General Robotti, of Slovenian fame, at about the same time that Ambrosio replaced Cavallero as chief of the general staff. Without the German "Quisling" at the CS, the Italian military team in Yugoslavia could afford to be less accommodating to its Axis partner, which reduced the friction between Rome and Sušak. The Italians were at one in questioning the German strategy to pursue Balkan guerrillas relentlessly across the breadth of Italy's "zones of occupation."

Notwithstanding the Italian determination to avoid costly engagements with either Tito or Mihailović, military operations took a nasty turn in mid-February when the partisans captured the town of Prozor in the Neretva River valley, destroyed a small Četnik contingent there, and shattered elements of the widely dispersed *Murge* Division holed up in isolated forts.[18] The battle was vicious with atrocities committed by both sides. The Italians lost 2,300 men.[19] A large cache of supplies fell into the hands of the attacking partisans, who were now poised for an assault on Mihailović's bastion in Herzegovina.[20]

Weiss I ended inconclusively on 15 February, leaving the fate of the noncombatant population up in the air and the Četnik problem unresolved. The Germans prepared to launch Weiss II against the partisans on the 20th at the same time as the joyless Italian experience at Prozor.[21] To prevent the partisans from crossing the Neretva, the Wehrmacht assigned Italy the task of blocking

15. Srdja Trifkovic, *Ustaša: Croatian Separatism and European Politics, 1929–1945* (London: The Lord Byron Foundation for Balkan Studies, 1998), p. 186.
16. Loi, *Le operazioni*, p. 212; *The Ciano Diaries*, 6 January 1943.
17. PP, *Diario*, 6 January 1943.
18. Francesco Fatutta, *La campagna di Iugoslava, aprile 1941-settembre 1943* (Campobasso, 1996), p. 127.
19. AUSSME, N I-II, b. 1222, Robotti to Piazzoni, 5 March 1942.
20. Matteo J. Milazzo, *The Chetnik Movement & the Yugoslav Resistance* (Baltimore and London: The Johns Hopkins University Press, 1975), p. 122.
21. NAW, T-501, 264, 000518-29, Glaise to Shuchardt, 26 May 1943.

them from the south. General Robotti was not happy with this directive, for the Germans seemed determined to press on without taking into consideration the dispersion of his forces. And the situation in Herzegovina had dissolved into utter confusion. The Četnik leaders could not decide whether to resist or comply with Italian orders; Mihailović's attempt to mold a semblance of unity among his warlords conflicted with Italian efforts to bring them under the 2nd Army's control; and the Germans divided their attention between Četniks and partisans around Mostar, which created differing objectives between the Axis partners.

By the end of February, fed up with Italian dillydallying, the Germans decided to proceed with Weiss II on their own. As the Četniks in Herzegovina shifted their attention from the partisans to the imminent German threat, Tito's legions in early March marshaled their forces for a breakthrough across the Neretva to Herzegovina in the direction of Montenegro. The odds were long, but fortune smiled on them when a large portion of the 2,000–5,000 Četniks in their way unexpectedly broke and ran during the early weeks of March. In a "biblical exodus" during this final stage of Weiss II, the partisans escaped the Axis pincers movement.[22]

Although Weiss II inflicted a heavy defeat on the partisans, the Germans were unhappy that they had not been able to deliver a knockout blow. The Italians had even less reason to celebrate. When the smoke cleared from the Battle of the Neretva, the partisans had gained a decisive advantage over the Italian ally, the Četniks, in Yugoslavia. Meanwhile Italian troops were dispersed raggedly all over the map, which ruined their plan to withdraw from the nether regions of the country. Exhausted by the Wehrmacht's constantly shifting battle plans, the troops also had been dangerously weakened by orders from Rome to send weapons and units back across the Adriatic for homeland defense. Rather than having Četniks move into Italian-abandoned fortresses in the Lika area, partisans competed with Croats in taking them over. In spite of their brush with outright destruction, the partisans quickly reassembled, replenished by a brief respite in the fighting and the acquisition of captured heavy weapons. Partisan morale soared while the Italian troops only wanted to go home. The future of Italian Dalmatia trembled in the balance.

To clean out the remaining nests of insurgency, the Germans activated Operation Schwarz, which was launched on 17 May in Montenegro and the Sandžak. This time the German juggernaut would proceed unhampered by Italian vacillation and backstairs deals with the insurgent Četniks.

---

22. Vladimir Dedjer, *Tito* (New York: Simon & Schuster, 1953), pp. 191–94.

The Italian 2nd Army commander, Robotti, met General Alexander Löhr, commander of German Army Group Southeast, on 5 May to discuss the disposition of the 200,000-odd German, Italian, Bulgarian, and Croatian troops armed with heavy artillery, tanks, airborne forces, and planes preparing to launch Operation Schwarz against approximately 19,000 partisans. The Germans spelled out their purpose of protecting the bauxite mines in Herzegovina and the lead and chromium ore lodes in the southern parts of Serbia, Kosovo, and Macedonia. They refrained from informing the Italians of their intention to destroy the Montenegrin Četniks and capture Mihailović, and then finish off the partisans.[23] This concealment was by order of the Führer, who, under the impression that the partisan forces had been broken, considered Mihailović his chief remaining enemy in the area.[24] Whatever motive Hitler had to protect the persona of the Duce was overridden by what he deemed a paramount strategic necessity. Reliance was placed on the Ustaša, Muslim SS units, and German trained anti-guerrilla mountain forces to get rid of insurgents of all stripes.

Although the Italians suffered 2,106 soldiers dead, wounded, or missing, they hailed Operation Schwarz a success.[25] The Germans knew otherwise, for both Tito and Mihailović were still at large. The partisans lost more heavily, perhaps thirty-five percent of their troops.[26] In Montenegro, still under Italian occupation until the fatal days of September, both Axis partners behaved brutally toward captured prisoners and the inhabitants. One Italian soldier noted that there was destruction everywhere. "This war is continually degenerating to ever lower depths and we can no longer see it as a war between civilized peoples."[27]

During the first half of 1943, whatever spirit existed among the Italian troops had been drained during long and exhausting battles. Still, Italy's generals persisted. Mussolini's fall did not occasion much soul-searching, for the 2nd Army pursued counterinsurgency as if by rote. The dazed Italian troops fought half-heartedly, wanting to abandon the desolate Balkan front lines for home. But they followed orders and stayed in the lines with few defections before the Armistice. Throughout the occupation period the 2nd Army doggedly carried out its military assignments in an ethnic morass of religious clashes and ideological divisions.

23. Oddone Talpo, *Dalmazia: Una cronaca per la storia (1943–1944)* (Rome: SME US, 1994), D. 1, Robotti to SME, 8 May 1943, pp. 661–62.
24. Trifkovic, *Ustaša*, p. 190.
25. Loi, *Le operazioni*, p. 254.
26. Joso Tomasevich, *War and Revolution in Yugoslavia, 1941–1945: The Chetniks* (Stanford CA: Stanford University Press, 1975), p. 254.
27. Cited in Verna, "Yugoslavia Under Italian Rule," p. 263.

Last Days in Greece

In Greece Italian counterinsurgency experienced marked setbacks in late 1942. Encouraged by the turn of the tide of war in favor of the Allies, the insurgents spread into the Pindus Mountains to sabotage railroads, disrupt the arteries of Axis communications, and undertake hit-and-run tactics against outlying posts. The cumbersome Italian military machine answered by rambling forward to do its job of repression, employing no less than five infantry battalions. Following the ambush of an Italian convoy by a local band of partisans on 16 February 1943, General Cesare Benelli, commander of the *Pinerolo* Division, ordered the destruction of the town of Domenikon, a small rural center in Thessaly, and the massacre of all men of the village, aged fifteen to eighty.[28] The following month General Geloso, the commander of the 11th Army, called on his men to undertake systematic aerial bombardment, artillery barrages, and deportation to concentration camps of village chiefs.[29]

In his spyglass search for "rebels," Geloso spelled out instructions on 3 April 1943 that seemed to be taken out of Roatta's 3C handbook: uproot village communities suspected of disloyalty to the occupier, bomb and burn property, plunder food reserves, destroy farm implements, and round up hostages.[30] Remember, reminded Geloso, "that hunger is the rebels' worst enemy and therefore it is necessary to deprive them of every source of sustenance"—a particularly cold-hearted order given the famine-struck Greek population. In what amounted to collective punishment, the Italian raiders set up concentration camps housing thousands of people who suffered from cold, malnutrition, and malaria.[31] In the same month Geloso wrote that the enemy had exceeded the infamy of savages. Against such "wild beasts," the troops must carry out the most pitiless vengeance and brutal reprisals.[32]

During the course of this prolonged punitive expedition, the soldiers did what they were told. Greek peasants and mine workers fled from their homes for refuge in the mountains.[33] Units of the 11th Army succeeded in destroying many partisan hideouts and broke up "bandit" clusters, but the overall results were disappointing, for the partisans, aided by Allied airdrops, quickly regrouped for further assaults on the Italian army. So much for Geloso's frenetic attempts to

---

28. Lidia Santarelli, "Muted Violence: Italian War Crimes in Occupied Greece," *Journal of Modern History*, vol. 9, no. 3 (Fall: 2004), p. 293.

29. Ibid.

30. AUSSME, L-13 (96), Geloso memorandum, "Lotta contro i banditi," 3 February 1943.

31. Rodogno, *Fascism's European Empire*, pp. 358–60.

32. Rodogno, "Les conquérants de l'espace vital fasciste (1940–1943)," *Relations Internationales*, no. 110 (Spring 2002), pp. 165–66; AUSSME, N I-II, DS, b.1237, XI Army memorandum, 7 April 1943.

33. Etmektoglou-Koehn, "Axis Exploitation of Wartime Greece, 1941–1943," p. 243.

smother resistance in the hinterlands before a suspected imminent Allied landing at Salonica.

During Geloso's last days in Greece, he presided over a country rising up as one against the occupying Italians. Sensing disarray in Italian ranks, the partisans in latter March overwhelmed Carabinieri camps and isolated Guardia di Finanza posts, while stepping up sabotage of train service and communication lines.[34]

The 11th Army was unraveling. Of the 93,000 Italian troops on mainland Greece, 12,000 had malaria. Another 70,000 demoralized soldiers manned the islands. There were "20,000 rebels in Thessaly" and "the *Pinerolo* was very tired." "All my troops," Geloso wrote Ambrosio, "have antiquated arms and lack almost any anti-tank or anti-air guns, or armored transport." With no coastal artillery or bombers, they were utterly unprepared for an expected Allied landing. Britain, he believed, eyed Salonica for two purposes: to block a Russian drive into the Balkan Peninsula and thence to the Mediterranean, and to utilize Greece as a launching pad for an invasion of Italy.[35]

Geloso's forces in tatters, he was in sore need of German reinforcements. But the Wehrmacht in March 1943, still having only a small number of occupation troops in Greece, had few to spare. That did not stop the Germans in Italian-occupied territory from flouting the Carabinieri, controlling railroad rolling stock, monopolizing Greek shipping, dominating strategic rail lines and communication centers, flying in Italian air space, and bleeding the Greek economy white.[36] Geloso warned that an influx of German reinforcements would cause overall control to pass out of Italian hands.[37]

Like Italian generals elsewhere, the last thing Geloso wanted was to fall under the sway of domineering Germans. Along with his colleagues, however, he knew survival was not possible without them. Still, there were limits. When the OKW and General Löhr strove to place his troops under Wehrmacht command, Geloso refused to be moved from "coordination" to subordination. Hence, in the absence of a common command structure, Geloso and Löhr resorted to ad hoc meetings.

Geloso clarified his position to Ambrosio in mid-March 1943. "In our war," he should be the supreme commander over a unified Balkan force of Italian troops assembled together from Montenegro, Albania, and Greece. Turning the tables on General Löhr, he proposed placing Wehrmacht troops under his command as well! This would require a speedy movement of Italian units from

34. USSME, DS, IV, D. 114, Promemoria for the Duce-Report on Greece, 16 April 1943.
35. AUSSME, L15, DS, R/28, f. 10, Geloso promemoria, 21 March 1943.
36. Ibid., L13, b. 108, Geloso reports of 27 and 28 October 1942, 2 March 1943.
37. Ibid., N I-II, b. 1393 A, Geloso report, 2 July 1943.

their scattered outposts and remote regions in the Balkans to key points in Greece. Ambrosio countered by pointing out that the Allies just as easily might land in Albania, which precluded any withdrawal of Italian troops from those remote redoubts.

Complicating the matter was the appointment of a new lieutenant-general in Albania, Alberto Pariani, who had political clout in Rome. Geloso remarked: "The nomination of Pariani as Governor is a hindrance." Ambrosio agreed: "Pariani is like Pirzio Biroli." The military was forever struggling to get "political" appointees out of their hair. Whereas Geloso and Ambrosio aimed to safeguard the lower Balkans from a possible Allied invasion, the governors were bent on safeguarding their provinces from insurgency by moving around Italian troops at their discretion. Just as the "politicians" had slowed down Roatta's withdrawal of troops from remote areas in Croatia, so would these two governors hinder Geloso's effort to take generals Dalmazzo and Mentasti from under their thumbs for his command. Ambrosio, too, would like to have placed the governors totally under the military, but felt that he could not press the point in Rome. Insurmountable logistics stared the two generals in the face as well. Already burdened with the huge problem of provisioning troops in Tunisia, Ambrosio realized that he lacked the wherewithal to transport large numbers of troops from outlying Balkan areas into Greece.

In the far reaches of the Balkans, the sole enemy of the Italians were partisans, who posed no threat to the Italian mainland as long as the Axis held the Adriatic coastline and Greece, "the natural landing wharf of the enemy's access to the Balkan peninsula." In the losing endeavor of stamping out partisans in remote mountainous regions, the CS had spread Italian troops thinly and had created an excessive number of autonomous regional outposts. Concerned with their own security against partisan raids, the local political/military leaders ignored the larger strategic picture. Having seen no progress in the implementation of his "radical" reform—a Balkan unified command under his generalship—Geloso was left with this pessimistic prophecy: an enemy landing in Greece "could not be resisted."[38]

General Vecchiarelli, who replaced General Geloso as commander of the Italian forces in Greece on 3 May 1943, detailed a restricted mission that required a general pullback of occupation troops from the partisan-dominated areas in Thessaly. Primary emphasis was placed on the organization of coastal

---

38. On the meetings in Rome, see NAW, T-821, 125, 000825–38, Meeting between Ambrosio and Geloso, 13 March 1943; 000839-42, Meeting between Ambrosio and Geloso, 14 March 1943.; AUSSME, DS, b.1054, allegao 6, 19 Oct 1942 and B1442, 22 Nov 1942; L 15, R/28, f. 10, Geloso report, 21 March 1943; ACS, Segretaria Particolare del Duce, b.174 (1942-43).

defenses against a possible Allied landing, surveillance of attacks on major lines of communication, and heightened security of the main Italian fortresses.

In pondering a more moderate approach, Vecchiarelli attempted to cut back on harsh counterinsurgency in favor of conciliation. Consistent with this new strategy, he replaced the notorious General Benelli of the *Pinerolo* Division with the milder General Adolfo Infante. Vecchiarelli fulfilled previous promises of clemency, slowed down the pace of *rastrellamenti*, listened sympathetically to Greek charges of Italian abuses and illegalities, and exercised tighter control over arbitrary violence. Slowly he emptied the concentration camps of "less compromised" internees in a belated effort to disassociate the innocent population from the insurgency.[39] But it must be said that Vecchiarelli emphasized persuasion and goodwill because his army was run-down and because the Germans were perfectly willing to take on the burden of counterinsurgency in abandoned Italian-occupied territory. His moderation came in for harsh criticism at the Palazzo Chigi. Vecchiarelli lacked "vigor," held Pietromarchi; "It was a grave error to remove Geloso from his command post at this most critical moment."[40]

There is some question as to whether Vecchiarelli actually downgraded terror in the last months of Italian occupation. Recent evidence drawn from the Italian foreign ministry and United Nations Commission on War Crimes indicates that actually there was hardly any slowdown in search-and-destroy missions and the inevitable toll they took in civilian casualties. In retaliation for a partisan success in blowing up a tunnel of Kournovo, which killed 600 Italian soldiers on a troop train, the Italian command on 5 June massacred 106 hostages.[41] In a desperate effort to suppress an increasingly well-organized and equipped partisan force, Vecchiarelli in June ordered air bombardments that randomly damaged villages and carried out reprisal executions of prisoners and innocent people.[42] And, on 17 August, three weeks after Mussolini's fall from power, the not so "mild" General Infante of the *Pinerolo* masterminded the destruction of a town

---

39. As Filippo Cappellano, who has researched this period in the Italian occupation, admits, his description of Vechiarelli's tenure as commander of the 11th Army is based on evidence in the Italian military archives in spring and summer 1943 that is very sketchy. His account includes extracts from Vecchiarelli's report dated June 1947: "Comportamento delle forze italiane d'occupazione in Grecia, Estate 1943." Filippo Cappellano, "L'occupazione italiana della Grecia (1941–43)," *Nuova storia contemporanea*, no. 4 (2008), p. 38 and f. 71, p.39 and f. 72.

40. PP, *Diario*, 9 June 1943.

41. Elena Aga Rossi and Maria Teresa Giusti, *Una guerra a parte: I militari italiani nei Baclani 1940–1945* (Milan: Il Mulino, 2011), p. 82.

42. Davide Conti, *L'occupazione italiana dei balcani: Crimini di guerra e mito della "brava gente!" (1940–1942)* (Rome: Odradek, 2008), pp. 178–79; Lidia Santarelli, "Muted Violence," pp. 288–99; Brunello Mantelli, "Gli italiani nei Balcani 1941–1943: occupazione militare, politiche persecutore e crimini di guerra," in *Qualestoria*, n. 1 (June 2002): pp. 23–24.

and the execution of about fifty men as reprisal against the partisans.[43] Moreover, there was no letup in the dispatch of Greeks to internment camps and prisons where they received dreadful treatment.[44] On the other hand, the Italian foreign ministry at the end of August instructed General Vecchiarelli to refrain from handing over prisoners and hostages to the Germans. In a belated effort to clean up the Italian record, Pietromarchi ordered that the use of reprisals against hostages be at once abandoned.[45]

The Germans were quite dissatisfied. They could not abide Italian-style counterinsurgency because it was undisciplined, blasé, and lacking "German thoroughness."[46] There were no large-scale reprisals and no ruthlessness in breaking strikes. German diplomats and generals implored the Italians to toughen up against the "bandits," but concluded that their allies were incorrigibly indolent. In March German plenipotentiary Günther Altenburg reported that the Italians hardly lifted a finger in preventing resistance fighters from assuming control of whole areas in Thessaly. In May the Reich's expert on economic matters, Hermann Neubacher, suggested that a few good Germans could replace the entire ramshackle Italian army. For the OKW, the presence of Italian troops in Greece was a burden rather than a support.[47] The more the Germans feared an Allied landing in the lower Balkans, the more they harped on Italy's questionable fighting value and allegiance.

Corruption permeated Italian military ranks in Greece, which undoubtedly cut into military efficiency. Praised in several quarters for having a high intelligence, the "little and ugly" General Geloso took a relaxed view of the moral standards expected of an army of occupation. Along with Ghigi, the Italian minister in Athens and other top-ranking military, he was recalled to Rome in May 1943 and subjected to a commission of inquiry headed by Admiral Cavagnari for black-marketing in the acquisition of Greek rugs and silver. Pietromarchi recounts a story going the rounds that a plane carrying trunks of Geloso's stolen goods from Greece crash-landed with the loss of all his contraband. Added to this were embarrassing charges of orgies in luxurious villas and rendezvous with local women, many of whom were allegedly enemy spies gathering valuable information in their private boudoirs. The Italian general consul in Salonica, Guelfo Zamboni, who did so much in saving Jews, was alleged to have sent home trunk after trunk containing a total of 900 bottles of champagne and

---

43. Santarelli, "Muted Violence," p. 294.
44. Rodogno, *Fascism's European Empire*, pp. 358–61.
45. Aga Rossi and Giusti, *Una guerra a parte*, p. 85.
46. Etmektsoglou-Koehn, *Axis Exploitation of Wartime Greece, 1941–1943*, p. 244.
47. Mazower, *Inside Hitler's Greece*, p. 147.

300 of whisky. Ghigi got off thanks to Bastianini's intervention with Mussolini.[48] Geloso, however, was not so lucky.

A Fascist carnival ensued. The charges brought against Geloso, observed Pietromarchi, could easily have been covered up rather than exposed for public curiosity, which made the 11th Army look like *L'armata dell'amo* ("the army of love").[49] The Commission of Inquiry, he complained, was a leftover relic utilized by liberal governments that, unable for political reasons to remove esteemed authoritarian leaders from public power, would trump up base charges to bring them down. No totalitarian regime, he moralized, should allow people to draw the conclusion that the government was incapable of weeding out corruption. When the country faced grave danger, the army, Pietromarchi believed, was obliged to act with unquestioned integrity. And there should be no sensational scandals to shred the army's morale and the respect of soldiers for their officers. Drop the case against Geloso, Pietromarchi implored. Bastianini agreed, but told him that Mussolini, who was "furious" over the military's "lax" behavior, was unyielding. The inquiry would go forward.[50] Geloso's reaction: "I have never thought that an officer in wartime ought to be expected to be chaste and pure, the more so as I am firmly convinced that those who are such can neither fight nor command."[51] After the fall of Fascism, Geloso was recalled to active duty without having to submit to discipline of any sort.

In the litany of criticisms of the Italian troops, *L'armata ti amo* is joined by the more ambiguous term *l'armata s'agapò*. The latter bears the disagreeable connotation of an army of ragamuffins much more dedicated to chasing down women rather than pursuing insurgents. In February 1953 screenwriter Renzo Renzi, an ex-officer veteran of the Greek campaign, wrote an article in the journal *Cinema Nuovo* of a film to be produced on the occupation of Greece entitled *L'armata s'agapò*, in which he described his experiences there, including the personal testimony of Italian soldiers killing hostages, looting recklessly, and taking advantage of Greek women reduced by hunger to selling themselves for a loaf of bread. This produced a furor in Italy. Seven months later Renzi and the director of the journal, Guido Aristarco, himself an ex-NCO, were arrested and put on trial by a military tribunal for having defamed the reputation of the armed forces. Convicted, Renzi was sentenced to seven months in military prison, Aristarco to six.

---

48. PP, *Diario*, 11 May 1943.
49. Ibid.
50. This story is drawn from Pietromarchi's *Diario*, 11, 12, and 13 March 1943.
51. AUSSME, N I-II, b. 1393A, Geloso, "Due Anni in Grecia," p. 42.

Moral laxity in the ranks, as the Italians themselves admitted, was as vexing as the breakdown in military discipline. Instead of setting a warrior's example, officers had lost respect of their troops by settling into an easy and lavish life-style financed by forays into the black market.[52] How much these habits engendered corruption in the Italian ranks is not easy to measure, but the slackness that existed perhaps resulted in some perhaps avoidable disasters, for example, when Italian guards allowed a team of Greek partisans to blow up the Gorgopatomos Bridge on the night of 25–26 November 1942.[53] Geloso himself was full of complaints about his soldiers' lackadaisical behavior, reporting, for instance, that an infantry regiment in the middle of Athens walked all over the road in disorder.[54] Such behavior was corroborated by many British sources.[55] There is enough evidence to suggest that, in spite of the frightful damage Italian soldiers wrought, many had mentally drifted out of the war and were not involved in carrying out Geloso's more inhumane orders.

As in Yugoslavia, the Italian soldiers in Greece, sensing defeat by late 1942, struck back blindly against both real and imagined enemies. Having gone without leave for months on end and sometimes well over two years, and lacking supplies and clothing from the motherland, they resorted to thievery to ward off privation. Endless tours of unremitting warfare in deplorable conditions for no clearly visible purpose turned them into disillusioned losers. As opposed to the exultant Fascist refrain "Long live death," the typical soldier's attitude had become "I don't give a damn."

As opposed to Yugoslavia and Albania, Italian Fascists made only sporadic efforts to impose their unique institutions on the Greeks or to rob them of their traditions and civilization. This was not due to self-restraint but to lack of resources and an inability to remove the omnipresent Germans. Although Hitler had frequently referred to Greece as lying in the Italian sphere, he refused, upon the Wehrmacht's arrival in the country, to yield his ally any significant power in formulating occupation policy. Therefore no Fascist governor was appointed to initiate the process of Italianization. Authority *in loco* remained in the hands of the Italian military, which had no interest in acquainting Greeks with Fascist institutions. As elsewhere, their single-minded purpose was to institute a "Roman" peace by crushing dissent and insurgency without mercy.

There is, however, another side to the story in Greece: Italian defense of its Jewish population. On the Italian side of the demarcation line, Jews, 3,500 of

---

52 USSME, DS, IV, D. 37, General Magli to the Superior Command in Greece, 9 December 1942.

53. Steinberg, *All or Nothing*, p. 104.

54.. AUSSME, N I-II, DS, b. 634, Geloso to his commanders, 7 February 1942; b. 736, Allegato, 4, 23 March 1942; b. 840, Allegato 6, 12 June 1942.

55. Mazower cites such evidence in his *Inside Hitler's Greece*, p. 145.

whom resided in Athens, went about their business unharmed. By 1943 their numbers had swollen to 8,000, consisting mainly of Jewish refugees fleeing the Bulgarian and German zones for safety in the Greek capital. Smaller Jewish communities were scattered about in areas of Italian occupation. The grand total of Jews living in the Italian zone was 12,500.[56]

The Germans, bent on persecuting Jews everywhere, were greatly irked that the Italian occupation had brought about no substantive change in the Jews' legal status of full equality in civil rights.[57] Worse still, in their view, the Italian plenipotentiary in Athens, Pellegrino Ghigi, was on the lookout for any action taken by Germans in their zone aimed at depriving Jews of Italian citizenship. Indeed, the arrest and internment of Greek Jews, Ghigi felt, was politically counterproductive.[58] Since the Jewish communities were peaceable and easily controlled, he could see no reason why time and energy should be wasted in rounding them up.[59] This argument was the standard one applied by Italians throughout the Mediterranean area.

In areas comprising the Italian empire, Jews constituted an important imperial and economic outpost in the Mediterranean. Hence Rome would not listen to German insistence that they be handed over for deportation. What was Berlin to do with the wayward Italians, whose commander, General Geloso, had a Jewish girlfriend connected with anglophile circles and gave parties in luxurious villas?[60] Under German eyes, the Italian consul in Salonica, Guelfo Zamboni, who was an ardent Fascist and admirer of German Nazism, helped to place 350 Jews of Italian citizenship in July 1942 on a train to Athens and safety.[61] Every Jew who had the remotest kinship to an Italian subject was declared eligible for a certificate of nationality. Such a relaxed attitude on an issue so basic to the Nazi creed compelled the Germans to ramp up the pressure. Maddened by the sight of Jews unmarked by the Star of David and untouched by segregation laws, the Germans, stymied by Italian recalcitrance, demanded that they be repatriated to Italy.[62]

It was not until March 1943 that the Germans got down to business in implementing the Holocaust in Greece. When they swept into Salonica to collect the 60,000 Jews living there, Zamboni, on instructions from Rome, intervened to

---

56. Daniel Carpi, "Notes on the History of the Jews in Greece During the Holocaust Period. The Attitude of the Italians (1941–1943)," in *The Conduct of the Air War in the Second World War*, ed. Horst Boog (New York/Oxford, Oxford University Press, 1992).

57. Ibid., p. 31.

58. DDI, 9, X, 3, Ghigi to Mussolini, 8 February 1943.

59. Rodogno, *Fascism's European Empire*, p. 390; Carpi, "Nuovi documenti," p. 190, d. 16.

60. Steinberg, *All or Nothing*, p. 102.

61. Ibid., p. 100.

62. Ibid., p. 98.

secure the release of Italian Jewish citizens earmarked for Auschwitz. In early April Bastianini ordered that Italian nationality should be granted even in dubious cases, and that deportation of Italian Jews should be prevented by relocating them to the Italian-occupied zone. In spite of these brave efforts, however, only "some hundreds of persons" were transported to the Italian zone. Over Italian protests and obstructions, the Germans rounded up 48,974 Jews for shipment to Auschwitz.[63]

Doubtless, hard economic reality, pride, and resentment of German interference told much in determining Italian behavior toward Jews, as did their growing awareness of an imminent end to the war. In a reckoning with the victorious allies, the Italians decidedly did not want to be associated with Holocaust horrors.[64] But political expediency was not the only motive. In giving Jews shelter, Pietromarchi, Bastianini, Ghigi, Zamboni, and their collaborators showed real bravery by exposing themselves to Nazi wrath. If General Löhr could "tremble from head to foot" in a Nazi environment, so could they,[65] but they did not.

In closing the chapter of the 11th Army's harsh occupation of Greece, we can conclude the following: the average soldier's bravery was mixed with indifference; he appeared as much a "ragamuffin" as redoubtable fighter; and he sensed a kinship with fellow Mediterraneans rather than seeing them, as the Germans did, as racial inferiors. Although examples of Italian atrocities are legion, they did not reach German machine-like cruelty and thoroughness. No doubt the Italian imperialists meant to milk the Greek economy as much as possible, but they were not indifferent to the starvation of the Greek people toward whom the Germans showed the utmost callousness in their relentless pillaging and exploitation.

Meltdown of Ciano's Albanian Fief

By January 1943 the Albanian resistance movement, having grown to 3,000-4,000, had seized control of much open land in the southern part of the country. Communists under Enver Hoxha were the main driving force of the insurgency that by June 1943 claimed 30,000 fighters. The Italians finally woke up to the reality that they were the hunted, not the hunter. Mussolini asked the lieutenant-general Jacomoni how the Albanians sized up the course of the war. Jacomoni replied forthrightly that after the Allied landings in Africa, no Albanian believed

---

63. Ibid., p. 100.
64. PP, *Diario*, 2 February 1943.
65. Steinberg, *All or Nothing*, p. 99.

any longer in an Axis victory.[66] Hatred of the occupiers, which daily threatened to turn into open defiance, was inescapably evident in all walks of Albanian life.

To offset the escalating disenchantment, the Italian military bestirred itself to track down the growing insurgent movement, which was swelled by discontented nationalists. However, guerrilla fighters who typically avoided any open clash with large Italian units stymied the troops by melting away when outnumbered. Frustrated by the inability to corner them, the military burned villages and killed many civilians. Reinforcements streamed in. In February 1943, 55,000 Italian and 17,000 Albanian troops launched a number of search-and-destroy forays that wrought more damage than success. In addition to these undistinguished military measures, Jacomoni, the man who supposedly treated Albanians with a velvet glove, put suppression of daily civilian dissidence into the hands of his hand-picked prime minister, Mustafa Kruja. The move backfired when many of Kruja's police defected to the resistance, taking their weapons with them.[67]

Undeterred, Jacomoni pressed on with rapid changes of the guard aimed at further "reform." Against a background of spiraling vendettas among Albanian factions, he dismissed Kruja in favor of the unpopular Eqrem Bey Libohova, a feudal highlander from the south, who took office in January.[68] The Italians surrounded Libohova with "experts" to offset the loss of previously reliable nationalists who had taken stock of heavy Axis military setbacks in Russia and North Africa.[69] To encourage moderates to rally around Libohova, Jacomoni played down the importance of military repressions and reprisals.[70]

The "light hand" of the Libohova government, unsurprisingly, did not head off a Fascist shipwreck The failure of so many makeshift moves encouraged Jacomoni to abandon tinkering in favor of radical change by converting the Albanian Fascist party—an obvious creature of the parent party in Rome—into a "twin," renamed the "Guard of Great Albania." An Albanian gendarmerie took over law enforcement tasks from the Italian Carabinieri. This was accompanied by the creation of an Albanian army, police force, and militia, measures taken to bring about an "Albanianized" Fascist state.[71] Discriminatory economic agreements were revised to treat the country more equitably.

Opposed to an open declaration of war against Albanian dissidence carried out by military authority, Jacomoni preferred leaving the initiative to the govern-

---

66. Jacomoni, *La politica dell'Italia in Albania*, p. 308.

67. Fischer, *Albania at War*, p. 139.

68. *The Ciano Diaries*, 13 January 1943. See also Jacomoni, *La politica del Italia Albania*, pp. 305–6; Eichberg, *Il fascio littorio e l'aquila di Skanderbeg*, p.106.

69. DDI, 9, IX, 512, Jacomoni to Ciano, 18 January 1943.

70. Ibid., 551, Jacomoni to Ciano, 26 January 1943; 555, Jacomoni to Ciano, 27 January 1943.

71. Ibid., X, 2, Jacomoni to Mussolini, 7 February 1943; Jacomoni, *La politica dell'Italia in Albania*, pp. 314–19.

ment. In those areas where the police was lax or too few in numbers to check disorder, he would entrust the military with the authority of restoring public order. By keeping this power firmly in the hands of the government, Jacomoni hoped to secure the collaboration of the population and the obedience of the military to his directives.[72]

Mussolini warmed to the idea of forming a *Guardia Nazionale Grande Albania* to absorb the *Partito Fascista Albanese.* A Spanish-style Falange would emerge in this renovated, strictly Albanian party, he hoped, that would become the driving force behind rehabilitation of the country.[73]

Apart from Mussolini's lingering support of Jacomoni, Fascists and the military both in Rome and Albania were ready to ditch him for his aimless scheming, simplicity, and lofty attitude. His expulsion of 12,000 Montenegrins from Kosovo to their homeland did not help his reputation.[74] Nor did the corruption over which Jacomoni presided. Pietromarchi noted the shortcomings of his governance: "Albania is abundantly provided with every gift of God: wheat, pasta, rice and sugar," which, via the black market, fell into the hands of the Italian rulers and their Albanian minions, creating an oasis of privilege in a country struggling in misery.[75] "It is said of Jacomoni," noted Pietromarchi, "that he has all the vices of the regime. This description is exact. What makes the greatest impression on me is the simple-minded ego of this man who is not pre-occupied by the severe repercussions in Italy that his policy of satisfying the interests and amour propre of the Albanians produces in Italy. Few men are as hated as he. But he proceeds undaunted."[76]

Ciano, Jacomoni's former friend and partner, had become equally disenchanted with his leadership: "I talked to the Duce on the problem of Albania. The situation is such that I think it is necessary to replace Jacomoni. For a certain period he did very well, but now his policies should be superseded. We need a man who can talk about force, and who can also employ it. I propose Guzzoni or Pariani, two generals who know the country and are well thought of. Mussolini said he would think about it and decide,"[77] but he had another idea: to cashier Ciano as foreign minister and put him in Albania in place of Jacomoni! On this notion, an appalled Ciano wrote: "Among the various solutions of a personal nature that he offers me I decisively reject the position of governorship

---

72. ASMAE, Albania, 1938–1945, Anno 1940, b. 107, fascicolo "rapporti dal Luogotenenza," 11 March 1943.
73. DDI, 9, X, 8, Bastianini to Jacomoni, 10 February 1943.
74. Rodogno, *Fascism's European Empire*, p. 294.
75. PP, *Diario*, 8 January 1943.
76. Ibid.
77. *The Ciano Diaries*, 3 February 1943.

of Albania, where I would be going as the executioner and hangman of those people to whom I promised brotherhood and equality."[78]

Police reports from Albania dwelled on the bankruptcy of Jacomoni's "reforms." Under his lax leadership, guilty people who had been dismissed from their government posts were left unpunished, while other "criminal elements" remained at large, which the Albanians took as a patent confession of weakness. Italian acts of clemency left the Albanian people cold.

Jacomoni's Albanian lackeys increasingly defied Italian law and order. While demonstrators sang *"Abbasso il Fascismo, abbasso l'Italia"* and hissed at the "barbarous" killings by the Fascist usurper, Albanian police stood hands in pocket. For stalwart Italians in Albania habituated to the Fascist club, this represented a shameful abdication in the use of power to crush dissent. Jacomoni had demonstrated no Fascist élan in letting the opposition run on destructive rampages. His failures cried out for passage of all power to the military.[79]

Still worse news arrived in Rome. On 28 February 1943 Colonel Edmondo de Renzi of the Army Information Service wrote a remarkably straightforward account of the Italian occupation in Albania. Communism had penetrated the university campus, the Albanian gendarmerie, and army. Since the nationalists had written Italy off as losers in the war, they were passing over to the insurgents. "The country people are stupefied and diffident; they perceive the invader throwing money away in building Roman monuments to dull the pain of a lost freedom. The instillation of a superb network of roads suitable for vehicles has left the masses indifferent. They affirm: 'the roads you have constructed are for yourselves, your automobiles, and your troops. We, with our mules and horses, have no need of them.' In substance, Italian and Albanian interests are distinct, often divergent, and mostly contradictory. The promise of a spiritual order embodied in viable political institutions has turned out to be a fallacy."[80]

De Renzi cut to the core of major contradictions and flaws in Fascist imperialism: "The sovereignty conceded to the Albanian state seems to have been sidelined by the interferences—intolerable appointments by the *Luogotenenza*—of the permanent Italian advisors to the individual ministries and the large number of PNF Italian advisors who flank Albanian officials." When the war against Greece raged on Albanian territory, "their country constituted a land of Italian occupation, which rendered the creation of Albania as a free and independent state merely a juridical fiction. The constitution of an imperium by the

---

78. Ibid., 5 February 1943.
79. NAW, T-821, 248, 000105–108, report by the permanent advisor of the police, G. Travaglio, 5 February 1943.
80. NAW, T-821, 250, 000087-97, Colonel Edmondo de Renzi to SME, 28 February 1943.

PNFA, and the imposition of doctrines and political methods not consistent with the tradition and mentality of the people, have traumatized the masses by disrupting the traditional customs of their lives." Jacomoni's "liberal" measures intended to grant Albanians more autonomy merely put nationalists, whom he hoped to win over, in a better position to challenge the Italian occupation. Instead of overcoming the distinctive Albanian traits of clan loyalties—self-reliance, attachment to the land, family, and religion—by inculcating in the people concepts of commonweal and nationhood, Jacomoni encountered a stubborn resistance. By means of a Fascist education, the Italians in his administration were unable to develop a military and national *esprit de corps* "in the framework of an Italo-Albanian union and of the Roman Empire." Inadvertently, the Italian occupiers had swung the door open to the insurgents.[81]

Many high-ranking military officers agreed with De Renzi in believing that the empire-builders sent out by Rome were amateurish, uninformed, and naïve. The only way out of the Fascist-created mess, in their view, was for the army to take over control of the forces of order and the administration of justice. In accordance with the military's standard thinking, only the generals, as in Greece and Yugoslavia, had the expertise to carry out a clean-cut and "exemplary" repression.[82] General Giuseppe Pièche, on a fact-finding mission in Albania, likewise described the country as a disaster area, whose remedy demanded a "clean sweep of the Albanian political regime and administration."[83]

Albanian Kosovo was faring no better. Serbs loyal to Mihailović, reported the Italian trouble-shooter Pièche, approached him for cooperation against Albanian Muslims, but, as he pointed out, this would be difficult since the Albanian prefects pursued anti-Serb policies. Still, thought Pièche, Mihailović's forces could be quite useful in the struggle against the Communist insurgents since many Albanians were actually cooperating with them in their general antipathy toward Italy.[84]

The same story obtained in Albanian Macedonia. To resolve the tangle of ethnic conflicts, said Pièche, Italy must take over the military power and end Albanian authority. The local population of whatever race or religion would be grateful for the end of violence and therefore collaborate with Italy against the Bolshevik peril.[85] Pièche pointed out that Muslims holding the power in Kosovo

---

81. Ibid., Colonel Edomondo De Renzi to SME, 28 February 1943; Piero Crociani, *Gli Albanesi nelle forze armate italiane (1939–1943)* (Rome: SME US, 2001), D. 21, The Superior Commadant FF.AA. Albania, Camillo Mercalli to the Comando Superiore FF.AA. Albania, 14 July 1943, pp. 296–98.
82. NAW, T-821, 248, 000132–43, Promemoria for the head of the SME. Signed by Colonel Edmondo de Renzi, 28 February 1943.
83. Ibid., 000114–17, Pièche report, 12 February 1943.
84. Ibid., 000118–120, Pièche report on Kosovo, 15 February 1943.
85. Ibid., 000121–22, Pièche report on Albanian Macedonia, 27 February 1943.

committed the most savage abuses and brutal persecutions against local Serbs, the people of order, on the pretext that the Orthodox religion was the declared enemy of the Muslims.[86]

In the Palazzo Chigi, Pietromarchi had had enough: "The policy of Jacomoni has been a failure. In this moment of crisis we don't have a single friend. We have bought Albanians and now we watch as they offer themselves to the highest bidder. In such a difficult situation whom do they propose to send in place of Jacomoni? The elderly Pariani. For he is one of the authors of the current halfhearted policy toward the Albanians and the one principally responsible for the grave situation in which our army found itself when entering the war. This shows that the malaise of which Italy suffers is incurable. The same discredited old men are rotated; the same errors committed. Italy has returned to the worst immobility. From the Italy of the Vittorio Veneto, it has returned to the Italy of Franceschiello [the last king of Naples]."[87]

On 18 March Mussolini sacked Jacomoni. His legacy is that of a dutiful Fascist who avoided the worst practices of the exuberant fanatic. He did not treat Albanians as *Untermenschen* or turn the country into a vast concentration camp. Neither did he propose the drastic military crackdowns that found so much favor among the generals and police, preferring instead "political" solutions worked out with "reliable" collaborators, of which there were few. Jacomoni was cut from the same cloth as Pietromarchi, a "moderate," or "idealistic," Fascist colonizer aiming at "Italianization." If not equality, faithful collaborators could find a rewarding niche as reliable vassals presiding over their own subject peoples under Fascist Italy's lordly watch. When Jacomoni in his memoirs constantly referred to this setup as "parity" or "equality" between Italians and Albanians, he was either being duplicitous or fantasizing. From all his obfuscations one Fascist theme stands out. As in the case of Italy's other imperial governors, Jacomoni required that the conquered peoples who wished to qualify for Italian largess be loyal and take no notice of Italian economic exploitation. If they showed the slightest disrespect or eschewed Fascist "reforms," there would be no Italian "civilization" for them—only serfdom.

Taking Jacomoni's place as lieutenant-general of Albania was the elderly and bungling General Alberto Pariani, the former chief of the Italian military mission in Albania and an undersecretary of state in the ministry of war—a man who once urged Mussolini to "wage a *guerra brigantesca* [a brigands' raid] on the fat and

---

86. Ibid., 000075–78, Pièche report, 28 May 1943. A SC officer commented in the margin: "It's incredible what you can dream up when you don't know the facts."
87. PP, *Diario*, 16 February 1943.

unwarlike democracies."[88] The new viceroy's mission was to undo the damage of his predecessor and restore a "Roman" peace. Since Jacomoni's devolution of authority to Albanians had broken down, such "reforms" were to be instantly abrogated. But Pariani did nothing more than lurch from crisis to crisis. His decrees prohibiting fraternization between Albanians and Italians, coupled with a general purge of Jacomoni's Albanian camp following from positions of political power, satisfied only the small Italian community in the country.[89]

In reports to Rome in early April, Pariani turned on those formerly favored fellow Italians who reaped fortunes from engaging in scams with Albanians. In sullying Italy's good name, such profiteers made an ugly situation truly "gangrenous." Military officers enjoying cushy lives in Tirana did not cut much ice with him either. Having to deal simultaneously with Italian corruption and Albanian insurgency, Pariani arrived at the conclusion that Italian imperialism had reached a dead end.[90]

A report of the same period belatedly owned up to a trail of mistaken decisions. Instead of constructing so many showy buildings and boulevards, the Italians should have concentrated on what might have earned Albanian gratitude, such as improvement of farm conditions and production aimed at narrowing the gap between the ongoing poverty of the masses and the enormous fortunes amassed by a few Italian and Albanian swindlers.[91]

The head of the Italian police, the solidly Fascist Renzo Chierici, implored Pariani in mid-April "to disprove the legend of our 'impotence' in order to convince the '*dubbiosi*' that Italy is ready to fight."[92] Pariani, however, devised a compromise. In zones where normality prevailed, public order would be entrusted to the Albanian government, relying solely on the police. In "abnormal" zones, power would pass to the military, which would have the responsibility for ruthlessly tracking down the insurgents. But care should be taken to pursue only the guilty and to avoid useless destruction of houses and property.[93] In early May, urged on by Rome, Pièche, and the police in Albania, Pariani divested the government of power and declared the country a war zone, which meant an all-out military undertaking to quell disorder.[94] The head of the Italian Carabinieri

---

88. Cited in Knox, *Hitler's Italian Allies*, p. 86.

89. NAW, T-821, 248, 000079-82, unsigned memorandum, March 1943.

90. Pariani's reports in DDI, 9, X, 178 and 207, Pariani to Bastianini, 1 April and 7 April 1943.

91. NAW, T-821, 248, 000058–64, unsigned memorandum, 10 April 1943

92. ASMAE, Albania, b. 1, Renzo Chierici, head of the police in Italy, to Pariani, 18 April 1943.

93. Ibid., Gabinetto Albania, 1938–1945, Anno 1943, b. 180, Pariani to the MAE, 29 April 1943.

94. Ibid., Albania b.1, Report of Gr. Off. Dr. Epifanio Pennetti, direttore capo della divisione A.G.R, 18 April 1943. Foreseeing a big uprising, Pariani wanted to head it off by sending about a thousand "dangerous" people to concentration camps in Italy.

advised: "Fifty Albanians should be shot for every one Italian."[95] Pariani intensified reprisals to be conducted "with the kind of violence and inflexibility that
can restore tranquility, where such action can overcome criminal minds and
enemy propaganda."[96] As elsewhere in the Balkans, Italian overkill merely
prompted the fence-sitters to become insurgents.

Reliance on the military was a desperate ultimate solution. According to
Pariani, the armed forces in Albania consisted of about 85,536 Italians and 7,760
untrustworthy Albanians. Of the Italian figure, 41,220 were engaged in sedentary
jobs and territorial duty. For search-and-kill operations against a rising insurgency, there were only 13,428 infantry and Blackshirts on hand. Having such a
small force, the Italian command glumly approached its task of repression.[97]

In this hopeless enterprise, the military itself was crippled by corruption that
seeped ever deeper as the end of Italian rule approached. According to the SME,
"In the various commands there is not always a lively, active, and firm mentality
of war, which must be manifested in prompt replies to the sudden attacks of the
rebels."[98] Too many soldiers were surrendering to them. After stripping captured
soldiers of arms, shoes, and equipment, the rebels set them free, a clever ploy to
drain the Italians the will to fight. General de Renzi's solution: "After a
responsible and discreet verification of the surrenders, commanders should hand
down exemplary sentences to demonstrate that the risk of surrender is greater
than the risk of fighting."[99]

Against this background of military ineptitude, Pariani had second thoughts
over unrestrained repression. The iron fist must be accompanied by acts of
clemency to temper the alarm felt by Albanians.[100] Such belated appeasement
was far overdue and had no consequence. In the swirl of defeatism engulfing
him, Pariani did not lose his reverence for Mussolini: "There is a reward, if small,
in all this: a gratifying tribute for what I have been able to achieve. Based on a
history of satisfying experiences, I have the certainty that the Duce will give me
his full support."[101] In carrying out the will of Mussolini, the Italian conquerors
had nicely fertilized the ground in Albania for Fascist-haters and die-hard
Communists.

On 27 July 1943, the day after Badoglio replaced Mussolini, King Victor
Emmanuel declared the whole territory of Albania an operational war zone,

95. Cited in Fischer, *Albania at War*, p. 136.
96. ASMAE, Gabinetto Albania, 1938–1945, Anno 1943, b. 180, Pariani to Bastianini, 18 July 1943.
97. USSME, DS, IV, D. 103, Pariani to Ambrosio, 26 March 1943; NAW, T-821, 250, 000078-82, unsigned
promemoria for the head of the SME, 22 February 1943.
98. NAW, T-821, 250, 000084-86, 4 March 1943, SME Undersecretary Francesco Rossi to SME, 4 March 1943.
99. Ibid., 000087-97, Edmondo de Renzi, SME Army Intelligence, to SME, 28 February 1943.
100. ASMAE, Albania 1938–1945, Anno 1943, b. 195/1, f. 42, Pariani appunto for the Duce, 11 June 1943.
101. DDI, 9, X, 294, Pariani to Bastianini, 5 May 1943.

which meant that all executive powers were to be turned over to the military, commanded by General Dalmazzo. After the Italian surrender, Dalmazzo met with Allied representatives and partisan leaders in former king Zogu's old palace to discuss plans for a joint resistance against the Germans poised to take over Albania. A plan was worked out. Dalmazzo would seize Tirana and Durazzo in preparation for an Allied landing, while partisans would hold off the Germans. But while this conversation was taking place, Dalmazzo slipped into an adjacent room to make arrangements with senior German officers for the evacuation of himself and his family.[102]

---

102. Fischer, *Albania at War*, pp. 162–63.

Chapter XII

Lights Out in Tunisia

Tunisian Intrigues
Deceits and Delusions in Rome
Axis Combat Ingenuity
"Tunisgrad"
Wasted Military Deeds

Tunisian Intrigues

When the Germans parachuted into Tunisia on 9 November 1942, Vichyite French Vice-Admiral Jean-Pierre Estéva, the resident-general of Tunisia, extended his hand as a pliant collaborator in the belief that the Axis troops had arrived to defend the colony from further "aggression" on the part of the Allies. However, when twenty-two Italian Macchi 202 planes flew in, they received an entirely different reception. Vichy officials greeted them with outright hostility and Kesselring wondered why they were there. This pressure constrained Mussolini to order the planes flown back to Sicily—proof positive of Vichy preference for the Germans over the Italians and German preference for Vichy collaborators over the Axis ally.[1]

---

1. *Operazioni*, IV: 100–101.

The Tunisian Moncef Bey, whose family had long ruled the country under the firm hand of French guardians, pledged loyalty to Berlin. While the French ground forces in Tunisia, some 12,000 in number, retreated toward the Algerian border on the order of their commander, General George Barré, the naval forces in Bizerte, led by Vice-Admiral Louis Derrien, yielded to Axis pressure on 12 November by opening up this important base for their use, which enabled the Italians to land troops a couple of days later.

After it became clear that the French in Algeria and Morocco were about to throw in their lot with the Allies, the Germans contrived the fiction that the Axis forces had arrived in Tunisia officially to prop up the Vichy colonial government.[2] The Italians were therefore unable to haul down the tricolor in favor of their own flag in a colony that was supposed to be theirs. The tone for the Axis occupation of Tunisia had been set.

If the formalities of government were left untouched to assure loyal French collaborators of their safety, the Germans quickly dispelled any doubt over who was in charge. The Italians were diverted to menial tasks and given time to frequent local bars and cafes. In the military sphere, the Wehrmacht took control of the battlefield assisted by Italian subalterns, while a representative of the German foreign office, Rudolf Rahn, accompanied by a crew of SS officers, managed the body politic. Rahn, who had previously served as the right-hand man of Otto Abetz, the German ambassador in Paris, was known to share his pro-Vichy sentiments.

In occupying Tunisia, the Axis Powers had made an ominous decision. Recoiling from the Allied invasion in North Africa and encountering stiff Russian resistance at Stalingrad, Hitler reiterated his strategic vision: "North Africa, being the approach to Europe, must be held at all costs." For him, everything depended on the fate of Stalingrad. Anticipating the capture of the beleaguered city, Hitler expected that a general collapse of Soviet resistance would follow. Turkey would react by joining the Axis and assist in the passage of German air and troop reinforcements through the Orient for an attack on Egypt, relieving Allied pressure on Tunisia. Mussolini needed no encouragement: "The occupation of Tunis is of decisive importance for the further conduct of hostilities in the Mediterranean, and therefore our first and most urgent task is to build up the Tunis bridgehead."[3] He said emphatically: "If we do not gain time, the game is up."[4]

---

2. Hitler reassured Pétain on 26 November: "I am firmly resolved to help France to regain possession of its colonial domain....neither Germany nor Italy has the intention of destroying the French colonial empire." Rainero, *La politica araba di Mussolini nella seconda guerra mondiale*, p. 228.
3. Cited in Deakin, *The Brutal Friendship*, p. 78.
4. Cited in De Felice, *Mussolini l'alleato*, II: 1093.

The Italian determination to hold on to Tunisia is explained both on strategic grounds and by the power of historical memory. Just as the Italians had viewed Nice, the birthplace of Garibaldi, as the cradle of the Risorgimento, they regarded Tunisia, which had harbored a large and flourishing Italian community for hundreds of years, as a symbol of unfulfilled colonial demands.

Ever since unification Italy had longed to found an empire. As a latecomer to the European balance of power, the fledgling country had to start from scratch. In the general scramble for empire that marked European life down to World War I, Italian nationalists scoured Africa for leftovers to enhance the reputation of their imperial *arriviste* country. Tunis was high on the list. But the French preempted the Italians by pouncing on the coveted colony in 1881. By the Treaty of Bardo, the French forced a protectorate on the bey of Tunis, a far less intrusive rule than that in Algeria, where no semblance of an independent state was maintained. Italy's masquerade as a Great Power was exposed by its obvious inability to counter the French move in a colony that contained 20,000 or so Italian settlers as against 200 French. Retaliation came immediately in May 1882 when Italy abandoned cautious neutrality in favor of membership in Bismarck's Triple Alliance. This, they were convinced, would secure Italy's boundary in northern Europe, while the country, with Berlin and Vienna holding the ring, slaked its appetite for colonies. But instead of granting its new ally free rein, Germany and Austria-Hungary declared Italy's imperialist ambitions off-limits. They did not want their restless new alliance partner to entangle them in controversies with the Entente in areas outside their own national interests.

Italy opted for neutrality in 1914, but as the war ground on the country's leadership decided to abandon their alliance partners by joining the Triple Entente in May 1915. The Allies paid a high price for bribing Italy to enter the war: the promise of large imperial gain for its new partner incorporated in the 1915 Pact of London. With this promise, Italian revenge against France was deferred. Following a victorious outcome, the nation expected to be paid off handsomely for the huge sacrifices of war at the Paris Peace Conference. Though nothing had been said about Tunis in the wartime treaties, the Italians anticipated that it would be handed over to them, along with the pledge of territories owed their country in the Pact of London. The French ridiculed such an extravagant expectation. Although far more aroused over territory denied in the Adriatic, the Italians smarted from the rebuff. Prodded by Mussolini, Italy's imperialists longed to avenge themselves against the French for the ongoing national humiliation administered by the Bardo treaty.

The French protectorate over Tunisia did not stop a heavy flow of Italian immigrants over the years. And so it came as a surprise when Mussolini casually signed an agreement with France on 7 January 1935 that included a protocol whereby Italy agreed to a progressive liquidation of Italian rights and privileges in Tunisia. The die-hard nationalists looked at the Duce's handiwork with furrowed brows. As Pierre Laval put it, "Tunisia is for Italy what Alsace-Lorraine was for France." But Mussolini had bigger fish to fry. In exchange for his veritable renunciation of the colony, he believed that France would give him a "free hand" to launch an invasion of Ethiopia.

The necessities of politics did not, however, eliminate Tunisia from the imperialist agenda—further reason why Mussolini's cohorts were so shocked when, capitulating to Hitler's appeasement of France in the armistice agreements of June 1940, Mussolini deferred his claim on Tunisia to an indefinite future. Finally, in November 1942, the Tunisian pearl seemed close for the taking, but this time it was not the French enemy but the Axis ally that would snatch it from the Italian grasp.

During that month Tunisia buzzed with the intrigues of rival Arab factions, German occupiers, and French Vichyites. All were opposed to Italy, save the country's settler colony. Rome was faced with a perennial question: how to protect the Italian community from French authority. Since the armistice with France in 1940, the Axis ally had been of no help, for the Vichy regime had been able to coax accords from the Germans that foresaw certain collaboration in exchange for promises to honor the integrity of the French empire in North Africa. The upshot of this tenuous collaboration were Montoire and the Paris Protocols, which certainly did not harmonize with the timeless Italian imperialist claim on Tunisia. Mussolini's belief in the *guerra breve* promised on 10 June, to be followed by a harvest of former British and French colonies, had become a monstrous joke. In what had turned out to be a *guerra lunga,* the Vichy government cleverly used the German "new policy" to postpone, then annul, Italian demands to disarm its soldiers in North Africa. French force levels there grew from 30,000 to 125,000, Bizerte and Constantine were never evacuated, and French ships and planes freely roamed the skies. In asking for Hitler's support against Mussolini's territorial claims, the Vichy regime openly acknowledged Germany as the dominant Axis partner in the French Mediterranean areas.

Italy's position in Tunisia was further complicated when, after the Axis Powers landed on 10-11 November, the Arab genie escaped from the French imperialist bottle to demand Tunisian independence. An old Italian ally, the unenlightened zealot ex-Mufti of Jerusalem Hajj Amin el-Husseini, asked Rome for permission to increase his support of the Maghreb Arabs in Tunisia, who were fighting for liberation from French imperialism. For him the Axis Powers were a good bet because they hated French secularism and practiced what he preached:

an unflinching struggle against "the Jews, the Anglo-Saxons, and the influence of Judaism."[5]

Although feeling a kinship with the Mufti's fanaticism, the Italians, dead-set on fixing a protectorate over Tunisia, were not about to release a formal declaration of freedom and independence for Maghreb Arabs, and granting the Mufti permission to visit Tunisia was simply out of the question. Yielding to Rome's wishes—a rare occasion indeed—Ribbentrop solemnly proclaimed Italian predominance in Tunisia,[6] which left the Mufti hung out to dry.[7] His efforts to assume leadership of a broad liberation movement encompassing Arab countries in North Africa and the Middle East had captured the imagination of neither Axis power. They were concerned only about Arab insurrection behind Allied lines or the formation of an Arab legion to fight them. In effect, the Mufti episode was merely a digression, for he cut a small figure in Tunisian Arab politics.

The neo-Destour movement led by Habib Bourguiba provided far more political muscle. Languishing in a French jail, Bourguiba was sprung free by the Germans after the Wehrmacht had moved into non-occupied France. On 18 December Klaus Barbie, the Gestapo chief from Lyon, had him taken to Chalon-sur-Saône, and on 9 January he was turned over to the Italians. This, for the Italians, was a bad idea since his goal was untrammeled Tunisian independence. They tried to cajole him into accepting a diluted version of protectorate status, but Bourguiba stood his ground. In pursuing independence, he insisted that the first step should be the legal forfeiture of the French protectorate and the suppression of the Vichyite resident-general. The benefit for Italy, he pointed out, was that the bey, once liberated from French tutelage, would negotiate a new treaty with Italy to align Tunisia on the side of the Axis.[8] This was an effort to catch Italy off guard, but the Palazzo Chigi would never allow independence in whatever guise to supplant a protectorate.[9] Bourguiba went on to become an autocratic sovereign in Tunisia, ruling in a fiercely secular style as an Arab Ataturk for the first three decades after the country had wrung independence from France in the mid-1950s.

While the stubborn Italian imperialists failed in recruiting reliable Arab collaborators in Rome, their influence in Tunisia slipped badly as the conniving Rudolf Rahn contrived a workable relationship with a collaborating French gov-

5. Daniel Carpi, "The Mufti of Jerusalem, Amin el-Husseini, and His Diplomatic Activity during World War II (October 1941–July 1943)," in *Studies in Zionism*, no. 7 (Spring 1983), p. 125.

6. DDI, 9, IX, 402, Lanza d'Ajeta to Ciano, 12 December 1942.

7. Ibid., 465, Vitetti to Ciano, 2 January 1943.

8. Ibid., 506, D'Ajeta to Alfieri, 17 January 1943.

9. Ibid., X, 15, Vitetti to Mussolini, 12 February 1943.

ernment. To gain the allegiance of local Vichyites, he set about the formation of a French civil commission headed by "our trusted friend," the journalist Georges Guilbaud. A confidante of Pétain,[10] Guilbaud was the founder of the Tunisian pro-Nazi organization Comité d'Unité d'Action Révolutionnaire and of an extremely pro-Nazi and anti-Semitic newspaper, *Tunis-Journal.* Scheming to buttress his authority, he brought on board the pro-German Jacques Doriot, who, creating the Phalange Africaine, a Nazi-type militia operating in Tunisia during the Nazi presence, assisted in mobilizing greater Vichy support for the Axis military fighting machine.[11] On another occasion Rahn thought of summoning the notorious pro-Nazi Joseph Darnand to activate anti-Gaullist forces.[12] A favorite gambit of the Wehrmacht was the recruitment of an Arab legion to stir up trouble behind Allied lines.

All these doings were anathema to the Italians since they were intended to reinforce French political movements that professed to be collaborationist but, in truth, had the aim of defending the French empire. Equally incongruent with Italian interests was Rahn's supposed readiness to throw out lines to Arab nationalists, the Mufti, the political neo-Destour movement, and other insurrectionary conspiracies. To beat off these schemes, the Italians looked to a strictly military regime supervised by Rahn and the Italian consul Giacomo Silimbani in cooperation with local French authorities, whose power would be chipped away by sending home functionaries not indispensable for the operation of public services.[13]

Rahn ended up discarding many of these ideas, but that did not alter the fundamental realities. Suave and affable, he won over many Vichy collaborators and, since Germany had no visible claims on Arab land, was able to befriend elements of the indigenous population too. As for the Italians, they were dismissed as undignified and incompetent.

However, Rahn experienced a setback at Italian hands in Germany's push to carry out drastic anti-Semitic policies against the Tunisian Jewish population. The Jews were already under the gun. As early as the beginning of 1941, Vichy authorities dismissed them from their posts in education, journalism, and the civil service, and placed strict limits on their business and professional enterprises. Still, Admiral Estéva did what he could to ward off Nazi agents bent on carrying out violence against Jews.[14] Undeterred, SS agents fanned out to round

---

10. Ibid., IX, 419, Silimbani to Ciano, 19 December 1942; 563, Vitetti to Ciano, 30 January 1943.
11. Ibid., 465, Vitetti to Ciano, 23 December 1942, 2 January 1943.
12. Ibid., X, 124, Vitetti to Bastianini, 16 March 1943.
13. Ibid., IX, 419, Silimbani to Ciano, 19 December 1942; 432, Ciano to Silimbani, 23 December 1942; X, 124, Vitetti to Bastianini, 16 March 1943.
14. Mallmann and Cüppers, *Nazi Palestine*, p. 184.

up Jews for forced labor and to lay plans for their extermination. But when Rome insisted that Jews bearing Italian citizenship be left alone, the Germans acquiesced.[15]

The protection afforded Jews by the Italians grew out of an untidy concoction of opportunism, pride, and resentment suffused with a touch of humanitarianism. Ciano spelled out a vitally important economic imperative: "It will be very difficult for us to find immediately in Tunisia Aryan Italian citizens with the qualifications required to manage the commercial and industrial enterprises to be expropriated, at the present level of profitability and success."[16] In defending Italian Jewry, the Italians would not tolerate outside interference in their imaginary domain. But on their own, they set up a certain number of work camps for Jews, which, by March, numbered 150–200.[17] Still, the Italian authorities granted protection to the small community of Jews holding Italian citizenship, which stood in sharp contrast with the shameful and discriminatory policy of the Vichy government and the violence and persecution exercised by the Germans at the expense of Tunisian Jewry.

After having been bullied and belittled by both French and Germans, the Italians were on the constant lookout for retaliation against their many tormentors by reasserting their title to Tunisia, a task that had never been easy. Back in July 1941 Ciano noted Silimbani's assessment: "Even the stones [in Tunisia] support De Gaulle, and 80 percent of the middle classes believe in a British victory. They hate the Germans but admire them; they simply despise us."[18]

While barely hanging on in Tunisia, the Italians did not let up in their pursuit of Fascist-style imperialism, which had the effect of hardening the many disparate factions of the country against them. Surrounded by hatred and fearful of expulsion, the Italian colony grasped for Fascist standards. But the imperialists in Rome were hapless bystanders, unable to repress the political turmoil wracking the country. French Gaullists and Vichy supporters might have viewed each other as mortal enemies, but they were united in their aim to preserve the "Frenchness" of the country against any Italian, or Arab, intrusion. The Tunisian Muslims, desiring true independence, rejected outright the galling thought of an Italian protectorate replacing a French colonial regime. And in spite of all the superficial concessions and banal assurances that Tunisia belonged in Italy's sphere of influence, Germans supervised public services and local government, stoked Tunisian nationalism, propped up the Vichy administration, and picked

15. Ibid.; Daniel Carpi, "L'atteggiamento italiano nei confronti degli ebrei della Tunisia durante la seconda guerra mondiale: giugno 1940–maggio 1943," in *Storia contemporanea*, XX, No. 6 (October 1969), pp. 1243–44.
16. Cited in Carpi, *Between Mussolini and Hitler*, p. 224.
17. Daniel Carpi, "L'atteggiamento italiano," pp. 243–44.
18. *The Ciano Diaries*, 5 July 1941.

the country clean to feed the Wehrmacht war machine. Vichyites, Arabs, and Germans, derisive of Italy's defeats on the battlefield, gave the nation's unquenched imperialist craving a deprecatory shrug.

In their delusion, Italy's hyper-nationalists noisily voiced their views. Among them was the new Italian consul, Enrico Bombieri, a radical Fascist, who replaced Silimbani in early February. He encouraged his local Italian counterparts to put out the newspaper *L'Unione*, with the masthead *"Vincere!"*—high comedy when measured against the backdrop of faltering Axis fortunes on the battlefield. The phrase "We are all Tunisians" was a popular refrain coined to convince the local Italian settlers that they would not be betrayed. Paradoxically, Fascist imperial sloganeering became ever more barefaced as the Italian military took on a cadaverous appearance in the last stages of "Tunisgrad." Rahn's theme song rang loud and clear: "Let us Germans take care of matters now; after the war your country will have a free hand in Tunisia." *"Va bene,"* muttered the disbelieving Italians.

Deceits and Delusions in Rome

In the endeavor of bringing Tunisia under their control, the Italians, lacking military leverage, had to resort to guile and diplomatic trickery. On 18–20 December 1942 Mussolini sent Ciano and his entourage to meet at Rastenberg with their German counterparts, hoping for a mutually profitable dialogue. Hitler assured Ciano that there would be no retreat either from Tunisia or from Stalingrad. After pledging four more divisions for North Africa, he placed on Italy the obligation to secure the sea routes to Bizerte and Tunis.[19] This was no longer possible. Lacking air superiority and with a dwindling number of merchant ships, the Italians could not solve the transport problem; the defense of Tunisia would ultimately prove unsustainable without heavy support from the Axis ally.[20] The two sides were at loggerheads.

According to Lanza, Ciano lost his composure at the meeting. "The Germans don't listen to reason, the Germans have lost the war."[21] Alfieri, the Italian ambassador in Berlin, wondered whether it was time to find a way out. Ciano looked at him with a tired eye, then said irately: "Never, never! There is nothing to do but wait for the collapse!"[22]

19. Deakin, *The Brutal Friendship*, I: 103.
20. DDI, 9, IX, 410, Mussolini to Ciano, 16 December 1942.
21. Simoni, *Berlino, Ambasciata d'Italia*, pp. 299–300.
22. Ibid., pp. 300–301.

As the Italian hold on Libya hung by a thread, Mussolini, according to Ciano, lived in a fool's paradise: "He is very unhappy over the fall of Tripoli," Ciano notes, "but [he] isn't at all convinced that we can't counterattack from Tunisia and retake it. Thus he continues to lull himself with many dangerous illusions, which distort his clear vision of reality—a reality which is now apparent to everybody."[23]

On 23 January 1943, the day that Tripoli fell, Mussolini informed General Messe that he had been chosen to replace Rommel, who by this time had lost his aura of invincibility, as commander of ACIT: "The army you are to command is in good shape and still has excellent firepower, seven hundred artillery pieces and seven thousand vehicles.... Cavallero, who has seen it march, says that the soldiers are well dressed." Messe was instructed to block the enemy coming from the west and south. "During the summer you will resume the initiative with a great offensive toward Algeria and Morocco and the reconquest of Libya."[24] Then he added: "Resist at any cost to delay an attack on Italy that will inevitably follow the fall of North Africa. You must resist till autumn, which will force the Allies to postpone their attack till the following year. I am certain that you will succeed!"[25] Behind these arid exhortations, Mussolini knew that in Messe he was playing his last card. Stupefied by Mussolini's charade, Messe thought the appointment was the doing of Cavallero, who, he imagined, shunted him off to Tunisia expecting that his reputation would suffer in the inevitable defeats to come or that he would end up in a prison camp.[26]

Although he had been relieved of his post, Rommel defied all intrigues to oust him from Tunisia until 9 March. When Messe finally took up his command, he brought with him two veterans of counterinsurgency fame in Yugoslavia, Generals Orlando and Berardi.

Rankled by the loss of Tripoli, Mussolini told the Council of Ministers on 23 January to brace for a war of three or four more years. Following this defiance, Churchill and Roosevelt announced at the Casablanca Conference on the 27th that they would force the Axis powers to surrender unconditionally, a decision that would dishearten those Italians who were hopeful of negotiating a change of sides in the war. A few days later, at a meeting of the military brass, a chastened Mussolini owned up to the hostility surrounding Italy. In Greece: "We know that everybody is against us.... If the Anglo-Americans land the Greeks will make common cause with them." In Albania: "The situation is getting continuously

---

23. *The Ciano Diaries*, 22 January 1943.
24. Messe, *La mia armata in Tunisia*, p. 140.
25. Ibid., p. 141–42.
26. *The Ciano Diaries*, 28 January 1943.

worse." In Provence: "they hate us, almost as much as they hate the Germans." Stubborn to the end, Mussolini called on the troops to "resist for the sake of resisting."[27] "We will never yield," he proclaimed to 6,000 legionnaires on 2 February.[28]

While the Axis troops were learning how to fight in mixed units, Cavallero tried to steal a march on the Germans on 26 January by setting up an African general staff under the aegis of the CS. Hitler, however, foiled this scheme by naming General Hans-Jürgen von Arnim to provide a German unity of command. Outmaneuvered, Cavallero commented lamely: "It is a problem that needs to be pondered and then taken up for examination again."[29] Mussolini eased Cavallero's embarrassment by rubberstamping Hitler's dictate, which left matters as before. Von Arnim would take charge in North Africa. But since there was no fixed command structure, and von Arnim continued formally to be under the ultimate authority of the CS, the actual delineation of responsibility remained as fuzzy as ever.[30]

Cavallero's machinations to be the principal leader of the Axis forces in North Africa had been successfully thwarted; only Germans would crack the whip. Kesselring proceeded to enhance his dictatorial power in Rome by crowding his operatives into CS headquarters, and, under Hitler's instructions, by coordinating the operations of the two Axis armies in Tunisia. But this did not amount to a unified command and would have nefarious consequences during tough campaigning in February.

The dysfunctional CS structure posed a monumental obstacle to Cavallero's control over the military branches, which felt free to negotiate their own contracts with industry and shunned common planning of military strategy. Absent strong hierarchical lines of authority, Cavallero resorted to wire pulling, which he did not so much to advance Italy's military competency as to build up his own power. With Mussolini standing by him, Cavallero could dish out favors to incompetent friends and eliminate capable rivals. The daring General Gambara was pulled from his African command for exercising "intellectual indiscipline" in a dispute between himself and Rommel. And in early 1942 Cavallero exiled Roatta, who supported a rival of his, General Guzzoni, to Yugoslavia where he would lose himself in the wilderness of partisan insurgency.

In pandering to Mussolini, Cavallero made unpardonable military decisions by scattering Italian forces on far too many fronts. Overcome by Fascist folklore,

---

27. *Operazioni*, IV: 254–55.
28. *OO*, XXXI, pp. 147–48.
29. *Operazioni*, IV: 260.
30. Ibid.: 259–60.

Cavallero held by its precepts that waves of infantry would overwhelm armor and that will power would triumph over technology. These were peculiar positions for a man who had been chief of the Ansaldo armaments combine. Strange too that Cavallero should ultimately fail in an area where, in Albania, he had established a reputation for expertise: developing existing resources and the nation's war potential.

Finally the time had come when Cavallero could no longer survive the accumulation of battlefield defeats so damaging to the regime's prestige. On 31 January Mussolini cashiered him, a decision that did not displease the other Italian generals. Ciano had a hand in bringing him down. But if, in fact, Cavallero had consorted with the Germans, as Ciano maintained,[31] he still had shown guile in the endeavor to establish control over the Axis armies in North Africa.

Not surprisingly, the Axis ally was distressed over Cavallero's departure. Bismarck, who had become his "mouthpiece,"[32] commented: "Cavallero's dismissal from the German point of view is very regrettable. Because of his energy, intelligence and gift for making quick decisions, co-operation with him was particularly smooth and characterized by the fact that he fell in willingly with German requests and attempted to implement them with an energy unusual in conditions there."[33]

Mussolini's habitual changing of the guard was typical of his style of government. In this case, it rose from a growing need to challenge Hitler in across-the-board problems of high military and diplomatic import—a challenge beyond Cavallero, and one that he, Mussolini, was loath to undertake on his own. Not one to accept responsibility for the military disaster in Africa and the imminent collapse of the Russian front, the Duce, to retain an image of infallibility in the eyes of the nation, needed someone to blame for the wearying string of military defeats in Africa and Russia. Cavallero was the perfect fall guy.

Ambrosio's appointment as the new military chief-of-staff is perplexing because his antipathy toward the Axis ally was not well hidden. The German interpreter Eugen Dollmann remarked that "Mussolini had taken the first step toward political suicide."[34] Ciano questioned Ambrosio's savvy.[35] Pietromarchi was even less complimentary. "He has narrow ideas, without intellectual élan, without enthusiasm, and without creative impulses. He is a man of routine, while

---

31. *The Ciano Diaries*, 20 January 1943.
32. Ibid.
33. Cited in Deakin, *The Brutal Friendship*, p. 147.
34. Eugen Dollmann, *The Interpreter: Memoirs of Doktor Eugen Dollmann* (London: Hutchinson, 1967), p. 202.
35. *The Ciano Diaries*, 30 January 1943.

what is needed is someone inventive, who transforms passion and faith, and who resuscitates the spirit and shows innovation."[36]

Since Ambrosio has left no archives, memoirs, or testimonials, we know little about this rather gray figure except that he held a strong loyalty to king and army, and that he bore an air of authenticity so lacking among Italy's generals, notably General Roatta.

One wonders whether there could have been worse conditions in which to take up a military command. Everywhere Ambrosio looked Italian war fronts were crumbling. The military smashup in Russia and the failure of counter-insurgency in the Balkans did not immediately imperil the homeland, but Tunisia, which was a hop, skip, and a jump from Sicily, posed a threat that demanded immediate attention. Ambrosio looked glumly on the paltry Italian naval resources that could be marshaled to keep the Axis forces provisioned there: twenty destroyers, thirty motor torpedo boats, thirty submarines, and six heavy cruisers lacking fuel for transporting 10,000 German troops to Tunis by the end of February, with 36,000 to follow.[37] There was no getting around the need for substantial German military assistance. The jovial Kesselring's unful-filled promises aside, Ambrosio knew that even with the best intentions the Germans would be unable to sustain Italian resistance as long as their military fortunes on the Eastern Front continued to sink. Ambrosio hoped to assemble a strategic reserve in Italy for protection of the motherland by withdrawing divi-sions from far-flung fronts. This was much easier said than done. The troops were randomly scattered in remote posts and lacked the modern equipment needed for an effective defense against invading well-armed Allies. Moreover, the Germans were opposed to Rome's pulling out troops still deployed in the lower Balkans for home defense.

Axis Combat Ingenuity

General Walter Nehring, who commanded the Axis troops that had hastily landed in Tunisia in early November 1942, was under enormous pressure to form a battle line quickly against an Allied force bearing down on Tunis and Bizerta. He profited from Pétain's last major service to the Germans, which was to order Resident-General Admiral Estéva to stand down while the Axis forces in November widened their beachhead in Tunisia. Nehring also benefited from a crucial Allied decision to land a small force east of Algeria, giving the Axis army breathing space to build up its forces. In a back-and-forth struggle at the end of

---

36. PP, *Diario*, 31 January 1943.
37. Deakin, *The Brutal Friendship*, p. 159.

the year, Nehring and his successor, General Hans-Jürgen von Arnim, who took over the newly formed Fifth Panzer Army, were able to thwart the Allied drive on Tunis, but not their advance deep into the hinterland.

In mid-January, as the Allies poured in troops and equipment, von Arnim barely had the forces for anything but a desperate defense. During the late winter months, the Axis sent a large convoy that the Allies, assisted by radar and Ultra, mostly destroyed. A heavy Allied bombardment of Naples disrupted a vital railhead, blasted shipping yards, and damaged warships at anchor. To avoid further losses, the Italian navy dispersed, which left very few ships available for convoy duties. The Allies laid many mines in the corridor and their planes combed the sea-lanes for Axis shipping. Logjams at Italian ports impeded the movement of goods. Loading a ship often took a full month, while damaged vessels were laid up unattended in Italian shipyards. French cargo and railway workers refused to unload those ships that did get through to Tunisia, which left the job up to the arriving Axis troops.

It was the Luftwaffe, flying from first-class airfields outside Bizerta, which came to the rescue by recapturing air superiority. Under this cover 99,000 tons of much-needed equipment arrived during January and February that included 100 tanks, 4,300 vehicles, and 320 guns. By mid-February von Arnim's forces numbered 110,000 troops organized into the 10th and 21st panzer divisions, the old nucleus of the German Afrika Korps, the 334th and Hermann Göring divisions, the XXX Italian Army Corps, comprising the *Superga* Division, the 50th special brigade, and numerous smaller units.

Once landed, the Axis troops and equipment were easily moved over relatively short distances from the principal Tunisian ports and airfields to the armies in the interior, whereas the Allies had to haul supplies over routes that ran from distant Algerian ports to their troops advancing deep into Tunisia. In a miracle of improvisation, the Axis had brought over a formidable force from Italy by the end of the month. Instead of a cakewalk, the Allies faced a tough struggle. Von Arnim was so buoyed that he talked up the idea of a "dash to Casablanca" which, among other things, would blot out the Canal fiasco of the previous year. This appealed to the dictators who were grasping at straws and perhaps willfully underestimated the forces arrayed against them.[38]

In southeast Tunisia, the second Axis front, General Rommel still held sway over ACIT, renamed First Italian Army on 30 January. It consisted of the Italian XX Army Corps (*Giovani Fascisti, Trieste*), the 90th German Light, and the Italian XXI Army Corps (*La Spezia* and *Pistoia*), which included 164th German Light.

---

38. Ibid., pp. 160–61.

The Italian armored *Centauro* and German 15th Panzer comprised separate units. At the end of January Rommel arrived at Mareth, a Maginot-like defense system in the southeastern part of the country constructed in the interwar years to repel an Italian attack from Libya, then left in abeyance by the Vichy French and overhauled by Axis engineers. But Rommel viewed the Mareth defenses unfavorably when compared with the Akarit Line farther north, which he considered harder to encircle. It also presented a smaller and more manageable area for consolidation of his positions. But the CS, suspecting retreat to be his guiding motive, ordered him to defend the Mareth Line whatever the cost.

The Italians had misread Rommel, for once safely ensconced in Tunisia his derring-do spirit revived. His eye fixed on the raw American troops facing him, Rommel conceived a strike aimed at transforming the entire complexion of the North African war by turning the Allied southern flank in Tunisia. He would launch an attack from the Mareth Line toward Tebessa, an important Allied airbase, supply and transport center in the northwest, enabling him to reach the port city of Bône, which he hoped would throw the entire Allied line into disarray and force a general retreat back to Algeria. Rommel gathered together a strong force, the best of his hard-bitten desert veterans whose old fighting zeal was rekindled by the arrival of powerful tanks from Germany.

For his offensive the Desert Fox was given command over the "Rommel Group."[39] At the outset his attack plan lost punch when von Arnim decided to keep the 10th Panzer in his sector, which showed his reluctance to accept Rommel's strategic thinking.[40] The CS added to his problems by changing the direction of his attacking force. Playing the role of arbiter, Kesselring negotiated a compromise. Instead of Tebessa, Rommel should drive due northward in a less ambitious attack through the Kassarine Pass toward the mountain towns of Thala and Le Kef.[41] Rommel was scandalized by these changes, an "appalling and unbelievable piece of shortsightedness" bound to slow down Axis momentum.[42]

Belatedly reinforced by units of the 21st Panzer and half of the 10th Panzer finally released by von Arnim, Rommel unleashed his attack on 19 February and immediately smashed through inexperienced American forces manning the Pass. A battalion of *Bersaglieri*, black cock-fighting feathers nodding on their helmets, distinguished themselves in the battle.[43] As the enemy floundered, Rommel,

---

39. Kitchen, *Rommel's Desert War*, p. 149.
40. *The Rommel Papers*, p. 401; Longo, *Giovanni Messe*, p. 230.
41. Longo, *Giovanni Messe*, p. 230.
42. *The Rommel Papers*, p. 402.
43. Ibid., p. 407.

much to the chagrin of Kesselring, called off his offensive.[44] Thwarted by von Arnim's refusal to release nineteen Tiger tanks of the 10th Panzer Division during a critical phase of the operations around Thala,[45] Rommel felt his flanks dangerously exposed, and he was running short on ammunition and fuel. Since both Rommel and von Arnim acted independently of one another, uncertainty characterized the fragmented command structure. A long way from Tunisia, the CS was in no position to synchronize the movement of the armies, but probably missed a chance by failing to support Rommel's original plan of heading directly toward Tebessa. Kesselring, meanwhile, spent his time trying to referee differences between his two antagonistic commanders. But nothing could lessen the ill will these three powerful egomaniacs held for each other. When measured against this discord, the divergence of opinion aired among American and British commanders seem like animated conversation.

By 23 February Rommel had slipped back through the Kassarine Pass. Unhurried, indomitable, and armed with new multiple rocket-launchers (the *Nebelwerfer*), his troops destroyed bridges and sowed mines as they filed toward the Mareth Line to the rear. Out of the blue, Hitler on that day appointed Rommel commander of a unified Army Group Africa to cover all Axis forces in Tunisia. Rommel took heart with this latest appointment by turning southward on 6 March to take on General Montgomery. Armed with Ultra decrypts, the British general was ready for him. In the ensuing battle of Medenine, Rommel, denied the 10th and 21 Panzer divisions,[46] launched an undisguised frontal attack and suffered defeat. In losing a large number of tanks, he opened the gates for a future powerful and coordinated Allied counter-offensive.

When Rommel left North Africa for good on 9 March, the dictators were glad to see him go. No longer would they have to hear that the Allies could not be resisted at Mareth, or that his troops should retreat to the Akarit line to shorten the front; no longer would they have to live with the suspicion that behind Rommel's drawback proposals lay an "African Dunkirk";[47] and no longer would they have to put up with his guarantee to defend "our southern European flank" with the African veterans re-equipped in Italy.[48] After Rommel's departure, command of Army Group Africa was handed to von Arnim. General Messe, the commander of the First Italian Army, was designated as his subordinate.

---

44. Messe, *La mia armata in Tunisia*, p. 166.
45. *The Rommel Papers*, p. 406.
46. Longo, *Giovanni Messe*, p. 233.
47. *Operazioni*, IV, Allegato 20, Kesselring report, 10 March 1943, pp. 648–50.
48. Deakin, *The Brutal Friendship*, p. 210.

"Tunisgrad"

During March, when it was already too late, Mussolini puzzled over how to save Tunisia. In the early part of the month, admonishing his ministers not to expect a drastic turnaround, he still exhorted them to "keep afloat, endure." By some magic a way would be found to increase the flow of fuel and supplies for Tunisia.[49] In a letter to Hitler on the 9th Mussolini displayed his military grit: "We must remain in Tunisia, whatever the cost.... In order to hold Tunisia, we must extend our bridgehead and not shrink it."[50] On the 26th he wrote him: "The Allied expedition to North Africa would become a disaster if the Axis resisted to the end."[51] Added to this reverie, Mussolini suggested an equally unrealistic proposal of a major operation to the rear of the Allies across Spain into Morocco. Gibraltar would be captured and the Balearic Islands occupied to give the Axis control of the western Mediterranean. "Cut off from supplies, the fate of the Anglo-French-American troops would be sealed," thus negating the threat of an Allied landing in Italy. No matter that the Axis lacked aircraft and soldiers, or that the Allies held the key ports in the western Mediterranean; "fortune favors the audacious."[52] As for Italy's loyalty, Hitler need not be concerned: "Italy will march with Germany to the end."[53] But it was far too late in the day. With the Allies sitting on his doorstep, Franco would obviously not move, so Hitler simply let Mussolini's letter drop. The CS was relieved, for under the Duce's madcap order to scramble together a plan for a Gibraltar expedition, only motorized units of the *Piave* could be provided followed by the dispatch of *Nembo* parachutists.[54]

On 8 March Hitler provoked a *strappo nell'alleanza* (tear in the alliance) by appointing Kesselring as the highest Wehrmacht representative to the CS with responsibility for all matters of combat in the central and western Mediterranean. This strengthened authority gave Kesselring license to burrow more deeply into the crypts of power in Rome. On the 14th he told Mussolini to make way for the real connoisseurs of warfare—Admiral Karl Dönitz and his entourage of experts, who would take charge of a timid Italian navy that refused deployment for a robust defense of Tunisia.[55]

---

49. *Operazioni*, IV: 570.
50. DDI, 9, X, 95, Mussolini to Hitler, 9 March 1943.
51. Ibid., 159, Mussolini to Hitler, 26 March 1943.
52. Ibid., Mussolini to Hitler, 26 March 1943.
53. Ibid., Mussolini to Hitler, 26 March 1943.
54. Ibid., 220, Ambrosio to Mussolini, 12 April 1943; Ceva, "Italia in guerra," p. 124.
55. De Felice, *Mussolini l'alleato*, II: 1111; Deakin, *The Brutal Friendship*, p. 215; Puntoni, *Parla Vittorio Emanuele III*, pp. 125–26.

To make the German case, Hitler rambled on to Mussolini about his navy's superb exertions in the infinite stretches of the Atlantic as opposed to the lackluster Italian effort to provision Tunisia in the narrow spaces of the Mediterranean. Mussolini replied that he would never hand over command of a single Italian ship to the German navy admirals. Since Italy did not have enough vessels for the Tunisian run, it was imperative to carry troops and supplies across to Tunisia by air—in German planes. Kesselring had no better luck in vigorously lobbying Ambrosio to release torpedo boats to protect Tunisian convoys.[56] The Führer countered with a refusal to give guns and weapons to the Italians without close scrutiny, fearing that many would simply vanish, end up in enemy hands, or be turned on German troops. He simply dismissed the Italians as "gutless," incapable of "a struggle to exist or not exist." He might have had something here, for the percentage of the Italian gross domestic product directed to the war effort reached twenty-three percent in 1941 and hardly rose further, as compared to Germany's sixty-four percent in 1942.[57]

On 13 March Ambrosio told the king's adjutant Puntoni: "Tunisia is by now lost. It is only a question of time."[58] Riveted on the need to extricate the Italian troops from Tunisia for the defense of the homeland, the hard-pressed Italian general wrote Mussolini on 24 March: "Does it make more sense to play the enemy's game by continuing to throw men and equipment into the Tunisian furnace, or rather to save them for the heavy tasks to come?" He knew Italy's Axis partner well. "Our ally does not feel directly or immediately threatened by an attack on the Italian peninsula and will care little if it is put to fire and sword; thus once Tunisia is evacuated, he won't send us a thing."[59]

Fear of Germany's abandonment and Hitler's revenge if Italy sought to leave the war paralyzed Ambrosio and the entire Italian leadership up until Mussolini's fall on 25 July 1943. To ward off the invasion of Italy, Tunisia had to be held, and this could not be done without heavy German reinforcements and aid.[60] Complaining about German arrogance, Ambrosio sported defiance but acted no differently from Cavallero by following Kesselring's lead in a fight to the finish in Tunisia. There was one notable exception. For Ambrosio, if retreat became inevitable under threat of annihilation, he wanted to orchestrate a move home of Italian troops to save lives and equipment, whereas the hard-boiled Kesselring,

56. De Felice, *Mussolini l'alleato*, II: 1112; DDI, 9, X, 116, Hitler to Mussolini, 14 March 1943; Deakin, *The Brutal Friendship*, p. 215.
57. Richard J. Bosworth, *Mussolini's Italy: Life Under the Fascist Dictatorship, 1915–1945* (New York: The Penguin Press, 2006), p. 466.
58. Puntoni, *Parla Vittorio Emanuele III*, p. 125.
59. *Operazioni*, IV, Allegato 27, Ambrosio memorandum for Mussolini, 24 March 1943, pp. 694–97.
60. Ibid.: pp. 441–42.

who had no concern for the fate of Italian soldiers, only wanted to use them as throwaways in an outer perimeter defending the Fatherland. But Kesselring's callousness did not stop at Italy's door. When Hitler decreed that Germans should die at their posts in this useless cause, Kesselring looked at his compatriots stonily, making no move to oppose his revered Führer while humoring the Italians into carrying out his crazed orders.

While the dictators were crossing swords over transport problems, General Montgomery on 20 March launched a furious attack on the Mareth line over desert land, salt lakes, and rugged terrain. Realizing that his troops could not long resist a determined assault, Messe continued to favor a speedy retreat to the Akarit line to save his infantry, but was constantly opposed by von Arnim, who seemed determined to defend the Mareth line to the last Italian soldier.[61] As to be expected, the First Italian Army, lacking reinforcements, cracked under Montgomery's massive assault, throwing the Axis armies into disarray. When von Arnim hastened to order a swift fallback, he ignored the plight in store for the slow-moving Italian infantry. Messe strenuously argued for a delay, but von Arnim remained immovable.[62] Nonetheless, having adroitly placed deadly mines and booby traps, Messe was able to foil Montgomery by arriving at the fortified gap at Akarit in reasonably good order on 31 March. Italian divisions bore the brunt of the fighting and showed an improved ability to react quickly, but still had to leave many thousands of infantry behind. It was primarily the German anti-tank squads that slowed down the British armor and thwarted Montgomery's aim to destroy the First Italian Army.[63]

General Messe filed a secret report to Ambrosio summarizing these recent battles, which Mussolini, surprisingly, made public. The report detailed deep fissures in the Italian war effort, the inferior conditions in which the Italian soldier was required to fight, the vast and perilous lacunae in army preparations, the lack of air support, and differences between himself and von Arnim that hampered Axis cooperation—all good talking points for enemy propaganda. Included was Mussolini's command for his soldiers to drive themselves "to the extreme end," which, as the Italian military historian Mario Montanari suggests, amounted to a callous "Dying, I salute you!"[64] In 1944 Mussolini accused Messe of "a particularly opprobrious betrayal" in reporting on the battle of Mareth, overlooking the inconvenient fact that it was he who leaked to the press what was supposed to be a secret report.[65]

---

61. Messe, *La mia armata in Tunisia*, pp. 198–200.
62. Colacicchi, *L'ultimo fronte d'Africa*, p. 65.
63. Messe, *La mia armata in Tunisia*, p. 219.
64. *Operazioni*, IV: 418–19.
65. Benito Mussolini, *My Rise and Fall* (New York: Da Capo Press, 1998), p. 12.

On 29 March, in a meeting with Ambrosio and Kesselring, Mussolini reversed himself and suggested a retreat to the line further north of Akarit to avoid the loss of the First Italian Army. Kesselring, vigorously dissenting, replied that such a shortening of the defense lines would render the Axis bridgehead even smaller, thus hastening surrender.[66] Taking a contrary position, Ambrosio, echoing Rommel, argued that von Arnim be given more leeway to disengage if further resistance would compromise the fate of Messe's army. To terminate further discussion, Kesselring played his favorite trump card, Hitler: "The Führer had said that the Sciott Line must be considered as the last position."[67] The Luftwaffe would deliver everything needed, and the fragmented and incompetent Allies would be a setup for counterattack. Kesselring's nattering could hardly lift Ambrosio from his forebodings.

No Italian on the battlefield shared Kesselring's rosy outlook. What was to be done with the edict from Rome that the Akarit line be held? Messe brushed aside the nonsensical order by arguing for a disengagement from the enemy and a retreat northward to Enfidaville. Von Arnim granted Messe permission to do this. But a few days later Messe was surprised to learn that von Arnim's changed view was unknown to the CS, which, when informed, was greatly displeased. Had Messe absorbed the "spirit of Rommel" in wanting to avoid battle in order to reach the ultimate redoubt at Enfidaville at breakneck speed?[68]

Indeed, Ambrosio on 5 April warned von Arnim that any conspicuous preparation for a fallback from the Akarit positions to the Enfidaville line would have a chilling effect on the army's morale. "It is better," he wrote, "to lose a part of the materiel than undermine the spirit of the units by a premature withdrawal."[69] Messe wryly commented that it was "easier to give an order than to translate it into reality."[70] While Ambrosio squirmed in Rome from Kesselring's exhortations, von Arnim and Messe, in spite of their tactical differences, looked to do their best while sensing the ineluctability of the fates running against them.

On 6 April Kesselring, chastising Ambrosio over the lack of planes for ferrying troops to Tunisia, commented on the battlefield superiority of Germans and expressed dismay that the CS would ponder withdrawal to the Enfidaville line instead of holding firm at Akarit. What better time for a counterattack!

Exasperated by Kesselring's empty promises, upbeat projections, and irritating citations of the Führer's war strategy, Ambrosio replied in a faultfinding historical disquisition. He had a lot to get off his chest. The Axis forces had

---

66. *Operazioni*, IV: 435–36.
67. Ibid., Allegato 30, Conversation between Ambrosio and Kesselring, 29 March 1943, p. 706.
68. Messe, *La mia armata in Tunisia*, pp. 226–27.
69. *Operazioni*, IV: 455–56.
70. Ibid.: 456.

retreated so quickly to Akarit because Rommel, in defiance of Italian generals, had failed to put up resistance against the 8th Army in North Africa. "I cannot forget that if Rommel had stayed put, we would still be at Tobruk." Moreover, a date had been fixed for the Malta operation that the Germans willfully disregarded. "In a nutshell, in this long retreat over 2,000 kilometers, we have started to resist only after Rommel has departed the scene." When the Desert Fox revealed his intention of an immediate retreat to Enfidaville, "I supported the idea that Rommel should not return to Africa." True, Kesselring too wanted to be rid of the Desert Fox, but was embarrassed by talk of Malta in light of Hitler's opposition to the expedition for which he had been an ardent exponent.[71]

The two dictators met on 8 April at Schloss Klessheim in Salzburg to work on a common approach. Hitler drove home the point that Tunisia, since it protected Italy and the rest of southern Europe, must be defended aggressively. A loss of North Africa, he warned, would seriously imperil the Duce, the regime, and the Italian homeland. Hastening to buoy Mussolini's spirits, Hitler told him: "Rest assured, Duce, there will be no invasion of Sicily. The fortress of Verdun withstood every onslaught for months on end during the last world war, and I shall ensure that our enemies meet with as little success this time, on the shores of the Mediterranean: Tunis must become the African Verdun!" Mussolini nodded in agreement, Dollmann recalls, while German and Italian officers visibly paled.[72]

Notwithstanding the German determination to stand fast, the First Italian Army, reeling from strong enemy attacks, began on 7 April to withdraw from its positions at Akarit-Chotts toward the Tunis bridgehead at Enfidaville, the most formidable position occupied by the Axis since the losses at El Alamein. Once again Montgomery was denied a complete victory when his 8th Army, expecting to deliver a *coup de grâce*, discovered that Messe's forces had slipped away. Montgomery recovered quickly enough to chip away at the mostly Italian infantry straining to keep up with the main body of Messe's retreating forces. As the two Axis armies, thrown back on each other, settled in the small perimeter of northern Tunisia, they confronted the huge Allied force advancing inexorably against them. Despair reigned. In mid-April twenty Allied divisions besieged Axis forces in Army Group Africa, which numbered some 200,000 (with Germans outnumbering Italians). There were 70,000 Italians and 43,000 Germans in the First Italian Army; 34,000 Italians and 18,000 Germans in DAK; and 1,800 Italians and 34,000 Germans in the 5th German Army. The Italians

---

71. Ibid., Allegato 31, Conversation between Ambrosio and Kesselring, 6 April 1943.
72. Dollmann, *The Interpreter*, pp. 208–9.

were down to fifty planes; the Luftwaffe had 328 operational.[73] On 13 April von Arnim was told that there would be no mass evacuation, which made him wonder about continued resistance without hope.

But for Kesselring the game was never up. On 12 April he implored Ambrosio and Mussolini for the umpteenth time to redouble their efforts in assembling an assortment of small vessels and torpedo boats that would be sent as reinforcements to North Africa. "There was no time to lose; *'it is a question of hours.'"*[74] Mussolini needed no persuasion—as long as Germans provided the transportation: "WE MUST resist as long as possible," the Duce insisted. "The Führer has provided us with an example: 'Stalingrad.' Twenty-two sectors of the city were in our hands; only two remained outside a definitive occupation. The Russians not having yielded, we have witnessed a turnaround. WE MUST resist not only till the clock strikes twelve but till a quarter after twelve;"[75] that is, to the last merchant ship, the last standing soldier.

There was no letup in the squabbling between Messe and Kesselring when they met on 16 April. Kesselring, reading passages that decreed "no retreat" to Messe from the dictators' strategic gospel, chastised him for falling back from the Chott-Akarit position. The German general added: "There was another solution, which was to withdraw the mobile forces and abandon the infantry to their own destiny." Messe replied: "Thus the Italian divisions would have paid the price again as at El Alamein." Taken aback, Kesselring hastily wound up the discussion: "I have the authority to inform you that the Tunisian positions must be maintained at all cost."[76]

Messe held that the order to resist to the very end was a recipe for disaster without strong reinforcements in men, arms, and materiel. Kesselring retorted that the loss of Tunisia would distress both Mussolini and Hitler. And it was not possible to carry away 300,000 men, who, to their everlasting credit, would prefer to go down fighting than surrender their arms. Hearing the name "Mussolini," Messe snapped to: "Tell the DUCE and the FÜHRER that for this energized Army there will be no giving up, and that its Commandant would certainly be the last hold-out." Kesselring: "I don't know a better message for the DUCE and the FÜHRER."[77] Out of loyalty to Mussolini, Messe, in spite of deep misgivings, was prepared to send his army to a martyr's death.

---

73. *Operazioni*, IV: 502.
74. Ibid.: 487.
75. Ibid., Allegato 36, Mussolini meeting with Kesselring, 12 April 1943; DDI, 9, X, 220, Ambrosio to Mussolini, 12 April 1943.
76. This is the account found in Messe, *La mia armata in Tunisia*, p. 270, but not in the official summary of their meeting in *Operazioni*, Allegato 37, pp. 734–39, a report written by Ten. Col S. M. Mario Revetria, 16 April 1943.
77. *Operazioni*, IV: 503, and Allegato 37.

The next day Kesselring carried his bonhomie back to Rome by reporting that the troops were highly motivated to fight; "their morale was good." When Ambrosio questioned this sunny observation, Kesselring backtracked, but insisted that "certainly, morale would increase if the troops were allowed to fire," that is, if they were not issued orders to retreat.[78]

At the battle of Enfidaville, 19–30 April, Italian and German forces, dug in hilly terrain and craggy peaks behind screens of mines and protected by deadly accurate artillery in a semicircle protecting Tunis and Biserta, repulsed the Allies time and again. The British military expert Liddell Hart acknowledges that the "Italians fought as vigorously as the Germans"; a dispatch sent by General Alexander held that the Italians "outdid them."[79] But it was German armor and anti-tank guns, the famous 88 that put real spine into the defense.

Nonetheless, given the increasingly catastrophic supply crisis, morale sank fast.[80] The First Italian Army labored painfully. On 26 April Lieutenant Colonel Dogliani wrote: "For the troops to resist *à outrance* was meaningless without reinforcements and supplies."[81] Doubtless, he observed, Messe had animated the spirit of the troops. They acquitted themselves splendidly in defending the motherland, but, worn out, knew that the end was near. Italians found solidarity with the Germans on the front, but acrimony raged behind the lines. Von Arnim hardly shored up camaraderie when on the 27th he began to ransack Messe's legions for men and equipment for his own army.[82]

As the Allies tightened the noose around the penned-up Axis forces in the Enfidaville redoubt, panic seized Rome. On 30 April Mussolini wrote Hitler: "If, as I have already several times indicated, the air problem in the Mediterranean is not solved at once by sending air support to counterbalance the shattering air superiority of the enemy, it will no longer be possible for any warship, or supply ship, or plane, to arrive in Tunisia. This means losing Tunisia at once, without saving anything."[83] The Italians knew that the Germans, unable to handle the Eastern Front and North Africa simultaneously, had written Tunisia off.[84]

Opposition to the regime in the military ranks was rising in Rome. An unsigned minute initialed by Bastianini on 2 May reads: "The order of the Duce to reinforce Tunisia at all costs with warships has produced a sharp reaction in the Italian High Command. The reaction at navy headquarters has been the most

---

78. Ibid.
79. Liddell Hart, *History of the Second World War*, p. 425; Ceva, *Guerra mondiale*, pp. 45–46.
80. *Operazioni*, IV: 530–32.
81. Ibid.: 531.
82. Ibid.: 514.
83. DDI, 276, 9, X, Mussolini to Hitler, 30 April 1943; Deakin, *The Brutal Friendship*, p. 284.
84. Deakin, *The Brutal Friendship*, p. 284.

open and lively, and has in this regard clearly and insistently expressed a contrary view in the use of naval vessels for transporting troops." Warships loaded with troops, read the minute, had recently been sunk. "Lively resentment has also been provoked by the direct interference of Marshal Kesselring, whose influence on the Duce in the conduct of operations is a subject of open comment. The conduct of the war, which is a preeminently amphibious one, is confided to the exclusive direction of the General Staff Officers of the army, whose incompetence in such matters is well known."[85]

On 4 May Mussolini was compelled once again to tell the relentless Kesselring that he would not release destroyers to send supplies to Tunisia. Not to be denied, Kesselring sprung the idea of assembling three hundred motor-powered rafts to speed up the flow of reinforcements. To this outlandish suggestion Mussolini commented: "If we could send two armored divisions, we could revolutionize the situation in Tunisia."[86]

Down the home stretch to the fall of Tunisia, it was Kesselring, not Mussolini, who was the boss of Axis operations in North Africa. His cocksure attitude alienated everyone, but nothing could be done to bridle him since the nearly prostrate Italy lay at the mercy of its overbearing ally.[87] At every meeting Kesselring acted as if his orders for Italian ships and planes to carry the goods could be executed straightaway by sailors and pilots blissfully oblivious to the heavy odds stacked against them in plying the "Death Route." Word spread that Kesselring regularly administered cocaine to the CS, but that the action of the drug was always fleeting, leaving behind a cold awareness of deception and hatred.

Kesselring was slowed but not stopped by the dull-witted Ambrosio, who wanted to liberate himself from German tutelage but did not know how. Rintelen, who saw what was happening, tried stiffly to mediate, but without success. Kesselring smugly reviews this history: "When Cavallero was succeeded as Chief of the General Staff by General Ambrosio, formerly C-in-C of the army, the situation became intolerable. The trustful relationship that had existed between Cavallero and myself deteriorated to the opposite extreme. I warned the Duce before the new appointment, and as my warnings remained unheeded I asked to be relieved myself. Unfortunately I yielded to the Duce's insistence and his assurance that we would 'trust each other like brothers.'"[88]

---

85. Ibid., p. 285.
86. Ibid., pp. 285–86.
87. *Operazioni*, IV: 561.
88. Kesselring, *Memoirs*, p. 157.

Mussolini was an unapologetic imperialist to the end. On 5 May when Italian guns in Tunisia were falling silent, he proclaimed from the balcony of the Palazzo Vecchio: "Millions and millions of Italians suffer from indefinable pain, which is called the pain of Africa." There was only one remedy: "to return, and return we shall."[89]

On 12 May General von Arnim raised the white flag. Mussolini informed Messe: "As the aims of your resistance can be considered achieved, your Excellency is free to accept an honorable surrender. To you and the heroic remains of the 1st Army I once again emphasize my admiration and most heart-felt praise."[90] (One can see an interesting comparison between Mussolini's tribute to Messe and Hitler's heartless condemnation of Paulus for cowardice following his surrender at Stalingrad.) On his own, Messe first tried to wheedle an armistice out of the Allied command but was given a much less heroic choice: unconditional surrender or annihilation. Messe struck his colors. The number of prisoners taken totaled approximately 250,000—157,000 Germans and 87,000 Italians—more than the German force that downed arms at Stalingrad.[91]

At the time of the surrender, the Italians were hated, or at least held in contempt, by everyone: their German comrades, the victorious Allies, the indigenous Tunisians, and particularly the French of all political persuasions. Italian prisoners who managed to escape "prefer anything, even death, to being returned to the French. At Camp n.131, when fifty-eight prisoners were ordered returned to their care, men groveled on the ground, begging that Americans intercede and refuse their return. One asked to be shot. Finally [they] had to be forced into French buses."[92]

At the surrender ceremonies, New Zealand Major-General Bernard Freyberg gallantly observed that in the end the war was one of materiel, with the winner having been the side that had the most. Messe replied that, beyond guns, it was spirit that counted. Freyberg: "The marshal is perhaps a Fascist?" Messe: "Naturally." Freyberg: "*Naturally*? Why?" Messe: "Because the king whom I have the honor of serving accepted the head of a fascist government. If my king accepted him, *naturally* I accept him too."[93] Paolo Colacicchi, a fellow prisoner in Britain, made an interesting point. "Our oath of faith, as all the troops, the navy, and the air force, was to the king. I respect those who, when they were asked,

89. *OO*, XXXI, p. 178.
90. *Operazioni*, IV: 548.
91. Ibid.: 550–51.
92. Cited in Rick Atkinson, *An Army at Dawn: The War in North Africa, 1942–1943* (New York: Henry Holt 2004), p. 527.
93. Cited in Colacicchi, *L'ultimo fronte d'Africa*, p. 111.

responded: 'Yes, I am a Fascist because I believe in Fascism.'"[94] This blinkered thinking partially explains why Messe had traveled down a potholed road. Back in November 1942 he expressed the opinion that a bridgehead in Tunisia was a lost cause and implied that he wanted no part of it.[95] Yet when called on by Mussolini the following January to take up the Tunisian command, he did so without hesitation.

Many people in Rome had thought the gallant marshal would be expatriated in order to take charge of the Italian army facing the expected Allied invasion. Instead, against the strong advice of Ambrosio, Mussolini gave the order that he be taken prisoner.[96] Pietromarchi was devastated by this news: "The impression that has been awakened in me by this notice has been disastrous. I have seen the last hope vanish. It is an error that will be fatal to Italy and to the Regime. Thus is the country lost…. Messe would have been accepted by the crowd as the Savior. He would have galvanized the country and created a heroic atmosphere, the same atmosphere in which the 1st Army lived."[97] Bastianini's secretary Egidio Ortona concluded: "It is the final disengagement of Italy from Africa. We have returned to the era prior to Adua."[98]

Wasted Military Deeds

On the whole the Italians fought better in Tunisia than in North Africa, where the immobile infantry were easily mowed down in open desert by enemy tanks maneuvering at will. Tunisia's terrain of craggy hills, ditches, and scrubby rock-strewn land was hostile to highly mechanized forces, and the Italian infantry found shelter from which to fire on tanks that now appeared more like sitting ducks than terrifying steamrollers. They held exemplary defensive positions at Mareth, Wadi Akarit, and Enfidaville, each a bottleneck where the coastal plain narrowed and the mountains or a salt marsh came close to the sea. Although the Italian units still came up short in skill and equipment—machine guns, mortars, and anti-tank guns—they managed to deny the enemy easy passage notwithstanding the overwhelming numbers and superior armor brought to bear against them. In view of the acrimonious arguments between the two Axis partners who plainly did not like each other, it is surprising the two armies would fight so coherently and well under such immensely trying circumstances.

---

94. Ibid.
95. *The Ciano Diaries*, 14 November 1942.
96. PP, *Diario*, 14 May 1943.
97. Ibid.
98. Egidio Ortona, *Diplomazia di guerra: diari 1937–1943* (Bologna: Il Mulino, 1993), p. 231.

As in the desert, major differences arose in field strategy between the two Axis partners on the Tunisian battlefield, differences dictated by their widely divergent capabilities and makeup. The didactic Messe heatedly questioned von Arnim's usual tactic that called for slow retreat in fits and starts followed by a more rapid pace. This strategy, Messe argued, afforded the enemy possessing ultra-mobilized and powerful armor ample opportunity to crush successive waves of Italian infantry worn down by continuous combat and entirely without resources for conducting counterattacks. Hence the motorized Germans were always able to get away in relatively good shape. In the future, Messe argued, an initial bound backward that put space between the two contending armies would make for a more orderly withdrawal. A robust motorized rearguard could form a covering force able to beat off enemy pursuit until the slower-moving units had reached a safer place, for example the strong fortified positions at Enfidaville whose jagged hills and craters were unfriendly to pursuing heavy armor.[99]

General Messe was so buoyed by the tenacity and valor of his Italian troops that he believed they endured the weight of the last battle at Enfidaville better than Germany's battalions. "One did not see the shadow of supine resignation on the faces of our troops who felt hope running out." They fought to the last as defenders of "family, home, and country."[100] Especially galling to Messe was the British predisposition to overshadow him and his warriors by creating the "myth" that Italy's "marvelous" resistance and "bloody counterattacks" were instead German characteristics.[101]

General Messe emerged from the war angry that General Montgomery in his memoirs would not credit, but only deprecate, Italian troops who actually fought hard without hope of final victory or escape from Mussolini's "Tunisgrad."[102] Colacicchi describes the encounter between Messe and Montgomery on the day of the Italian surrender. Still believing he was fighting the Desert Fox, Montgomery met Messe with "Who is this?"[103] In his memoirs Montgomery gives scant attention to Messe, but writes admiringly of the Englishman's champion, Rommel.[104] Any admission that Messe had fought valiantly would have taken luster off his victory over the celebrated Desert Fox in the ex-post facto judgments of the war by Rommel aficionados. Lord Strabolgi had earlier come to Messe's rescue in his *The Conquest of Italy*, by writing that at the end of the Axis

---

99. *Operazioni*, IV, Allegato 37, Conversation between Messe and Kesselring, 16 April 1943, pp. 734–39.

100. Messe, *La mia armata in Tunisia*, p. 289.

101. *Operazioni*, IV: p. 764.

102. Messe, *La mia armata in Tunisia*, p. 291.

103. Colacicchi, *L'ultimo fronte d'Africa*, pp. 112–17.

104. Bernard L. Montgomery, *The Memoirs of Field-Marshal Montgomery* (London and Glasgow: Fontana Monarchs, 1958), p. 187.

debacle, "the Italians fought better than the Germans. The German morale collapsed completely towards the end of the campaign."[105]

Proof exists on this point. Alan Moorehead, an eminent and discerning journalist and eyewitness, describes the horde of surrendering Germans: "The prisoners I saw—and I suppose I passed thirty thousand on this first day, mostly Germans—were not exhausted; they were not hungry or shell-shocked or wounded; they were not frightened. I saw their dumps under the trees from Soliman to Grombalia and way up the peninsula, and the weapons they had thrown away—they had ammunition and food and water; they had enough weapons and supplies to make a series of isolated stands in the mountains for weeks had they chosen to do so."[106] Moorehead goes on to reflect: "The Italians at the end showed much more initiative. Indeed, the young Fascists were indignant at several places when their German companions gave up. A few of the Italians at least wanted to fight it out, guerrilla fashion, to the death."[107] Yet we must remember that, apart from those final days, it was the Germans, not the Italians whom they outnumbered, who did the heavy lifting throughout the Tunisian campaign.

Besides the weapon inferiority on the ground, Messe suffered from a lack of air support. Since the Italian air arm was determined to go its own way, cooperation with the Luftwaffe hardly existed, depriving him of support for important ground operations or air cover during retreats. Bombing squadrons from Sicily would occasionally show up without warning and fly back after releasing their loads in empty spaces.

The navy, too, has come in for some heavy criticism on the part of contemporaries and scholars who have deplored its lack of imagination and technical ineptitude. Their censure is not far-fetched. The naval authorities failed to upgrade night fighting or to defend convoys against air attacks, anti-aircraft firepower, and anti-submarine devices like sonar and depth charges. By early 1943 the navy had only rudimentary radar and nothing to match Ultra's searching eye. As a result of primitive technology, a lot of valiant sailors went down, hapless victims in an unfair fight.

The main battle fleet, demoralized by the many disasters on the high seas and crippled by a chronic shortage of fuel oil, hardly ventured out of port during the last stages of the war. Mussolini had a hand in this. Instead of committing the fleet to provide convoy escort on the Tunisian run, he kept what capital ships were left in reserve in order to thwart any attempt at invasion of the Italian

---

105. Lord Strabolgi, *The Conquest of Italy* (London & New York: Hutchinson & Co., 1944), p. 17.
106. Alan Moorehead, *Desert War* (New York: Penguin Books, 2001), p. 626.
107. Ibid., p. 629.

coasts. But when the Allies landed in Sicily, the Italian naval commanders showed no more enterprise than they had during the North African campaign.

Rommel, throughout the campaign in North Africa, repeatedly paddled the Italian navy for failing to supply him enough equipment and troop reinforcements. During the summer and fall of 1942, he groused over the insufficient help ACIT received when the losses in navy ships were around 12.5 percent. Instead of provisioning his needy forces, the Axis power brokers in November sent over 13,302 men, 1,600 vehicles, and 17,000 tons of materiel to Tunisia. Rommel was convinced that had he been the beneficiary of the comparatively large contingent of troops and supplies earmarked for Tunisia, ACIT would have been in a position to administer a sharp defeat on Montgomery's 8th Army.

Notwithstanding its faults and deficiencies, the navy acquitted itself well in performing what had become the primary mission of ferrying over supplies and troops to Tunisia on a route infested with enemy submarines and skies dominated by Allied aircraft. The figures don't lie. Losses in maritime traffic headed for Libyan ports from November 1942 to January 1943 in gross net tonnage was about 10 percent in November, 42 percent in December, and 46 percent in January. Convoys that headed for Tunisia from November 1942 to May 1943 lost 2.5 percent in November, 16 percent in December, 14 percent in January, 20 percent in February, 16 percent in March, 31 percent in April, and 72 percent in May. In all, an average of 71 percent of materiel, trucks, tanks, and artillery, sent from Italy arrived in Tunisia—306,500 tons out of the 433,169. The amount of fuel oil that landed in Tunisia was 94,000 barrels out of 133,000 sent. From 1 December 1942 to 31 May 1943, 157,000 men, 8,500 vehicles, and at least 400 tanks and armored cars arrived in Tunisia safely.[108]

During the final moments of "Tunisgrad," Mussolini stumbled and fell as Italy's warlord, his days in power ticking away. At the beginning of January there was still time to undertake a painful reappraisal of a strategy that was leading directly to the unconditional surrender of the flower of the Italian army. But the Duce did not order a timely evacuation to avoid this disaster. If undertaken earlier in December, the two dictators might have extricated their beaten but valiant armies from Tunisia, gained a Dunkirk-like propaganda victory, preserved their dwindling resources, and consolidated their defenses on Europe's southern shore. The irony is this: from the beginning of Germany's intervention in the African campaign, Hitler and his general staff were fearful of embarking on a major expedition overseas under the guns of the British navy and unwilling to divert troops and equipment from Barbarossa. Taking half-measures to keep

---

108. *Operazioni*, IV: 569.

Mussolini in the war, they dispatched a small expeditionary corps and insufficient supplies that prevented Rommel from exploiting his partial victories, let alone deliver a knockout blow. As the curtain rang down in Tunisia, the Axis forces embarked on a lost cause by flooding the area with materiel and troops that could have been employed for a more robust defense of Europe. Had Hitler ordered the Axis troops back to Europe instead of defending Tunisia *à outrance*, however, it hardly would have mattered in the long run. Even if the Axis had conducted an exemplary campaign in North Africa by seizing the Canal, they would eventually have succumbed to the huge American war machine that was just beginning to swing into high gear.

As Hitler's resentful but unresisting subaltern, Mussolini deprived himself of the chance for an independent military strategy. The outcome of "Tunisgrad" was entirely negative: needless consumption of precious materiel, loss of the remaining merchant marine, captivity for prize units of the Italian army, and capture of his best general. In holding off inevitable calamity, Mussolini's strategy mimicked Hitler's—an irresponsible resistance for the sake of resisting—"keep afloat, persist."[109] One is tempted to say in this case that the Axis leaders, during the unfolding events of battle, should have deferred to the commanders on the spot. But would they have been better off leaving everything in the hands of Kesselring? To emerge from a no-win situation, Mussolini gave General Messe the thankless task of plugging up a dike threatened by a tidal wave. The Duce's call for resistance to the point of total exhaustion, capitulation, or certain death was the sterile and irresponsible strategy of a desperate leader paralyzed by fear of enemy capture and the hangman's noose.

---

109. Ibid.: 570.

The Tunisian Front 1942-1943.

Chapter XIII

Endgame

Whirlwind Diplomacy
Denouement

Whirlwind Diplomacy

Mussolini's hourglass began to run out in November 1942 with the Axis set-back at El Alamein and the Allied invasion of North Africa, followed in January by the calamitous defeats before Stalingrad. Rome was enveloped in gloom. Seeking a way out, Mussolini sent Ciano on 16-18 December 1942 to the Wolf's Lair, Hitler's forest headquarters in East Prussia, with the charge of urging the Führer to pursue a separate peace with Russia, thus paving the way for a new Brest-Litovsk. If Stalin should prove obdurate, a defensive line could be set up and held by a small force, enabling the Axis Powers to shift substantial troops for the decisive battles shaping up in the West and North Africa.[1]

Did Italian diplomacy have a ghost of a chance in pulling off such a miracle in Berlin? There is some evidence to suggest that Mussolini was not completely deluded. At Salzburg on 29 April 1942, Hitler had stated that his objective was limited to "annulling Bolshevism as a military power," which, if accomplished,

---

1. DDI, 9, IX, 415, Conversation between Ciano and Hitler, 18 December 1942.

would enable Germany to shift forces for a showdown against the Allies.[2] Stalin might even be ready to parley. The two dictators knew that he was concerned by the Allies' "interminable and inexcusable delay" in opening up a second front in Western Europe. And they were not wrong in perceiving Stalin's fear of being double-crossed: that the Allies would wait, before launching an amphibious landing in the West, until the two mammoth armies on the Eastern Front had slaughtered each other, thus bringing about both the destruction of Nazism and the end of the Bolshevik menace. At little cost to themselves, the Allies would find a devastated Europe at their feet.

But Hitler would not be swayed. For the unity and autarky of Europe, he informed the Italians in December, the Ukraine with its grain and minerals was indispensable.[3] He told Ciano on the 18th, during their meeting in the forest of Görlitz, that any opening toward the Kremlin was damaging and futile. Moscow would never renounce its expansionist aims in Eastern Europe and the Straits. If handed a ceasefire, the Soviets would take advantage of the pause by overhauling their mauled forces for a future assault against a Germany further weakened by the ongoing campaign against the Allies.[4]

Left unsaid was the truism that peace talks were bound to yield little if undertaken while two powerfully equipped armies were carrying out frightful vengeance against each other in a battlefield of constantly changing fortunes. There were also complicated logistics to be resolved, such as shipping large troop contingents and their mountain of supplies huge distances westward and the building of new landing fields to receive Luftwaffe squadrons flying in from the Russian front. This would take months while Mussolini was forced to think in terms of weeks. All such thorny practical considerations aside, for the uncompromising Führer nothing mattered other than "victory now" over the Soviets, the fulfillment of Lebensraum and the destruction of Jewry. Hitler's war of annihilation in the East was incompatible with compromise, which rendered Mussolini's efforts to persuade him to observe the centrality of the Mediterranean a lost cause.

During the Görlitz conference Alfieri told Ciano that the moment had arrived to break with the Germans. "Ciano looks at him with tired eyes....then lets fall these textual words: 'Nothing, nothing! It remains only to wait for the collapse.'"[5] On the evening of the 18th, a grave Ciano cabled Mussolini not to expect that Germany would ever arrive at terms with Russia.[6] News bulletins in-

---

2. Ibid., VIII, 492, Conversation between Mussolini and Hitler, 29 April 1942.
3. PP, *Diario*, 23 December 1942.
4. DDI, 9, IX, 415. 18 December 1942, Conversation between Ciano and Hitler, 18 December 1942.
5. Simoni, *Berlino ambasciata d'Italia*, p. 300.
6. Ibid., p. 299.

dicating the disintegration of the German front at Stalingrad unsettled the conference attendees. "Pansa [Mario Pansa, Italian vice chief of protocol]: 'Had our army many losses?' Hewel [Walter Hewel political adviser attached by the German foreign office to Hitler's headquarters]: 'no losses at all; they are running.' Pansa: 'As you did in Moscow last year?' Hewel: 'Exactly.'"[7]

As the barometer kept falling at remorseless speed on the Eastern Front, the "Beresina Wind," fatal to Napoleon, was blowing across Europe from the steppes of Asia to punish the Axis invaders.[8] Once again Mussolini ignored what was happening, telling Bastianini that Russia was defeated. Caught off balance, Bastianini replied: "'And yet, Duce, a month ago you told me that Russia was far from having exhausted its resources'…. The Duce nodded: 'And in fact it has advanced sixty kilometers. But that is all. Observe the symptoms are the same as in the past war when they arrived at Prezemysl and were stopped as if struck blind. They lacked then as now cannon, units were composed of men of fifty and youth under twenty years, badly equipped and badly armed.'"[9]

This nonsensical reflection reveals that Mussolini could not make up his mind on what to do. On the one hand, he wanted to prevail on Hitler to make peace with the Soviets in order to save Italy from imminent disaster in North Africa. Pietromarchi, for one, saw only harm should the Duce align "with the devil" to save his country. If Hitler has been an incautious ally, he remarked, "Stalin would be nothing other than a dominator."[10] At the same time Mussolini was very reluctant to abandon the anticipated harvest of raw materials in the Donetz Basin and the Caucasus, which were desperately needed to make the Italian factories hum again. Bilateral negotiations with the Axis partner aimed at committing Berlin to deliver a whole array of materiel—steel, iron, and oil flowing from German-controlled territory—had so far left them starving.

In the latter part of 1942 the long-dormant Palazzo Chigi took on a daunting challenge. The Romanians in December brought up with Baron Renato Bova Scoppa, the Italian minister in Bucharest, the possibility of a "Latin Axis" to include Italy, France, Spain, Portugal, and Romania—a bloc "destined to contain German expansion and Slav impulses."[11] Deputy Premier of the Romanian council Mihai Antonescu "was very explicit about the tragic condition of Germany and foresees the need for Romania and Italy to contact the Allies in order to establish a defense against the bolshevization of Europe."[12] In his view,

7. *The Ciano Diaries*, 18 December 1942. Conversation carried on in English.
8. Deakin, *The Brutal Friendship*, p. 103.
9. PP, *Diario*, 17 December 1942.
10. Ibid., 6 February 1943.
11. Deakin, *The Brutal Friendship*, p. 139.
12. *The Ciano Diaries*, 19 January 1943.

cautious preliminary steps should be taken to prevent the total disaster that would inevitably result from Hitler's obsessive desire to annihilate Russia. (Ciano gained a similar impression on the part of the Hungarians from his former chef de cabinet, Filippo Anfuso, now Italian minister in Budapest.) Ciano delivered Antonescu's ideas to Mussolini, who was not drawn to the Romanian's "overly subtle" language. He concluded: "The Danube is not the way we must follow."[13] Rather, he would "march with Germany to the end."[14] His Italian-led Danubian Union composed of Axis satellites emphatically rebuffed, Ciano had played his last card.

Ciano's wish to part from the Axis alliance was shared by the *classe dirigente*. Not unknown to Mussolini, throughout 1943 diplomats, generals, and "moderate" Fascists were devising cloak-and-dagger schemes aimed at opening peace negotiations with the Allies. But not peace at any price. As watchdogs of national unity and independence, the elite of the regime deemed "unconditional surrender" ignoble and a formula that would lead to social chaos and perhaps Communist revolution. Pietromarchi saw these disparate peace initiatives as amounting to harmless prattle that provided only "conspiratorial twaddle" since the Allies were totally unresponsive. After much hand-wringing moderate Fascists, old liberals, and military generals fell back on the hope that either the Duce would stumble on a solution, or the king would step in to save the country and reinstate conservative government. The Fascist maverick Dino Grandi had his own plan. Without informing the Duce, he schemed to bring about a consti-tutional crisis by promoting a coup, after which the king would resume his lawful military and political powers and replace Mussolini with a government that would immediately join the Allied cause. But his following was small and his influence scant.

Italy was left trapped in a no-win situation, destined to be dragged along by events to a tragic denouement. But not for any lack of effort on Ambrosio's part. To head the country into a different direction, he implored Mussolini during the 7–10 April meeting at Klessheim Castle with Hitler and his entourage to con-front the Germans with stark alternatives: they must either give priority to rein-forcing Tunisia and defending Italy by providing the necessary military aid, or Italy would be obliged to leave the alliance and ask for a separate peace. The Axis military plight, he emphasized, could be greatly eased if Hitler arrived at a truce with the Russians, following which large German forces could be shifted to the Mediterranean and arms provided to the pitifully equipped Italian military forces. For his part, Bastianini pointed out that Italy could not continue the war

---

13. Ibid., 20 January 1943.
14. Ibid., 21 January 1943.

in the face of strikes causing work stoppages in Turin and Milan and Allied bombing raids pulverizing industrial plants and railheads.

Mussolini, however, let his colleagues down. Although bravely stating, "At present Hitler has engaged in a monologue; tomorrow I will speak," the following day he hardly uttered a word.[15] His silence was understandable. Urging Hitler to ponder new approaches toward the Soviet Union would only have incurred the Führer's wrath. And since Hitler had issued orders in mid-March for a spring offensive against the Kursk salient on the Eastern Front, he was not about to oblige Italy by instigating peace talks with the hated Bolsheviks.

On a related tack, as Italy's answer to Hitler's Lebensraum and the Allies' Atlantic Charter, Bastianini pressed on Ribbentrop his "European Union," a declaration of rights for the small European nations that would assure them safety under the benign supervision of the Axis Powers. But what chance did Bastianini have when faced with Hitler's obvious unwillingness to hear any more about respect for small nations, which the Führer would consider to be sentimental rubbish? As Ribbentrop told him: "The only way that is uniquely suited to the difficult situation created by this war has been to proceed with extreme firmness and brutality. This is a war of extermination that will only be won by paying no heed to means."[16] Egidio Ortona noted that Bastianini's diplomacy was "complicated above all by a swarm of foolish and rhetorical initiatives emanating from certain environments where one speaks of a new order as if dealing with changes in railroad schedules."[17]

Bastianini's diplomacy was not only simplistic but imbued with prejudice. Like Mussolini, he bore ideological baggage that for years had dogged Italian negotiations. In urging Germany to make peace with the Soviets, Bastianini told Ribbentrop that the Axis war should be primarily waged against the Allies' monopoly of the world's resources.[18] This was not simply sand thrown in Ribbentrop's eyes but an expression of Bastianini's ageless Fascist resentment over Britain and France's refusal to share the world's riches. As one who yearned to break this Allied monopoly, Bastianini, in an aside to his Italian understudy, pointed out that the fight was against plutocracy, not Europe.[19]

These were exactly Mussolini's views. When the Allies stepped up bombardment of Italian cities, his cup of bitterness overflowed. The Duce resented the prospect that British bombers would turn Sicily and Sardinia into graveyards, thus revealing the Italian air fleet's inability to reduce Malta to rubble. Mussolini

---

15. Paolo Monelli, *Roma 1943* (Rome: Migliaresi, 1945), p. 77; Alfieri, *Face to Face*, p. 225.
16. DDI, 9, X, 203, Conversation between Bastianini and Ribbentrop, 7 April 1943.
17. Ortona, *Diplomazia di guerra*, p. 212.
18. DDI, 9, X, 210, Conversation between Bastianini and Ribbentrop, 8 April 1943.
19. PP, *Diario*, 8 April 1943.

also liked to imagine that the United States was teetering on the brink of a break-down brought on by open racial conflict between whites and blacks.[20]

The final upshot of the Salzburg talks was predictable. The Germans were put on further notice that the Italians were looking to separate from the Axis. Obviously Ambrosio wanted to cut and run, and Mussolini stood against any large influx of German troops under Wehrmacht command on Italian soil. The Duce was not unaware that Hitler intended to reduce him to a figurehead by taking over military operations. Himmler added to Germany's open mistrust by telling Mussolini that he had no more support in Italy; he therefore had nothing to lose by adopting ruthless coercion by means of an Italian SS.[21] Prompted by a rapidly deteriorating situation, Hitler ordered his generals to draw up Operations Alaric and Constantine for a military takeover of Italy and the Balkans in the event of a sudden collapse of Mussolini's government. Characterized by mounting distrust and crossed swords over strategy, the Salzburg meeting resulted in a further tear in the alliance.

In a speech on 17 April to party leaders, Mussolini took out his frustration on fellow Italians: "This backward nation is burdened by many people who are mentally, physically, and morally deficient. It is filled with blind, crippled, and toothless characters; cretins, draft dodgers, and half-wits; in sum, by those in-capable of waging war. These are the people who search for alibis to appease their consciences by decrying that this war should never have been fought. Dear comrades, we must have the courage, we who have made revolutions, to seize these defeatists by the neck and denounce them."[22] The next day Mussolini appointed Carlo Scorza to replace Vidussoni as party secretary. A tough man of action, he would reconstitute the *squadristi* to fire up the nation for a fight to the finish. Scorza boasted: "If we are going to fall, let us do it in style."[23] This attempt to resuscitate the fighting spirit of the early days was met with derision. Party propagandists were playing their tunes on a worn-out piano.

During the early summer of 1943, with defeat staring Italy down, Bastianini set ideology aside by reviving the idea of a Danubian alignment consisting of Italy, Hungary, and Romania as a prelude to sounding out the West for a com-promise peace. Supposedly the Allies would be interested in having this Italian-led bloc to stand as a bulwark against an eventual Russian attack on the Balkans. Bastianini assembled these ideas under the rubric: "The collaboration between Italy and the Danubian Countries in seeking a political solution of the war."

20. Ibid., 7 July 1943.
21. Wiskemann, *The Rome-Berlin Axis*, p. 349.
22. Cited in Bocca, *Storia d'Italia nella guerra fascista*, p. 475.
23. Ibid., pp. 475–76.

Conceived not as a challenge to Germany but as an add-on to the Axis,[24] the proposal was sent to Mussolini during the second week of June. Already under Berlin's pressure to break off from the "traitorous" Antonescu,[25] the Duce declined to mastermind a "Munich of the War," and he would not listen to the Romanian argument that they proceed alone should the Germans turn them down. For Mussolini there would be no last gamble in seeking terms from the West. Rejecting a serious offer from the Vatican to mediate a peace with the United States in May provided more proof of his intransigence.[26]

Bastianini's flurry of diplomacy was based on a mirage: that the Allies, fearing above all else the postwar domination of Europe and Italy by the Soviet Union, would welcome the support of such an Italian-led Danubian union. As an expression of their gratitude, and as a reward for breaking with the Third Reich, they would, in spite of the Casablanca formula, treat Fascist Italy as a newfound ally. When spring turned, only the most deluded still held out such hopes. As for Mussolini, he allowed Bastianini to act out his musings unimpeded.

Denouement

On 10 June the Allies landed on the Italian island of Pantelleria unopposed. How could a supposedly impregnable bastion, bristling with coastal guns and 11,000 soldiers, succumb without a fight? Ever since early May, Pantelleria had been battered unmercifully by clouds of Allied planes to soften it up for invasion. Even though the Italian troops were able to find shelter underground, their artillery suffered heavy damage, and the exposed civilians had become deprived of provisions and water. Mussolini hastily ordered the commanding officer, Admiral Pavesi, to surrender. The only military casualties were two Allied soldiers shot in error and one Italian kicked by a mule. The effect in Italy was catastrophic. Mussolini was heard to murmur: "Pantelleria is an alarm bell, I would say almost a wild ringing at the gates." When receiving the suggestion that it was time for Italy to leave the war, he replied: "Now all discussion is useless. Italy has only one alternative: to conquer or fall at the side of Germany."[27] Later, Mussolini expressed the view that Pantelleria had represented the gravest example of Italian cowardice in the war. But that did not stop him from conferring the Military Order of Savoy on the disgraced Pavesi. Pietromarchi remarked: "Promotions to marshalhood and military medals rain on the heads of

24. Ortona, *Diplomazia di guerra*, p. 243.
25. Ibid., p. 224.
26. Morgan, *The Fall of Mussolini*, p. 24.
27. Quotes above cited in Bocca, *Storia d'Italia nella guerra fascista*, p. 477.

the defeated, the conquered, and the cowardly. Thus ends the Regime."[28] A few days later the island of Lampedusa also fell without a fight.

On 24 June at the Palazzo Venezia, Mussolini presided over a meeting of the Fascist party and spoke these words: "The enemy must play his card. He has proclaimed high and low that he will invade the continent. This invasion must be attempted because otherwise he will face defeat even before fighting. Clearly this attempt will fail.... As soon as the enemy attempts to land, he will be frozen at the line the sailors call *il bagnasciuga*, that line in the sand where the water stops and land begins.... Having an iron, unshakeable, and granite will, the Fascists will prevail."[29] Many Italians laughed, for the word *bagnasciuga* means the water-line of a ship's hull; *battigia* is the word for shoreline or water's edge. Hence the speech became known derisively as the *Discorso del Bagnasciuga*. But Mussolini's meaning was clear. Filled with combative spirit, the Italian nation would stop the Allies "at the shoreline." The speech, recorded Pietromarchi, "was vigorous, of irrefutable logic, and opportune, a solemn and praiseworthy acknowledgement of the quality and solidity of the Italian people, and proof of their spirit of sacrifice. The speech represents an act of complete faith in the resistance that they will put up against the invader."[30]

To lend weight to this resolve, the CS asked the Germans for armored units to be incorporated into Italian divisions. Berlin replied tersely that if German generals were not placed in command, no Wehrmacht troops and no armaments would be handed over to the Italian army.

The Allies, in Operation Husky, launched the invasion of Sicily on 10 July. The 300,000 badly armed and ill-equipped Italian troops put up a tepid resistance, which made the Duce's summons for a defense to the knife of *la patrie en danger* in his *bagnasciuga* speech look even more ridiculous. Plagued by deplorable hygienic conditions, shabby clothing, and paltry rations, the demoralized Italian troops disappeared or deserted as their commanders accused them of lacking moral fiber. Only the *Livorno* Division, composed of troops from the mainland, acquitted itself well, as did the two tough German divisions fighting at its side. Mussolini urgently asked for Luftwaffe fighter aircraft. But once again, out of pride, he refused to request armored units that would not be incorporated in Italian divisions. For the Germans, the timing could not have been worse, since five days earlier in Russia the famous tank battle of Kursk had commenced in a fiery storm of twisted metal and smoke.

---

28. PP, *Diario*, 22 June 1943.
29. Text of the speech can be found in De Felice, *Mussolini l'alleato*, pp. 1466-79.
30. PP, *Diario*, 5 July 1943.

Terrified that Germany was dragging Italy down in flames, Bastianini, in a meeting with Mussolini on the 15th, suggested a desperate change of course by sounding out enemy intentions directly.[31] Mussolini replied that nothing should be done without German approval, and added: "I will never deliver Italy to England."[32] But when Bastianini promised to bear the full burden of responsibility, Mussolini hesitated, thus providing the undersecretary an opening to send a banker by name of Nino Fummi, who had represented the House of Morgan in Italy, to contact the Allies in London via Lisbon in the search for an exit from the war. Bastianini sought out the Holy See to play its part by telling the Allies that since Mussolini was the only person who could prevail on Hitler to withdraw troops from Italian territory, he should not be removed from power.[33] Fummi, however, could not perform this mission since he was stranded in Portugal, unable to secure a British visa before Mussolini's fall.

During these fast-paced days, the Italians and Germans planned to meet on 19 July at Villa Gaggia, near Feltre. Ambrosio prepared a letter for Mussolini to send Hitler in advance that bore some hard truths: Italy, having burned out its resources in Africa, Russia, and the Balkans, must not be the one charged with delaying the Allied offensive aimed at Germany. It behooved the two Axis partners to sort out responsibilities and find acceptable means of cooperation that would serve the interests of both countries. But Mussolini at the last minute decided not to send this forthright letter.[34]

When the Italians arrived at the villa, a labyrinthine edifice that Mussolini described as a crossword puzzle frozen into a house, the generals must have felt uneasy, for they were preparing to come out in the open against the regime. Ambrosio, for one, had been kept au courant by General Giuseppe Castellano of a plot to capture and arrest Mussolini, and Ambrosio had in turn already informed the king of a plan to depose him.[35] (Parallel to this, the king and Badoglio were putting the final touches on an agreement to form a cabinet that would replace the Fascist government.)

Nonetheless, both Ambrosio and Bastianini bravely prepared for a showdown. While Mussolini shifted idly on the sidelines, they made the point to their German interlocutors that Italy must receive massive German arms or seek Hitler's permission for a tidy withdrawal from the war. Before having a chance to press their case, the Führer harshly reprimanded them for the feeble defense of Pantelleria and Sicily; Italy, he sourly noted, would get no more equipment

31. Bastianini, *Volevo Fermare Mussolini*, Preface, p. XVI.
32. Ortona, *Diplomazia di guerra*, pp. 248–49.
33. Deakin, *The Brutal Friendship*, p. 392.
34. Corvaja, *Hitler and Mussolini*, p. 291.
35. Puntoni, *Parla Vittorio Emanuelle III*, p. 137; Deakin, *The Brutal Friendship*, p. 340.

unless placed under direct German control. In the middle of Hitler's monologue, an aide rushed into the room and whispered to the Duce: "Rome is under violent bombardment by the enemy."[36] Taking no notice of this interruption, Hitler did not break stride in his effort to inspire Mussolini with courage by telling him that Sicily could become for the enemy what Stalingrad was for Germany. Have patience, hang on, Hitler implored, for Germany was about to launch secret weapons like the V2, which would turn the tide of the war. This was exactly what he had disclosed to Mussolini in early April, a ploy that did not fail to revive his hopes. Don't waste time, Hitler advised the Duce; liquidate the traitors of Fascism and keep a careful eye on the king.

Under this salvo, an unkempt Mussolini retreated into a weary silence, unable to broach with Hitler the idea of a German armistice with Russia. In any event, Hitler, having received the doleful news of the Wehrmacht's setback in the gigantic tank battle at Kursk, would not have been persuaded to parley with the Communist adversary. Riding on the crest of victory, Stalin, he suspected, would be dismissive of any Axis-launched "peace offensive" that called for concessions to a battered German war machine. Still, the Führer was prepared to wind down his tank attack in order to send major reinforcements to Italy—but only if Mussolini placed his forces in the Mediterranean under Wehrmacht command, an abandonment of Italian sovereignty that the Duce would not tolerate.

Mussolini was similarly unwilling to ask Hitler for a release from the Axis in order to pursue a separate peace with the Allies. Even at this agonizing moment ideological conviction did not abandon him. "Democracy was a reality, a civilization to overthrow and destroy," he told a confidante Edgardo Sulis during the conference. "Bolshevism was instead only a disease, a prodigal son of democracy."[37] Even as Italy staggered toward the abyss, the Duce did not modify his view of the world divided between the Young Peoples—bearers of a new and superior morality embodied in the "proletarian nations Italy and Germany"— and the old and decrepit pluto-democracies. Hatred against Britain reached new heights because of the heavy bombardment of Italian cities.[38]

For the Italians, the conference with the Germans exposed their country's grave failings and helplessness before Hitler's arrogance and unforgiving nature. What diplomatic cards they had to play were played badly, or not at all. As for Mussolini, his rigid loyalty to ideological principle shackled innovative diplomacy. But since he was more or less an invisible figure, this hardly mattered. And

---

36. Alfieri, *Face to Face*, p. 241.
37. Cited in De Felice, *Mussolini l'alleato*, p. 1287.
38. Ortona, *Diplomazia di guerra*, p. 239.

the more "pragmatic" Ambrosio, in holding fast to ideas of a separate peace with the Allies and a gracefully negotiated withdrawal from the Axis, turned out to be merely a nuisance to stonefaced Germans. To be sure, the time had long passed for a diplomatic solution. Hitler would not let Italy withdraw from the war, and, since the Allies had locked Italy into dependency on Germany by their declared goal of unconditional surrender, neither would they.

Feeling boxed in, Mussolini confided to Alfieri: "Behind my mask of apparent indifference, there is a deep, troubling anxiety. Can you suppose that I have not long been tormented by this problem? My apparent indifference masks an intense agony of spirit. For the sake of argument, suppose we were to make a separate peace. It looks so simple. One fine day, at a specified hour, we broadcast a message to the enemy. But what would be the result? The enemy, quite justly, would demand our capitulation. Are we prepared to obliterate twenty years of Fascism at a single stroke? To undo all that we have achieved by so much unremitting effort? To acknowledge our first military and political defeat? To vanish from the international scene? It's so easy to talk about a separate peace. But what would Hitler's attitude be? Can you believe that he would allow us to retain our freedom of action?"[39] Unwilling to accept the seriousness of Sicily's loss, Mussolini hoped to hang on until Germany's secret weapons reversed the course of the war, just as he had expected the Third Reich to invade Britain and Rommel to reach the Canal, thus winning the war for Italy. In a meeting that featured a battle between Hitler and Ambrosio for influence over the spiritless Duce, the Führer had easily prevailed.

Mussolini returned to Rome where he had to deal with an unhappy people afflicted by Allied bombing. Their desire to put an end to the war was stronger than the humiliation of losing it. Seized by a feeling of impotence, they were exhausted, resigned, and apathetic. But since depressed peoples generally do not flock to the streets demanding revolutionary changes, Mussolini did not have to worry about massive demonstrations against him or a violent overthrow. Italians who were prepared to wait on events merely reinforced the Duce's contempt. But he, in turn, had earned their contempt by his failure of nerve to face Hitler down. The warlord, who supposedly left for Feltre to find a way out of Italy's predicament, "returned a wreck of a man."[40] He had done nothing to ward off Italy's exposure to death and destruction, for it was now a battleground between the invading Allies and the fanatical Germans.

Faced with a floundering Duce, many Fascists and a vast majority of the people knew it was time for him to go. Small cabals behind the scenes drew

---

39. Alfieri, *Dictators Face to Face*, p. 246.
40. PP, *Diario*, 24 July 1943.

daggers. Still, all eyes were on the king to make the first move. Although no one was prepared to act without his consent, impatience was mounting. Ambrosio and Castellano despaired over their sovereign's constant hemming and hawing. Finally, forced by the pressure of events to take a position, the king decided on the evening of the 19th to withdraw his support from Mussolini—the same day that the Duce, in response to a request by a group of Fascists a week earlier, had issued a call for the Grand Council of Fascism to meet on the 24th. Ambrosio and Castellano went to Badoglio's splendid villa, given to him by Mussolini for having gassed his way to victory over Ethiopia, to say that the king was preparing to cashier the Duce, and that he, Badoglio, would replace him. According to Puntoni, on the 22nd the king told him that he had tried to reason with the Duce: "only his persona….stood in the way of internal recovery…. He did not understand, or he did not want to understand. It was as if I had spoken to the wind."[41]

The Fascist Grand Council meeting, which started at 5:00 p.m. on the 24th, sprang no surprises. Dino Grandi, who many days before had shared his intentions with co-conspirators, was prepared to challenge the Duce. His program envisaged the abolishment of Mussolini's dictatorship and the immediate re-activation of the authority and functions of the state's traditional and collegial organs: the Council of Ministers, the Grand Council, and the Chamber. The king would resume his constitutional powers. Of equal importance, Mussolini would be required to hand back command of the armed forces, which he had usurped in 1940, to the crown. By a nineteen-to-eight vote with two abstentions, the Duce's comrades passed Grandi's motion. The Fascist system that rested on the principle of charismatic leadership by an infallible Duce had been abruptly ended.

Mussolini returned home in the wee hours of the 25th where he was told by his wife to arrest the traitors. Although ignoring this advice, the Duce was not yet finished, for he had convinced himself that the Grand Council's order of the day was only advisory, not binding, which left him room for maneuver.[42] Unaware that he was about to be detained by order of the king and military, Mussolini contrived a plan of using the Grand Council vote against him for leverage in Berlin. Since he had nothing to lose, he would salvage survival from the wreckage of Italian military defeats and draw renewed hope from a seemingly lost war by urging Hitler yet again to re-orient his primary military effort toward the Allies. This time Mussolini would add the ultimate threat: unless Germany made peace with Russia, Italy would withdraw from the war. On the chance that

41. Puntoni, *Parla Vittorio Emanuele III*, p. 142.
42. Monelli, *Roma 1943*, pp. 183, 185.

the Führer should yield, he would be able to utilize such a stunning switch in Axis military priorities to demand that the Grand Council reverse its vote stripping him of power.

To reinforce this tortuous undertaking, Mussolini looked to the Japanese for support. Seeking relief from Anglo-American pressure in Asia, Japan, as far back as March 1942, had aimed at bringing Germany and Russia to a peace accord by acting as a mediator, but had been flatly turned down by Berlin.[43] It appears from Japanese sources that Mussolini, in his talks with Hitler at Klessheim in April 1943, had pointed out that Japan was prepared to offer its good offices between the Axis Powers and Russia, but these were once more put off by Berlin.[44]

Mussolini and the new Japanese ambassador Shinrokuro Hidaka took up this idea yet again on 25 July 1943 soon after the Grand Council meeting.[45] According to the Italian summary of the meeting: "He [Mussolini] had repeatedly attempted, on various occasions, to make the Führer understand the need for political solutions but nevertheless had not succeeded in persuading him.... The Duce had therefore decided that in the course of the coming week, he would undertake an energetic approach to the Führer to draw his most serious attention to the situation that had recently developed, and to induce the Führer, as he had already attempted to do on previous occasions, to cease hostilities on the Eastern Front and thus arrive at a settlement with Russia. Once this had been obtained, the Reich would be able to bring the whole weight of its military potential to bear against the Anglo-Americans in the Mediterranean, and thus restore a situation that today was undoubtedly compromised." In this endeavor, Mussolini asked for the support of Hideki Tojo, the president of the Japanese Council: "Otherwise the conditions in which Italy was fighting were such that she would, in a short space of time, find herself absolutely unable to continue hostilities and would be obliged to examine a solution of a political character."[46] Göring, the least enthusiastic German of high standing for the continuation of the war on Russia, was another ally the Duce hoped to enlist in his campaign to put pressure on Hitler.

43. De Felice, *Mussolini l'alleato*, pp. 1290–1.

44. Deakin, *The Brutal Friendship*, p. 269.

45. De Felice, *Mussolini l'alleato*, p. 1387 and n. 2. According to De Felice, the Duce spoke of the Germans in the harshest tones, defining them as "stupid madmen.... The next time I see Hitler I will tell him clearly and categorically that he must conclude the fight against Russia. And I ask you Japanese to do the same. Tell him [Hitler] to wind it up. It is possible that we together can succeed in wrenching this obsession from Hitler's mind. If we still hope to win this war, we must do it." As Eugenio Di Rienzo and Emilio Gin point out, in their article "Quella mattinia del 25 luglio 1943, Mussolini, Shinrokuro Hidaka e il progetto di pace separate con L'URSS," *Nuova rivista storica*, XCV, 95, n. 1 (January–July 2011), p. 27, n. 74, De Felice here was referring to other decrypts dated 31 July and 4 August 1943.

46. DDI, 9, X, 551, Conversation between Mussolini and Hidaka, 25 July 1943.

Mussolini had also taken renewed heart from the current buzz in diplomatic corridors over German and Russian agents secretly discussing a cease-fire or separate peace on the Eastern Front. Perhaps the Führer was at long last ready to change course. But, since Mussolini had always shied away from confronting the Führer directly on the matter,[47] would he have been emboldened to do so if given another chance?

The fact remains, however, that no matter how much Rome or other European capitals feasted on such rumors—or how many people in Berlin were desperately searching for a way out of pending disaster in the East—the appalling German-inflicted sufferings on the Soviet people and prisoners-of-war, superimposed on the devouring distrust and unmitigated hatred between the Nazi and Communist regimes, had rendered any viable diplomatic settlement unattainable. Mussolini's hope that Hitler would bend to his arguments by shifting the epicenter of the war from the Russian front to the Mediterranean would therefore once again have been garroted by the Führer's single-minded-ness. Nor could the Duce ever have managed a dignified withdrawal of Italy from the war without charge of betrayal or violent retribution. In any event, the press of time denied Mussolini his hoped-for meeting with Hitler.

On 25 July the king finally summoned the courage to take decisive action. During an afternoon meeting with Mussolini, after observing that he was the most hated man in Italy, the king dismissed him as head of government. As the unnerved Duce exited, expecting to be met by his chauffeur, he was accosted by a group of Carabinieri who, by prearrangement, whisked him off to prison. His old friend Manlio Morgagni, director of the Agenzia Stefani, shot himself dead in grief, leaving the following note: "The Duce has resigned. My life is finished. *Viva Mussolini!*"[48] But his was practically a lone act, for the departure of Musso-lini from the government and the end of the regime were greeted by celebrations throughout the country. Former hard-nosed Fascists slunk into the shadows to escape retribution. On receiving the news, Hitler in a fit of temper prepared to punish the Italians by invading their country. To avert this calamity, Badoglio, the newly appointed prime minister, issued the order: "the war goes on."

---

47. Ibid., 95, 9 March 1943, Mussolini to Hitler, 9 March 1943, and 158, 26 March 1943, 159, Mussolini to Hitler, 26 March 1943.
48. Cited in Farrell, *Mussolini*, p. 406.

Chapter XIV

The Warlord's Legacy

Crackup of the Empire
The Duce and the Military: An Uneasy Partnership
Mussolini's Enslavement to Hitler

Crackup of the Empire

Ever since coming to power, Mussolini had contemplated empire. Italy would be master of the Mediterranean, sandwich Libya between Tunisia and Egypt, and carve out "living space" in the Balkans. And that was only the beginning. But the Western Powers stood in his way. Since Mussolini had despaired of cajoling or intimidating them into sharing their imperialist real estate, he would take what he wanted by force. During the 1920s Italy was far too weak for anyone to fear his warlike rants. But when Hitler came into power, it appeared that the Duce's dreams might be fulfilled through alignment with the kindred regime of the Third Reich against Italy's erstwhile and "decadent" allies of World War I. Although Mussolini recognized the peril to Italy of a runaway Nazi Germany, the expansionist impulse caused him to throw caution to the winds. In profiting from Germany's victories against the Western Powers, he would fulfill Fascist Italy's imperialist destiny.

But that was not to be. Mussolini launched wars against France, Britain, Yugoslavia, and Greece that turned out to be disasters. The Italian nation was in no position to initiate military operations anywhere, and the Duce's absurd leadership did not address the mountain of obstacles he faced. Fought under the banner of a "parallel war," Italy's attack on Greece resulted in humiliating losses and accomplished nothing more than to make clear that hereafter Italy would perform military duty as Germany's subaltern. But the Duce would not be stopped. After having been battered on one front, he would hurl troops in another, and then still another, until bogged down or in retreat everywhere. Incapable of learning from his mistakes, Mussolini threw away the lives of his soldiers and his country's resources in wars that had little to do with Realpolitik or national interest.

Whatever the obstacles, Mussolini was adamant in pursuing a "New Mediterranean World," a euphemism for imperial penal colonies of oppression and economic plunder. This was, however, a job that could only have been completed under cover of Hitler. In Mussolini's incomplete empire, those whom the Italians conquered experienced a humiliating life as helots. There was only one escape hatch for the occupied peoples: a willingness to become exemplary Italians through assimilation. But the vast majority refused to give up their own culture and way of life, and thus had to take comfort in mere survival as suppressed peoples. Mussolini's efforts to expand Italy's empire heroically by war resulted in heavy destruction of much of the Balkans and a profusion of deaths. Under Mussolini (and, later, Badoglio), 355,000 Italians died in battle, yielded to wounds, or breathed their last in captivity.[1]

The Duce and Military: An Uneasy Partnership

The old values, as found in the code of Italian military honor, preached that an officer was a gentleman. Decorum, courtliness, professional competence, deference, and respect toward both enemy and ally meshed humanity with firmness. World War I destroyed many of these chivalrous attitudes, and colonial wars in Africa obliterated them altogether. In Ethiopia, the Fascist regime, by affirming Italian domination, had discarded every compromise solution with "inferior peoples." The military was given the task of conquering, pacifying, and breaking any resistance by force of arms and terror. There would be no pity in the suppression of "backward" black peoples. To eliminate hidden rebels, informants, and spies, the Italian generals were bent on forcing them out in the

---

1. Sullivan, "The Italian Soldier in Combat," p. 205

open by making dwelling places uninhabitable. Such a cruel approach could only be undertaken if the troops comported themselves with the pride of conquerors imbued with a sense of spiritual and cultural superiority. Eventually the army generals turned the imperial Roman civilizer of Italian mythology into the barbarian their propaganda depicted as characteristic of the partisan warrior. Having experienced without protest a long period of implementing Mussolini's hateful policies toward Africans, it is no wonder that they fit snugly in a Fascist environment. They fawned before the Duce to harvest promotions, medals, and personal glory in Italy's far-flung war theaters.

There is no doubt that the Fascist regime aided and abetted the cruelty that is inherent in counterinsurgency warfare and fostered a culture of violence that would make the homicidal instinct a normal one. Mussolini made a point of enticing his warriors to feel a fraternity with Fascism through a shared veneration of war and conquest. At the same time, he grudgingly respected the autonomy of the military. He had neither the daring nor the resources to bend the military to his Fascist lifestyle by subjecting the soldiers to close political scrutiny. Nonetheless, the soldiers shared many of the Duce's prejudices, such as his views on the barbarous nature of African and Slav peoples. This prejudice did not originate with him. Many European armies, in the scramble for colonies at the turn of the century, waged inhumane imperialist wars toward native peoples around the globe and handed down such notions to the latecomers in the game, Germany and Italy. "We proceeded systematically, village by village, and we destroyed the houses, filled up the wells, blew down the towers, cut down the shady trees, burned the crops and broke the reservoirs in punitive devastation."[2] These were the words not of an Italian general or *squadristi* leader but of Winston Churchill taking part in "a lot of jolly little wars against barbarous peoples" during the turn of the century.[3]

Compared to the constant hectoring the Nazis inflicted on the Wehrmacht, Fascist Italy's military propaganda was sporadic and lacking the well-defined ideology that shaped the Nazi Weltanschauung. Also absent was a powerful and well-organized bureaucracy to impose discipline and conformity. Nor were there SS or Communist-style political commissars looking over the shoulders of the Italian officers and troops to make sure they were closely adhering to party principles. This placed limits on Fascism's ability to indoctrinate the troops.

---

2. Title of chapter 2 of Richard Toye's book, *Churchill's Empire* (New York: Henry Holt, 2010).

3. Johann Hari, "The Two Churchills: The man who led the charge against Hitler had his own disturbing history of conquest, racism and brutality," a review of *Churchill's Empire*, by Richard Toye, *New York Times Book Review*, 15 August 2010, p. 11.

Simply put, the average Italian soldier was not naturally disposed to be an indomitable Fascist warrior. He was not happy to be drafted and showed little stomach for military service, let alone performing duty on firing squads against all and sundry so-called partisan suspects. Bewildered by his presence in a bitter insurgency, the soldier was unsure of the reasons for war. Unaware that he was an aggressor bringing war to a land of which he knew little, he thought mainly about survival and getting out alive. Most Italian troops, fighting without a clear sense of ideological mission, felt no great ardor for the principles underlying Mussolini's imperialist surge. Bastianini confided to Ciano: "Except for the Militia our armed forces are deplorable. They show no energy and no spirit."[4] This is an unfair charge, for many Italian soldiers, compelled to fight in wretched conditions, and feeling that they were flinging arrows against steel, comported themselves well. In fact, their incompetent generals and not a few officers failed to match their durability and perseverance. Brian Sullivan summarizes: "That he [the Italian soldier] fought for an evil cause in 1940–1943 is incontestable. That he fought heroically is undeniable."[5]

Still, the ordinary Italian soldier more than occasionally engaged in abominable behavior toward the occupied peoples. This derived not so much from Fascist indoctrination aimed at convincing him that he represented a "master race" as from duty and the need to get on with the ugly business of putting down an implacable rebellion that enjoyed widespread civilian support. Before having to face the partisan insurgency, he was unexpectedly immersed in the terrible cycle of death and destruction wrought by sectarian strife, which, confirming images handed down over generations of the "dark and gloomy Balkans," left him with the fear that he would be a victim of unseen hostile and wild brutes bent on torture and massacre. No Fascist missionary could do what battlefield experiences accomplished in extinguishing human pity from the hearts of many Italian soldiers. In their mind, "counterinsurgency" violence was justified, because they were dealing with combatants who in their view observed no law of war and abided no ethical principle.

Neither were the generals, on the whole, "fascistized" in the sense demanded by Farinacci and his gang of ultras. Although they hardly needed Mussolini to persuade them that their country had the duty and right to expand the empire, the generals did not consider themselves a phalanx of indoctrinated Fascists determined to build a New Order on the graveyard of destroyed Slavic civilizations. Nor did they feel kinship with the Blackshirt units attached to their divisions. Quite the contrary, to a man they were irritated by the behavior of the

---

4. *The Ciano Diaries*, 15 March 1942.
5. Sullivan, *The Italian Soldier in Combat*, p. 205.

rogue militia legions, whose wanton violence violated their notions of methodical repression. Many beseeched Rome to recall the Blackshirts. In the main, the generals were hard-boiled, old school imperialists who looked disapprovingly as a wave of Fascists poured into the annexed provinces to govern in the image of the Duce in Rome.

In line with the traditional notion that the Italian military remained a law unto itself, Giorgio Rochat defines the relationship between the *regio esercito* and Fascism during the war as an "alliance." According to this view, the army essentially supported Mussolini in a tacit understanding whereby the officers would refrain from involvement in politics and the regime would not encroach on their space. This resulted in a certain military accommodation, manifested in the adoption of Fascist rituals and practices, such as the *passo romano*, songs, gymnastics, inflammatory circulars, and obligatory party membership decreed in 1940.[6] One by one, as Rochat notes, these doings amounted to small potatoes but together made a visual impression. Still, through this *conformismo di facciata* the military was able to ward off substantive Fascist reforms, with one major exception. With deplorable submissiveness, the officers accepted without protest the Duce's orders to eliminate Jews from the ranks of the armed forces.[7]

Nonetheless, twenty years of Fascist rule resulted to a certain extent in the *Gleichschaltung* (political coordination) of the military. Since the officers shared a common culture, aspirations, and values of the middle classes—and, above all a fierce hatred and fear of Communism—the military became an "ally" of Fascism. As the Italian historian Osti Guerrazzi shrewdly observes, there was a team spirit between the military and regime that sometimes carried collaboration beyond "alliance."[8]

From the regime's point of view, the "alliance" that existed was born of necessity, not choice. Throughout his reign, Mussolini and his Fascist cohorts held the military in disdain. Heralding the Fascist showman Achille Starace for his agility in jumping through rings of fire, they were repelled by the flabby physique of many generals and contemptuous of their stiff, old-fashioned ways. Annoyed by the arrogance of his generals, Mussolini viewed the military as the bedrock of the monarchy and an expression of the despised conservative classes. Mired in the past, they were unable to adapt themselves to modern times. There was only one remedy: Fascistization. To lessen the distance between officers and common soldiers, the Duce and the radical Fascists around him yearned to inculcate a true comradeship, a more "frequent and cordial" rapport.

---

6. Rochat, *Le guerre italiane*, pp. 191–95; 248–49.
7. Giovanni Cecini, *I soldati ebrei di Mussolini. I militari israeliti nel periodo fascista* (Milan: Mursia, 2008), pp. 114–15.
8. Osti Guerrazzi, *Il Regio esercito italiano in Slovenia*, p. 95.

General Ambrosio showed that he was initially not opposed to reforms by encouraging initiatives from below. But in the end he shrank from such radical departures from army tradition. Mitigating formalism, he believed at heart, would result in subalterns who showed a lack of respect toward their superiors. His generals shared this view. On 20 November one day after the Soviets unleashed Operation Uranus, General Zanghieri, commander of the 2nd Army Corps, read his troops passages from the "old school" handbook regarding appropriate relations between officers and troops: "Respect the formalities scrupulously with clear-headed communications and direct relations. No familiarity when not on duty. Camaraderie and comprehension yes, but exercised tactfully. Pay heed to hierarchy and the vestments of authority."[9] The old authoritarian spirit of General Cadorna having prevailed, Mussolini fell far short of either replacing the military hierarchy with Fascist militia or in infusing a Fascist spirit in the comportment of the troops.

Like Mussolini, the military failed lamentably in upgrading equipment and battlefield strategy. The regime and military bowed before industrial manufacturers whose factories produced ineffectual armaments in small amounts at inflated prices. For a regime that boasted about modernization, both Mussolini and his generals showed a remarkable inability to grasp the importance of technology and resources. Until it was too late the army neglected medium tanks, the navy disdained radar, and the air force opposed the all-metal monoplane fighter. Inadequate training, doctrinal lethargy, and a rigid-top-to-bottom command structure stifled individual creativity on the part of the officers and produced a junior officer corps incapable of making wise decisions during shifts in the tide of battle. The imperviousness of the regime and the resistance of much of Italian industry to modernization explain many of the technical failings of the military. Mussolini and his generals covered up this flagrant irresponsibility by putting major emphasis on élan and will power, hoping that would carry the day against their better-armed and better-equipped opponents.

Generals Messe and Roatta stood out among the few major military reformers in the Italian army during World War II. Messe had perhaps the easier task in retraining ill-taught troops for what was still traditional warfare. Roatta's mission was more challenging, for he had to craft an entirely new combat mission, counterinsurgency, with which his troops had no familiarity. His circular of 1 March 1942, bristling with didactic instructions on how to improve fighting skills, outlined novel tactics and maneuvers by smaller units

---

9. Scotoni and Filonenko, *La disfatta*, D. 86, Zinghieri directive, pp. 293–94, 20 November 1942.

in commando-style action against a mobile and unseen enemy.[10] What seemed higher on the to-do list of the typical general, however, was to toughen up the troops. That good-natured soldiers should mingle easily with the local inhabitants, whom they were supposed to oppress, annoyed many an Italian commander for their failure to "feel" the war.[11] If the troops lacked the certainty of victory, the Italian conqueror would lose the respect of the enemy.[12] Lassitude and sloppy deportment, Roatta sternly wrote, must yield to a "forbidding face" and a steely determination to destroy the enemy.[13] In June 1942 Roatta issued Circular 5C on the organization of the Italian forts. "In general the defensive works are abysmal and *absolutely unworthy of a modern army*. Some, although having been worked on for months, are not up to what sturdy troops are able to do in two hours."[14] But beating combativeness into troops who lacked rigorous training and were too easily duped and captured was a tough chore. Against the more reliant and ideologically motivated opponent, could the typical Italian recruit far from home reply with equal ardor? As matters turned out, instead of taking pains to retrain their troops, most army generals passed time disparaging them.

Just as the generals hardly moved to overcome incompetence and technical backwardness, they took few measures to address the deepening corruption that sapped morale and effectiveness. An army report of 1943 denounced a vast contraband commerce in currency, foodstuffs, animal furs, spirits, cigarettes, and leather that shamefully enriched privileged insiders while causing resentment among the less well-placed, who were "constrained to see but not touch."[15] Clad in shoddy boots and tattered clothes, the troops took on a ragged and dissolute appearance. Without adequate medical care and faced with a dwindling supply of food and equipment, morale sank and the troops turned to theft, speculation, and the black market to provide for their needs. All this rendered the troops a far cry from the ideal demanded by the officers, let alone the *uomo nuovo* whom the regime wished to showcase. Frequently generals lectured their officers to uphold military dignity and emphasize the victor's superiority by a tidy appearance and

10. A copy of the 3C Memorandum, a small booklet, can be found in AVII, b. 93, f. 1. It is reproduced in Massimo Legnani, "Il 'ginger' del generale Roatta: Le diretrive della 2ª armata sulla repressione antipartigiana in Slovenia e Croazia," in *Italia contemporanea*," 209–210 (December 1997–March 1998): 159–74.
11. S. Bianchini and F. Privitera, *6 aprile 1941: L'attacco italiano alla Jugoslavia* (Milan: Marzorati, 1993), p. 72.
12. NAW, T-821, 000395, 71, Ambrosio to the XI Army Command, 26 September 1941.
13. Teodoro Sala, "Guerriglia e controguerriglia in Jugoslavia nella propaganda per le truppe occupanti italiane (1941–1943)," in Sala, *Il fascismo italiano e gli Slavi del sud*, pp. 45–68; Enzo Collotti, *L'Europa nazista: Il progetto di un nuovo ordine europeo (1939–1945)* (Florence: Giunti, 2002), p. 266.
14. Cited in Osti Guerrazzi, *Il Regio esercito italiano in Slovenia*, p. 52.
15. Ibid., p. 56.

proper deportment. But many officers themselves were hardly role models, given their forays into corruption and licentiousness.

As Italy marched from defeat to defeat, the generals began to question Mussolini's disposition to wage senseless wars that had brought the country to its knees. The Duce's dismissal of Badoglio, who was popular among the generals, and the hiring of Cavallero, deemed a "Fascist general" who, decidedly, was not one of them, marked a parting of the ways.[16] The generals were further incensed by Mussolini's habit of foisting responsibility on them for the humiliating Greek disaster while covering up the real culprits, Ciano and Farinacci.[17] But as long as the king stayed in the shadows, they—Fascists, *fiancheggiatori*, the apolitical, or anti-Fascists—would obediently follow orders, for any action taken against Mussolini would have constituted a revolt against the sovereign. Nonetheless, as Osti Guerrazzi reminds us, we should not assume that the military held an undying loyalty to the crown. Until disaster struck Italian armies on all fronts in early 1943, the military had become used to promotions and medals handed out directly by the Duce, not the monarch, who during the war had remained in the background. In their memoirs, the generals obsess about Mussolini but barely mention the king.[18]

Notwithstanding the king's fading from view during the war, however, the generals, if put to the choice between Mussolini and the crown, would have opted for Victor Emmanuel III. They were, at heart, monarchists, not dyed-in-the-wool Fascists.

The Duce's Enslavement to Hitler

In spite of his many anti-German tirades, Mussolini sacrificed his country to the German colossus in the belief that he would end up as Hitler's equal in an Axis-dominated world. In the process he would become the revered leader of a warrior nation welded together by unflinching devotion. But the outcome for his "totalitarian Fascism" was not a happy one. Having tottered into the war sclerotic and hidebound, Italy, much to the Duce's disgust, turned out to be only a sad replica of a Führer state.

Responsibility for Italy's enduring loyalty to Hitler, however, was not Mussolini's alone. Complicity nationwide allowed Nazi Germany to decide Italy's fate because Hitler's helping hand was conceived to be needed in expanding the

---

16. Ibid., p. 127.
17. Ibid., p. 58.
18. Ibid., p. 100.

empire. No more need be said about the obvious pro-Nazi predisposition of a small hard-core group of diehard Fascists from the petit bourgeois classes. The upper crust too, despite its fear and dislike of Nazis, was drawn to the Third Reich by what it perceived to be qualities embodied in Hindenberg and Prussia: individual discipline, devotion to the commonweal, and self-sacrifice. Real kinship was provided by a common hatred of liberalism and Communism—evils to be destroyed in alliance with Hitler if need be. When the true Nazi essence emerged gradually from a conservative and reactionary matrix into blatant nihilism during the war, many of these same Italians hurried to disassociate themselves from the Third Reich, claiming that their original image of Nazism had been distorted. Nazism was not the legacy or prolongation of pan-Germanism, as they had once understood, but an unprecedented form of racist imperialism that had caught them by surprise. Mario Luciolli spoke for many when he stated: "The undeniable wrong of Fascism was its support of German dynamism without having the vaguest idea of its real nature."[19]

Coming from someone who had denied the destructive features of Hitler's Weltanschauung because he did not want to doubt his own Fascist creed, Luciolli's comment seems more an apologia than an explanation. The German historian Jens Petersen points out that Mussolini, his disciples, and the Italian ruling classes could not plead ignorance or incomprehension of Hitler's ambitions, for irrefutable evidence about Nazi atrocities piled up on their desks during the course of the war that simply could not be dismissed as Allied propaganda.[20]

Certainly, many highly placed moderate Fascists were aware of Nazi barbarism and had deeply mixed feelings over tying Italy's fate to Germany. Such "respectable" Fascists as Pietromarchi, enamored of the glittering achievements of the Italian Renaissance, felt a decided cultural superiority over a coarse and uncivilized Nazi Germany. As opposed to the base essence of Lebensraum outlined in *Mein Kampf,* Pietromarchi firmly believed that Fascist Italy was engaged in a civilizing mission that emphasized the *latinità* of Roman imperialism. At the same time, he felt acute pain over Italian military inferiority and fashioned an image of the Axis ally as a greedy bully. Anxiety over the real aims of German expansion and suspicion over what place would be reserved for Italy in the New European Order characterized Rome's relationship with the Third Reich from the Pact of Steel down to Mussolini's fall from power. In early March 1938

---

19. Mario Donosti (Mario Luciolli), *Mussolini e l'Europa. La politica estera fascista* (Rome: Leonardo, 1945), p. 79.
20. Jens Petersen, "Italia e Germania: due immagini incrociate," in Francesca Ferrantini Tosi, Gaetano Grassi, Massimo Legnani, eds., *L'Italia nella seconda guerra mondiale e nella resistenza* (Milan: Franco Angeli, 1988), pp. 45–63.

Pietromarchi wrote: "We are prisoners of the Germans, tied to our worst enemy for fear of being struck down by him—a situation both humiliating and embarrassing."[21] Reading the tea leaves incorrectly, Mussolini found his destiny: to stand or fall with the Führer. Thoughts of a separate peace occurred to him, but only fleetingly; there would be no changing sides for one who followed Hitler's lead out of ideological belief, fatalism, fear, or a lingering hope that Germany would pull off a miracle by staging a last-minute rally for a come-from-behind win with an array of new miracle weapons.

It is abundantly clear that Nazis in general belittled Fascists. Whatever his own anti-German sentiments, however, Mussolini had to accept the Third Reich in order to have the Axis carry out Italy's war aims. In turn Hitler felt that he had to prop up Mussolini to avoid a Fascist collapse that would badly tarnish the reputation of the Axis. Since Italy's destiny was wrapped up with Hitler's, Mussolini was ready to toast every Wehrmacht victory if it paid off in the advancement of Italian imperialism. But when the German armies stumbled, he took delight in seeing Hitler taken down a peg or two. Still, along with many radical Fascists, Mussolini admired Hitler and invariably was buoyed by him when his own élan flagged. The two men were drawn together spiritually since *il duce* wished to do with Italians what Hitler was brilliantly doing with Germans: creating a totalitarian nation of hardened and disciplined warriors.

Although both felt bonded by a blood vow of solidarity, the two dictators acted toward each other in distinctive ways owing to their country's far different war-making capacities. Hitler, though esteeming the Duce, lied to him, while Mussolini, mesmerized by Nazi power and totally reliant on the Third Reich for his program of conquest, swallowed his fear of the Führer. Ultimately the Duce chose to link Italy's fate with Germany from a position of weakness. Driven by precepts of war and empire-building, he ignored national interests that dictated a foreign policy of limited aims consonant with Italy's paucity of natural resources and an underdeveloped industry incapable of supplying the armed forces with the sinews of modern warfare. Hitler, on the other hand, dealt with Mussolini from a position of overwhelming strength. Doubtless, the Führer thought that Germany would benefit from having Mussolini as an ally, first in 1939-40, then in 1942 when he needed troop reinforcements on the Eastern Front. With a mighty war machine and a militarized nation behind him, he enjoyed having the Duce on board for sentimental reasons, for his fellow dictator once had been an inspiration and beacon of light. Whatever the power disparities between the two countries, Mussolini and Hitler were attracted to each other by a shared fascina-

---

21. *I diari e le agende di Luca Pietromarchi*, diary entry 18 March 1938, p. 108.

tion for war, a common antipathy toward the Western Democracies, and an insatiable ambition to dominate. In the absence of any scruples, both men fell victim to their greed for unlimited power.

One important dividing line between Hitler and Mussolini in the areas that they had conquered was the ultimate fate of Jews living in occupied lands. Luca Pietromarchi records over and over in his diary the horror he felt over the Holocaust and the Nazi destruction of European life and culture. Most Italians agreed. When braced up by his subordinates, Mussolini himself episodically showed courage in standing against the Nazi order to turn Jews over for shipment to the gas chambers. Humbling Jews by undisguised discrimination, which had become accepted practice in Fascist Italy, is unacceptable by any code of public conduct, but this did not turn into complicity in the German Holocaust throughout the occupied territories.

Although both Führer and Duce wrote new and terrible chapters in the history of imperial conquest, they envisioned the Axis New Order somewhat differently. Hitler's plan was to annihilate inferior races. In this he made a successful beginning but did not have time to settle conquered territory with the master race. Mussolini stopped far short of outright massacre—except for Africans, a notable exception—but frequently talked about clearing out native peoples for Italian settlement. World War II provided him the opportunity to realize Fascism's goal of reinventing European civilization. Against the Western Powers, Mussolini was ready to fight with no holds barred. Whereas Hitler planned to occupy the apex in the "New Europe" hierarchy of peoples and aimed at world domination, the Duce would preside as an emperor over the Mediterranean and the Balkans. While the single-minded Hitler demonstrated a boundless capacity for evil, Mussolini's absences of morality made him appear by comparison a charlatan. Hitler reveled in homicide and for that was idolized by a large hypnotized following, while Mussolini ruled a people that still needed a thorough whipping to participate in pogrom-style violence.

As opposed to the majority of the Italian people, war, for Mussolini, was the normal condition of life. The Fascist *uomo nuovo* was expected to thrive as a fierce warrior. Driven by this article of faith, Mussolini hoped to throw troops into battle who bore a spiritual belief in ultimate victory and were steeped in relentless hatred of the enemy.[22] When the adversary replied in the same coin, Mussolini brimmed over with pride and accomplishment. Fascism provided the impetus: "It is evident that the character of this war is exactly one of religion. There will be booty, of which we will have our share….but this war's preeminent

---

22. *OO*, XXXI, 2 December 1942, p. 130; 3 Jan 1943, p. 144.

character is defined by principle. In this war, victory will be won by armies animated by profound faith."[23]

In the end Mussolini's glorifaction of war and the savagery of which he was capable made him much worse than an uncompromising radical Fascist imperialist. Black Africans and Arabs suffered from large-scale killings and apartheid; some 30,000 Slovenes were driven off their lands into filthy concentration camps; and the Balkan peoples were intermittently subjected to indiscriminate killing. Mussolini's Fascism held that the experience of war would eradicate residual pernicious traits in the national character like laziness, whining, and flightiness, and that hatred would supplant sentimentality and pietism. The Duce intended to normalize the killer instinct by depicting war as a continuation of the "surgical violence" that had characterized *squadrismo*. His life's work would be accomplished when the Italian people had become thoroughly inculcated with a "warrior conscience" and conducted themselves pitilessly toward opponents of the regime both at home and abroad.

An admirer of force, an atheist in a Catholic country, Mussolini was both presumptuous and vain and became increasingly corrupted by power. His judgment regarding his subordinates was flawed, and he surrounded himself with dishonest followers and profiteers. Instead of welding his cohorts together as a capable team to wage efficient warfare, he played them off against one another, thus assuring fragmented authority and administrative disharmony. Men of talent were rarely seen among the crew forging an empire. Bottai noted on the eve of the fateful Grand Council meeting: "It is no longer a question of 'betraying' or not 'betraying' but of having the courage to confess the treachery that he [Mussolini] has committed, going on day by day, from the first delusion to this moral collapse. There was not one idea, one agreement, one institution, or one law to which he has remained faithful. Everything has been broken, distorted, corrupted by him, in the wake of a conceited yet cunning empiricism, founded on a contempt for men and their ideals."[24] Pietromarchi wrote later: "The makeup of this man can be summarized in two words: brain-damage and cowardice. From the end of the Ethiopian campaign, of the old Mussolini only bits and pieces remained. The man was finished, pared down to the marrow, a pitiable shell."[25] Such statements might be described as sour grapes on the part of two formerly fervent followers who, with the nation's elite, kept the Duce afloat by an unwillingness to bring him to account for his transgressions until it was too late. But their post-mortems were not wrong.

---

23. Ibid., 5 March 1942, p. 70.
24. Bottai, *Diario*, p. 406.
25. Pietromarchi, *Diario*, 7 June 1944.

Given the irrefutable facts of Benito Mussolini's disastrous leadership during World War II, it would seem inconceivable to any student of history that he would have a following today. However, rightist Italian politicians like Gianfranco Fini and Silvio Berlusconi still fawn before the Warlord. "Mussolini was the greatest Italian of the 20th century." Renzo De Felice, who in his many writings has been known to give Mussolini due credit, curtly dismissed Fini's aside:

> How commonplace! I prefer Winston Churchill. Let me be candid about this: if Nazism was defeated, if Hitler did not devour the Soviet Union, and if the Allies won the war, it was because of Churchill's political resistance. His was a moral force built on an understanding of his own cultural, historical, and national values.[26]

Those qualities gave the British prime minister the standing to defend resolutely democracy and constitutional government against totalitarianism. Mussolini, on the other hand, was determined to become a conquistador of brutal aggression and expansion—a man who carelessly threw away the lives of his soldiers and did irreparable harm to his country. The contrast between the two warlords is striking.

What led the Duce down the path of destruction to self and nation? His successful conquest of Ethiopia certainly emboldened him, as did the great popularity he basked in after proclaiming the new Italian empire in May 1936. It was when Mussolini irrationally concluded that his country had reached military parity with the Western Powers and then linked forces with Adolf Hitler in the Pact of Steel to acquire Italy's mastery of the Mediterranean that his grip on reality began to disintegrate. His decision to enter World War II for predatory gain turned out to be a disaster. In attacking an already prostrate France, undertaking naked aggression against Greece, and mindlessly pitching a quarter of a million Italian soldiers of the Armir into Russia, the Duce reached his nadir. These momentous decisions guaranteed him a place in history as a war criminal.

---

26. Renzo De Felice, *Rosso e nero*, ed. by Pasquale Chessa (Milan: Baldini & Castoldi, 1995), pp. 166–67.

Bibliography

Archival Materials

Microscopy No. T-821: Collection of Italian Military Records, 1933–1943
N I-II. Diari storici of the Second World War.

State Archives

Presidenza del Consiglio dei Ministri 1940–1943. I.I.3. 16452. 1-189 (Governatorato della Dalmazia), 36146, 57412.
Graziani Papers

Foreign Ministry Archives

Gabinetto Armistizio-Pace (GABAP)

Croatia: files 28–47
France: files 1–4
Greece: files 21–24
Montenegro: files 48–54

Affari Politici 1931–1945

Jugoslavia: files 105–107
Albania: New files in the Foreign Ministry Archives that have recently been opened: Busta 104, 107, 117, 125.

Archivio storico dello stato maggiore dell'esercito

Fondo M 3, L13, L 15, N I-II (Diari storici of the Comando Supremo Regio Esercito)

Documentary Works issued by the Ufficio Storico dello Stato Maggiore dell'Esercito Italiano

Biagini Antonello and Fernando Frattolillo, eds. *Diario storico del Comando Supremo*. Rome: USSME DS, 1997.
Crociani, Piero. *Gli Albanesi nelle forze armate italiane (1939–1943)*. Rome: SME US, 2001.
Gallinari, Vincenzo. *Le operazioni del giugno 1940 sulle Alpi occidentali*. Rome: SME US, 1981.
La prima controffensiva Italo-Tedesca in Africa Settentrionale. Rome: SME US, 1974.
Le truppe italiane in Albania (1914–1920 e 1939). Rome: SME US, 1978.

Loi, Salvatore. *Le operazioni delle unitá italiane in Jugoslavia 1941–1943*. Rome: SME US, 1978.

Montanari, Mario. *La Campagna di Grecia*, 3 vols. Rome: SME US, 1980.

——. *Le Operazioni in Africa Settentrionale*, 4 vols. Rome: SME US, 1990.

Seconda controffensiva Italo-Tedesca in Africa Settentrionale da El Agheila a El Alamein, gennaio-settembre 1942. Rome: SME US, 1951.

Seconda offensiva britannica in Africa Setttentrionale e ripiegamento Italo-Tedesco nella Sirtica Orientale (18 november 1941–17 gennaio 1942. Rome: SME US, 1949.

Schipsi, Domenico. *L'occupazione italiana dei territori metropolitani francesi, 1940–1943*. Rome: SME US, 2007.

Talpo, Oddone. *Dalmazia: Una cronaca per la storia (1941)*. Rome: SME US, 1995.

——. *Dalmazia: Una cronaca per la storia (1942)*, 2nd ed. Rome: SME US, 2000.

——. *Dalmazia: Unca cronaca per la storia (1943–1944)*. Rome: SME US, 1994.

Terza offensiva britannica in Africa. Rome: SME US, 1961.

Diplomatic Documents

Akten zur deutschen auswärtigen Politik, series E (1941–1945).

Archives of the Slovene Republic, Ljubljana, Slovenia.

Documenti diplomatici italiani, series IX (1939–1943).

Documents on German Foreign Policy, 1918–1945, series D (1937–45)

Hitler-Mussolini, *Lettere e documenti*. Milan: Rizzoli, 1948.

Mussolini, Benito, *Opera omnia*, edited by D. Susmel, 44 vols.

Zbornik dokumenata i podataka o Narodnooslobodilač kom ratu jugosloveskih naroda, Institute of Military History, Belgrade.

Selected Bibliography

Alfieri, Dino. *Dictators Face to Face*. London: Elek, 1954.

Anfuso, Filippo. *Dal Palazzo Venezia al Lago di Garda 1936-1945*. Bologna: Cappelli, 1957.

——. *Roma, Berlino, Salò*. Milan: Garzanti, 1950.

Ansaldo, Giovanni. *Il giornalista di Ciano: Diari 1932–1943*. Bologna: Il Mulino, 2000.

Archer, Laird. *Balkan Journal*. New York: W. W. Norton, 1944.

Armellini, Quirino. *Diario di guerra. Nuove mesi al Comando Supremo*. Milan: Garzanti, 1946.

Arnold, W. Vincent. *The Illusion of Victory: Fascist Propaganda and the Second World War*. New York: Peter Lang, 1998.

Atkinson, Rick. *An Army at Dawn: The War in North Africa, 1942–1943*. New York: Harry Holt and Co., 2002

Avramov, Smilja. *Genocide in Yugoslavia*. Belgrade: BIGZ, 1995.

Badoglio, Pietro. *L'Italia nella seconda guerra mondiale*. Milan: Mondadori, 1946.

Bambara, Gino. *Jugoslavia settebandiere: Guerra senza retrovie nella Jugoslavia occupata (1941–1943)*. Brescia: Vannini, 1988.

Bastianini, Giuseppe. *Volevo Fermare Mussolini: Memorie di un diplomatico fascista*. Milan: BUR, 2005.

Battistelli, Pier Paolo. *La "guerra dell'Asse." Condotta bellica e collaborazione militare Italo-Tedesca, 1939–1943*. Ph.D. diss. University of Padua, 1999-2000.

Bianchini, S. and F. Privitera. *6 aprile 1941: L'attaco italiano alla Jugoslavia*. Milan: Marzorati, 1993.

Bierman, John and Colin Smith. *War Without Hate: The Desert Campaign of 1940–1943*. New York: Penguin Books, 2004.

Bitzes, John. *Greece in World War II to April 1941*. Manhattan, Kansas: Sunflower University Press, 1989.

Bocca, Giorgio. *Storia d'Italia nella guerra fascista 1940–1943*. Milan: Mondadori, 1996.

Boog, Horst, Werner Rahn, Reinhard Stumpf, Bernd Wegner. *Germany and the Second World War*, vol. VI: *The Global War*. Oxford: Clarendon Press, 2001.

Borgogni, Massimo. *Italia e Francia: Durante la crisi militare dell'asse (1942–1943)*. Siena: Nuova Immagine Editrice, 1994.

——. *Mussolini e La Francia di Vichy*. Siena: Nuova Immagine Editrice, 1991.

Bosworth, R. J. B. *Alto Polo: Intellectuals and Their Ideas in Contemporary Italy*. Sydney: F. May Foundation, 1983.

——. *Mussolini's Italy: Life Under the Fascist Dictatorship, 1915–1945*. New York: The Penguin Press, 2006.

Bottai, Giuseppe. *Diario 1935–1944*. Milan: Rizzoli, 1989.

——. *Vent'anni e un giorno (24 luglio 1943)*. Milan: Garzanti, 1977.

Breccia, Alfredo. *Jugoslavia 1939–1941: Diplomazia della neutralità*. Milan: Giuffrè, 1978.

Broucek, Peter. *General in Zwielicht: Die Lebenserinnerungen Edmund Glaises von Horstenau*. 3 vols. Vienna: Boehlhaus, 1980, 1983, 1988.

Burgwyn, H. James. *Empire on the Adriatic: Mussolini's Conquest of Yugoslavia 1941–1943*. New York: Enigma Books, 2005.

——. *The Legend of the Mutilated Victory: Italy, the Great War, and the Paris Peace Conference, 1915–1919*. Westport CT and London: Greenwood Press, 1993.

Burrin, Philippe. *France Under the Germans: Collaboration and Compromise*. New York: The New Press, 1996.

Capogreco, Carlo Spartaco. *I campi del duce: L'internamento civile nell'Italia fascista (1941–1943)*. Turin: Einaudi, 2004.

——. *Renicci. Un campo di concentramento in riva al Tevere (1942–1943)*. Cosenza: Fondazione Ferramonti, 1998.

——. "Una storia rimossa dell'Italia fascista: L'internamento dei civili jugoslavi (1941–1943)." *Studi storici* XLII, no. 1 (January–March 2001): 203–230.

Cappellano, Filippo. "L'occupazione in Grecia (1941–1943)." *Nuova storia contemporanea*, no. 4 (2008): 19–46.

Carpi, Daniel. *Between Mussolini and Hitler: The Jews and the Italian Authorities in France and Tunisia*. Hanover and London: University Press of New England, 1994.

——. "The Mufti of Jerusalem, Amin el-Husseini, and His Diplomatic Activity during World War II (October 1941–July 1943). *Studies in Zionism*, no. 7 (Spring 1983): 101–131.

——. "Notes on the History of the Jews in Greece during the Holocaust Period. The Attitude of the Italians (1941–1943)." In *The Conduct of the Air War in the Second World War*, edited by Horst Boog. New York/Oxford: Oxford University Press, 1992: 25-62.

Cavallero, Ugo. *Diario 1940–1943*, edited by Giuseppe Bucciante. Rome: Ciarrapico, 1984.

Cavallo, Pietro. *Italiani in guerra: Sentimenti e immagini dal 1940–al 1943*. Bologna: Il Mulino, 1997.

Cecini, Giovanni. *I soldati ebrei di Mussolini: I militari israeliti nel periodo fascista*. Milan: Mursia, 2008.

Cervi, Mario. *The Hollow Legions: Mussolini's Blunder in Greece*. New York: Doubleday, 1971.

Ceva, Lucio. *La condotta italiana della guerra. Cavallero e il Comando Supremo 1941/1942*. Milan: Feltrinelli, 1975.

——. *Guerra mondiale: Strategie e industria bellica 1939–1945*. Milan: Franco Angeli, 2000.

——. "The North African Campaign 1940–1943: A Reconsideration." In *Decisive Campaigns of the Second World War*, edited by John Gooch. London: F. Cass, 1990.

Churchill, Winston S. *Their Finest Hour*. Boston: Houghton Mifflin, 1950.

——. *The Grand Alliance*. Boston: Houghton Mifflin, 1950.

Ciano, Count Galeazzo. *The Ciano Diaries 1939–1943*, edited by Hugh Gibson. Garden City, NY: Doubleday, 1946.

——. *Ciano's Diplomatic Papers*. London: Oldham's Press, 1948.

Clissold, Stephen. *Whirlwind: An Account of Marshal Tito's Rise to Power*. London: Cresset Press, 1949.

Cohen, Philip J. *Serbia's Secret War*. College Park, TX: Texas A&M University Press, 1996.

Colacicchi, Paolo. *L'ultimo fronte d'Africa. Tunisia: novembre 1942–maggio 1943*. Milan: Mursia, 1977.

Collotti, Enzo. *L'Europa nazista: Il progetto di un nuovo ordine europeo (1939–1945)*. Florence: Giunti, 2002.

Conti, Davide. *L'occupazione italiana dei Balcani: Crimini di guerra e mito della "brava gente" (1940–1943)*. Rome: Odradek, 2008.

Conti, Giuseppe. *Una guerra segreta: Il Sim nel secondo conflitto mondiale*. Milan: Il Mulino, 2009.

Cornwell, John. *Hitler's Pope. The Secret History of Pius XII*. New York: Penguin, 1999.

Corvaja, Santi. *Hitler and Mussolini: The Secret Meetings*. New York: Enigma Books, 2001.

Coverdale, John F. *Italian Intervention in the Spanish Civil War*. Princeton, NJ: Princeton University Press, 1975.

Creveld, Martin L. *Hitler's Strategy, 1940–1941: The Balkan Clue*. Cambridge: Cambridge University Press, 1973.

——. *Supplying War: Logistics from Wallenstein to Partition*. Cambridge: Cambridge University Press, 2007.

Cuzzi, Mario. *L'occupazione italiana della Slovenia (1941–1943)*. Rome: SME US, 1998.

Dassovich, Mario. *Fronte Jugoslavo 1941–'42*. Udine: Del Bianco, 1999.

——. *Fronte Jugoslavo 1943*. Udine: Del Bianco, 2000.

Deakin, F. W. *The Brutal Friendship: Mussolini, Hitler and the Fall of Italian Fascism*. Garden City, NY: Doubleday Anchor Books, 1966.

Dedjer, Vladimir. *Tito.* New York: Simon & Schuster, 1953.

Delarue, Jaques. *Trafics et crimes sous l'occupation.* Paris: Fayard, 1993.

De Felice, Renzo. *Mussolini l'alleato: L'Italia in guerra.* Turin: Einaudi, 1990.

——. *Mussolini il duce: Gli anni del consenso,* Turin: Einaudi, 1974.

Della Volpa, Nicola. *Esercito e propaganda nella 2a guerra mondiale.* Rome: SME US, 1998.

Di Rienzo, Eugenio and Emilio Gin. "Quella mattina del 25 luglio 1943. Mussolini, Shinrokuro Hidaka e il progetto di pace separata con L'URSS. In *Nuova rivista storica,* XCV, n. 1 (2011), pp. 2–87.

Di Sante, Costantino, *Italiani senza onore: I crimini in Jugoslavia e i processi negati (1941–1951).* Verona: Ombre Corte, 2005.

Dollmann, Eugen. *The Interpreter: Memoirs of Doktor Eugen Dollmann.* London: Hutchinson, 1967.

Donosti, Mario (Mario Luciolli). *Mussolini e l'Europa: La politica estera fascista.* Rome: Leonardo, 1945.

Eichberg, Federico. *Il fascio littorio e l'aquila di Skanderbeg: Italia e Albania 1939–1945.* Rome: Apes, 1997.

Etmektsoglou-Koehn, Gabriella, "Axis Exploitation of Wartime Greece 1941–1943." Ph.D. diss., Emory University, 1995.

Evans, Richard. *Third Reich at War.* New York: The Penguin Press, 2009.

Fabei, Stefano. *Il Fascio, la svastica e la mezzaluna.* Milan: Mursia, 2002.

——. "Il collaborazionismo anticomunista nella Dalmazia 'italiana.'" *Nuova storia contemporanea* no. 4 (2008): 47–74.

Faldella, Emilio. *Revisione di giudizi: L'Italia nella seconda guerra mondiale.* Bologna: Capelli, 1967.

Farrell, Nicholas. *Mussolini: A New Life.* London: A Phoenix Paperback, 2004.

Fatutta, Francesco. *La campagna di Iugoslava, aprile 1941–settembre 1943.* Campobasso, 1996.

Ferenc, Tone. *Rab-Arbe-Arbissima: Konfinacije, Racije in Internacije v Lubljanski Pokrajini 1941–1943.* Ljubljana Inštitut za novejšo zgodovino, 2000.

——. *"Si amazza troppo poco": Condannati a morte-ostaggi-passati per le armi nella provincia di Lubiana 1941–1943.* Ljubljana: Istituto per la storia moderna, 1999.

——. *La provincia 'italiana' di Lubiana: Documenti 1941–1943.* Udine: Istituto friulano per la storia del movimento di liberazione, 1994.

Fischer, Bernd J. *Albania at War 1939–1945.* West Lafayette, Indiana: Purdue University Press, 1999.

——. "The Jews of Albania During the Zogist and Second World War Periods." http// www.ipfw.edu/news/resources/speakers/bios/f/fischer.shtml.

Focardi, Filippo. "'Bravo italiano' e 'cattivo tedesco': riflessioni sulla genesi di due immagini incrociate." *Storia e memoria* I (1996): 55–83.

——. "La memoria della guerra e il mito del 'bravo italiano.' Origine e affermazione di un autoritratto collectivo." *Italia contemporanea* 220–21 (settembre–decembre 2000): 393–399.

Focardi, Filippo and Lutz Klinkhammer. "The Question of Fascist Italy's War Crimes: The Construction of a Self-acquitting Myth (1943–1948). *Journal of Modern Italian Studies.* 9(3) 2004: 330–348.

François-Poncet, André. *Au palais Farnèse: Souvenirs d'une ambassade à Rome, 1938–1940.* Paris: Fayard, 1961.

Gabriele, Mariano. *Operazione C 3: Malta.* Rome: Stato Maggiore della Marina, Ufficio Storico, 1965.

Giusti, Maria Teresa. *I prigionieri italiani in Russia.* Bologna: Il Mulino, 2009.

Glantz, David M. and Jonathan House. *When Titans Clashed: How the Red Army Stopped Hitler.* Lawrence: University of Kansas Press, 1995.

Gobetti, Eric. *L'occupazione allegra: Gli italiani in Jugoslavia (1941–1943).* Rome: Carocci, 2007.

Goda, Norman J. *Hitler, Northwest Africa, and the Path Toward America.* College Station, TX: Texas A & M University Press, 1998.

Gooch, John. *Mussolini and His Generals: The Armed Forces and Fascist Foreign Policy, 1922–1940.* Cambridge: Cambridge University Press, 2007.

Gorla, Giuseppe. *L'Italia nella seconda guerra mondiale: Diario di un Milanese ministro del Re nel Governo Mussolini.* Milan: Baldini and Castoldi, 1959.

Grazzi, Emanuele. *Il principio della fine (L'impresa di Grecia).* Rome: Editrice Faro, 1945.

Green, Jack and Alessandro Massignani. *The Naval War in the Mediterranean 1940–1943.* London: Sarpedon, 1998.

Guariglia, Raffaele. *Ricordi, 1922–1946.* Naples: Edizione scientifiche italiane, 1950.

Halder, Franz. *War Diary, 1939–1942.* 2 vols. Novato, CA: Presidio Press, 1988.

Hamilton, Hope. *Sacrifice on the Steppe: The Italian Alpine Corps in the Stalingrad Campaign, 1942–1943.* Philadelphia & Newbury: Casemate, 2011.

Hehn, Paul. *The Struggle Against Yugoslav Guerrillas in World War II.* Boulder, CO: Eastern European Monographs, 1980.

Hitler and His Generals: Military Conferences 1942–1945. Helmut Heiber and David M. Glantz, eds. New York: Enigma Books, 2004.

Hoare, Marco Attila. *Genocide and Resistance in Hitler's Bosnia: The Partisans and the Chetniks 1941–1943.* Oxford: Oxford University Press, 2006.

Hull, Cordell. *The Memoirs of Cordell Hull,* 2 vols. New York: Macmillan, 1948.

Innocenti, Marco. *L'Italia del 1940: Come eravamo nel primo anno della guerra di Mussolini.* Milan: Mursia, 1996.

Jackson, Julian. *France. The Dark Years 1940–1944.* Oxford: Oxford University Press, 2001.

Jacomoni di San Savino, Francesco. *La politica dell'Italia in Albania.* Cappelli: Rocca San Casciano, 1965.

Kent, Ralph. "I Saw Greece Looted." In Homer W. Davis, *Greece Fights. The People Behind the Front.* New York: American Friends of Greece, 1942.

Kesselring, Albert. *The Memoirs of Field-Marshal Kesselring.* London: Greenhill Books, 2007

Kitchen, Martin. *Rommel's Desert War.* Cambridge: Cambridge University Press, 2009.

Klinkhammer, Lutz, "La politica di occupazione nazista in europa: Un tentativo di analisi strutturale." In *Crimini e memorie di guerra,* edited by Luca Baldissara and Paolo Pezzino. Naples: L'ancora del mediterraneo, 2004: 61–88.

Knox, MacGregor. *Common Destiny: Dictatorship, Foreign Policy, and War in Fascist Italy and Nazi Germany.* Cambridge: Cambridge University Press, 2000.

——. *Hitler's Italian Allies: Royal Armed Forces, Fascist Regime, and the War of 1940–1943.* Cambridge: Cambridge University Press, 2000.

——. *Mussolini Unleashed 1939–1941: Politics and Strategy in Fascist Italy's Last War.* Cambridge: Cambridge University Press, 1982.

Lanza, Michele (pseudo. Leonardo Simoni). *Berlino ambasciata d'Italia 1939–1943.* Rome: Migliaresi, 1946.

Liddell Hart, B. H. *History of the Second World War.* Old Saybrook, CT: Konecky & Konecky, 1970.

Longo, Luigi Emilio. "Profili di capi militari tratteggianti da uno di loro." *Studi Storico-Militari* (1994). Rome: USSME, 1996.

——. *L'ultimo maresciallo d'Italia.* Rome: SME US, 2006.

Mack Smith, Denis. *Mussolini's Roman Empire.* London and New York: Longman, 1976.

Mallmann, Klaus-Michael and Martin Cüpers. *Nazi Palestine.* New York: Enigma Books, 2009.

Manoschek, Walter, "'Coming Along to Shoot Some Jews?' The Destruction of the Jews in Serbia." In *War of Extermination: The German Military in World War II, 1941–1944,* edited by Hannes Heer and Klaus Naumann. New York and Oxford: Berghahn Books, 2000: 39–54.

Mantelli, Bruno. "Gli italiani nei Balcani 1941–1943: Occupazione militare, politiche persecutore e crimini di guerra." *Qualestoria,* no. 1 (June 2002): 23–37.

Marrus, Michael R. and Robert O. Paxton. *Vichy France and the Jews.* New York: Basic Books, 1981.

Massignani, Alessandro. *Alpini e Tedeschi sul Don.* Vicenza: Edizioni Gino Rossato, 2010.

Mazower, Mark. *Hitler's Empire: How the Nazis Ruled Europe.* New York: The Penguin Press, 2008.

Mellenthin, F. W. *Panzer Battles: A Study of the Employment of Armor in the Second World War.* Old Saybrook CT: Konecky & Konecky, 1956.

Messe, Giovanni. *La guerra al fronte russo.* Milan: Mursia, 2005.

——. *La mia armata in Tunisia.* Milan: Mursia, 2004.

Milazzo, Matteo J. *The Chetnik Movement & The Yugoslav Resistance.* Baltimore and London: The Johns Hopkins University Press, 1975.

Monelli, Paolo. *Mussolini: An Intimate Life.* London: Thomas and Hudson, 1953.

——. *Roma 1943.* Rome: Migliaresi, 1945.

Montanelli, Indro and Mario Cervi. *L'Italia della disfatta.* Milan: Rizzoli, 1979.

Montgomery, Bernard L. *The Memoirs of Field-Marshal Montgomery.* London and Glasgow: Fontana Monarchs, 1958.

Moorehead, Alan. *Desert War.* New York: Penguin Books, 2001.

Morgan, Philip. *The Fall of Mussolini.* Oxford: Oxford University Press, 2007.

Moseley, Ray. *Mussolini's Shadow: The Double Life of Count Galeazzo Ciano.* New Haven CN: Yale University Press, 1999.

Mussolini, Benito. *My Rise and Fall.* New York: Da Capo Press, 1998.

Nattermann, Ruth, ed. *I diari e le agende di Luca Pietromarchi (1938–1940): Politica estera del fascismo e vita quotidiana di un diplomatico romano del '900.* Rome: Viella, 2009.

O'Hara, Vincent P. *Struggle for the Middle Sea: The Great Navies at War in the Mediterranean Theater, 1940–1945*. Annapolis MD: Naval Institute Press, 2009.

Orlandi, Rosita. "Giovanni Messe: da volontario a Maresciallo d'Italia." In *Il Maresciallo d'Italia Giovanni Messe*. Mesegne: Congedo, 2003.

Ortona, Egidio. *Diplomazia di guerra: Diari 1937–1943*. Bologna: Il Mulino, 1993.

Osti Guerrazzi, Amedeo and Thomas Schlemmer. "I soldati italiani nella campagna di Russia. Propaganda, esperienza, memoria." *Annali dell'Istituto storico italo-germanico in Trento"* 33 (2007): 385–417.

Osti Guerrazzi, Amedeo. *Il Regio esercito Italiano in Slovenia. Documenti 1941–1943*. Unpublished Manuscript.

Panicacci, Jean-Louis. *L'Occupation italienne: Sud-Est de la France, juin 1940–septembre 1943*. Rennes: Press Universitaires de Rennes, 2010.

Paoletti, Ciro. *A Military History of Italy*. Westport CN: Praeger, 2008.

Pavlowitch, Steven K. *Hitler's New Disorder: The Second World War in Yugoslavia*. New York: Columbia University Press, 2008.

———. *Yugoslavia*. New York: Praeger, 1975.

Paxton, Robert O. *Parades & Politics at Vichy*. Princeton, NJ: Princeton University Press, 1966.

Payne, Stanley G. *Franco and Hitler*. New Haven and London: Yale University Press, 2008.

Perona, Gianni. "Aspetti economici dell'occupazione italiana in Francia." In *8 settembre: lo sfacelo della IV Armata*. Turin: Istituto storico della resistenza in Piemonte, 1978.

Petersen, Jens. "L'Afrika-Korps." In *L'Italia in Guerra: il 1° anno—1941*. Rome: Commissione italiana di storia militare, 1992.

———. "Italia e Germania: Due immagini incrociate." In Tosi, Francesca Ferrantini, Gaetano Grassi, Massimo Legnani, eds. *L'Italia nella seconda guerra mondiale e nella resistenza*. Milan: Franco Angeli, 1988: 45–63.

Pirelli, Alberto. *Taccuini 1942/1943*. Bologna: Il Mulino, 1984.

Playfair, I. S. O. *The Mediterranean and the Middle East*, 4 vols. Uckfield, England: Naval and Military, 2004.

Poliakov, Léon, and Jacques Sabille. *Jews Under the Italian Occupation*. Paris: Éditions du Centre, 1955.

Pricolo, Francisco. *La regia aeronautica nella seconda guerra mondiale*. Milan: Longanesi, 1971.

Puntoni, Paolo. *Parla Vittorio Emanuele III*. Bologna: Il Mulino, 1993.

Pupo, Raoul. "Le annessioni italiane in Slovenia e Dalmazia 1941–1943." *Italia contemporanea* no. 243 (giugno 2006): 181–211.

———. "Slovenia e Dalmazia fra Italia e Terzo Reich 1940–1945." *Qualestoria* XXX, no. 1 (June 2002): 129–141.

Rainero, Romain H. "La campagna contro la Francia, l'armistizio e la CIAF." In *L'Italia in Guerra: il 1° anno—1941*. Rome: Commissione italiana di storia militare, 1992.

———. *Mussolini e Pétain: Storia dei rapporti tra l'Italia e la Francia di Vichy (10 giugno 1940–8 settembre 1943)*, 2 vols. Rome: SME US, 1990.

———. *La politica araba di Mussolini nella seconda guerra mondiale*. Padova: CEDAM, 2004.

Rintelen, Enno E. *Mussolini e l'alleato. Ricordi dell'addetto militare Tedesco a Roma, 1936–1943*. Rome: Corso, 1952.

Roatta, Mario. *Otto milioni di baionette: L'esercito italiano in guerra 1940–1944*. Milan: Mondadori, 1946.

Rochat, Giorgio. *Le guerre italiane 1935–1943*. Turin: Einaudi, 2005.

Rodogno, Davide. *Fascism's European Empire: Italian Occupation During the Second World War* (Cambridge: Cambridge University Press, 2006.

Sadat, Anwar. *In Search of an Identity*. Glasgow: Collins, 1978.

Sadkovich, James J. *The Italian Navy in World War II*. Westport CN: The Greenwood Press, 1994.

Sala, Teodoro. *Il fascismo italiano e gli Slavi del Sud*. Trieste: Istituto regionale per la storia del movimento di liberazione, 2008.

Santarelli, Lidia, "Fra coabitazione e conflitto: invasione italiana e popolazione civile nella Grecia occupata (primavera-estate 1941)." *Qualestoria* no. 1 (June 2002): 143–155.

———. "Muted Violence: Italian War Crimes in Occupied Greece." *Journal of Modern Italian Studies* vol. 9, no. 3 (Fall 2004): 280–299.

Salerno, Reynolds. *Vital Crossroads: Mediterranean Origins of the Second World War, 1935–1940*. Ithaca, NY: Cornell University Press, 2002.

Schlemmer, Thomas. *Invasori, non vittime: La campagna italiana di Russia 1941–1943*. Rome-Bari: Laterza, 2009.

———. "Die Comandi Tappa Der 8. Italienischen Armee Und Die Deutche Besatzungs-herrschaft Im Süden Der Sowjetunion." *Quellen Und Forschungen* no. 88 (2008): 512-546.

Schmider, Klaus. "The Mediterranean in 1940–1941: Crossroads of Lost Opportunities?" *War and Society* vol. 15, no. 2 (1997): 19–41.

———. *Partisanenkrieg in Jugoslawien 1941–1944*. Hamburg: Mittler, 2002.

Schreiber, Gerhard. "Due popoli, una vittoria? Gli italiani nei Balcani nel giudizio dell'alleato germanico." In *L'Italia in guerra 1940–1943*, edited by P. P. Poggio and B. Micheletti. Brescia: Fondazione "Luigi Micheletti," 1992: 95–124.

Schreiber, Gerhard, Bernd Stegemann, Detlef Vogel. *Germany and the Second World War*, vol. III: *The Mediterranean, South-east Europe, and North Africa 1939–1941*. Oxford: Oxford University Press, 1995.

———. "The Mediterranean in Hitler's Strategy in 1940. Program and Military Planning." In *The German Military in the Age of Total War*, edited by Wilhelm Deist. Dover, NH: Berg, 1987.

———. "La partecipazione italiana alla guerra conto l'URSS. Motivi, fatti, conseguenze." *Italia contemporanea* 191 (1993): 245–75.

Scotoni, Giorgio. *L'Armata Rossa e la disfatta italiana (1942–1943)*. Trento: Panorama, 2007.

Scotoni. Giorgio and Sergej Ivanovich Filonenko. *Retroscena della disfatta italiana in Russia nei documenti inediti dell 8° Armata*. vol 1: *L'occupazione* and vol. II: *La disfatta*. Trento: Casa Editrice Panorama, 2008.

Scotti, Giacomo. *Buono Taliano: Gli Italiani in Yugoslavia 1941-1943*. Milan: La Pietra, 1977.

Scotti, Giacomo and Luciano Viazzi. *L'inutile vittoria: La tragica esperienza delle truppe italiane in Montenegro*. Milan: Mursia, 1989.

———. *Occupazione e guerra italiana in Montenegro: Le aquile delle montagne nere*. Milan: Mursia, 1987.

Stahel, David. *Operation Barbarossa and Germany's Defeat in the East*. Cambridge: Cambridge University Press, 2009.

Steinberg, Jonathan. *All or Nothing: The Axis and the Holocaust 1941–1943*. London and New York: Routledge, 1991.

Strabolgi, Lord. *The Conquest of Italy*. London & New York: Hutchinson & Co., 1944.

Sullivan, Brian R. "Downfall of the Regia Aeronautica, 1933–1943." In *Why Air Forces Fail: The Anatomy of Defeat*, edited by Robin Higham and Stephen J. Harris. Kentucky: The University Press of Kentucky, 2006.

———. "The Italian Soldier in Combat, June 1940–September 1943: Myths, Realities and Explanations." In *The Soldiers Experience of War in the West 1939–1945*, edited by Paul Addison and Angus Cronin. London: Pimlico Press, 1997.

———. "The Path Marked Out by History: The German-Italian Alliance, 1939–1943." In *Hitler and His Allies in World War II*, edited by Jonathan R. Adelman. London and New York: Routledge, 2007.

Tolloy, Giusto. *Con l'armata italiana in Russia*. Milan: Mursia, 1968.

Tomasevich, Jozo. *War and Revolution in Yugoslavia, 1941–1945: Occupation and Collaboration*. Stanford, CA: Stanford University Press, 2001.

———. *War and Revolution in Yugoslavia, 1941–1945: The Chetniks*. Stanford: Stanford University Press, 1975.

Toye, Richard. *Churchill's Empire*. New York: Henry Holt and Company, 2010.

Tranfaglia, Nicola, ed. *Ministri e giornalisti: La guerra e il Minculpop (1939–1943)*. Turin: Einaudi, 2005.

Trifkovic, Srdja. *Ustaša: Croatian Separatism and European Politics, 1929–1945*. London: Lord Byron Foundation for Balkan Studies, 1998.

Umiltà, Carlo. *Jugoslavia e Albania: Memorie di un diplomatico*. Cernusco sul Naviglio: Garzanti, 1947.

Valori, Aldo. *La Campagna di Russia CSIR-ARMIR*, 2 vols. Rome: Grafica Nazionale Editrice, 1950–1951.

Verna, Frank Philip. "Yugoslavia Under Italian Rule 1941–1943: Civil and Military Aspects of the Italian Occupation." Ph.D. diss., University of California, 1985.

Voigt, Klaus. *Il Rifugio precario: Gli esuli in Italia dal 1933 al 1945*. Florence: La Nuova Italia, 1996.

Walker, Ian. *Iron Hulls from Hearts*. Ramsbury: Crowood Press, 2006.

Weinberg, Gerhard L. *A World at Arms: A Global History of World War II*. Cambridge: Cambridge University Press, 1994.

Zanussi, Giacomo. *Guerra e catastrophe d'Italia*, 2 vols. Rome: Corso, 1945.

Index